Blue Metros,
Red States

David F. Damore
Robert E. Lang
Karen A. Danielsen

WITH CONTRIBUTIONS FROM

William E. Brown Jr.
John J. Hudak
Molly E. Reynolds

THE SHIFTING

URBAN-RURAL DIVIDE

Blue Metros, Red States

IN AMERICA'S

SWING STATES

BROOKINGS INSTITUTION PRESS
Washington, D.C.

The Brookings Institution is a private nonprofit organization devoted to research, education, and publication on important issues of domestic and foreign policy. Its principal purpose is to bring the highest quality independent research and analysis to bear on current and emerging policy problems. Interpretations or conclusions in Brookings publications should be understood to be solely those of the authors.

Library of Congress Control Number: 2020943121
ISBN 9780815738473 (pbk)
ISBN 9780815738480 (ebook)

9 8 7 6 5 4 3 2 1

Typeset in Kepler

Composition by Elliott Beard

Contents

Foreword

Ruy Teixeira

The 2020 election is shaping up to be hugely consequential, with a wide range of states in play between the two parties. I will be keeping a copy of *Blue Metros, Red States: The Shifting Urban-Rural Divide in America's Swing States* close at hand as I follow all of the action and try to make sense of it—both in terms of gaming out the election itself and thinking about what the results might tell us about America's political future.

This is because David F. Damore, Robert E. Lang, and Karen A. Danielsen, the principal authors of the volume, with additional contributions from William E. Brown Jr., John J. Hudak, and Molly E. Reynolds, provide a depth and quality of information about the thirteen swing states they cover that you literally cannot find anywhere else.

Let me enumerate some of the book's unique qualities. First, the theme of the volume—that swing states' overall political trends cannot be understood without considering the interplay between large (million-plus) blue and blue-trending metros and the less dense, redder parts of these states—is spot on. You cannot understand Arizona without understanding the Tucson and, particularly, the Phoenix metros; Colorado without Denver; North Carolina without Charlotte and Raleigh; Georgia without Atlanta; and so on. The push and pull between these metros and the outlying parts of their states is the big political story in election after election.

But the analysis of individual states in this volume further embeds the story of the million-plus metros into a regional analysis of every state (with regions clearly delineated on maps). Each region has a distinct political identity and those identities help unpack political trends in a given state. Speaking as someone who has conducted some regional analyses of swing states, I find the authors' regional designations uniformly plausible and helpful.

The coverage of individual states also benefits from a uniform set of tables for every state. One table compares the demographics of the state as a whole with the demographics of the million-plus metros within the state. This allows you to see not only how nonwhites might be concentrated in the large metros, but also how much diversity within diversity—a key theme of the volume—there is among the nonwhite population, which turns out to have significant political implications. Another table shows the results of statewide elections 2012–2018, again comparing the state as a whole to the million-plus metros, and another presents the party affiliation of the state's governor and the partisan composition of the state's legislative bodies and Senate and House representation. These at-a-glance tables are enormously helpful and by themselves are worth the price of admission as reference material.

Governance structures are not neglected either. Both the relative fragmentation and local autonomy of decisionmaking within million-plus metros is examined, as well as the extent to which large metros are typically disadvantaged in state politics and policymaking. The latter dynamic explains a great deal of currently salient political conflict within these states.

Finally, the write-up for each state includes a deep dive into the state's cultural and demographic evolution via interviews with an expert or experts on that state. This provides another lens of a state's recent political trends, situating each in a rich historical context.

The chapter authors also synthesize all of the information about a given state, provide what they term the "state of play" for the state, and suggest some possible outcomes going forward. I find these assessments judicious and insightful, based both on the data the authors provide and previous analyses I have conducted of these states' politics. It will be interesting to see the outcomes of the coming election and how they may have been foreshadowed by the analyses in this book. I will not be surprised if many of them are quite prescient.

As this sketch makes clear, the coverage of each state in this volume constitutes a mini-handbook about the state and its politics. I cannot think of a better, more accessible way to anchor one's understanding of the political situation within a swing state of interest than to consult the appropriate chapter in this book. It's that good.

Preface

THE ORIGINS OF BLUE METROS, RED STATES

Robert E. Lang

The "blue metros, red states" concept originated in discussions at a meeting of Sun Belt center directors organized by the Kinder Institute at Rice University in Houston, Texas, in June 2017. William Fulton, Kinder Institute's director, organized the meeting so the directors of academic public policy centers located in metropolitan areas within Sun Belt states could share their experiences and review recent projects. The intent was to see if these centers could combine resources and perhaps work on regional-to-national-level research projects. Sun Belt states represented included Arizona, California, Colorado, Florida, Georgia, Nevada, North Carolina, and Texas, among others. Big metros represented at the meeting included Atlanta, Austin, Charlotte, Denver, Houston, Las Vegas, Miami, Phoenix, and San Diego.

Part of the Rice discussion included a concern for how the largest metropolitan regions in mostly swing Sun Belt states interacted with their often more conservative state governments. This meeting took place a year after the North Carolina legislature passed the "bathroom bill" mandating that people use a facility consistent with the gender identified on their birth certificate. The legislation preempted an ordinance passed by the city of Charlotte (see chapters 1 and 4) allowing people to use the facilities matching their current gender identity. The idea that a state legislature could dictate to a major city such as Charlotte where its residents could go to the bathroom proved a provocative and vivid example of the split in blue metros and red states politics.

As the discussions continued about how big Sun Belt metros were often at loggerheads with their state legislatures, many examples of bills tapping into the sociocultural, urban/rural divide—such as abortion, gun control, and marijuana legalization—were noted. Participants also expressed concerns about state tax resources that were often generated in large part by big metros but not returned to such places in proportion to their revenue contributions. This involved everything from infrastructure investment to school funding.

A common theme emerged from the Rice meeting—large metros in the Sun Belt, including their urbanized suburbs, are often politically opposed by smaller metros, exurbs, and rural areas. I suggested we collectively explore this matter. However, there was some trepidation among policy center directors to tackle the issue directly. Many policy centers rely on state funding and must avoid politically controversial research. I then asked if there was interest in and relevance to a study that reviews the major metro versus rest-of-state divide in depth. There was agreement that such a study was both relevant and welcome. Because Brookings Mountain West and The Lincy Institute, policy centers located at UNLV where I serve as the executive director, do not rely on state funding, they are well positioned to take on what some see as a controversial topic.

Thus was born the blue metros, red states project. While many of the places covered in the volume are in the Sun Belt, key swing states such as Michigan, Pennsylvania, and Wisconsin are located in the Rust Belt. To make the project national in scope, we include all states that contain at least one metropolitan region that exceeds a million residents and where the 2016 presidential election was decided by ten points or less.

The blue metros, red states framework was not intended to address only the impact of the swing states on the Electoral College or to predict presidential outcomes—although that is a big component of the analysis. Rather, the concept was devised as a way to understand state-level political and policy dynamics that revolve around conflicting interests between blue (or mostly Democratic-voting) million-plus metros and the mostly red (or Republican-voting) balance of their states. Assessing the causes and consequences for these sectional divides is a major focus of the book. As we note in chapter 1, some of the analysis presented here is local in origin and was provided by state experts (including some policy center directors) via structured interviews. The material from these interviews allows the book to go beyond descriptive analyses of intrastate voting and demographic differences to understand how blue metros navigate their state's cultural, political, and policy terrain.

Blue Metros, Red States was completed in early April 2020, the moment COVID-19 had shut down most of America. Coronavirus politics are touched on briefly here, but the full impact of the COVID-19 pandemic and its corresponding economic fallout could not be known at the time. Obviously, the virus and its consequences could potentially reshape America's political landscape in the early part of this decade and perhaps for years to come. What we do know already is that COVID-19 pitted blue metro municipal and county leaders against red state governors in Arizona, Florida, Georgia, and Texas. Mayors in metros such as Atlanta, Dallas, Houston, Miami, and Phoenix issued orders for their residents to stay at home and practice social distancing. Many red state governors were late to act in a similar fashion and, in some instances—such as Florida—actually preempted local actions to manage the pandemic. It appears that even a national emergency does not override the political divide between blue metros and red states.

Finally, the 2020 Democratic presidential primaries resulted in a presumptive nominee just as *Blue Metros, Red States* was finished. Former Vice President Joe Biden will face Republican Donald Trump in November 2020 in a contest likely to be decided by the thirteen swing states covered here. Independent Vermont senator Bernie Sanders, Biden's last major opponent, quit the Democratic race on April 8. As noted in chapter 10, Biden gained an insurmountable delegate lead in nominating contests through early March 2020. He won Michigan's primary, held on March 10, by a wide margin. The race was closely watched given that Sanders had won in the Wolverine State over Hillary Clinton in 2016. Biden also won the Idaho, Mississippi, Missouri, and Washington primaries held that same day. As with Super Tuesday's nominating contests on March 3, Biden performed especially well in the swing suburban districts from which the Democrats gained control of the U.S. House in the 2018 midterm election.

Robert E. Lang

Lincy Endowed Chair in Urban Affairs
Greenspun College of Urban Affairs, UNLV
Executive Director, Brookings Mountain West
Executive Director, The Lincy Institute

Acknowledgments

The development and completion of *Red States, Blue Metros* would not have been possible without the contributions and efforts of many people.

Throughout the book, we incorporate concepts and ideas offered in a variety of forums by analysts, journalists, and scholars, including Michael Barrone, Bill Bishop, Ron Brownstein, Richard Florida, Bill Frey, Bruce Katz, Mark Muro, Ruy Teixeira, and everyone involved with the "States of Change" project led by the Bipartisan Policy Center in Washington, D.C. Our book attempts to systemize their insights and place them into a common geography. The end result, we hope, is a geographic almanac of political competition in swing states that will interest analysts, instructors, journalists, and those studying national, state, and local politics.

Participants in the June 2017 Sun Belt policy center directors meeting organized by Bill Fulton at the Kinder Institute at Rice University in Houston, Texas, provided initial feedback about the value of the blue metros, red states framework. Several of those attending the meeting also participated in the project as state experts. Their willingness, and that of the other state experts—all of whom are listed in the appendix—to be interviewed and share their knowledge made the state case analyses possible.

Some of the book's preliminary work was presented at academic meetings, such as the Southwestern Political Science Association. We thank the discussants and panelists at those meetings for their comments. We also thank the anonymous reviewers who were selected by the Brookings Institution Press to review the manuscript. Their suggestions vastly improved the final product.

A special note of gratitude is due our colleagues at Brookings Mountain West and The Lincy Institute at UNLV. Throughout the project, Bill Brown, who authored chapter 7, served as a sounding board, copy editor, and compiler of all materials blue metros, red states. Jaewon Lim created the state regional maps, and Kelliann Beavers, Ashley LeClair, and Caitlin Saladino organized the preparation of the manuscript. Kaylie Pattni and Ember Smith assisted with data collection and tabulation, and Elaine Silverstone conducted and transcribed the interviews with the state experts. We cannot thank Elaine enough for her diligence and care in overseeing the twenty state expert interviews that are incorporated into the state case analyses.

We also thank the leadership of the College of Liberal Arts and the Greenspun College of Urban Affairs at UNLV for providing us with the time and space to complete the manuscript. Likewise, we thank our generous donors for their continued support of Brookings Mountain West and The Lincy Institute.

John Hudak and Molly Reynolds at the Brookings Institution not only contributed to the book but also suggested many of the state experts and provided early advice about the book's thesis and organization. We thank John and Molly for their contributions. Bill Finan, the director of the Brookings Institution Press, was an early champion of the project. Bill's patience and assistance, and that of his staff, made it possible for us to bring the project to fruition.

Last, we thank our families—Andrea, Jacob, and Nicholas Damore and Aidan Lang—for their love and support and for tolerating our endless preoccupation as we worked on the project, especially when we were all sheltering in place and trying not to drive each other crazy.

Blue Metros,
Red States

1

INTRODUCTION

David F. Damore
Robert E. Lang
Karen A. Danielsen

> Where we once had two parties, each sprawled across
> the country, north and south, east and west, we now have
> two distinct coalitions defined primarily by density. The
> old dichotomies—red state/blue state, city/suburb—are
> just too simplistic to capture today's much more complex
> picture, which often as not is painted in shades of pink,
> purple and mauve. Welcome to America's new map.[1]

—*Richard Florida*

While colored state maps have been a staple of media coverage of presidential elections for decades, the colors used to identify candidates and parties have been inconsistent over time.[2] However, starting with the 2000 presidential election, the red state, blue state configuration became the manner by which Republican- and Democratic-voting states are more-or-less universally categorized. In the subsequent two decades, the red state, blue state motif has become so firmly entrenched that it is now used as shorthand to account for outcomes as diverse as the prevalence of Lyme disease, divorce, teen pregnancy, and a host of consumer and lifestyle behaviors.[3]

Yet, just because the red state, blue state framework is ubiquitous does not mean it accurately captures the fissures defining contemporary American politics. Most obviously, while state boundaries define the spaces by which votes in presidential and other statewide elections are aggregated, there is variation in every state's levels of par-

1

tisan support and representation. An entire state is never completely red or blue. There have always been blue parts of red states and vice versa.

Take, for instance, Utah. Although the state is regarded of as one of the most Republican in the nation, Utah ranks second in the nation for protections for LGBTQ people (lesbian, gay, bisexual, transgender, and queer) and its largest city, Salt Lake City, is led by Democrat Erin Mendenhall.[4] In fact, the last time a Republican served as the mayor of Salt Lake City was in 1974.[5] On the other end of the spectrum are Maryland and Massachusetts, two of the most liberal states in the country. Yet, in 2018, Maryland Democrat Ben Cardin won reelection to the U.S. Senate with nearly 65 percent of the vote and the Democrats picked up a handful of seats in the statehouse, even as Republican governor Larry Hogan was reelected by nearly twelve points. In Massachusetts, Republican governor Charlie Baker cruised to a second term, while Democrat Elizabeth Warren was reelected to the U.S. Senate with more than 60 percent of the vote. The Democrats also maintained control of all nine of Massachusetts's U.S. House seats and strengthened their majorities in both chambers of that statehouse.

We are not the first to note the shortcomings of the red state, blue state paradigm. Many others, inside and outside of academia, make this point.[6] We add a new dimension to this literature by disentangling the spatial underpinnings of intrastate electoral and policy competition. We also examine how the political, cultural, demographic, and economic differences distinguishing Democratic-voting blue metros from Republican-voting outlying rural and exurban areas reverberate in electoral politics and state policymaking. While we focus our analysis on thirteen selected swing states, our thesis addresses the tensions between liberal urban spaces and conservative rural spaces that not only underlie red state, blue state voting patterns in statewide elections but also affect statehouse, county commission, mayoral, city council, and congressional races and the policies promoted by these candidates and elected officials. Our analysis goes beyond the use of red states versus blue states in the Electoral College and applies the concept to the political and policy dynamics within states.

An effort to implement background checks for private gun sales in Nevada captures these dynamics. In 2013, Republican governor Brian

Sandoval vetoed SB (Senate Bill) 221, passed by the urban-dominated, Democratic-controlled legislature, requiring background checks for private gun purchases or transfers. In response to the governor's veto, Question 1, requiring background checks for private gun sales or transfers, qualified for the November 2016 ballot.[7] The initiative passed by fewer than 10,000 votes after receiving majority support in one county—Clark County—home to Las Vegas, where Question 1 passed by more than 100,000 votes. However, the state's Republican attorney general, backed by the Republican governor, refused to implement the initiative over technical issues stemming from the initiative's language. Consequently, the initiative languished and remained unimplemented for more than two years.

In the aftermath of the 1 October (2017) mass shooting on the Las Vegas Strip, Nevada Democrats campaigned in support of stronger gun regulations. After the party's 2018 rout of Republicans, which delivered unified control of state government, one of the first bills signed into law by Democratic governor Steve Sisolak was SB 143 (2019) implementing Question 1's background check requirements. Following the bill's signing, Republican legislators opined that the bill was rushed, even though SB 143 implemented an initiative passed more than two years earlier and the bill received an eight-hour joint chamber hearing. Republican legislators suggested the bill did not reflect their belief that "most of our state is rural," ignoring the fact that a small percent of Nevadans reside in the state's rural (or non-core-based) counties.[8] Rural county sheriffs pledged not to enforce the law, and rural county commissioners passed resolutions declaring their counties as "Second Amendment Sanctuary" zones.[9]

The background check example highlights a number of the key themes in this book. Although Nevada is considered a swing state, outside of Clark County, Democratic candidates typically lose by significant vote deficits. However, nearly three-quarters of all Nevadans reside in Clark County, and when unified, Clark is large enough to impose its preferences on all Nevada. Indeed, given the limited scope of the background check policy,[10] what seemed to be a greater concern of some opponents to the measure was that urban Democrats were ignoring the concerns of the rural counties.[11] This perspective, of course, is at odds with the principle that "legislators represent people, not trees or acres," but it is consistent with research suggesting that the country's diversifying population fosters perceptions of status loss among those who feel threatened by America's changing demographics.[12] County-level maps of partisan support showing scattered blue islands amid seas of red reinforce this view.

The battle in swing-state North Carolina over bathroom access provides another example of blue metros, red states politics. In February 2016, the Charlotte city council voted to protect gay and transgender people by allowing them to use public restrooms consistent with their preferred gender identity. Because of a successful gerrymander, Republicans dominated the statehouse and soon thereafter used their stranglehold on state government to call a special session. Republicans, in a single day, introduced, passed, and signed into law HB (House Bill) 2, the "Public Facilities Privacy and Security Act." The legislation required individuals in government buildings to use restrooms corresponding to the sex identified on their birth certificate. The bill also overturned local anti-discrimination LGBTQ protection ordinances and prohibited local governments from strengthening such ordinances moving forward.[13]

Examining the vote for HB 2 suggests a geographic asymmetry. Within the seventeen-member Mecklenburg delegation (the county in which Charlotte, the largest metro in North Carolina, sits), six Republicans voted in favor, four Democrats voted in opposition, and five Democrats and two Republicans were either absent or did not vote. Thus, of the 114 total votes in favor of the bill, Mecklenburg legislators cast just six of these votes (roughly 5 percent of the total). In contrast, a fifth of the legislators who were absent, voted no, or abstained represented districts in Mecklenburg County. In addition, nine legislators representing districts in North Carolina's other major metro region, Raleigh, either voted no or did not vote.

A controversy that began in North Carolina with a single municipality seeking to present itself as a tolerant community reverberated far and wide. Despite legal challenges to the North Carolina law, Republican state legislators across the country proposed similar legislation. Not content to sit by idly as a new front in the country's culture war opened, legislatures in some blue states then pushed bills strengthening LGBTQ protections.

The issue also resonated economically. After the bill's passage, Adidas, Deutsche Bank, Eli Lilly, PayPal, and other companies withdrew plans for investments in North Carolina. Entertainers canceled concerts. The National Basketball Association (NBA), the National Collegiate Athletic Association (NCAA), and the Atlantic Coast Conference (ACC) relocated sporting events from the state. In total, the Associated Press estimated that the legislation cost North Carolina close to $4 billion in lost business.[14]

In an effort to save face, the North Carolina legislature revised the "Public Facilities Privacy and Security Act." The replacement legislation eliminated the "bathroom ban," but maintained the prohibitions on local governments from enacting nondiscrimination ordinances (also known as "preemption"), a restraint that ensured that local governments would not overstep their bounds by promoting policies repellent to the Republican legislative majority.[15] Years later, Charlotte still spends millions on marketing to restore the city's image in the aftermath of HB 2.[16] Some blue states maintain policies prohibiting state-funded travel to North Carolina.

It is no accident that both state examples stem from disputes over sociocultural issues. As explored in chapter 2, such value-driven disputes are ground zero for partisan and, by extension, geographic polarization. Las Vegas, with its overwhelming population relative to the rest of Nevada, secured its interests through recently obtained hegemony over state government via the 2018 election. In contrast, even though Mecklenburg is the largest county in the state, it accounts for just 10 percent of North Carolina's population. Mecklenburg's delegation is not large enough to drive outcomes in the North Carolina legislature. Moreover, because of a Republican gerrymander, the county's delegation at the time of the HB 2 vote split 9-8 in favor of the Democrats even though Democrats held a 20-point voter registration advantage over the GOP in the county. Charlotte may be small relative to the rest the state, but when combined with other metros along North Carolina's I-85 Corridor, which includes the Research Triangle (Raleigh, Durham, and Chapel Hill), it contributes to a larger blue urban space that makes North Carolina a swing state.

More generally, the Nevada background check and the North Carolina bathroom bills are examples of the conflicts between what journalist Ron Brownstein calls "the coalition of transformation" versus "the coalition of restoration."[17] We unpack how geography and demographics underlying these diverging world views interact with electoral and policymaking institutions to determine political outcomes. While these tensions exist across the country and at all levels of government, we focus our analysis on the swing states that currently hold the balance of power in the Electoral College and the U.S. Senate. In the next sections, we specify our case selection criteria, present the framework that guides our examination of the urban/rural divide in the swing states, and provide a brief overview of our data and measurements. The chapter concludes with a summary of how the remainder of the book is organized.

BLUE METROS, RED STATES CASES

In 2016, Republican Donald Trump was elected president despite losing eighty-eight of the 100 most populated counties in America. Collectively, these counties accounted for the bulk of Democratic presidential candidate Hillary Clinton's popular vote advantage.[18] Two years later, the Democrats took majority control of the U.S. House of Representatives, mostly by flipping seats in suburban districts that ring the nation's largest metros. These gains came not just in blue states such as California and New Jersey or in swing states such as Colorado, Michigan, and Virginia, but even in red states such as Kansas, Oklahoma, and Utah.

By accelerating the conflation of density, race and ethnicity, and partisanship, the 2016 and 2018 elections fortified the urban/rural delineation of the parties' electoral bases. For most voters, the partisanship of their geography in statewide elections is baked in depending on the relative sizes of the urban and rural blocs in their respective states. From this perspective, Nebraska and Utah are red states because Omaha and Salt Lake City lack the diversity and scale to offset the Republican advantages in the outlying areas. California and New Jersey are blue states because their diverse, massive urban population centers dwarf each state's less diverse and less populated hinterlands. Swing states are places where neither bloc dominates, and as our analysis demonstrates, outcomes in these states are often determined by the degree to which infrequent voters participate in elections and how much short-term political influences shuffle the preferences of suburban voters—especially those residing in fast-growth, urbanizing suburbs, what Robert Lang and Jennifer LeFurgy label "boomburbs."[19]

While our analysis certainly has implications for how the swing states may shape the composition of the federal government come January 2021 and beyond, that is not the book's sole focus. We also examine the political dynamic within the swing states by considering how swing state metros navigate the intrastate urban/rural divide. In total, our case analysis considers thirteen swing states and twenty-seven million-plus metros (see table 1-1). The swing states were determined by two criteria: a 2016 presidential vote margin within ten points and at least one metropolitan area exceeding 1 million residents. The second criterion excludes three northern swing states—Iowa (Trump +9.4), Maine (Clinton +2.9), and New Hampshire (Clinton +0.4)—that had 2016 margins within ten points. In total, the thirteen swing states covered in this volume contain over 40 percent of the country's total population and include seven of the ten most populous states.

We use the 1 million population threshold to differentiate large, high-density metros from smaller-scale regions (as of 2019, there are fifty-three such metros in the United States).[20] Large metros maintain extensive public infrastructure, including multimodal transportation networks; are responsible for delivering significant public services; and are supported by substantial administrative apparatuses. The metros also generate most of the nation's foreign trade and GDP and account for the vast share of patents and new technology.[21] Almost every major seaport and airport, which manage the nation's logistics and supply chains, is found within a million-plus metro. The core cities within large metros house large concentrations of minorities and liberal whites. The urban/rural divide is not a significant characteristic in places such as Maine, New Hampshire, or Iowa, which feature smaller-scaled metros and less-diverse demographics.[22]

Table 1-1 organizes the states regionally to capture their dispersion across the country's physical space as well as to highlight geographic clusters. The states' number of Electoral College votes are included in the table to provide a sense of their relative populations and their ability to influence presidential elections.

TABLE 1-1. Blue Metros and Red States Case Studies

State	2016 Margin	Electoral College Votes	Metros
Mid-Atlantic			
Pennsylvania	Trump +0.7	20	Philadelphia and Pittsburgh
Virginia	Clinton +5.3	13	Northern Virginia, Richmond, and Virginia Beach
South Atlantic			
Georgia	Trump +5.2	16	Atlanta
North Carolina	Trump +3.7	15	Charlotte and Raleigh
Midwest			
Michigan	Trump +0.2	16	Detroit and Grand Rapids
Ohio	Trump +8.1	18	Cleveland, Cincinnati, and Columbus
Upper Midwest			
Minnesota	Clinton +1.5	10	Minneapolis
Wisconsin	Trump +0.8	10	Milwaukee
Mountain West			
Arizona	Trump +3.5	11	Phoenix and Tucson
Colorado	Clinton +4.9	9	Denver
Nevada	Clinton +2.4	6	Las Vegas
Florida and Texas			
Florida	Trump +1.2	29	Jacksonville, Miami, Orlando, and Tampa
Texas	Trump +9.0	38	Austin, Dallas, Houston, and San Antonio

Notes: States were selected based upon two criteria: A 2016 presidential vote margin of ten points or less and at least one million-plus metro. Note that million-plus metro regions are labeled by their principal cities. The only expectation is we label the "Arlington-Alexandria" section of the Washington, D.C., MSA as "Northern Virginia." We used metropolitan statistical areas as the metro unit of analysis. We did not use the larger census regional unit of combined statistical areas. Thus, even though the smaller Durham-Chapel Hill, NC MSA is adjacent to the larger Raleigh, NC MSA and maintains significant economic linkages with its neighbor, data for the Durham-Chapel Hill, NC MSA are not added to the Raleigh MSA. We recognize that North Carolina's "Research Triangle" has a common regional identity, but we sought to maintain consistent statistical definitions throughout the book.

Sources: 2017 American Community Survey 1-Year estimates as aggregated by censusreporter.org and secretary of state websites.

Collectively, the states provide differing contexts for studying how the urban/rural divide affects state politics and policy. Pennsylvania and Virginia are ground zero for the partisan battle for the suburbs. Wisconsin and Minnesota are fading blue states with little diversity outside of their metro regions, but both have histories of progressivism and are culturally Northern.[23] The industrial states of Ohio and Michigan illuminate the economic challenges facing former industrial powers in a digital age. Georgia and North Carolina feature emerging economies, diverse demography, and large shares of college-educated graduates concentrated in their metros. The rapidly diversifying and urbanizing Mountain West states of Arizona, Colorado, and Nevada have fast growing metropolitan regions that constitute the majority of their states' populations. With multiple million-plus metros, Texas and Florida are massive, highly diverse states that, together, account for nearly a quarter of the Electoral College votes needed to win the presidency. Both states are so large in scale that they are the equivalent of nation states in economic terms and surpass the GDP output of most other countries.[24]

In the chapters that follow, we explore these states and their million-plus metros to show how patterns of intrastate diversity, density, and economic concentration affect electoral outcomes and shape policy decisions. These case studies consider how institutional variables (for example, legislative professionalism, redistricting, and home rule) affect the distribution of political power within states and how these arrangements either hinder or facilitate metro influence in policymaking. In the next section, we provide an overview of our thesis detailing how sociocultural geography shapes how diversity is experienced and the consequences it has for how million-plus metros versus smaller regions and rural areas respond to their state's changing demographic and economic landscapes.

DIVERSITY AND ITS GEOGRAPHY

At the federal level, the institutional arrangements that allocate political power, particularly the state-driven apportionment of the U.S. Senate and its effects on the allocation of Electoral College votes, underrepresent urban America's interests. A similar dynamic exists at the state level. As we highlight in chapter 2, in state politics, major metros often punch below their demographic and economic weight, allowing rural and exurban voters to impose policies potentially adverse to the interests of blue metros. North Carolina's preemption of Charlotte's efforts to implement an antidiscrimination ordinance is one example of these undercurrents. In Georgia, another swing state, the decision by Republicans to sharply restrict access to abortion by passing a fetal-heartbeat bill—legislation that led to television and movie production companies pulling projects from the state—is another.[25] This is no small concern. Atlanta recently emerged as "Hollywood East" and is now second to Los Angeles in film and television production.

In both instances, the actions of Republicans, often representing voters outside million-plus metros, imposed policies that inflicted both reputational and economic costs on their states' blue metros. That both of these examples come from southern states speaks to the essence of our thesis: the geography within the geography and the diversity within the diversity matters.

In every swing state with a million-plus metro, some variant of the urban/rural divide exists. But at what latitude and, to a lesser extent, at what longitude the blue metro, red state pairing is situated determines how race, immigration, and the country's changing demography are experienced and perceived. Geography shapes not just the composition and dispersion of a state's nonwhite population but also what these patterns engender culturally and how value differences manifest themselves at the ballot box and in policy. To achieve their agendas, major metros need to be integrated, open, and forward thinking. To the degree that there is a metro ethos, diversity acceptance is a key component, a value that is mostly not shared outside million-plus metros.

Table 1-2 groups the thirteen swing states in terms of the distribution of diversity in their million-plus metros versus smaller metros and rural areas and the major composition of their minority populations. As we detail in chapter 2, one of our building blocks is research examining the causes and consequences of regional cultural geography, particularly as it relates to the establishment, development, and migration from the northern and southern parts of the country. These

TABLE 1-2. Regional Patterns of Diversity and Composition among the Thirteen Swing States

Regions	States	Diversity Dispersion	Diversity Composition
Midwest/ Mid-Atlantic	MI, MN, OH PA, WI	Semi-diverse metro Nondiverse nonmetro	Black
South/ Mid-Atlantic/ Texas	GA, NC, TX, VA	Diverse metro Diverse nonmetro	Black, Latino, and emerging Asian
Mountain West/ Florida	AZ, CO, FL, NV	Diverse metro Semi-diverse nonmetro	Latino, some Black, Native, and Asian

cultural differences affect regional variation in the composition and dispersion of the states' diversity and how these differences structure cultural and social schisms.

The four Midwestern states—Michigan, Minnesota, Ohio, and Wisconsin (and Mid-Atlantic Pennsylvania)—have white populations exceeding the national average. To the degree to which these states have diversity, it is predominately African American and concentrated in the larger metros. Rural areas and smaller cities are mostly white, creating the starkest urban/rural demographic difference among our three state groupings. Pennsylvania partly follows the same pattern. There are, however, differences between Pennsylvania's metros. Pittsburgh's white population share exceeds the national average, while Philadelphia's is consistent with the national average. Philadelphia also has greater diversity within its diversity compared to Pittsburgh because it lies within the Mid-Atlantic region.

The states in the south also have diverse metros, but unlike the first grouping, these states also have substantial diversity in rural areas. Consequently, diversity is patterned differently in the Midwest and Pennsylvania compared to the south. In the north, diversity exists mostly in major metros, while in the south, it extends to smaller metros and rural areas. Thus we include Texas in this group. Yet, because of its physical expanse, Texas's rural population mix differs from most other southern states. Akin to Georgia, North Carolina, and Virginia, in east Texas, rural diversity generally is African American. However, in rural central and western Texas, Latinos dominate, a demographic group that recently increased in many southern states, including Georgia and North Carolina. Texas is a hybrid state. In the east, its demography aligns more with the south, but by San Antonio, the state is similar to the west. Still, as former Confederate states, Georgia, North Carolina, and to a lesser extent Texas and Virginia, remain rooted in the Southern Black/white slavery-post-slavery context. The history creates a very different cultural legacy compared to the swing states in the Midwest, Mid-Atlantic, and Mountain West.

Mountain West states differ from the other two groups in three important respects. First, Arizona, Colorado, and Nevada have diverse million-plus metros and some diversity in their smaller cities and rural towns. Although the diversity dispersion in these states is less than what exists in the south and in Texas, it is greater than what we observe in the Midwest and Mid-Atlantic states. Second, what Robert Lang, Andrea Sarzynski, and Mark Muro call the "Mountain Megas,"[26] Denver, Phoenix, and Las Vegas, form dominant population centers accounting for roughly one-half, two-thirds, and three-quarters of their state's population, respectively. By comparison, Dallas is the fourth largest American metropolitan statistical areas (MSA), but constitutes less than 30 percent of Texas's population. Third, Mountain West states' diversity features large shares of Asian Americans, Native Americans, and Latinos. Only Nevada has a sizeable African American population, which resides almost exclusively in Las Vegas.

We group Florida with Mountain West swing states because it, too, has diversity within its diversity (the states also were settled at roughly the same time, booming in the post-WWII decades). Like the southern and northern states, Florida has a substantial African American population (15 percent), but Florida's Black population is dwarfed by the state's Latino residents, and roughly two-thirds of all Florida African Americans reside in the state's four million-plus metros. Like Mountain West states, Florida has a large share of immigrants and some diversity in its smaller metros and rural areas, but the diversity is less extensive when compared to the other southern states.

Certainly, the case can be made for either swapping Florida and Texas or placing them in a separate category. Unlike the western states with highly concentrated population centers, Florida and Texas each contain four separate million-plus metros. Similar to the Mountain West states, however, each state has diversity within its diversity but divergent patterns of rural diversity. Regardless of which set of considerations one chooses to elevate over the others, Florida and Texas defy easy classification—a conclusion that cultural geographers such as Wilbur Zelinsky came to fifty years ago.[27]

To a lesser degree, these classification difficulties extend to Virginia. Unlike Florida and Texas, the one-time Confederate capital has voted strongly Democratic in recent elections. The transition has occurred so rapidly that *Politico* writer Charles Mahtesian argues that Virginia hardly had time to be a true swing state.[28] In terms of population, Virginia is much less populous than Florida or Texas. But like Florida and Texas, Virginia contains multiple million-plus metros, and, similar to those states' major metros, Virginia has significant inter-metro differences in terms of diversity composition.

Analytically, the existence of multiple million-plus metros within some of our states is advantageous. In chapter 2, we present data from the 2016 presidential election demonstrating how the diversity within the diversity affects statewide voting patterns. We find a negative relationship between a state's Black population share and support for Hillary Clinton. In states where African Americans are a smaller share of the minority population—that is, where there is diversity within the diversity—Clinton performed much stronger. These patterns track with geography and are attributable to spatial differences in the voting behavior among whites. In the southern states, where Blacks form the largest minority group and there is spatial integration among Blacks and whites, Donald Trump's margin among white voters increased (see figures 2-1 and 2-2). In states where there is greater diversity within the diversity, Trump's support among whites was much weaker. Our analysis shows that whites who are exposed to the hyper-diversity of big metros vote more Democratic than whites from regions with less complex diversity.

The metros in Florida, Texas, and Virginia allow us to assess if similar effects exist within states. For instance, while all three of Virginia's metros have similar nonwhite population shares, in Richmond and Virginia Beach, this diversity is largely African American. However, in Northern Virginia, which is part of the larger Washington, D.C., MSA, there is much greater diversity within the diversity, and similar to metros such as Austin, Denver, Raleigh, and Tucson, it has a large share of college-educated residents. Florida's metros provide similar contrasts. The diversity in Jacksonville and Tampa is primarily African American, while Orlando and Miami feature smaller shares of Blacks and larger numbers of Latinos. The four Texas metros offer another set of comparisons. Austin is overwhelmingly white, but the culture of its geography differs from the rest of Texas due to its founding by Central Europeans as opposed to the Scots-Irish who migrated into much of the rest of the state.[29] San Antonio has the largest share of Latinos, while Dallas and Houston have large shares of African Americans. Thus, while we expect all of these metros to be more Democrat oriented compared to their state's nonmetro areas, these effects should be stronger in the metros with greater diversity within their diversity.

Ohio, with its three million-plus metros, offers a different type of intrastate comparison. Lacking the variation in diversity composition and dispersion of Florida, Texas, and Virginia, the spatial variation of Ohio's three metros—Cleveland in the north, Columbus in the center, and Cincinnati in the south—cut across the Northern, Midland, and Southern cultural zones according to a map of the cultural regions of the United States by Zelinsky.[30]

Figure 1-1, which plots the nonwhite population shares in each state against the share of each states' nonwhite population that resides within the states' million-plus metros, demonstrates the degree to which diversity is clustered in large urban regions. Note that for states with multiple million-plus metros, the data are combined. These data do not control for variation in the composition of each state's minority populations.

The positive slope of the trend line suggests that, in general, the more diverse the state, the higher the concentration of diversity in the biggest metros. However, due to regional variation, the slope is not particularly steep. In terms of our thirteen swing states, as expected, Pennsylvania and the four Midwestern states are clustered on the left side of the figure, suggesting they have limited diversity and that this

FIGURE 1-1. Concentration of Statewide Nonwhite
Population Shares in Million-Plus Metros (2017)

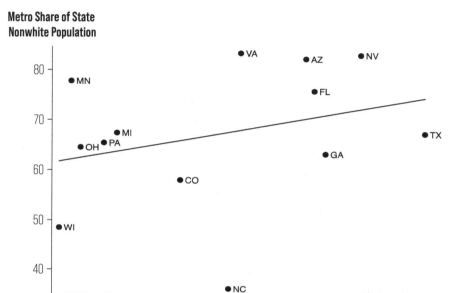

Metro Share of State
Nonwhite Population

State Nonwhite Population Share

diversity is largely within the million-plus metros. This is particularly the case for Minneapolis, which constitutes 62 percent of Minnesota's population but houses over three-quarters of the state's minority population. In Wisconsin, which has the smallest major metro population share of the thirteen states, Milwaukee constitutes 27 percent of the state's population but maintains nearly half Wisconsin's nonwhite population, the largest percentage point discrepancy among any of our million-plus metro/rest of state pairings.

Due to the differences in the size of major metros relative to their state populations, the relationships for the other groups of states is less obvious. For instance, over 82 percent of Arizonans live in metro Phoenix and Tucson compared to 34 percent of North Carolinians who reside in Charlotte and Raleigh. Arizona's million-plus metro population is so dominant that there is little population to be dispersed in smaller metros and rural areas. In North Carolina, however, both the bulk of the state's population and the state's nonwhite population resides outside of Charlotte and Raleigh, with many North Carolinians living in a larger, extended urban region known as the Piedmont or the I-85 Corridor.[31]

In Texas and southern swing states, except for Virginia, each state's million-plus metros have diversity concentrations that are more-or-less consistent with their share of total population. In Georgia, Texas, and North Carolina, 37 percent, 33 percent, and 64 percent, respectively, of those states' nonwhite populations are located outside of their major metropolitan areas. Within this group of states, Virginia, the most urbanized one, is the outlier. The state's three million-plus metros constitute 71 percent of Virginia's population but are home to more than 83 percent of Virginia's minorities. As suggested, there also is growing divergence in terms of the minority composition of Virginia's metros. Northern Virginia, which includes Asian American, Latino, and foreign-born population shares that are all roughly twice the state average, has a demographic profile similar to Mid-Atlantic states, such as New Jersey. The demographics of Richmond and Virginia Beach are more like the rest of the south. Despite the state's changing demography and urbanization, Black rural pockets persist in Virginia's coastal plains region.

In the three Mountain West swing states and Florida, diversity concentrates in million-plus metros but they maintain greater relative diversity dispersion compared to Pennsylvania and the Midwest. This is particularly the case for Colorado. Because of the large rural, Native American and Latino populations, more than 40 percent of minorities in Colorado reside outside of metro Denver. Although Arizona and Nevada have highly concentrated urban populations (82.1 and 73.5 percent of state population share, respectively), roughly 18 percent of each state's nonwhite population is located in smaller metros and rural areas. In Florida, another highly urbanized state, a quarter of the minority population resides outside of the state's four million-plus metros.

DEFINITIONS AND DATA

The book uses qualitative and quantitative data to examine electoral and policy differences between million-plus metros and smaller metros/rural areas in thirteen swing states. Comparing and contrasting major metropolitan areas and smaller/nonmetro regions necessitates defining each. We use the terms major metro, city, or urban interchangeably to refer to the MSAs designated by the U.S. census. Except for Northern Virginia, we identify million-plus metros by their principal or largest cities rather than by their formal MSA titles (for example, Orlando instead of Orlando-Kissimmee-Sanford, FL MSA). Because six of our metro regions—Northern Virginia, Charlotte, Cincinnati, Minneapolis, Philadelphia, and Virginia Beach—extend into multiple states, except for table 2-3, we adjust the data of these metros to include only the counties within the thirteen swing states. Box 1-1 defines the geographic terms derived from the census data that we use throughout.

Spaces not within major metros are referred to as smaller metros, rural, nonmetro, or nonurban. This bifurcation of space means that MSAs with populations below 1 million are classified as "smaller metros" and their data are included with the "rest of state" outside the major metros. The effect of this on our analysis depends on a state's size. In a small state, a smaller metro may constitute a fairly large share of state population, while a similar-size or larger metro in a more populated state may be less consequential for understanding intrastate politics and policy dynamics. For instance, in Nevada, the least populated of the thirteen swing states we consider, metro Reno, with 425,000 residents, accounts for 15 percent of Nevada's population. However, it is a fifth the size of Las Vegas, and it is the 114th largest metro in the country. By comparison, Austin, which is slightly smaller than Las Vegas, is home to less than 8 percent of Texans.

In total, seventeen of the 100 largest metros with populations below 1 million are in the swing states. These smaller metros are concentrated primarily in the more populated states.[32] The largest two such metros, McAllen and El Paso, are in Texas. With five such metros, Florida has the most (Sarasota, Fort Myers, Lakeland, Daytona, Palm Bay), followed by North Carolina with three (Greensboro,

BOX 1-1. Geographic Definitions

Throughout the book, we employ a number of geographic concepts, the most important of which is the Office of Management and Budget (OMB)-defined "metropolitan statistical area" (MSA).[a] An MSA is one of three "core-based statistical areas" (CBSA) established by OMB to classify American population clusters. The other CBSAs are "combined statistical areas" (CSA) and "micropolitan statistical areas" (MicroSA). OMB also identifies "urban cores," and subregional geographic constructs such as "principal cities," the largest city in an MSA or MicroSA, and "census-designated places," unincorporated communities, often proximate to principal cities, with significant populations.[b] The census began tracking these spaces in 1980.

The building blocks for all CBSAs are counties. OMB defines an MSA as having an "urban core" exceeding 50,000 residents that maintains an economic interdependence via commuting, either within or to adjacent counties, based on an "employment-interchange measure" (EIM). If a county maintains at least 25 percent of its households commuting to a "central county" (a 25 percent-plus EIM), then the two counties join in a common MSA. The same is true for a MicroSA, only the urban core contains between 10,000 to 50,000 residents. A CSA is defined as a combination of MSAs and/or MicroSAs that maintain an EIM of between 15 to 25 percent.[c] EIMs and MSA county components are updated annually via the American Community Survey.

In addition to OMB-defined urban places, scholars affiliated with the Metropolitan In-

---

a. The OMB is responsible for codifying the geographic definitions used by the Bureau of the Census, which is under the U.S. Department of Commerce.

b. Because the 2000 "Millennium Census" introduced such a radically altered population geography from the preceding 1990 census, scholars at the Brookings Institution developed a "field guide" to assist researchers using the new categories; see William H. Frey, Jill H. Wilson, Alan Berube, and Audrey Singer, "Tracking Metropolitan America into the 21st Century: A Field Guide to the New Metropolitan and Micropolitan Definitions," in *Redefining Urban and Suburban America: Evidence from the Census 2000*, volume 3, edited by Alan Berube, Bruce Katz, and Robert E. Lang (Washington: Brookings Institution Press, 2006), pp. 191–234. In the same volume, Robert E. Lang and Dawn Dhavale published the first comprehensive analysis covering micropolitan areas; see Robert E. Lang and Dawn Dhavale, "Micropolitan America: A Brand New Geography," in *Redefining Cities and Suburbs: Evidence from the Census 2000*, volume 3, pp. 235–58.

c. A detailed summation of these concepts can be found in Robert E. Lang and Arthur C. Nelson, "Megapolitan America: Defining and Applying a New Geography," in *Megaregions: Planning for Global Competitiveness*, edited by Catherine Ross (Washington: Island Press, 2009), pp. 107–26.

stitute at Virginia Tech in Alexandria, Virginia,[d] developed multiple geographic constructs based in census and commercial data.[e] Under the Metropolitan Institute's "new metropolis" research initiative, they advanced ideas such as "megapolitan areas," "boomburbs," "edgeless cities," "metroburbs," and "world cities."[f] Part of the Metropolitan Institute's new metropolis thinking has been applied to politics. In 2008, Robert Lang, Thomas Sanchez, and Alan Berube published a metropolitan classification system based on a county's density and diversity that tracked presidential and congressional voting trends since 2000 for all U.S. urban regions exceeding 1 million residents.[g] However, this book represents the first effort to apply multiple new metropolis concepts to comprehensively analyze state and

---

d. Robert Lang began as director of the Metropolitan Institute in 2001 and was later joined by urban planner Arthur C. Nelson as codirector in 2004. Urban geographers Paul L. Knox, who was dean of Virginia Tech's College of Architecture and Urban Studies, and Peter J. Taylor, who ran Loughborough's Globalization and World Cities (GaWC) research network, were Metropolitan Institute faculty affiliates for several years in the mid 2000s.

e. For a discussion of explosion of these labels, see Peter J. Taylor and Robert E. Lang, "The Shock of the New: 100 Concepts Describing Recent Urban Change," *Environment and Planning* 36 (June 2004), pp. 951–58.

f. See Robert E. Lang, *Edgeless Cities: Exploring the Elusive Metropolis* (Washington: Brookings Institution Press, 2003); Robert E. Lang and Jennifer B. LeFurgy, *Boomburbs: The Rise of America's Accidental Cities* (Washington: Brookings Institution Press, 2007); Robert E. Lang, Edward J. Blakely, and Megan Zimmerman-Gough, "Keys to the New Metropolis: America's Big, Fast-Growing Suburban Counties," *Journal of the American Planning Association* 71 (Autumn 2005), pp. 381–91; Arthur C. Nelson and Robert E. Lang, *Megapolitan America: A New Vision for Understanding America's Metropolitan Geography* (Chicago: American Planning Association Press, 2011); Paul L. Knox, *Metroburbia, USA* (Rutgers University Press, 2008); Peter J. Taylor and Robert E. Lang, "U.S. Cities in the 'World City Network,'" Brookings Institution Metropolitan Policy Program Report, February 2005. For a history of the megapolitan concept, see Robert E. Lang, Jaewon Lim, and Karen A. Danielsen, "The Origin, Evolution, and Application of the Megapolitan Area Concept," *International Journal of Urban Sciences* 24 (January 2020), pp. 1–12.

g. Robert E. Lang, Thomas W. Sanchez, and Alan Berube, "The New Suburban Politics: A County-Based Analysis of Metropolitan Voting Trends since 2000," in *The Future of Red, Blue, and Purple America: Election Demographics, 2008 and Beyond*, edited by Ruy Teixeira (Washington: Brookings Institution Press, 2008), pp. 25–49. A similar typology was first used in Robert E. Lang and Thomas W. Sanchez, "The New Metropolitics: Interpreting Recent Elections using a County-Based Regional Typology," *Metropolitan Institute at Virginia Tech 2006 Election Brief Series* (Metropolitan Institute at Virginia Tech), pp. 1–19, www .researchgate.net/publication/230820734_The_new_metro_politics_Interpreting _recent_presidential_elections_using_a_county-based_regional_typology.

national politics, including intrastate conflict between million-plus metros and the rest of the state.

Finally, it is worth noting that, during the Clinton administration, the OMB considered the idea of creating a large-scale metropolitan category that it labeled "megapolitan areas."[h] The metropolitan area category had grown so broad that it lost meaning because it included places ranging from the New York MSA, with nearly 20 million residents, down to the Carson City MSA, with just 55,000 people. The U.S. Census Geography Program proposed that metropolitan areas with urban cores exceeding a million residents (about forty regions in 2000) be reclassified as megapolitan areas. Thus the census would feature a three-tier, core-based urban hierarchy: micros (with 10,000 to 50,000 population cores); metros (with 50,001 to 1,000,000 population cores); and megas (with 1,000,000 or more population cores).[i] George W. Bush's OMB nixed the megapolitan areas in 2001 but retained the micropolitan area geography developed under the Clinton administration.

---

h. Robert E. Lang and Arthur C. Nelson, "Megapolitan America," *Places Journal* (November 2011), https://doi.org/10.22269/111114.

i. Ibid. Lang and Nelson used the label for their largest urban clusters.

Durham, and Winston-Salem). Ohio (Akron and Toledo), Pennsylvania (Allentown and Harrisburg), and Texas each have two. The other smaller-scale metros in the swing states are Augusta, Georgia, Colorado Springs, Colorado, and Madison, Wisconsin. Given their population shares relative to their states, Colorado Springs and Madison are the two smaller metros that are likely to exert the greatest impact on outcomes, a point that is highlighted in the analyses of Colorado and Wisconsin, respectively.

Throughout the book, we present demographic, economic, electoral, and institutional data for our thirteen states and twenty-seven million-plus metros. These data were collected from publicly available sources, and the specific data sources used are noted in the tables and figures. While these data are insightful, they do not provide a complete picture. To better understand each state's intrastate cultural, policy, and political dynamics, we present data collected from interviews with state policy experts. The appendix provides a list of all the experts who participated. These experts are primarily academics, and they were selected because of their knowledge of their states' politics, demographics, and histories.

After participation was secured via an email solicitation, interviews were conducted by phone, recorded, and transcribed by a research assistant.[33] The interviews focused on five open-ended themes central to our thesis:

- Identifying the political dynamic between million-plus metros and the rest of the state and how this affects partisan patterns of voting

- Determining the degree to which million-plus metros and the rest of the state are divided socially and culturally and the implications this has for policy debates and outcomes

- Evaluating how continued demographic change is likely to impact the state's political dynamics in the future

- Examining how salient institutional features such as the location of the state capital, legislative professionalism, term limits, and Dillon's rule constraints on local governments empower or hinder major metros

- Assessing how much political clout a major metro exerts in state politics and how this affects the allocation of state resources

The state experts' responses are incorporated into the book via a qualitative analysis (inspired by the Delphi method of surveying expert opinion).[34] Our method identifies common themes that provide a contextual understanding of quantitative data associated with the thirteen states and the twenty-seven million-plus metros. By using a mixed methods approach that combines primary and secondary data, a geographic/historical analysis of each state and region, and the expert opinion of scholars whose knowledge spans politics, policy, urban affairs, and demography, we produce a comprehensive look at the dynamics between blue metros and their red states.

CHAPTER ORGANIZATION

The remainder of the book is organized into nine chapters. In chapter 2, we review prior research that informs our analysis and thesis. Here, we consider work examining sociocultural geography to understand the origins and persistence of regional political differences between and within states. The chapter also reviews scholarship examining how demographic, geographic, and economic sorting underlie the blue metros, red states urban/rural divide and how these differences manifest themselves attitudinally. The chapter concludes by evaluating how state and federal electoral and policymaking institutions can empower rural interests at the expense of metros and the implications this has for the representation and advancement of metro policy priorities.

In chapters 3 through 9, we present empirical analyses of the thirteen swing states and twenty-seven million-plus metros. These chapters use a common format. For each state, we provide a summary of the geopolitical "state of play" accompanied by a stylized state map highlighting each state's political sections, key transportation routes, major cities, and the state capital.[35] These discussions are augmented by the presentation of demographic, economic, and electoral data detailing differences between million-plus metros and smaller metros/rural areas in each state. We also show measures of metro governance fragmentation and local government autonomy. These data presentations and the state of play summaries provide the context for assessing the degree to which the preferences of the major metros reinforce or diverge from their states and the consequences this has for representation at the state and federal levels. Discussions of these dynamics are then further developed into a Delphi analysis provided by the state experts.

The state analyses are grouped by chapter, with the exceptions of Florida and Texas, which are covered in their own chapters. Chapter 3 groups the Mid-Atlantic states of Pennsylvania and Virginia together because the largest metro in each state is included in the blue-dominated Northeast Corridor that stretches from Boston to Washington, D.C. The fact that a major section of each state lies within that corridor is why Pennsylvania and Virginia are swing states. These blue sections offset what otherwise would be red states.

Georgia and North Carolina are examined together in chapter 4 because they anchor a new large-scale and urbanized south. Both states attract domestic and foreign migrants and businesses, as Atlanta and Charlotte have become major logistic and corporate hubs. Both states also support high-tech economies, in greater Atlanta and the Research Triangle of Raleigh, Durham, and Chapel Hill.

Chapter 6 examines the Midwestern states of Michigan and Ohio. Both have relied on heavy manufacturing that has suffered in recent decades. The declining union vote in both states, coupled with limited diversity, has made Michigan and Ohio more conservative and more open to protectionist trade policies.

Minnesota and Wisconsin are covered together in chapter 7 because they share a tradition of Upper Midwest progressive politics. Both states recently have experienced a shift in attitudes among rural voters, who have grown far more conservative in recent years, and outside of their largest metros, both states have very little diversity.

The three states in the Mountain West, Arizona, Colorado, and Nevada, are the focus of chapter 9. These states are fast growing, rapidly diversifying, and have one or two metro regions that account for a vast share of their residents.

Because Florida and Texas are so large scale, the second and third most populous American states, with each containing four separate million-plus metros, they are covered in their own chapters—chapters 5 and 8, respectively.

In the final chapter, we summarize our findings, evaluate their implications for future policy and electoral outcomes, and assess the likelihood that the blue metros will be positioned to move their states from swing states to blue states. In the epilogue, Brookings Institution scholar Molly Reynolds considers the blue metros, red states thesis from the perspective of Washington, D.C., and its consequences for representation and policy at the federal level.

NOTES

1. Richard Florida, "Welcome to Blueburbia . . . and Other Landmarks on America's New Map," *Politico Magazine*, November 2013, www.politico.com/magazine/story /2013/11/06/welcome-to-blueburbia-and-other-landmarks-on-americas-new-map -098957.

2. Ben Zimmer, "Thinking about Tim Russert, Red States and Blue States," *Visual Thesaurus*, June 17, 2008, www.visualthesaurus.com/cm/wordroutes/thinking-about -tim-russert-red-states-and-blue-states/.

3. Robert B. Nadelman and Gary P. Wormser, "Poly-Ticks: Blue State versus Red State for Lyme Disease," *The Lancet* 365 (January 2005), p. 289; Naomi Cahn and June Carbone, *Red Families v. Blue Families* (Oxford University Press, 2007), p. 21; Kiju Jung, Ellen Garabino, Donnel A. Briley, and Jesse Wynhausen, "Blue and Red Voices: Effects of Political Ideology on Consumers' Complaining and Disputing Behavior," *Journal of Consumer Research* 44, no. 3 (October 2017), pp. 477–99; Morning Consult, "Walmart vs. Target: A Political Divide among Shoppers," January 25, 2018, https:// morningconsult.com/2018/01/25/walmart-vs-target-a-political-divide-among -shoppers/.

4. Courtney Tanner and Scott D. Pierce, "Utah Ranks 2nd in the Nation for Supporting Laws that Protect LGBTQ Community," *Salt Lake Tribune*, July 22, 2019, www.sltrib.com/news/2019/07/22/utahns-support-laws/.

5. Salt Lake City's last Republican mayor was Jake Garn, who later represented Utah in the U.S. Senate for three terms.

6. For an overview of the utility and limitations of the red state, blue state paradigm, as well as a discussion of the various ways in which the paradigm is used, see Geiguen Shin and David J. Webster, "Red States, Blue States: How Well Do the Recent National Election Labels Capture State Political and Policy Differences?" *Social Science Journal* 51, no. 3 (September 2014), pp. 386–97; Edward L. Glaser and Bryce A. Ward, "Myths and Realities of American Political Geography," *Journal of Economic Perspectives* 20, no. 2 (Spring 2006), pp. 119–44.

7. With the Republicans gaining unified control of state government after the 2014 elections, similar legislation failed to advance during the 2015 session of the Nevada legislature.

8. Senator Scott Hammond, Senator Keith Pickard, Assemblyman Tom Roberts, Assemblywoman Melissa Hardy, and Assemblyman Glen Leavitt, "The Gun Background Check Bill was Rushed Through Too Quickly," *Nevada Independent*, February 9, 2017, https://thenevadaindependent.com/article/the-gun-background-check-bill -was-rushed-through-too-quickly.

9. Ben Margiott, "Rural Nevada Sheriffs Question Whether They Will Enforce New Gun Background Check Law," MyNews4, March 4, 2019, https://mynews4.com/ news/local/rural-nevada-sheriffs-question-whether-they-will-enforce-new-gun-background-check-law; Tim Burmeister, "Do We Stand Up Now . . . Or . . . When They

Come to Get the Guns?" *Elko Daily*, March 20, 2019, https://elkodaily.com/news/
local/govt-and-politics/do-we-stand-up-now-or-when-they-come-to/article_83f17
0d8-3183-50ba-9170-623bc2f949e6.amp.html?utm_medium=social&utm_source
=twitter&utm_campaign=user-share&__twitter_impression=true.

10. SB 143 (2017) extends background checks that already are required for purchases from licensed gun dealers to include private gun sales and transfers.

11. Legislators from districts within Clark County accounted for 90 percent of
the votes in favor of SB 143 (2017) and 33 percent of the votes in opposition to the bill.
See Ray Hagar, "Concern that Voice of Rural Nevada Not Being Heard," *Pahrump
Valley Times*, March 21, 2019, https://pvtimes.com/opinion/ray-hagar-concern
-that-voice-of-rural-nevada-not-being-heard-67596/.

12. Quote from *Reynolds v. Sims* 377 U.S. 533 (1964), the Supreme Court case that
extended the principle of one person, one vote to state legislative districts. For research assessing perceptions of status loss and its political consequence, see Diana
C. Mutz, "Status Threat, Not Economic Hardship, Explains the 2016 Presidential
Vote," *Proceedings of the National Academy of Sciences* 115, April 2018, pp. E4330–
E4339; Ashley Jardina, *White Identity Politics* (Cambridge University Press, 2019), pp.
21–49; Jonathan A. Metzl, *Dying of Whiteness: How the Politics of Racial Resentment
is Killing America's Heartland* (New York: Basic Books, 2019), pp. 1–22; Christopher
Parker and Matt A. Barreto, *Change They Can't Believe In: The Tea Party and Reactionary Politics in America* (Princeton University Press, 2013), pp. 20–65, 153–89; John
Sides, Michael Tesler, and Lynn Vavreck, *Identity Crisis: The 2016 Presidential Campaign and the Battle for the Meaning of America* (Princeton University Press, 2018),
pp. 201–20.

13. Michael Gordon, Mark S. Price, and Katie Peralta, "Understanding HB2:
North Carolina's Newest Law Solidifies State's Role in Defining Discrimination,"
Charlotte Observer, March 26, 2016, www.charlotteobserver.com/news/politics-
government/article68401147.html.

14. CNBC, "'Bathroom Bill' to Cost North Carolina $3.76 Billion," *CNBC.com*,
March 27, 2017, www.cnbc.com/2017/03/27/bathroom-bill-to-cost-north-carolina-
376-billion.html.

15. Barry Smith, "Cooper H.B. 2 Compromise Doesn't Address 'Home Rule'
Question," *Carolina Journal*, February 21, 2017, www.carolinajournal.com/news-
article/cooper-h-b-2-compromise-doesnt-address-home-rule-question/.

16. Katherine Peraltas, "Charlotte Still Has to Spend Money to Attract Visitors
Turned Off by HB2, Records Show," *Charlotte Observer*, December 17, 2018, www.
charlotteobserver.com/news/business/article223045445.html.

17. Ronald Brownstein, "The Coalition of Transformation vs. the Coalition of
Restoration," *The Atlantic*, November 21, 2012, www.theatlantic.com/politics/
archive/2012/11/the-coalition-of-transformation-vs-the-coalition-of-restoration
/265512/.

18. Ronald Brownstein, "How the Election Revealed the Divide between City and

Country," *The Atlantic*, November 17, 2016, www.theatlantic.com/politics/archive /2016/11/clinton-trump-city-country-divide/507902/.

19. A "boomburb" is defined as an incorporated city of more than 50,000 residents that experienced double-digit growth each decade since 1970. See Robert E. Lang and Jennifer B. LeFurgy, *Boomburbs: The Rise of America's Accidental Cities* (Washington: Brookings Institution Press, 2007).

20. Writing in 1965, the urban economist Wilbur Thompson developed "the urban-size ratchet" model to differentiate large-scale metro spaces that typically continue to grow and rarely, if ever, lose population from smaller urban areas that may operate at scales that are less sustainable. Thompson suggests that with scale comes industrial diversification, increased political clout, fixed infrastructure and capital investments, self-sustaining local markets, and innovation stemming from human capital that "almost ensure its continued growth and fully ensure against absolute decline," Wilbur R. Thompson, *A Preface to Urban Economics* (Johns Hopkins University Press, 1965), p. 24.

21. See Mark Muro and Jacob Whiten, "Geographic Gaps are Widening while U.S. Economic Growth Increases," *The Avenue* (blog), January 23, 2018, www.brookings .edu/blog/the-venue/2018/01/22/uneven-growth/; Adie Tomer and Joseph Kane, "Mapping Freight: The Highly Concentrated Nature of Goods Trade in the United States," Global Cities Initiative, The Brookings Institution, November 2014, www. brookings.edu/wp-content/uploads/2016/06/Srvy_GCIFreightNetworks_Oct24. pdf; Jay Shambaugh, Ryan Nunn, and Becca Portman, "Eleven Facts about Innovation and Patents," The Brookings Institution, The Hamilton Project, December 2017, www.brookings.edu/wp-content/uploads/2017/12/thp_20171213_eleven_facts_ innovation_patents.pdf.

22. Although with the Des Moines metro population at nearly 700,000, Iowa comes the closest to the blue metros, red states model that we posit here.

23. David F. Damore and Robert E. Lang, "Beyond Density & Diversity: Understanding the Socio-Cultural Geography of Contemporary Presidential Elections," Brookings Mountain West Policy Report, September 2016, p. 12, https://digitalschol arship.unlv.edu/brookings_pubs/42/.

24. Texas, for instance, has a larger GDP than Canada, while Florida's GDP approaches that of Mexico's.

25. Rodney Ho, "Multiple TV, Film Productions Not Coming to Georgia Due to 'Heartbeat' Abortion Bill as Backlash Builds," *Atlanta Journal-Constitution*, May 22, 2019, www.ajc.com/blog/radiotvtalk/multiple-film-productions-not-coming-georgia -due-heartbeat-abortion-bill-backlash-builds/tszYUlF6Pn20JCpf2XRMRI/.

26. Robert E. Lang, Andrea Sarzynski, and Mark Muro, "Mountain Megas: America's Newest Metropolitan Places and a Federal Partnership to Help Them Prosper," The Brookings Institution, Metropolitan Policy Program Report, July 20, 2008, pp. 1–68, 12–17, www.brookings.edu/wp-content/uploads/2016/06/IMW_full _report.pdf.

27. Wilbur Zelinsky, *The Cultural Geography of the United States* (Englewood Cliffs, NJ: Prentice Hall, 1973), p. 110.

28. Charles Mahtesian, "How Trump Rewired the Electoral Map," *Politico Magazine*, February 7, 2020, www.politico.com/news/magazine/2020/02/07/election-2020-new-electoral-map-110496.

29. Zelinsky, *The Cultural Geography of the United States*, pp. 118–19.

30. Ibid., p. 118.

31. See Arthur C. Nelson and Robert E. Lang, *Megapolitan America* (Chicago: American Planning Association Press, 2011), pp. 214–15.

32. Four of these metros in this group have populations that are greater than 800,000 (McAllen, Texas; El Paso, Texas; Allentown, Pennsylvania; Sarasota, Florida), five have populations exceeding 700,000 (Fort Myers, Florida, Greensboro, North Carolina, Colorado Springs, Colorado, Lakeland, Florida, Akron, Ohio) and 600,000 (Winston-Salem, North Carolina; Madison, Wisconsin; Daytona, Florida; Augusta, Georgia; Toledo, Ohio), and three have populations of 570,000 or greater (Palm Bay, Florida; Durham, North Carolina; Harrisburg, Pennsylvania). Note that roughly a third of the Augusta, GA MSA is in South Carolina and an eighth of the Allentown, PA MSA is in New Jersey.

33. All interviews were conducted by Elaine Silverstone, a research assistant and doctoral student in the Greenspun College of Urban Affairs at the University of Nevada, Las Vegas.

34. Bernice B. Brown, "Delphi Process: A Methodology Used for the Elicitation of Opinions of Experts," RAND Document No: P-3925, September 1968, www.rand.org/content/dam/rand/pubs/papers/2006/P3925.pdf.

35. The regions identified in the stylized state maps do not necessarily follow county boundaries since, in some instances, particularly in the western states that tend to have fewer counties that are geographically much larger compared to counties in the other regions, counties contained in the MSAs may have rural communities that are distinct from the urban spaces. However, the data we present throughout the book are aggregated at the county level within each MSA.

2

BLUE HORIZONS AND RED ROADBLOCKS

David F. Damore
Karen A. Danielsen

The place I'm talking about goes by different names.
Some call it America. Others call it Middle America. It
has also come to be known as Red America, in reference
to the maps that were produced on the night of the 2000
presidential election. People in Blue America, which is
my part of America, tend to live around big cities on the
coasts. People in Red America tend to live on farms or
in small towns or small cities far away from the coasts.
Things are different there.[1]

—*David Brooks*

Writing in 2001, just after the highly contested 2000 election, *New York Times* columnist David Brooks could see the emergent
red and blue geography and the sociocultural divide that undergirded
the split. This chapter explores the origins and current dynamics in
the geopolitics that has now firmly solidified into red and blue America and that inform our thesis.

We draw on scholarship grounded in a number of disciplines that
we organize into four sections. In the chapter's first section, we consider research examining cultural geography to understand the origins and persistence of spatial variation in sociocultural behavior and
attitudes. From there, we consider patterns of urban and rural demographic and economic clustering and their political consequences.

Next, we provide an overview of the attitudinal predispositions that permeate contemporary partisan conflict, particularly as related to social and cultural issues and race and ethnicity. In the chapter's final section, we examine how these inputs are filtered through electoral and policymaking institutions that often disadvantage million-plus metros. Throughout, we present descriptive analyses and data to place our thirteen swing states and twenty-seven million-plus metros in context.

In presenting this review, we limit discussion to the major themes and ideas that are most relevant to the thesis and cases as highlighted in chapter 1. This means that some bodies of research are noted in passing, while others are excluded altogether.[2] Readers seeking in-depth treatments of these topics are encouraged to explore the cited references and the references contained in those works.

CULTURAL GEOGRAPHY

There is a rich research tradition defining and differentiating the geography of America's cultural regions. The premise underlying this research is that place matters. Even in a country as commercially homogenized and as economically integrated as the United States, geographic differences, such as New York City's well-documented history of inclusion and tolerance or Minnesotans' propensity for being courteous to strangers ("Minnesota nice"), persist.

Donald Meinig's notable four-volume *The Shaping of America* provides a detailed 500-year accounting of the temporal and spatial development of North America.[3] His research offers a foundation for understanding how time and space interact with economic, technological, social, and political forces to shape regional settlement patterns. Meinig assembles a vast body of evidence to demonstrate how the settlement of different ethnic groups at specific points in time and in specific geographic spaces fostered distinctive regional cultures and norms. His work also details how these spatial tendencies remain even after these spaces repopulate in successive generations.

In *Albion's Seed*, David Hackett Fischer argues that the persistence of cultural variation in the United States stems from the importation, reinforcement, and adoption of distinct folkways from four British cultural hearths.[4] Collectively, the folkways shape societal and individual values, meanings, and norms as they relate to interpersonal relationships (for example, gender, marriage, sex, and family), community ordering and customs (for example, architecture, work, leisure, speech patterns, dress, and food), and the development and maintenance of institutions (for example, educational, religious, economic, and political). In Fischer's analysis, the stability of these folkways and the differences between them give way to conflicting conceptualizations of individual freedom that continue to permeate disputes about how and why governmental power should be exercised.

Colin Woodard steers the study of regional culture into the political realm. He identifies eleven regional cultures in North America and applies his regional framework to examine inflection points in American history such as the Revolutionary War, the adoption of the Constitution, the Civil War and Reconstruction, Westward Expansion, and on-going debates about foreign entanglements, immigration, and assimilation. His analysis demonstrates how these events can be understood in terms of "shifting coalitions of ethno-regional nations" seeking to capture and define governmental power and, by extension, our national identity.[5] By focusing on the endurance of interregional coalitions and alliances—anchored by the irreconcilable divisions between the "Deep South" and "Yankeedom"—Woodard traces the historical geographic underpinnings shaping current conflicts between red and blue states.

More generally, the connections unearthed in this literature are instructive. For instance, William Labov demonstrates how regional dialects correspond with cultural boundaries in the eastern United States and how these dialects propagated via east-west (and not north-south) transportation routes.[6] The settlements established along these dialect corridors, in turn, employed distinct building methods depending upon the scale and permanency of the initial settlement.[7] More than 150 years later, these dialect regions and the westward migration from these regions are predictive not only of patterns of urbanization but of a number of political behaviors, including Daniel Elazar's trichotomous measure of political culture,[8] the re-implementation of the death penalty, and county-level voting in presidential elections.[9]

The obvious criticism of this line of inquiry is that just because a set of factors indicative of cultural differences correlate with each other does not mean that one causes the other. Moreover, given that the regional cultures identified by scholars are, in some instances, centuries old, is it reasonable to use these constructs to explain contemporary political divisions?

In *The Cultural Geography of the United States*, Wilbur Zelinsky posits "the doctrine of first effective settlement" to explain how the preferences, behaviors, and institutions of those who are able to "effect a viable, self-perpetuating society" remain after they have been displaced by subsequent migrants and generations.[10] This framing provides a theoretical basis for understanding regional sociocultural differences that persist to this day. The classic example of Zelinsky's doctrine is New York City. Originally founded in 1624 by the Dutch, today little remains of the Dutch's original material presence. However, the Dutch ethos of cultural tolerance and diversity acceptance as a means to achieve commercial growth endures in New York City and throughout much of the urban North.

In our preliminary work for this project, David Damore and Robert Lang developed a measure that combines Zelinsky's doctrine with work on "Yankee cultural imperialism" to differentiate the degree to which states were settled by Northern and Southern interests,[11] and how these patterns account for spatial variation in attitudes related to diversity acceptance and inclusion (for example, support for same-sex marriage and the prevalence of interracial marriage). We then use our measure, which we call "northernness," to examine geographic variation in a number of partisan outcomes such as Electoral College voting, representation in the U.S. Senate and the House of Representatives, and individual vote choice.[12]

The geographic patterns we identify also track with other forms of politically significant spatial variation, such as the relationship between income and voting identified by Andrew Gelman and his co-authors in *Red State, Blue State, Rich State, Poor State: Why Americans Vote the Way They Do*.[13] Their analysis indicates that while wealthy voters everywhere are more likely to vote Republican, the relationship is strongest in poorer and rural states that support Republican candidates in presidential elections. As a consequence, in poorer and more religious Southern states, Republican support increases linearly with income. In contrast, in the more affluent, secular blue Northern states, electoral support for Republicans flattens across income levels. Gelman and his coauthors attribute these differences to sociocultural factors that vary from north to south, such as religiosity. They also suggest that these patterns may be driven by attitudes about race, a proposition considered in the next section.

The linkages between culture and geography also underlie the historical urban/rural divide and permeate inter- and intrastate sectionalism. During the early days of the American republic, "agrarian supremacy, political power, and political ideology were linked together."[14] But when manufacturing surpassed agriculture as the country's main economic driver, perceptions of cities changed.[15] For instance, writing to James Madison in 1787, Thomas Jefferson suggested that cites were a threat to the American way of life.[16] By 1816, as urban areas boomed with manufacturing, Jefferson rethought the importance of cities.[17]

Historian Arthur Schlesinger argues that over the course of American history, those on each side of the urban/rural divide reflected a distinct aversion for the other lifestyle. Country living was more individualistic and "yeomanlike." Urban areas became "increasingly unlike the countryside" by creating an environment where large diverse populations worked toward the mutual interests of the city.[18] Schlesinger also suggests that the adoption of the U.S. Constitution was a signal that cities had triumphed over rural areas. Business interests received tariff protections that benefited cities at the expense of rural economies. The urban/rural economic conflict provided the genesis for the country's original political party system.[19] These changes also "increased fear and resentment among country dwellers."[20] As cities grew more important, the rural "sturdy yeoman" increasing became a "hayseed" in the nation's esteem.[21]

These cultural differences may have been inevitable. As Schlesinger notes, Americans created their form of self-governance as a rural nation, and as a consequence, the county never learned how to govern cities.[22] Similarly, Richard Hofstadter suggests that the "United States was born in the country and has moved to the city," but the country's political values were inevitably "shaped by country life" because most early Americans were rural.[23] Along those same lines, Elazar notes that cities at the beginning of the nation were not strong enough to provide or demand more government services. He gives the example of Boston. Although it was then the third-largest city in the country, Boston did not incorporate until 1822, when its population reached 47,000.[24] Even as people continued to cluster in urban spaces, Americans have tried to have it both ways. In Elazar's opinion, there has been a "conversion of urban settlements into metropolitan ones" that combines rural and urban lifestyles into a geography more palatable to Americans that at least gives the appearance of maintaining agrarian ideals.[25] Historian Robert Fishman's work on "bourgeois utopias" identifies a distinct Anglo-American pattern to metropolitan development that preserves many elements of the rural ideal in the face of nineteenth-century urbanization.[26]

The urban/rural divide has deep roots in the expression of American sectionalism. Many scholars have argued that sectionalism is a fundamental building block of our two-party system, and sectional economic interests have exerted a significant effect on the country's political development.[27] Various regional, cultural, or economic differences and competition shape the nation's politics.[28] According to historian Frederick Jackson Turner, sectionalism has been one of the two most important factors in American history; the other, of course, being the frontier. Turner contends that sectionalism "was the dominant influence in shaping our political history upon all important matters," and that the perpetuation of sectionalism is politically problematic.[29]

Although Turner, among others, including Zelinsky,[30] identify several main sections within the United States, starting in the nineteenth century, sectionalism was conceptualized in terms of the North-South divide. In fact, sectionalism in the nineteenth century usually referred to the South and Southerners' fierce loyalty to the region and their common political views.[31] J. Clark Archer and Peter J. Taylor propose that a strong "North-South sectional cleavage" has dominated American politics since at least the 1920s, although not always in a predictable manner.[32] Political scientist V. O. Key suggests that sectionalism is not just a geographic phenomenon but a way to "mask territorially separated interests."[33] He argued that economic activity and economic differences between and within regions drive long-term sectional loyalty. Key predicted that sectionalism was a "rural and small-town phenomena" and, like many of his contemporaries, he expected it would slowly disappear as the country and the South urbanized.[34] Yet even today, the long-standing imprint of slave-holding states that imbued North/South sectionalism in the 1800s persists, according to our analysis (see figures 2-1 and 2-2).

While interstate sectionalism informs our expectations about states' diversity composition and dispersion (see chapter 1), our main thesis concerns the forces shaping *intrastate* regionalism. Here, too, the historical record suggests the persistence of within-state differences as they relate to political outcomes. For example, in analyzing county-level Midwestern voting returns during the second half of the 1800s, Turner finds that, despite significant social and economic changes and shifts in national political issues and personalities, counties more-or-less voted the same in 1900 as they did in 1856. Moreover, a 1989 update to Turner's original analysis by Fred Shelley and J. Clark Archer found that voting patterns in Turner's original electoral regions persisted well into the twentieth century.[35] Their analysis finds that urban and rural geography still shape the political landscape by creating clear voting "cleavages" between the economic core and periphery, farming and industrial regions, and cities and suburbs. Shelley and Archer find that Turner's observation that intrastate sectionalism in America was not dying is not only correct but still informs contemporary national and state politics.[36]

More recent work by James Gimpel and Jason Schuknecht examines the correlates underlying "the unevenness of partisan electoral strength across a state."[37] They argue that geographic variation in party support can be attributed to within-state "racial and ethnical sectionalism," "economic sectionalism," "ideological sectionalism," and "religious sectionalism." Their work also considers how migration and mobility within and between states alters state sectional divides.[38] The application of their framework to twelve state case studies, including six states that we consider, reveals that, despite "homogenizing forces" such as the nationalization of the media, the ubiquity of the internet, population mobility, and improved transportation, within-state sectionalism persists, and "the way these regional rivalries change over time tells us something about how underlying social and economic forces are transforming states and regions."[39] Although Gimpel and Schuknecht's analysis focuses less on the intra-state policy divides that state sectionalism foments, their work details how local conditions shape state regionalism and the implications that intrastate regionalism has for electoral outcomes and political representation.

With the country's continued urbanization and diversification, the political and cultural tug of war often expresses itself as a fight be-tween large liberal metros and their state's smaller cities and nonur-ban spaces. The conflicts echo historical intrastate rivalries that pitted a state's largest city against the rest of the state. In some instances, these conflicts were shaped by an upstate/downstate or an east/west political dynamic that mostly began as an urban/rural divide or as a conflict with a less populous region where perhaps the state capital is located. The most well-known, literal upstate/downstate monikers are in New York and Illinois, where the largest metros are geographically opposite from the region containing the capital.[40] For instance, in New York, *downstate* is metro New York, while *Chicagoland* is upstate in Illinois, but the rural area where the capital is located is referred to in terms of its geography vis-à-vis the big city (that is, Downstate Illinois or Upstate New York).

In the more rectangular or linear states, the labeling custom be-comes a little more complicated, where an east/west rivalry may fea-ture the larger cities opposite the rural areas between. Pennsylvania, where Philadelphia and Pittsburgh bookend the state, exemplifies this dynamic. In Minnesota, east/west regionalism takes the urban/rural division even further by categorizing places in the state as either part of the Twin Cities of Minneapolis-St. Paul or part of Greater Minne-sota, sometimes pejoratively referred to as "Outstate Minnesota,"[41] when a place is located outside the Twin Cities metro area.[42] In west-ern states such as California and Nevada, the regional fault lines are between the north, where the capitals are situated, and the south, where the largest population centers are located.

Regardless of the underlying geography shaping a state's sectional divisions, intrastate rivalries that originated from the often-inorganic process by which state boundaries were drawn, in many instances by bureaucrats in Washington, D.C., or in response to short-term polit-ical or economic considerations, persist into a new political reality

BOX 2-1. Tennessee's Formal Sectionalism

Tennessee's Grand Divisions

Source: www.tn.gov/content/dam/tn/health/documents/brfss/State%20Added%20Report%202016.pdf.

Tennessee's Three-Star Flag

Source: https://en.wikipedia.org/wiki/Flag_of_Tennessee#/media/File:Flag_of_Tennessee.

According to James Gimpel and Jason Schuknecht, for a "state to be sectional, there must be diversity across sub-state units" in terms of whether the various substate or intrastate areas support or oppose parties or their candidates, and such support must be uneven in its distribution.[a] Thus, a state cannot have political sections without distinct political clusters to define them. Tennessee offers an interesting twist on Gimpel and Schuknecht's sectional definition. In Tennessee, sectionalism is constitutionally delimited by the state's "Grand Divisions" (see figure 1 in this box). Tennessee's divisions are displayed symbolically in its "Three-Star Flag" (see figure 2 in this box). Tennessee is the only instance where political divisions are formally recognized, as opposed to all other states, where sections exist *de facto* but not *de jure*.

Tennessee's county-based Grand Divisions are: "West" (where Memphis is the main metro); "Middle" (where Nashville is the most populous metro and the state capital); and "East" Tennessee (where Knoxville is the largest metro). The sectional divisions were initially

a. James Graydon Gimpel and Jason E. Schuknecht, *Patchwork Nation: Sectionalism and Political Change in American Politics* (University of Michigan Press, 2014), p. 15.

based on the rough physical terrain and affiliations the areas had with neighboring states. There are also distinct cultural differences between the divisions; for example, in music, there is bluegrass in the East, country in the Middle, and blues in the West. Over time, the sections have taken on a strong political dimension. A political rivalry emerged between Middle and West Tennessee against East Tennessee stemming from each division's loyalties during the Civil War. Middle and West Tennessee, which were better suited for plantation agriculture, sided with the Confederacy and became strongly Democratic during Reconstruction. By contrast, East Tennessee's Republicanism resulted from it supporting the Union.

As Dewey W. Grantham notes, Tennessee is "unmistakably a Southern state" but "part of the peripheral South with a kind of a border state mentality."[b] These unusual sectional loyalties have had important political ramifications in both state and national elections. V. O. Key characterized this split as Tennessee having "not one one-party system but two one-party systems."[c] The long-standing sectional conflict has started to lessen only recently as Tennessee becomes more uniformly Republican.[d] Still, West Tennessee remains bluer than the rest of the state, with the exception of Davidson County (home to Nashville), while employment growth in Middle Tennessee, particularly in science, technology, engineering, and math-related sectors, eclipses growth in both West and East Tennessee.

---

b. Dewey W. Grantham, "Tennessee and Twentieth-Century American Politics," *Tennessee Historical Quarterly* 54, no. 3 (Fall 1995), pp. 210–29, p. 211.

c. V. O. Key, *Politics, Parties and Pressure Groups*, 5th edition (New York: Crowell, 1964; original 1942), p. 233.

d. Michael Nelson, "Tennessee: Once a Bluish State, Now a Reddish One," *Tennessee Historical Quarterly* 65, no. 2 (Summer 2006), pp. 162–83.

defined by "a stark division between cities and what remains of the countryside."[43] Contemporary conflicts between states and their large metros resemble the harsh anti-urban biases of the nineteenth century. However, while agriculture and agrarian ideals shaped national ideals then, that is no longer the case. In contrast to most million-plus metros, rural areas are losing population and languishing economically. Still, the residents of these spaces continue to oppose urban values, particularly as they relate to diversity acceptance and the speed of cultural change.[44]

In sum, cultural geography's extension to the political arena suggests how place instills values and attitudes that lead to asymmetrical spatial variation in political outcomes at the aggregate and individual levels. As detailed in chapter 1, we are particularly interested in understanding how these spatial differences affect diversity acceptance across the swing states and their million-plus metros. In the next section, we consider how geography interacts with diversity, urbanization, educational attainment, and economic output, and how these dynamics matter for electoral outcomes.

DEMOGRAPHIC AND ECONOMIC SORTING

Greeted with praise in the popular press but with skepticism from the academic community, Bill Bishop's *The Big Sort: Why the Clustering of Like-Minded America Is Tearing Us Apart* pushed the political and social notion of demographic sorting and its consequences into the mainstream.[45] Bishop argues that concentrating people who share similar demographic characteristics and lifestyle affinities in the same space breeds political division. Although choices about where to live may be motivated by nonpolitical factors, Bishop asserts that geographic sorting adds to the country's partisan polarization. For our purposes, the sorting framework provides a useful way to understand interstate and intrastate geographic, demographic, and economic differences, and the consequences these patterns have for partisan politics.

Consider John Judis and Ruy Teixeira's influential 2002 book *The Emerging Democratic Majority.*[46] They contend that the replacement of older, white voters with younger, minority ones provides Democrats more places to compete in coming decades. Brookings Institution demographer William Frey's research documents the enormous degree to which America's population recently diversified, or what he calls the "diversity explosion."[47] In particular, Frey finds that ethnic and racial diversity is most pronounced in the country's largest metropolitan areas (see table 2-1) and, increasingly, in the suburbs within these regions.[48] Frey's work, coupled with research examining the extent to which Democrats cluster in large cities, underlies the notion that diversity and density create pockets of strong Democratic support.[49] The corollary, of course, is that whiteness plus remoteness yields Republicans.[50] As is detailed in the swing state case studies that follow, the relative sizes and confluence of these demographic and geographic blocs is a defining feature of the blue metros, red states tension.

Still, the divergence in attitudes between urban and rural areas does not result from demographic or compositional differences alone but, rather, reflect a "mixture of selection and socialization processes."[51] Research by Gimpel and his coauthors suggests that regardless of an individual's education, income, race, ethnicity, or other demographic characteristics, population density and geographic distance exert independent effects on social and political opinions.[52] From this perspective, big cities are not liberal just because they are diverse. They are also liberal because they expose white and minority inhabitants to dense and diverse environments that facilitate social integration and reduce bias.[53] By contrast, people living in remote, rural spaces circulate in smaller and more homogenous networks and, unlike in cities, person-to-person social interactions are more frequent and tend to extend over time.

Because people residing in the same space often share political views, these preferences are regularly exhibited and fortified at the individual and collective levels. The nature of these differing social environments also promotes different sociocultural values, particularly as they relate to traditionalism and institutions supporting core values and behaviors. Thus, whereas selection effects account for the compositional differences between urban and rural America, the politically relevant behaviors and opinions manifested in these spaces also are shaped by differing patterns of social interaction.

To place our twenty-seven major metropolitan areas in context, table 2-1 summarizes their racial, ethnic, and foreign-born population shares. For comparison, the table includes data for the nation as a whole. The data shows the degree to which density and diversity covary. Just twelve of the metros feature white population shares above the national figure of 61 percent. These metros primarily are concentrated in the Midwest and the South. The remaining sixteen MSAs are more diverse than the nation, and eight feature populations that are majority-minority. Among the twenty-seven metros considered here, Tampa's demographics are closest to the United States as a whole.

Table 2-1 also highlights substantial regional differences in minority composition. In thirteen metros, Latinos form the largest mi-

TABLE 2-1. Racial/Ethnic Composition of Twenty-Seven Swing State Million-Plus Metros, 2017 (Percent)

		White	Black	Latino	Asian	Foreign-Born
United States		60.6	12.3	18.1	5.5	13.7
AZ	Phoenix	55.3	5.1	31.0	3.9	14.2
	Tucson	51.7	3.3	37.3	2.8	12.1
CO	Denver	64.2	5.5	23.1	4.3	12.3
FL	Jacksonville	63.0	21.0	8.8	4.1	9.4
	Miami	30.3	20.2	45.3	2.5	41.0
	Orlando	46.6	15.3	30.5	4.2	18.7
	Tampa	62.8	11.5	19.4	3.5	14.2
GA	Atlanta	47.0	33.5	10.8	5.8	14.1
MI	Detroit	66.4	22.2	4.4	4.3	10.3
	Grand Rapids	78.8	6.1	9.5	2.6	7.0
MN	Minneapolis*	74.9	8.9	6.0	6.9	11.3
NV	Las Vegas	42.3	11.4	31.3	10.0	23.1
NC	Charlotte*	59.7	22.5	11.2	4.0	11.2
	Raleigh	61.2	19.2	10.7	5.8	12.8
OH	Cincinnati*	76.2	14.7	3.4	3.0	5.5
	Cleveland	69.8	19.5	5.8	2.2	5.8
	Columbus	73.0	15.4	4.1	4.4	7.8
PA	Philadelphia*	60.3	21.8	9.1	6.6	11.8
	Pittsburgh	85.3	7.9	1.7	2.4	3.8
TX	Austin	52.0	6.8	32.5	5.8	15.1
	Dallas-Fort Worth	46.3	15.4	28.9	6.7	18.7
	Houston	36.1	16.9	37.3	7.8	23.6
	San Antonio	33.6	6.4	55.4	2.2	31.3
VA	Northern Virginia*	54.0	12.1	16.4	13.0	25.0
	Richmond	57.2	29.7	3.7	6.1	7.4
	Virginia Beach*	54.4	30.4	6.9	3.8	6.6
WI	Milwaukee	66.5	16.3	10.8	3.7	7.3

*Excludes counties outside of MSA primary state.

Note: Cell entries are within the MSA.

Source: 2017 American Community Survey 1-Year estimates as aggregated by census reporter.org.

nority group, while Blacks in the other fourteen regions comprise the largest minority. Only Northern Virginia and Las Vegas have Asian populations exceeding 10 percent. They are also the only two metros with double-digit shares of Blacks, Latinos, and Asians and, therefore, maintain the most diversity within diversity. Northern Virginia and Las Vegas, along with Atlanta, Miami, Orlando, Phoenix, Tampa, and the four Texas million-plus metros, have foreign-born population shares exceeding the nation as a whole. Among the twenty-seven metros in our study, Miami is the clear outlier, with a foreign-born population share that is 60 percent larger than Northern Virginia's, the next-highest metro.

Florida and Virginia, among the six states with multiple million-plus metros, provide the greatest contrast between regions. While Miami has the smallest share of white residents among the twenty-seven metros, Miami and Orlando have much greater diversity within their minority populations compared to Jacksonville and Tampa. The differences between Orlando and Tampa are particularly striking given their physical proximity. In Virginia, all three of the metros have similar shares of white residents. However, in Richmond and Virginia Beach, the racial composition is largely Black/white, whereas the diversity in Northern Virginia is more ecumenical. As we note in chapter 1, and the analyses of 2016 state-level presidential voting presented in figures 2-1 and 2-2 suggests, the different patterns of racial diversification yield divergent outcomes in partisan voting.

Frey's analysis also considers why the effects of the country's changing demographic political outcomes are uneven. Frey finds that the white share of the electorate is not decreasing as quickly as the white proportion of the population. This largely is due to lower levels of voter participation among Asians and Latinos. Therefore, whites continue to vote above their population share, creating what Frey labels a "voter representation gap."[54] The geographic concentration of white voters in rural spaces and minority voters in urban spaces also means that cities tend to underperform at the ballot box. Beyond demographics, characteristics of urban life such as commuting, residential mobility, and the nature of local governing institutions can undercut voter participation.[55]

The significance of the "voter representation gap" depends on the degree to which the preferences of whites and minority voters differ. Frey finds that whites are voting more Republican in presidential elections, while minority support for Democrats continues to increase.[56] However, akin to Gelman and his coauthors' "wealth paradox" indicating regional differences in partisan support among high-income earners, there is reason to suspect that these effects may be mitigated by geography and, by extension, the contours of a state's minority population.[57]

Starting with the work of V. O. Key, there is a robust literature examining how interracial proximity and density, primarily between Blacks and whites in the South, affects political behavior.[58] The research builds on Key's "racial threat hypothesis," which holds that in areas with higher concentrations of Blacks, and where Blacks are positioned to be politically powerful, whites will more aggressively seek to maintain political control. Although potentially mitigated by interracial contact[59] over time and across a variety of contexts, including those outside of the South, scholars have found that the greater the proportion of African Americans, the greater the likelihood that whites will grow racially resentful, if not racially prejudiced, and, therefore, more likely to vote Republican.[60] Scholarship extending this research to other racial and ethnic groups suggests that local Asian and Latino populations in general do not necessarily engender similar hostility from whites.[61] The effects of immigration can be more nuanced. Those living with large concentrations of immigrants do not consistently express anti-immigrant attitudes and, in fact, may resent efforts to scapegoat immigrants or to impose anti-immigrant policies.[62] Yet, in areas that experience rapid increases in immigrants, anti-immigrant attitudes become more prevalent.[63]

In presenting an overview of our thesis in chapter 1, we noted that regional geography shapes the composition and dispersion of states' nonwhite populations. Further, we argue that these differences matter for understanding electoral and policy outcomes. We expect that racial and ethnic partisan polarization will be greater in states where diversity is manifested in a Black/white political dialectic. In states where African Americans are one of many minority groups— where there is diversity within diversity—voting is likely less racially and ethnically polarized.

Figures 2-1 and 2-2 present data from the 2016 presidential election supporting these propositional statements. Note that to show the larger national context, these figures include all fifty states. For figure 2-1, the y-axis is the difference between Republican presidential candidate Donald Trump's and Democratic presidential candidate Hillary Clinton's statewide vote shares. The x-axis for figure 2-1a is the African American population share in each state. The x-axis for figure 2-1b is the share of each state's minority population that is not African American, an indicator of diversity within a state's minority population. Within each panel, the figures are presented separately for states that are below ("Low Diversity") and above ("High Diversity") the national median in terms of statewide nonwhite population. Washington, D.C., is excluded.

In the low-diversity states, an incidental relationship exists between diversity, however it is measured, and Clinton's vote margin. However, in the high-diversity states, the larger the African American population the less support Clinton received. Conversely, in states where African Americans constitute a smaller share of the state's overall minority population, Clinton performed much stronger.

Figure 2-2 extends the analysis using data from the thirty states, including our thirteen swing states, where exit polling data was collected during the 2016 presidential election to assess variation in support for Trump and Clinton among white voters. For figure 2-2, the y-axis is the difference in the margin of support among white voters for Trump and Clinton, and the x-axis in figure 2-2a is the African American population share. In figure 2-2b, the x-axis is the share of each state's minority population that is not African American. Because of noncoverage by exit polls, there are fewer states included in figure 2-2 and, therefore, we do not separate this analysis into low- and high-diversity states. Still, the pattern indicates that the larger the African American population share, the weaker the support among whites for Clinton. However, in states where there is greater ethnic and racial diversity, or where African Americans constitute a smaller share of a state's nonwhite population, support for Clinton among whites increases.

Closer inspection of figures 2-1 and 2-2 indicates that these effects sort by geography in a manner that is consistent with Damore

FIGURE 2-1. Relationship between State Diversity and Clinton Vote Share Margin (2016)

a. African American States

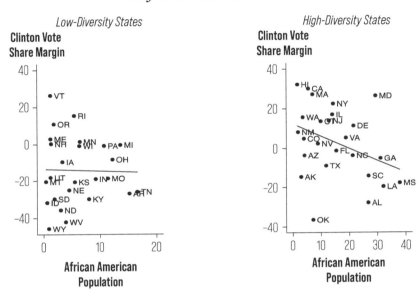

b. Diversity within Diversity States

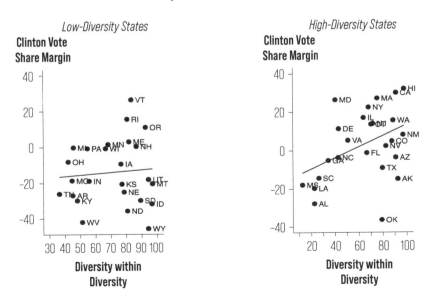

Source: Data from U.S. census and secretary of state websites.

FIGURE 2-2. Relationship between State Diversity and
Vote Share Margin among Whites (2016)

a. African American States

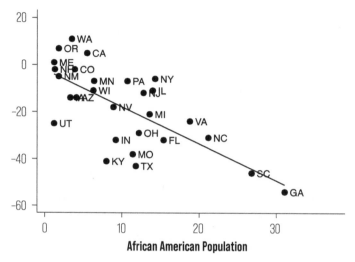

b. Diversity within Diversity States

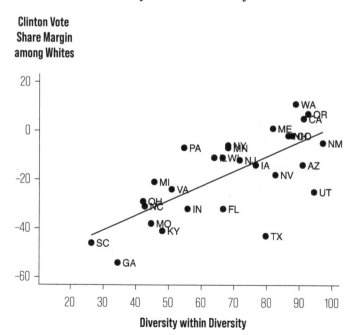

Source: Data from U.S. census and exit polls.

and Lang's measure of "northernness."[64] States settled by Northern interests and that feature either overwhelmingly white populations or where the diversity is more pluralistic tend to coalesce together in terms of vote margin (figure 2-1) and the degree to which voting is polarized among racial and ethnic blocs (figure 2-2). In contrast, states settled by Southern interests and where African Americans are the largest minority group exhibit stronger support for Trump and much higher levels of race-based voting. In general, density (urbanization) and diversity are drivers of partisan voting, and these effects are conditioned, in part, by sociocultural geography.[65]

The influence of geography and partisan support also are apparent at lower levels of aggregation. In a series of analyses for *CityLab*, David Montgomery uses a six-level measure of density, ranging from "pure rural" to "pure urban," to assess the partisan/spatial divide in U.S. House elections.[66] Not surprising, his analysis finds that density positively correlates with Democratic representation, a finding that is consistent with county-level analyses conducted by Robert Lang, Tom Sanchez, and Alan Berube ten years prior.[67] Within the competitive suburban, swing districts, Republicans tend to prevail in the less-diverse and less-dense districts, while the opposite holds true for Democrats. In 2008, Lang, Sanchez, and Berube offered the propositional statement that high population density plus high demographic diversity equals high support for Democrats (or, simply, D + D = D).[68] Our analysis, along with Montgomery's, supports these expectations.

The suburban swing districts identified by Montgomery tend to be wealthier and feature better-educated populations. These districts often vote Republican, but in 2018 swung heavily to the Democrats, allowing the party to secure its majority in the House of Representatives following the 2018 midterm elections. As a consequence, education and economic prosperity are further reinforcing the geography of partisan support. Indeed, perhaps one of the most stunning features of the 2016 presidential election is the finding by the Brookings Institution's Metropolitan Policy Program that Hillary Clinton carried just 16 percent of the nation's counties, but those counties generate nearly two-thirds of U.S. GDP.[69]

Follow-up research on the 2018 elections conducted by the Brookings Institution found that districts held by Democrats accounted for 61 percent of America's GDP.[70] The analysis also finds that the median income of Democratic-held House seats is $8,000 greater than Republican-held districts, and since 2008, the median income of Democratic seats increased by $7,000 while the median income in Republican-held districts decreased from $55,000 to $53,000. The finding suggests that districts held by Democrats and Republicans shifted from near income parity in 2008 to a growing divergence by 2018.[71] At the same time, the land area represented by Democratic House members decreased from four in ten to one in five square miles of the United States, offering further evidence that higher population density equals Democratic voting. It is important to note that, given the spatial concentration of wealth, fundraising from urban neighborhoods fuels campaigns for both parties,[72] despite the fact these places tend to elect Democrats.

Anchored by Walter Christaller's work examining central place theory and W. R. Tobler's "first law of geography," economists have long understood how space and density facilitate economic growth.[73] What is new is the degree to which intrastate differences in economic output between million-plus metros versus smaller regions and rural reinforce demographic and partisan sorting. Table 2-2 presents data summarizing the share of state population, the college educated, GDP, and jobs concentrated in our twenty-seven million-plus metros.

In general, the data demonstrate the degree to which high-skilled workers are concentrated in million-plus metros and the effects of this on employment and economic productivity. Atlanta, Austin, Denver, Northern Virginia, Philadelphia, Phoenix, Raleigh, and Minneapolis in particular have population shares of college-educated workers greater than their population shares. Atlanta, Dallas, Denver, Houston, Northern Virginia, Philadelphia, Phoenix, Minneapolis, and Milwaukee all generate shares of their state's GDP that are well above their population shares. Atlanta and Phoenix, followed by Northern Virginia, Dallas, and Denver, are metros with job shares exceeding their shares of their states' populations.

While the data presented in table 2-2 are useful for understanding the degree to which million-plus metros are demographic and economic powerhouses relative to the rest of their states, these data obscure important structural differences about the nature of red

TABLE 2-2. Economic Concentration in
Twenty-Seven Million-State Metros, 2017 (Percent)

State	Metro	Population	College	GDP	Jobs
AZ	Phoenix	67.5	71.0	75.5	73.2
	Tucson	14.6	16.6	12.4	14.4
CO	Denver	51.6	55.8	60.9	54.7
FL	Jacksonville	7.3	7.2	7.8	7.5
	Miami	29.3	31.7	35.6	30.9
	Orlando	12.0	12.4	14.0	13.0
	Tampa	14.7	15.0	15.4	15.0
GA	Atlanta	56.4	69.1	68.7	60.1
MI	Detroit	43.4	46.8	52.5	43.3
	Grand Rapids	10.6	11.8	12.1	11.9
MN	Minneapolis*	62.2	72.6	72.4	62.7
NV	Las Vegas	73.5	71.6	72.3	73.2
NC	Charlotte*	20.8	23.8	26.7	22.8
	Raleigh	13.0	18.8	15.4	14.2
OH	Cincinnati*	14.4	17.4	17.6	14.7
	Cleveland	17.7	20.0	21.3	17.9
	Columbus	17.8	22.5	20.6	18.8
PA	Philadelphia*	32.2	39.8	42.0	32.2
	Pittsburgh	18.2	21.1	19.7	18.7
TX	Austin	7.5	11.8	8.0	8.4
	Dallas-Fort Worth	26.1	30.9	30.3	28.2
	Houston	24.4	26.7	30.1	24.4
	San Antonio	8.7	11.6	7.3	8.7
VA	Northern Virginia*	35.3	49.7	45.3	37.7
	Richmond	15.4	14.8	15.9	15.6
	Virginia Beach*	19.9	16.3	18.9	19.2
WI	Milwaukee	27.2	31.9	37.1	26.4

*Excludes counties outside of MSA primary state.

Note: Cell entries are MSA share of state total.

Sources: 2017 American Community Survey 1-Year estimates as aggregated by censusreporter.org, Department of Commerce, Bureau of Economic Analysis, 2015 Real GDP (base = 2012) County Level Data, U.S. Department of Labor, and Bureau of Labor Statistics 2017 County Level Data.

and blue state economies that have important implications for a host of issues and policies, foremost being climate change. Absent federal leadership, blue states are aggressively implementing polices to reduce emissions and increase production of renewable energy.[74] By contrast, red states put little effort into addressing the causes and consequences of climate change. These differences can be accounted for in terms of economic self-interest. Among the fifteen states with the most carbon-intensive economies, only New Mexico voted for Hillary Clinton in 2016. Conversely, Trump carried only one of the fifteen states with the least carbon-intensive economies, North Carolina.[75] Among the swing states included in our analysis, the effects of climate change are most visible in Florida and North Carolina. Both states supported Trump and are represented by four Republicans in the U.S. Senate. Yet as is noted in chapter 5, on Florida, unlike most of their co-partisans, Republicans in the Sunshine State do not deny climate change or its effects.

ATTITUDINAL SORTING

The research examining red and blue attitudinal differences is vast, with much of it focused on the degree to which opinion formation and opinion holding fuel ideological and partisan polarization.[76] To that end, the conventional wisdom among pundits and journalists finds the United States in a period of unprecedented polarization. Evidence consistent with this perspective is ample. For instance, the Pew Research Center's longitudinal study of political values indicates that since the 1990s, when the survey began, the gap between Democrats and Republicans with respect to core political values and related issues such as racial discrimination, immigration, involvement in international affairs, economic fairness and government aid, and environmental protection continues to increase. These value differences, in turn, structure and reinforce ideological and partisan orientations.

However, due to differences in defining "polarization" and how the concept should be operationalized, the relevant academic research has produced more disparate findings. Some scholarship supports the view that the country is highly polarized at both the elite and popular levels,[77] while other research finds that assessments of polarization are exaggerated due to data and measurement limitations.[78] What is clear is that, compared to prior eras, Democrats and Republicans express more consistently liberal and conservative opinions, respectively, and as a consequence, Democrats and Republicans exhibit greater *average* opinion differences with respect to core values and policy preferences.[79] At the same time, because these effects are concentrated among partisans, the ideological distribution of the mass public remains unimodal, and substantial opinion overlap persists. Moreover, despite self-identifying as ideological conservatives or liberals, these identities for many voters "may not truly reflect any ideological policy commitments" but instead serve as little more than proxies for partisan loyalty.[80]

Given the degree of opinion overlap within the mass public, scholars have looked beyond issue positions and ideological orientations to consider how the emotional underpinnings of partisanship encourage polarization.[81] This research suggests that the stronger the emotional attachment to one's party, the greater the negative evaluations of the opposition party. The end result is an increase in "negative partisanship" such that a "growing proportion of Americans dislike the opposing party more than they like their own party."[82] Those holding strong partisan attachments may not only be less civil toward opposing partisans, but also less willing to support policy compromises if they believe the opposition may benefit, and they exhibit lower levels of trust in government when their preferred party is not in power.[83]

These attitudes can be further reinforced by the fact that the social groups that underlie the parties have largely become segregated. Whereas in the past, citizens' social identities may have created cross-pressures that mitigated the effects of partisanship, this is less likely today due to the increased homogeneity of individuals' social environments (or the Big Sort) that reduces exposure to groups and ideas not associated with their party. As the work of Lilliana Mason demonstrates, people's social identities and their partisan identities are now inextricably linked.[84]

A related line of inquiry considers the institutions and processes that prime these attitudes. This research suggests that polarization is largely a top-down process whereby party elites, perhaps responding to an increasingly polarized donor base,[85] disseminate partisan cues and talking points. The primary target for these messages are party activists who, through motivated reasoning, uncritically accept partisan dogma.[86] The key intervening variable linking partisan messaging to party activists is selective exposure to partisan-oriented media outlets, particularly cable news (that is, Fox News and MSNBC).[87] These effects are prevalent particularly among Republicans, who, all else equal, are less likely to deviate their news consumption from partisan sources.[88] Also note that while audiences that exclusively consume partisan-driven news are relatively small in a country of nearly 330 million, these audiences are politically influential, particularly in shaping party outcomes via their outsized influence over party nominations.[89]

The utility of this research is somewhat limited for our purposes by the fact that much of it draws on surveys derived from national samples. As a consequence, these data do not easily facilitate comparisons at lower units of analysis, and when these comparisons are made, they focus on interstate comparisons as opposed to intrastate (for example, rural versus urban) differences.[90] However, the behavioral implications of these effects, such as geographic patterns of partisan electoral support, can be accessed more clearly.[91] At the same time, it is important to remember that these effects are partially an artifact of a two-party system that by its structural nature manifests some degree of residual polarization. In addition, electoral institutions such as reapportionment and redistricting, primary elections, and plurality winners in single-member districts can magnify opinion differences such that "small shifts in *opinion* can translate into large differences in *outcomes*."[92]

Even with these caveats, the data presented in figure 2-3 demonstrate the divergence in partisan support between the twenty-seven million-plus metros and smaller regions in our thirteen swing states. Specifically, using county-level vote totals collected from secretary of state websites for the 2016 presidential election, the figure reports Clinton's and Trump's statewide, million-plus metro, and rest-of-state percentage point differences for our thirteen swing states. For states with multiple million-plus metro regions, the data are combined such that the metro values are the aggregate percentage point difference across all million-plus metros in a state.[93] The rest-of-state values are aggregated for all counties that are not in an MSA with a population over 1 million. Positive values indicate a bigger margin for Clinton, while negative values indicate more support for Trump.

While the overall patterns are not surprising, the magnitude of the differences in many of the states is stunning. In eleven states, Clinton dominated in million-plus metros, particularly in Colorado, Pennsylvania, and Virginia, and in the two states where she failed to carry the million-plus metros, Arizona and Texas, Trump's margin was 0.6 and 0.5 percentage points, respectively. However, by running up huge margins outside of the large metro regions, Trump carried nine of the thirteen states. In all but four states—Colorado, Michigan, North Carolina, and Wisconsin—his rest-of-state margin was less than ten points. Trump's twenty-three- and seven-point advantages in smaller regions and rural areas of Pennsylvania and Michigan, respectively, resulted in Trump becoming the first Republican presidential candidate to win those states since George H. W. Bush, in 1988. Trump's four-point advantage in Wisconsin (including Madison) outside of the Milwaukee metropolitan area was enough to move the Badger State's Electoral College votes into the GOP for the first time since Ronald Reagan's election in 1984. These three states, of course, decided the outcome of the 2016 presidential election by fewer than 78,000 total votes. More generally, these data suggest the degree to which the Southern worldview has penetrated much of the rural north and west and the Northern worldview has penetrated the big metros in the south and the west. As a consequence, sociocultural values that historically were associated with the Northeast and that were propagated to settlements founded by Northern interests, or what Damore and Lang call "northernness,"[94] now may be less tied to geography and more attributable to population density and distance from population centers.

The literature also demonstrates how changes in the political agenda can reshuffle existing demographic and, by extension, geographic electoral coalitions. Increases in partisan polarization and ideological sorting is a relatively new phenomenon, having materialized in the last thirty years. A primary catalyst for this shift is the growing saliency of cultural, racial, and other social issues and the increasing partisan divergence in how these issues should be addressed.

FIGURE 2-3. Comparison of Statewide Million-Plus Metros to Rest-of-State Voting in the 2016 Presidential Election in Thirteen Swing States

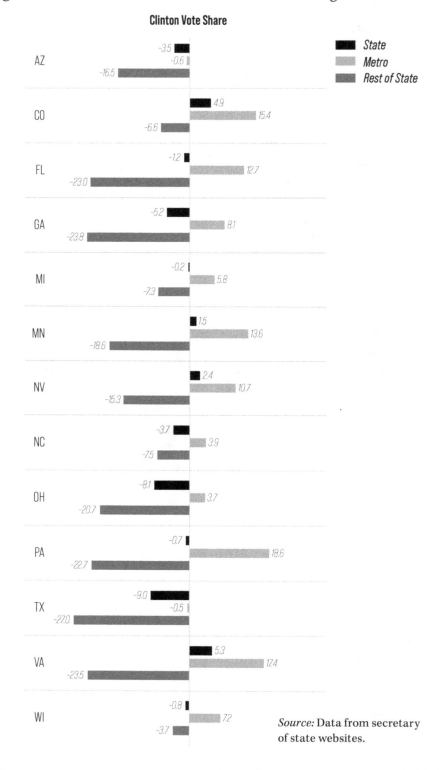

Clinton Vote Share

Legend:
- State
- Metro
- Rest of State

AZ: State -3.5, Metro -0.6, Rest of State -16.5
CO: State 4.9, Metro 15.4, Rest of State -6.6
FL: State -1.2, Metro 12.7, Rest of State -23.0
GA: State -5.2, Metro 8.1, Rest of State -23.8
MI: State -0.2, Metro 5.8, Rest of State -7.3
MN: State 1.5, Metro 13.6, Rest of State -18.6
NV: State 2.4, Metro 10.7, Rest of State -15.3
NC: State -3.7, Metro 3.9, Rest of State -7.5
OH: State -8.1, Metro 3.7, Rest of State -20.7
PA: State -0.7, Metro 18.6, Rest of State -22.7
TX: State -9.0, Metro -0.5, Rest of State -27.0
VA: State 5.3, Metro 17.4, Rest of State -23.5
WI: State -0.8, Metro 7.2, Rest of State -3.7

Source: Data from secretary of state websites.

These trends also move in tandem with increasing economic polarization and the growth in the country's immigrant population.[95]

Given our thesis, of particular interest is attitudinal sorting related to race and ethnicity. Traditionally, the study of race, ethnicity, and politics has focused on the formation of racial and ethnic minority group identification and the consequences these identities have for attitude formation, opinion holding, and political participation. Recent scholarship, however, has considered these processes through the lens of white-identity politics.[96]

In particular, work by political scientist Ashley Jardina suggests that white racial identity is more prevalent among the less educated and with those who support maintaining traditional hierarchies, adhere to authority, and resist changes to the status quo. Her work identifies geographic factors such as living in the south or in a rural context as weaker predictors.[97] White identity imbues exclusionary views about what it means to be an American, and whites who connect in terms of their race see themselves in a zero-sum competition with nonwhites for status and privilege. White identifiers oppose free trade, increased immigration, and social welfare, not necessarily because of racial resentment but because these policies threaten the status whites maintain at the top of the country's racial hierarchy. Those holding these views increasingly vote Republican, while whites with less salient racial identities and minority voters lean more and more Democratic.[98] Although largely anecdotal and descriptive in his approach, physician and sociologist Jonathan Metzl extends this line of inquiry by arguing that support for conservative social welfare, educational, and gun policies among racially resentful whites results in shorter life expectancies, increased gun suicides, higher school drop rates, and poorer health outcomes among whites from lower socioeconomic strata.[99]

Research on white identity politics explains Donald Trump's effective messaging during the 2016 presidential campaign and his outsized support among white racial identifiers. The Trump campaign emphasized the very issues that Jardina finds are strongly associated with status loss among whites. His campaign's tagline "Make America Great Again" clearly was aimed at voters seeking to preserve traditional hierarchies. Post-election autopsies found that Trump's victory was not driven by economic anxiety, a common media trope during the campaign, but rather by concerns about status threat among whites. Thus, Trump carried eighteen of the twenty states with the lowest shares of foreign-born residents while winning just two of the twenty states with the largest shares of foreign-born residents.[100]

The Trump campaign successfully revived many issues that had animated the Tea Party movement earlier in the decade. Media reporting on the Tea Party often framed it as a grassroots initiative driven by opposition to the Affordable Care Act. Yet, Theda Skocpol and Vanessa Williamson find that the Tea Party was substantially underwritten by conservative corporate interests, such as Koch Industries, and promoted by wealthy conservative media elites. Their analysis finds that most Tea Party members feared generational and demographic change (embodied by President Obama), resented the ascension of racial minorities in American society, and remain hostile to immigrants and immigration.[101]

INSTITUTIONAL FILTERING

Thus far, we have considered research assessing the geographic, demographic, economic, and attitudinal inputs underlying the tensions between blue metros and red states. Next, we explore the key intervening variables, electoral and policymaking institutions, through which these inputs are filtered, and review how institutional characteristics shape these outcomes. A central premise of the study of institutions is that they are needed to aggregate societal preferences and achieve stable outcomes. But institutions are rarely neutral. Rather, institutions "may have systematic biases in them so that they regularly produce one kind of outcome rather than another," and as such, political outcomes often do not reflect majority preferences.[102]

The manner by which institutions distort majority choice is seen in the electoral arena. At the federal level, the equal apportionment of seats in the U.S. Senate (two per state), the manner in which seats in the House of Representatives are distributed to the states, and the resulting allocation of Electoral College votes (determined by a state's total number of House and Senate seats) creates a bias that favors less populated states.[103]

Outside of the Northeast, the fact that less populated states tend to vote for Republicans results from a number of factors. For instance, while decisions to admit new states in the nineteenth and early twentieth centuries were driven by short-term political factors stemming from regional and partisan cleavages,[104] in the long term, the admission of states, particularly those that continue to have small, homogenous, and rural-oriented populations, provides Republicans a structural advantage. This is best exemplified by the decision to split the Dakota Territory into two states—North and South Dakota. Today, each Dakota has one seat in the House of Representatives, the minimum, but combined they have four seats in the Senate, representation equivalent to California and Texas combined, home to one in five Americans.

Economic transformation also played an important role in shaping geographic patterns of partisan support. The work of political scientist David Rodden demonstrates how the industrial revolution resulted in migration to the cities and the clustering of left-leaning voters and constituencies in urban spaces, a pattern that persists to this day.[105] The perpetuation and intensification of the geographic partisan patterns of electoral support that Rodden identifies, coupled with the allocation of political power via winner-take-all institutions, exert a significant influence on the contours of representation in government. Thus, even though the Democrats continue to gain support with the growth segments of the electorate, the concentration of Democratic voters in million-plus metros is electorally inefficient, resulting in many easy Democratic wins but also wasted votes. Conversely, the widespread geographic distribution of Republican voters allows the GOP to win more often even as the party's candidates receive less aggregate support compared to their Democratic counterparts. In short, the system is biased in that Republicans can often gain power without a majority of the vote.

Two of the last three Republican presidential wins, George Bush in 2000 and Donald Trump in 2016, came via the Electoral College and were accompanied by popular vote losses. Republican presidential candidates won the popular vote just once since 1988. Because of substantial population discrepancies between the states, Democratic U.S. senators represent roughly 40 million more people than their

Republican counterparts but remain the minority party. By some estimates, GOP dominance in the least populated states will allow the Republicans to maintain their U.S. Senate majority without having to win a single election in a swing state.[106] In the coming decades, the mismatch between representation and population in the U.S. Senate will get worse, as upward of 70 percent of the country's population is expected to live in the fifteen most populous states.[107]

Supreme Court decisions in the 1960s establishing the "one-person, one-vote" standard invalidated the malapportionment of U.S. House and state legislative seats that previously allowed district boundaries to be drawn with unequal populations.[108] Historically, these arrangements empowered rural interests at the expense of urban constituencies.[109] Even today, the trickling down of the more efficient distribution of Republican electoral support to state legislatures allows the GOP to use the redistricting process to further entrench their structural advantages in the U.S. House of Representatives and in state legislatures.[110] In most states, redistricting is still determined by state legislatures. As the legal challenges to a number of states' redistricting plans suggest, the process can be used to weaken the representation of urban constituencies by either packing these voters into a small number of districts or scattering such voters into multiple districts to dilute their power.

At the federal level, the institutional biases undermining the principle of equal representation yield inequities in policy outcomes, particularly with respect to the geographic distribution of federal outlays and tax burdens. The federal government transfers wealth from high-performing states, particularly in the Northeast and Pacific West, to poorer states largely in the south.[111] Ironically, Republican-voting states tend to be more dependent upon the federal government, contrary to the party's stated position of less government. For instance, an analysis of the balance of payments to the federal government for 2017 completed by the Rockefeller Institute of Government reports that among the ten states that contribute more to the federal coffers than they receive, only Nebraska and North Dakota are reliably Republican states.[112] The Tax Cut and Jobs Act of 2017 limited the amount of state and local property, income, and sales taxes that individuals can deduct from their federal taxes to $10,000 per household. The change impacted blue states much more than red ones, resulting in even more wealth transferring to Republican-voting places.[113] Blue state voters took notice. In 2018, a third of the House seats that the Democrats picked up came from California (seven), New Jersey (four), and New York (three), which all have high state and local taxes.

There is a large academic literature assessing the underperformance of cities in state policymaking. Prior to the 1960s reapportionment revolution requiring state legislative districts be equally populated, urban interests were systematically underrepresented in statehouses while rural areas were overrepresented. These arrangements, in turn, provided rural legislators with outsized influence over policy outcomes.[114] Yet, as the bathroom and abortion bills in North Carolina and Georgia suggest, the reapportionment revolution did not prove a panacea for urban interests in state policymaking. In fact, analyses of bill passage rates after *Reynolds v. Sims* requiring that state legislative districts be equally populated suggests that legislative success is inversely related to delegation size.[115]

There are multiple reasons cities continue to underperform in state politics. Big cities are complicated places composed of many interests that may conflict. Disagreements about legislative priorities can result in mixed cues being sent to urban delegations, particularly when they are split along party and generational lines.[116] As V. O. Key noted over sixty years ago, urban priorities may incite resentment from nonurban legislators, generating "a bipolarization of attitudes" within a legislature.[117] An extensive analysis of district bills passed in state legislatures conducted by political scientists Gerald Gamm and Thad Kousser finds that bills introduced by legislators representing cities with large foreign-born populations "fare most poorly in state capitals."[118] Moreover, while moderation still exists in state legislatures, these bodies increasingly polarize along partisan and ideological lines, making it more difficult to build policy coalitions.[119]

Million-plus metros may be hindered further by structural features of state government. In many states, legislatures are weak institutions relative to the governorship.[120] As a consequence, even in legislatures where urban representatives dominate, members may have limited ability to shape state budgets and other policy priorities.[121] In states with less professionalized legislatures, elected officials typically have fewer resources to assist with policymaking and tend to introduce fewer district-specific bills.[122]

Power in the United States is shared between states and the federal government. Local governments are not autonomous. Instead, as one of the architects of the doctrine of state preeminence, Judge John Dillon, famously opined in 1868, local governments are "creatures of the state."[123] In states with Dillon's Rule, local governments are extended limited autonomy to develop and implement local policies, including choosing or revising governmental arrangements (structural), exercising self-government (functional), raising taxes (fiscal), or determining employment conditions for municipal arrangements (personnel).[124] In these contexts, local governments must seek permission from state governments to attend to even minor local needs, a dynamic that allows legislatures with little connection to a city to influence urban policy priorities.

A salient example of this comes from Nevada, which extends very little home rule to its local governments. Part of the financing for Allegiant Stadium in Las Vegas, where the National Football League's Las Vegas Raiders and UNLV's football team play, comes from bonds backed by hotel room taxes collected exclusively in Clark County. Unlike Orlando, which has the authority to use locally generated tax sources to support its tourism and events infrastructure, stadium proponents in Las Vegas needed the governor to call a special session of the Nevada legislature to get the required bill passed to increase and direct local hotel room taxes to the project. During the session, legislators from outside the region not only were voting on a project that was clearly local in nature but also sought to squeeze the Raiders for training camp and practice facilities in Reno, located hundreds of miles away from Las Vegas.[125]

The ability of million-plus metros to chart their own course is often constrained by state-level preemption. A 2018 state-by-state report prepared by the National League of Cities examining trends in preemption finds states limiting action across a host of policy areas, including: minimum wage (twenty-eight states); paid leave (twenty-three states); anti-discrimination (three states); ride sharing (forty-one states), home sharing (five states); municipal broadband (twenty states); tax and expenditure limitations (forty-two states); as

BOX 2-2. State Capital Locations

State capitals are not typically the biggest city in their state. Consider, for example, the thirteen original states. The only states where the biggest city is also the state capital are Georgia (Atlanta), Massachusetts (Boston), Rhode Island (Providence). Most of the original states tried to locate the capital at their geographic center. A central location was the most democratic way to select the capital because legislators would have equal access to the statehouse at a time when transportation was difficult. The principle of equal access was sometimes carried too far, as several states rotated their capitals. For instance, Connecticut and New Jersey had two state capitals at the same time, Rhode Island rotated its state capital among five cities, and New Hampshire used six cities as capitals during the American Revolution. In time, the practice became unworkable, and a permanent home for the capital was selected. Because so many British North American colonies rotated their capitals, there was a state capital "removal movement" from 1776 to 1812.[a] In the early American republic, most states moved their original capital to a single city.[b] Eleven of the thirteen states succeeded at finding a fixed location, while two (Rhode Island and Connecticut) continued to rotate their capitals well into the nineteenth century. Note also that the U.S. capital, too, was located in various cities until it was permanently sited in the planned city of Washington, D.C., in 1801.

Outside the original thirteen colonies, newer states and territories continued to locate their capital at a geographic center, provided there was a sizeable population nearby. In those cases, the geographic center turned out to sometimes be the population center (as, for example, in Indiana). It is important to consider that a state's settled area may have not included what was to become the biggest city. Florida is such a case. Most of Florida's settlement at the time of its statehood in 1845 was in the north, the south being then mostly uninhabitable. Thus, Tallahassee, the state capital, was located halfway between Pensacola and St. Augustine (that is, the geographic center), the two largest cities. Oregon has a similar story in that its capital, Salem, lies in the geographic and population center of

a. Rosemarie Zagarri, "Representation and the Removal of State Capitals, 1776–1812," *Journal of American History* 74, no. 4 (March 1988), pp. 1239–56. Also see Rosemarie Zagarri, *The Politics of Size: Representation in the United States, 1776–1850* (Cornell University Press, 1989) and Rosemarie Zagarri, "The Emergence of the Extensive Republic: Representation in the United States, 1776 to 1812" (Dissertation, Yale University, 1984).

b. Erik J. Engstrom, Jesse R. Hammond, and John T. Scott, "Capitol Mobility: Madisonian Representation and the Location and Relocation of Capitals in the United States," *American Political Science Review* 107, no. 2 (May 2013), pp. 225–40.

the Willamette Valley, the settled portion of the state in the mid-nineteenth century. Much like in America's colonial period, territorial capitals had an advantage in eventually becoming the state capital. In some places, the territorial capital was the biggest city but not the geographic center, as in the case of Colorado and Minnesota. Finally, some states actually picked their biggest city as the capital. For instance, Arizona eventually moved its capital from Prescott to Phoenix when it gained statehood in 1912.

The three main drivers of state capital location are: geographic center; population center; and designation as the territorial capital. There also are cases where political jockeying and interurban rivalry determined the ultimate capital location. Sometimes it came down to a city offering more money to locate the capital or bribing legislators with the prospect of securing choice building lots near the statehouse. In Idaho, for instance, the capital was stolen from the territorial population center in Lewiston and moved to the more remote Boise (which later became the largest city in the state).c Finally, there are environmental and even security reasons for locating a state capital. Baton Rouge was selected over New Orleans because it was on higher ground and less prone to flooding. Richmond became Virginia's capital because it was thought to be better strategically protected from future British attacks. Indeed, its location proved useful during the Civil War, when Richmond was the capital of the Confederate States of America. It took the Union Army the better part of four years to finally occupy Richmond.

---

c. Eugene B. Chaffee, "The Political Clash between North and South Idaho over the Capital," *Pacific Northwest Quarterly* 29, no. 3 (July 1938), pp. 255–67.

well as plastic bag usage, gun safety, nutrition, and zoning and rent control.[126] Consistent with the Charlotte anti-discrimination controversy detailed in chapter 1, the report also finds that preemption is more common in states where Republicans have unified control of state government.[127] The consequences of preemption are particularly acute given that issues such as immigration, gun control, abortion, and ballot access are being addressed at the state level in the face of federal inaction.

Major metros also may be hindered by the remoteness of state government. Not only is distance between a state's population center and the capital associated with less oversight and accountability and higher levels of corruption,[128] remoteness creates an additional burden on legislative service that may disproportionately affect urban legislators. This, in turn, may result in higher turnover rates among urban lawmakers and less aggregate seniority and influence over the legislative process.

Urban underperformance in state policymaking contrasts with the influence cities once exerted in national politics, particularly in the mid-twentieth century. In *The Cities on the Hill*, urban politics scholar Thomas Ogorzalek demonstrates the role of cities in nationalizing politics and policy from the 1930s to the 1960s.[129] After largely being ignored for most of the county's history because rural interests dominated both state and federal policymaking, Ogorzalek details how cities, despite their internal divisions, particularly related to race, developed coalitions and institutions such as the U.S. Conference of Mayors to push urban priorities in Congress. His analysis details the pivotal role big city delegations played to expand federal power to address the urban economic dislocation caused by the Great Depression. Urban interests proved particularly successful in obtaining federal resources for housing, including the creation of the Federal Housing Administration in the 1930s, the forerunner to the current U.S. Department of Housing and Urban Development. These gains necessitated tolerating Jim Crow and supporting regional logrolls that delivered agricultural commodities to the south and the Midwest and power and water projects in the west. [130] Ogorzalek also examines how civil rights advocacy by big cities, particularly in the north, splintered the New Deal coalition and ushered in the current urban/rural, regional partisan divide.

In subsequent decades, the creation of what Ogorzalek calls the "metropolitan political order" has not been fully realized despite the increasing role major metros play in incubating innovation, growing the economy, addressing pressing policy challenges, and embracing the country's changing demography.[131] Certainly some of the reasons for this are the aforementioned institutional arrangements that penalize density and size and that "govern, administer, and legislate in two-year cycles, aligned more with the timeline of political elections than with social or market dynamics."[132] In addition, because most million-plus metros extend across broad swathes of space,[133] they are often fragmented by jurisdiction. By creating competition and disunity between localities within major metros, these municipal fragmentations may breed antagonism and conflict instead of cooperation and consensus.

To put our twenty-seven major metros in context, table 2-3 presents data from the 2017 Census of Governments detailing the number and types of governments that exist in each MSA. For the purposes of this analysis, we include data for the entirety of each region, including states and counties that are outside of the primary state.

These data make clear a number of important points relevant to our discussion about government fragmentation. First, in addition to the five metros that cross state borders, except for Las Vegas and Tucson, all metros cover multiple counties, and most counties contain multiple municipalities of varying sizes, each with its own politics and elected leadership. Moreover, because local government elections are mostly nonpartisan and often held in off years, local elected officials gain power in low-turnout contests with voters that tend to be older and less racially diverse.[134] As a consequence, local elected officials may be responsive to different constituencies compared to their state and federal counterparts.

Second, the disparity in the number of general purposes governments across the twenty-seven major metros is dwarfed by the variation in the use of special districts. In terms of the prevalence of special districts, Denver tops the list. Many of metro Denver's special districts are rather small in size and scope, created by developers to offset the infrastructure costs of building neighborhoods on undeveloped land in unincorporated spaces. Houston, too, has a large number of special districts, with many of these districts covering water systems that serve a handful of housing subdivisions. There also are substantial differences in the number of school districts across the million-plus metros, with Philadelphia, which contains parts of four states, maintaining the largest number of school districts.

Third, across all types of governments, Las Vegas is the outlier. Not only is the Las Vegas metropolitan area contained within a single county, that jurisdiction is served by just six local governments and a single school district. As a consequence, while the Las Vegas MSA is the twenty-eighth most populated in the United States, the Clark County School District is the fifth largest in the country. More Ne-

TABLE 2-3. Government Fragmentation in Twenty-Seven Swing State Metro Regions

MSA	State(s)	Counties	General Purposes	Special Districts	School Districts
Atlanta	GA	29	177	155	37
Austin	TX	4	54	221	30
Charlotte	NC, SC	7	81	39	19
Cincinnati	KY, OH, IN	15	243	125	84
Cleveland	OH	5	167	72	75
Columbus	OH	10	266	121	62
Dallas-Fort Worth	TX	13	219	238	117
Detroit	MI	6	213	63	105
Denver	CO	10	53	1,089	26
Grand Rapids	MI	4	112	25	40
Houston	TX	9	133	922	69
Jacksonville	FL	5	21	82	6
Las Vegas	NV	1	6	15	1
Miami	FL	3	107	191	6
Milwaukee	WI	4	94	56	53
Minneapolis	MN, WI	16	412	164	87
Orlando	FL	4	40	89	7
Philadelphia	PA, NJ, DE, MD	11	385	257	198
Phoenix	AZ	2	35	124	81
Pittsburgh	PA	7	463	297	109
Raleigh	NC	3	30	15	5
Richmond	VA	17	25	20	18
Tampa	FL	4	39	176	7
Tucson	AZ	1	6	24	20
San Antonio	TX	8	62	87	40
Virginia Beach	VA, NC	16	19	21	16
Washington, D.C.	DC, VA, MD, WV	24	113	37	29

Notes: "School Districts" includes independent school district governments and dependent school systems. MSAs where a state capital is located are shown in italic font. Note that, in this one instance, Washington, D.C., is included as a million-plus metro in place of Northern Virginia. This is because this table shows data for entire metropolitan areas and not simply the share of the region that lies with one of the thirteen swing states.

Source: Data from 2017 Census of Governments.

vadans (exceeding 1 million residents) live in unincorporated Clark County than any municipality in the state.[135]

| It is worth noting that despite the fact that many state capitals often were intentionally established away from large cities (see box 2-2), eight of the twenty-seven million-plus metros are state capitals. On the other end of the spectrum are Las Vegas and Miami, swing state million-plus metros that are geographically far removed from their state's capitals.

Metros more generally, as Bruce Katz and Jennifer Bradley argue in *The Metropolitan Revolution*, are led by region-wide informal leadership networks in contrast to the formal boundaries that delineate their fragmented governments. While federal and state governments often operate in silos and emphasize the development and implementation of one-size-fits-all policies, Katz and Bradley find that major metros are more integrated and better attuned to understand and respond to the distinctive cultural, economic, and social needs within their communities. Thus, large and integrated million-plus metros are well positioned to address their unique policy challenges, such as inclusion, affordability, transportation, and housing.[136] Still, leveraging metro connectivity requires working with federal and state government officials to develop policies to unlock this potential. Given the effects of the Tax Cut and Jobs Act of 2017 on blue states and the rise in preemption by state governments, it appears that not everyone is on board with this agenda.

SUMMARY AND CONCLUSION

In this chapter, we reviewed the scholarship relevant to our thesis outlined in chapter 1. We began with a discussion of cultural geography to understand how the development and persistence of geocultural proclivities continue to resonate in contemporary American politics. Of particular importance is how patterns of northern and southern westward migration and development inform geographic variation as they relate to diversity acceptance and tolerance. In the chapter's second section, we considered how the increasing convergence between demography and economic productivity underpin the geography of partisan electoral support, perhaps the most obvious manifestation of the blue metros, red states division. Next, we examined the attitudinal differences that inform the red, blue divide. As we detail, some of these differences stem from the increasing divergence among partisans with respect to core values as they relate to social issues. This, however, is not the whole story. The rise of negative partisanship and white identity politics amplify these differences so as to make election and policy outcomes a zero-sum competition. Last, we assessed how the unrelenting urbanization and diversification of the American population challenges the county's rurally oriented institutional arrangements.

All told, a picture emerges that can best be described as a decoupling of demographic and economic growth from formal political power, or what journalist Ron Brownstein dubs "the prosperity paradox." Brownstein notes:

> Even as economic growth is concentrating in Democratic-leaning metropolitan areas thriving in the information economy, Republicans rooted in non-urban communities largely excluded from these opportunities now control the levers of power in Washington and in most states. This disjuncture raises a pointed long-term question: How long can the places that are mostly lagging in the economy dictate the terms of politics and policy to the places that are mostly succeeding?[137]

In the following chapters, we apply our framework to our thirteen state and twenty-seven million-plus metro pairings. For each state case study, we begin with a geopolitical state of play that is supplemented with maps and data providing demographic, economic, and political comparisons between million-plus metros and the rest of their states. These discussions are followed by descriptive and qualitative analyses that draw from material obtained via structured interviews with state experts to understand the sociocultural and institutional contours of the urban/rural divide in each state and how these dynamics animate political and policy outcomes.

NOTES

1. David Brooks, "One Nation, Slightly Divisible," *The Atlantic*, December 2001, www.theatlantic.com/magazine/archive/2001/12/one-nation-slightly-divisible /376441/.

2. For example, in reviewing research examining demographic sorting, we do not discuss the erosion of ethnicity among whites after World War II. In our analysis of attitudinal sorting in section three, we do not cover the classic public opinion research examining attitude formation and opinion change. Instead, we focus our attention on more recent scholarship examining the causes and consequence of partisan opinion polarization. Similarly, in our discussion of institutional filtering in this chapter, we omit research assessing the consequences of different forms of municipal governance on representation and policy outcomes.

3. Donald Meinig, *The Shaping of America: A Geographical Perspective on 500 Years of History* (Yale University Press, 1986, 1992, 1994, 2004).

4. David Hackett Fischer, *Albion's Seed: Four British Folkways in America* (Oxford University Press, 1989), pp. 6–9.

5. Colin Woodard, *American Nations: A History of the Eleven Rival Regional Cultures of North America* (New York: Penguin Books, 2011), p. 295.

6. William Labov, *Principles of Linguistic Change*, vol. 3: *Cognitive and Cultural Factors* (Hoboken, NJ: Wiley-Blackwell, 2010).

7. For example, westward migration out of the Northeast often involved the migration of whole communities compared to the migration of single families or small groups in the midlands and the south. In the north, initial buildings were temporary and quickly gave way to permanent towns and cities, while in the south, sturdier cabins were erected in isolated locations. See Fred B. Kniffen, and Henry Glassie, "Building with Wood in the Eastern United States: A Time-Place Perspective," *Geographical Review* 56, no. 1 (January 1966), pp. 40–66.

8. Daniel Elazar, *American Federalism: A View from the States*, 2nd edition (New York: Thomas Crowell, 1972).

9. Labov, *Principles of Linguistic Change*.

10. Wilbur Zelinsky, *The Cultural Geography of the United States* (Englewood Cliffs, NJ: Prentice Hall, 1973), p. 13.

11. For discussions of Yankee cultural imperialism, see Zelinsky, *Cultural Geography of the United States* and Timothy C. Frazer, *"Heartland" English: Variation and Transition in the American Midwest* (University of Alabama Press, 1993).

12. David F. Damore and Robert E. Lang, "Beyond Density & Diversity: Understanding the Socio-Cultural Geography of Contemporary Presidential Elections," Brookings Mountain West Policy Report, September 2016, https://digitalscholar ship.unlv.edu/brookings_pubs/42/.

13. Andrew Gelman, David Park, Boris Short, Joseph Bafumi, and Jeronimo Cortina, *Red State, Blue State, Rich State, Poor State: Why Americans Vote the Way They Do*

(Princeton University Press, 2008). Also see Larry M. Bartels, *Unequal Democracy: The Political Economy of the New Gilded Age* (New York: Russell Sage Foundation, 2008).

14. Francis E. Rourke, "Urbanism and American Democracy," *Ethics* 74, no. 4 (July 1964), pp. 255–68.

15. Daniel J. Elazar, "Are We a Nation of Cities?" *Public Interest* 4 (Summer 1966) pp. 42–57, 47.

16. Arthur M. Schlesinger, "The City in American History," *Mississippi Valley Historical Review* 27, no. 1 (June 1940), pp. 43–66, 46.

17. Charles N. Glaab and A. Theodore Brown, *A History of Urban America*, (New York: The Macmillan Company, 1967), pp. 55–56. See also Morton White and Lucia White, *The Intellectual versus the City* (Harvard University Press and MIT Press, 1962), pp. 17–19.

18. Schlesinger, "The City in American History."

19. Ibid., p. 48.

20. Ibid., p. 54.

21. Ibid., p. 62.

22. Ibid., p. 59.

23. Richard Hofstader, *The Age of Reform: From Bryan to F.D.R.* (New York: Vintage Books 1960), pp. 23–66.

24. Daniel J. Elazar, "Urban Problems and the Federal Government: A Historical Inquiry," *Political Science Quarterly* 82, no. 4 (December 1966), pp. 505–27, 507.

25. Elazar, "Are We a Nation of Cities?" p. 48.

26. Robert Fishman, *Bourgeois Utopias: The Rise and Fall of Suburbia* (New York: Basic Books, 1987).

27. Richard Franklin Bensel, *Sectionalism and American Political Development, 1880–1980* (University of Wisconsin Press, 1984).

28. V. O. Key, *Politics, Parties and Pressure Groups*, 5th edition (New York: Crowell, 1964; original 1942), p. 229.

29. Frederick Jackson Turner, *The Significance of Sections in American History* (New York: Holt, 1932), p. 183. See also Frederick Jackson Turner, "Geographic Sectionalism in American History," *Annals of the Association of American Geographers* 16, no. 2 (June 1926), pp. 85–93; and J. Clark Archer and Peter J. Taylor, *Section and Party* (New York: Research Studies Press and John Wiley and Sons, 1981), pp. 11–15.

30. Zelinsky, *The Cultural Geography of the United States*, pp. 118–19.

31. James Graydon Gimpel and Jason E. Schuknecht, *Patchwork Nation: Sectionalism and Political Change in American Politics* (University of Michigan Press, 2014), p. 16.

32. Archer and Taylor, *Section and Party,* pp. 11–15.

33. Key, *Politics, Parties and Pressure Groups*, p. 233.

34. Ibid., p. 245.

35. Fred M. Shelley and J. Clark Archer, "Sectionalism and Presidential Politics: Voting Patterns in Illinois, Indiana, and Ohio," *Journal of Interdisciplinary History* 20, no. 2 (Autumn 1989), pp. 227–55, 252–53.

36. Ibid., p. 255.

37. Gimpel and Schuknecht, *Patchwork Nation*, pp. 18–19.

38. Ibid., pp. 28–29.

39. Ibid., p. 20.

40. Other states have these labels for parts of their states, but they are not always well-known or used outside the state with the same frequency that "Upstate New York" or "Downstate Chicago" are used. For this reason, only a few examples are covered here.

41. Ani Egbert and Susan Brower, "Greater Minnesota Refined and Revisited," Minnesota State Demographic Center, State of Minnesota: Department of Administration, January 2017, p. 4, mn.gov/admin/assets/greater-mn-refined-and-revisited-msdc-jan2017_tcm36-273216.pdf.

42. Local demographers, on the other hand, assert that there are six distinct regions in Greater Minnesota. See Minnesota Compass, Geographic Profiles, www.mncompass.org/profiles.

43. Josh Kron, "Red State, Blue City: How the Urban-Rural Divide is Splitting America," *The Atlantic*, November 30, 2012, www.theatlantic.com/politics/archive/2012/11/red-state-blue-city-how-the-urban-rural-divide-is-splitting-america/265686/.

44. David A. Graham, "Red State, Blue City," *The Atlantic*, March 2017, www.theatlantic.com/magazine/archive/2017/03/red-state-blue-city/513857/.

45. Bill Bishop, *The Big Sort: Why the Clustering of Like-Minded America Is Tearing Us Apart* (New York: Houghton Mifflin Company, 2008). After the publication of *The Big Sort*, scholars assembled a mountain of empirical data countering many of Bishop's claims (see, for example, Samuel J. Abrams and Morris P. Fiorina, "The Big Sort That Wasn't: A Skeptical Reexamination," *PS: Political Science & Politics* 45, no. 2 (April 2012), pp. 203–10). More recent work, however, supports some of Bishop's thesis (Jesse Sussell, "New Support for the Big Sort Hypothesis: An Assessment of Partisan Geographic Sorting in California, 1992–2010," *PS: Political Science & Politics* 46, no. 4 (October 2013); and Jesse Sussell and James A. Thomson, "Are Changing Constituencies Driving Rising Polarization?" (Santa Monica, CA: RAND Corporation, 2015), www.rand.org/pubs/research_reports/RR896.html. More generally, as Rodden notes, the heavy reliance on median voter models to study both electoral and economic outcomes and the emphasis on obtaining nationally representative survey samples to assess individual level behavior are methodologically at odds with studying the spatial clustering of voters. See Jonathan Rodden, "The Geographic Distribution of Political Preferences," *Annual Review of Political Science* 13, no. 1 (January 2010), pp. 321–40.

46. John B. Judis and Ruy Teixeira, *The Emerging Democratic Majority* (New York City: Scribner, 2002). The book's title and content evoke Kevin V. Phillips's *The Emerging Republican Majority* (New York: Arlington House Publishers, 1969). Democratic pollster Stanley Greenburg's recent book, *RIP GOP: How the New America Is Dooming the Republicans* (New York: Thomas Dunne Books, 2019), provides a bookend to both.

47. William H. Frey, *Diversity Explosion: How New Racial Demographics Are Remaking America* (Washington: Brookings Institution Press, 2015).

48. William H. Frey, "The Rise of the Melting-Pot Suburbs," Brookings Institution, *The Avenue*, May 26, 2015, www.brookings.edu/blog/the-avenue/2015/05/26/the-rise-of-melting-pot-suburbs/.

49. For an early analysis of these dynamics, see Robert Lang, Thomas Sanchez, and Alan Berube, "The New Suburban Politics: A County-Based Analysis of Metropolitan Voting Trends since 2000," in *Red, Blue, & Purple America: Changing Politics and Demographics in the Mountain West,* edited by Ruy Teixeira (Washington: Brookings Institution Press, 2008), pp. 25–50.

50. Also see Jowei Chen and Jonathan Rodden, "Unintentional Gerrymandering: Political Geography and Electoral Bias in Legislatures," *Quarterly Journal of Political Science* 8, no. 3 (2013), pp. 239–69.

51. James G. Gimpel, Nathan Loving, Bryant Moy, and Andrew Reeves, "The Urban-Rural Gulf in American Political Behavior," *Political Behavior* (online publication date March 5, 2020), p. 21.

52. Gimpel, Loving, Moy, and Reeves, "The Urban-Rural Gulf in American Political Behavior," pp. 2–3.

53. Gordon W. Allport, *The Nature of Prejudice* (Garden City, NY: Doubleday Anchor, 1954).

54. Frey, *Diversity Explosion.*

55. Jeffrey M. Sellers, "Place, Institution and the Political Ecology of U.S. Metropolitan Areas," in *The Political Ecology of the Metropolis*, edited by Jeffrey M. Sellers, Daniel Kübler, Melanie Walter-Rogg, and R. Alan Walks (Essex, UK: European Consortium for Political Research, 2013), pp. 37–86.

56. Frey, *Diversity Explosion.*

57. Gelman and others, *Red State, Blue State, Rich State, Poor State.*

58. V. O. Key, *Southern Politics in State and Nation* (New York: Alfred A. Knopf, 1984).

59. Lee Sigelman and Susan Welch, "The Contact Hypothesis. Black-White Interaction and Positive Racial Attitudes," *Social Forces* 71, no. 3 (March 1993), pp. 781–95.

60. See, for example, Michael W. Giles and Melanie A. Buckner, "David Duke and Black Threat: An Old Hypothesis Revisited," *Journal of Politics* 55, no. 3 (August 1993), pp. 702–13; James M. Glaser, "Back to the Black Belt: Racial Environment and White Racial Attitudes in the South," *Journal of Politics* 56, no. 1 (February 1994), pp. 21–24; Jonathan Knuckey and Myunghee Kim, "Racial Resentment, Old-Fashioned Racism, and the Vote Choice of Southern and Nonsouthern Whites in the 2012 U.S. Presidential Election," *Social Science Quarterly* 96, no. 4 (December 2015), pp. 905–22; and Seth C. McKee and Melanie J. Springer, "'A Tale of 'Two Souths': White Voting Behavior in Contemporary Southern Elections," *Social Science Quarterly* 96, no. 2 (June 2015), pp. 588–607.

61. Marylee C. Taylor, "How White Attitudes Vary with the Racial Composition of

Local Populations: Numbers Count," *American Sociological Review* 63, no. 4 (August 1998), pp. 512–35.

62. Shaun Bowler, Stephen P. Nicholson, and Gary M. Segura, "Earthquakes and Aftershocks: Race, Direct Democracy, and Partisan Change," *American Journal of Political Science* 50, no. 1 (January 2006); and Matt A. Barreto, Gary Segura, Elizabeth Bergman, David Damore, and Adrian Pantoja, "The Prop 187 Effect: The Politics of Immigration and Lessons from California," in *Latino America: How America's Most Dynamic Population Is Poised to Transform the Politics of the Nation*, edited by Matt Barreto and Gary M. Segura (New York: Public Affairs, 2014), pp. 173–88.

63. Daniel J. Hopkins, "Politicized Places: Explaining Where and When Immigrants Provoke Local Opposition," *American Political Science Review* 104, no. 1 (February 2010), pp. 40–60; and Benjamin J. Newman, "Acculturating Contexts and Anglo Opposition to Immigration in the United States," *American Journal of Political Science* 57, no. 2 (April 2013), pp. 374–90.

64. Damore and Lang, "Beyond Density & Diversity," pp. 14–17.

65. Ibid., p. 16.

66. David Montgomery and Richard Florida, "How the Suburbs Will Swing the Midterm Election," *CityLab*, October 4, 2018, www.citylab.com/equity/2018/10/mid term-election-data-suburban-voters/572137/. Also see Chen and Rodden, "Unintentional Gerrymandering: Political Geography and Electoral Bias in Legislatures."

67. Lang, Sanchez, and Berube, "The New Suburban Politics: A County-Based Analysis of Metropolitan Voting Trends since 2000."

68. Ibid.

69. Mark Muro and Sifan Liu, "Another Clinton-Trump Divide: High-Output American vs. Low-Output America," *The Avenue*, November 29, 2016, www.brookings.edu/blog/the-avenue/2016/11/29/another-clinton-trump-divide-high-output-america-vs-low-output-america/.

70. Mark Muro and Jacob Whiten, "America's Two Economies Remain Far Apart," Brookings Institution, *The Avenue*, November 16, 2018, www.brookings.edu/blog/the-avenue/2018/11/16/americas-two-economies-remain-far-apart/.

71. Mark Muro and Jacob Whiten, "America Has Two Economies—and They're Diverging Fast," Brookings Institution, *The Avenue*, September 19, 2019, www.brookings.edu/blog/the-avenue/2019/09/10/america-has-two-economies-and-theyre-diverging-fast/.

72. James G. Gimpel, Frances E. Lee, and Joshua Kaminski, "The Political Geography of Campaign Contributions in American Politics," *Journal of Politics* 68, no. 3 (August 2006), pp. 626–39.

73. See Walter Christaller, *Central Places in Southern Germany*, translated by Carlisle W. Baskin (Englewood Cliffs, NJ: Prentice-Hall, 1966, original 1933) and W. R. Tobler, "A Computer Move Simulating Urban Growth in the Detroit Region," *Economic Geography* 46, no. 2 (June 1970), pp. 234–40.

74. See Brad Plumer, "Blue States Roll Out Aggressive Climate Strategies. Red

States Keep to the Sidelines," *New York Times*, June 21, 2019, www.nytimes.com/2019/06/21/climate/states-climate-change.html.

75. Ronald Brownstein, "Why Red and Blue States Divide over Green Policy," CNN, September 4, 2018, www.cnn.com/2018/09/04/politics/climate-change-politics-red-blue-states/index.html.

76. For a comprehensive review of the polarization literature and a comparison of the current era of polarization to previous eras as they relate to extant theories of party change, see Geoffrey C. Layman, Thomas M. Carsey, and Juliana Menasce Horowitz, "Party Polarization in American Politics: Characteristics, Causes, and Consequences," *Annual Review of Political Science* 9 (June 2006), pp. 83–110.

77. Alan Abramowitz and Kyle Saunders, "Why Can't We All Get Along?: The Reality of a Polarized America," *The Forum: A Journal of Applied Research in Contemporary Politics* 3, no. 2, Article 1 (July 2005); Alan Abramowitz and Kyle Saunders, "Is Polarization a Myth?" *Journal of Politics* 70, no. 2 (April 2008), pp. 542–55; and Alan Abramowitz, *The Great Alignment: Race, Party Transformation, and the Rise of Donald Trump* (Yale University Press, 2018).

78. Morris P. Fiorina and Samuel J. Abrams, "Political Polarization in the American Public," *Annual Review of Politics* 11 (June 2008), pp. 563–88; Morris P. Fiorina, Samuel J. Abrams, and Jeremy C. Pope, *Culture War: The Myth of a Polarized America*, 3rd edition (New York: Longman, 2010); and Matthew Levendusky and Jeremy Pope, "Red States vs. Blue States: Going Beyond the Mean," *Public Opinion Quarterly* 75, no. 2 (Summer 2011), pp. 227–48.

79. Levendusky and Pope, "Red States vs. Blue States."

80. Michael Barber and Jeremy C. Pope, "Does Party Trump Ideology? Disentangling Party and Ideology in America," *American Political Science Review* 113, no. 1 (February 2019), pp. 38–54, 53. Also see Donald R. Kinder and Nathan P. Kalmone, *Neither Liberal Nor Conservative: Ideological Innocence in the American Public* (University of Chicago Press, 2017); and Yphtach Lelkes, "Mass Polarizations: Manifestations and Measurements," *Public Opinion Quarterly* 80, no. S1 (March 15, 2016), pp. 392–410.

81. Lilliana Mason, "'I Disrespectfully Agree': The Differential Effects of Partisan Sorting on Social and Issue Polarization," *American Journal of Political Science* 59, no. 1 (March 2014), pp. 128–45.

82. Alan Abramowitz and Steven Webster, "The Rise of Negative Partisanship and the Nationalization of U.S. Elections in the 21st Century," *Electoral Studies* 41 (March 2016), pp. 12–22, 21.

83. Marc J. Hetherington and Thomas J. Rudolph, *Why Washington Won't Work: Polarization, Political Trust, and the Governing Crisis* (University of Chicago Press, 2015).

84. Liliana Mason, *Uncivil Agreement: How Politics Became Our Identity* (University of Chicago Press, 2018).

85. See Carsey Layman and Menasce Horowitz, "Party Polarization in American

Politics: Characteristics, Causes, and Consequences," Raymond J. La Raja and Brian F. Schaffner (eds.), *Campaign Finance and Political Polarization* (University of Michigan Press, 2015).

86. Stephen P. Nicholson, "Polarizing Cues" *American Journal of Political Science* 56, no. 1 (January 2012), pp. 52–66; and James N. Druckman, Erik Peterson, and Rune Slothuus, "How Elite Partisan Polarization Affects Public Opinion Formation," *American Political Science Review* 107, no. 1 (February 2013), pp. 57–79. Also see John R. Zaller, *The Nature and Origins of Mass Opinion* (Cambridge University Press, 1992).

87. For an extensive review of this literature, see Marcus Prior, "Media and Political Polarization," *Annual Review of Political Science* 16 (February 2013), pp. 101–27.

88. Gregory J. Martin and Ali Yurukoglu, "Bias in Cable News: Persuasion and Polarization," *American Economic Review* 107, no. 9 (September 2017), pp. 2569–99. For an overview of the rise and consequences of conservative media, see Kathleen Hall Jamieson and Joseph N. Cappella, *Echo Chamber: Rush Limbaugh and the Conservative Media Establishment* (Oxford University Press, 2008).

89. Kathleen Bawn, Martin Cohen, David Karol, Seth Masket, Hans Noel, and John Zaller, "A Theory of Political Parties: Groups, Policy Demands and Nominations in American Politics" *Perspective on Politics* 10, no. 3 (September 2012), pp. 571–97.

90. See, for example, Gelman and others, *Red State, Blue State, Rich State, Poor State*; and David A. Hopkins, *Red Fighting Blue: How Geography and Electoral Rules Polarize American Politics* (Cambridge University Press, 2017).

91. See, for example, Sussell, "New Support for the Big Sort Hypothesis"; Ron Johnston, David Manley, and Kelvyn Jones, "Spatial Polarization of Presidential Voting in the United States, 1992–2012: The 'Big Sort' Revisited," *Annals of the American Association of Geographers* 106, no. 5 (April 2016), pp. 1047–62; Chad Kinsella, Colleen McTague, and Kevin N. Raleigh, "Unmasking Geographic Polarization and Clustering: A Micro-Scaler Analysis of Partisan Voting Behavior," *Applied Geography* 62, (August 2015), pp. 404–19; and Adam S. Myers, "Secular Geographical Polarization in the American South: The Case of Texas, 1996–2010," *Electoral Studies* 32, no. 1 (March 2013), pp. 48–62.

92. Levendusky and Pope, "Red States vs Blue States," p. 244.

93. Note that aggregating the data in this way simplifies the presentation, but it does obscure the fact that while Clinton carried most of the core counties in the twenty-seven metro regions, strong Trump support in the outlying suburban counties tipped some of the metros into his column.

94. Damore and Lang, "Beyond Density & Diversity."

95. See Bartels, *Unequal Democracy*; and Nolan McCarty, Keith T. Poole, and Howard Rosenthal, *Polarized America: The Dance of Ideology and Unequal Riches*, 2nd edition (MIT Press, 2016). Also note that Poole and Rosenthal track the rise of polarization to the 1970s. Other scholars find that partisan racial alignments began in the late 1960s or earlier, with the Republicans embracing the "Southern Strategy" under Richard Nixon that used race-based appeals as a means to convert white

Southern voters from Democrats to Republicans; see Phillips, *The Emerging Republican Majority*.

96. Ashley Jardina, *White Identity Politics* (Cambridge University Press, 2019); Jonathan M. Metzl, *Dying of Whiteness: How the Politics of Resentment Is Killing America's Heartland* (New York: Basic Books, 2019); Christopher S. Parker and Matt A. Barreto, *Change They Can't Believe In: The Tea Party and Reactionary Politics in America* (Princeton University Press, 2013); and John Sides, Michael Tesler, and Lynn Vavreck, *Identity Crises: The 2016 Presidential Campaign and the Battle for the Meaning of America* (Princeton University Press, 2018).

97. Jardina, *White Identity Politics*; also see Robert Wuthnow, *The Left Behind: Decline and Rage in Rural America*, (Princeton University Press, 2018) for a discussion of cultural antagonism in rural America.

98. William H. Frey, *Diversity Explosion*; and Sean Bowler and Gary Segura, *The Future Is Ours: Minority Politics, Political Behavior, and the Multiracial Era of American Politics* (Washington: CQ Press, 2012).

99. Metzl, *Dying of Whiteness*.

100. Ronald Brownstein, "Places with the Fewest Immigrants Push Back Hardest against Immigration," CNN, August 22, 2017, www.cnn.com/2017/08/22/politics/immigration-trump-arizona/index.html.

101. Theda Skocpol and Vanessa Williamson, *The Tea Party and the Remaking of Republican Conservatism* (Oxford University Press, 2013). Also see Parker and Barreto, *Change They Can't Believe in*.

102. William H. Riker, "Implications from the Disequilibrium of Majority Rule for the Study of Institutions," *American Political Science Review* 74, no. 2 (June 1980), pp. 432–46, 443.

103. George C. Edwards III, *Why the Electoral College is Bad for America* (Yale University Press, 2004); Michel L. Balinski and H. Peyton Young, "Apportionment," in *Operations Research and the Public Sector, Handbooks in Operations Research and Management Science*, volume 6, edited by Steven M. Pollock, Michael H. Rothkopf, and Arnold Barnett (Amsterdam: North-Holland, 1994); Michael L. Balinski and H. Peyton Young, "The Webster Method of Apportionment," *Proceedings of the National Academy of Sciences of the United States of America* 77, no. 1 (January 1980), pp. 1–4; and Frances E. Lee and Bruce I. Oppenheimer, *Sizing Up the Senate* (University of Chicago Press, 1999).

104. Nolan McCarty, Keith T. Poole, and Howard Rosenthal, "Congress and the Territorial Expansion of the United States," *SSRN*, July 4, 1999, https://ssrn.com/abstract=1154168 or http://dx.doi.org/10.2139/ssrn.1154168.

105. Jonathan A. Rodden, *Why Cities Lose: The Deep Roots of the Urban-Rural Political Divide* (New York: Basic Books, 2019).

106. David Wasserman, "The Congressional Map Has a Record-Setting Bias against Democrats," *FiveThirtyEight.com*, August 7, 2017, https://fivethirtyeight.com/features/the-congressional-map-is-historically-biased-toward-the-gop/.

107. Philip Bump, "By 2040, Two-Thirds of Americans Will Be Represented by 30 Percent of the Senate," *Washington Post*, November 28, 2017, www.washingtonpost .com/news/politics/wp/2017/11/28/by-2040-two-thirds-of-americans-will-be-rep resented-by-30-percent-of-the-senate/?utm_term=.6882a0ec4797.

108. In *Baker v. Carr*, 369 U.S. 186 (1962), the Supreme Court ruled that redistricting is within the purview of the federal courts. In *Wesberry v. Sanders*, 376 U.S. 1 (1964), the Supreme Court ruled that U.S. House districts be populated equally, and in *Reynolds v. Sims*, 377 U.S. 533 (1964), the Court extended this principle to state legislative districts.

109. For a historical analysis of the genesis of the rural/urban divide and congressional reapportionment, see Charles W. Eagles, *Democracy Delayed: Congressional Reapportionment and Urban-Rural Conflict in the 1920s* (University of Georgia Press, 1990). For analyses of the effects of malapportionment in state legislatures, see Manning J. Dauer and Robert G. Kelsay, "Unrepresentative States," *National Municipal Review* 44, no. 11 (December 1955), pp. 571–75; Thomas R. Dye, "Malapportionment and Public Policy in the States," *Journal of Politics* 27, no. 3 (August 1965), pp. 586–601; and John P. White and Norman C. Thomas, "Urban and Rural Representation and State Legislative Apportionment," *Western Political Quarterly* 17, no. 4 (December 1964), pp. 724–41. For analyses of the effects of malapportionment in the House of Representatives, see Andrew Hacker, *Congressional Districting*, revised edition, (Washington: Brookings Institution Press, 1964); and Gary W. Cox and Jonathan N. Katz, *Elbridge Gerry's Salamander* (Cambridge University Press, 2001).

110. For instance, in 2016, the Republicans won 55 percent of seats in the U.S. House while winning 50 percent of the vote; see Molly E. Reynolds, "Republicans in Congress Got a 'Seats Bonus' this Election (Again)," Brookings Institution, *FixGov Blog*, November 22, 2016, www.brookings.edu/blog/fixgov/2016/11/22/gop-seats-bo nus-in-congress/. In 2018, despite picking up forty-two seats, winning the national House vote by seven points, and gaining majority control of the House of Representatives, Republican gerrymanders in a number of states limited Democratic gains; see William T. Adler and Stuart A. Thompson, "The 'Blue Wave' Wasn't Enough to Overcome Republican Gerrymanders," *New York Times,* November 7, 2018, www.nytimes .com/interactive/2018/11/07/opinion/midterm-elections-2018-republican-gerry mandering.html; Associated Press, "GOP Redistricting Edge Moderated Democrats' 2018 Gains, Analysis Finds," March 21, 2019, www.nbcnews.com/politics/elections/ gop-redistricting-edge-moderated-democrats-2018-gains-analysis-finds-n985871; and Demetrios Pogkas, Jackie Gu, David Ingold, and Mira Rojanasakul, "How Democrats Broke the House Map Republicans Drew," *Bloomberg*, November 10, 2018, www .bloomberg.com/graphics/2018-house-seats-vs-votes/.

111. John Hudak, *Presidential Pork: White House Influence over the Distribution of Federal Grants* (Washington: Brookings Institution Press, 2014); Christopher R. Berry, Barry C. Burden, and William G. Howell, "The President and the Distribution of Federal Spending," *American Political Science Review* 10, no. 4 (November 2010), pp. 783–99; and Frances Lee, "Representation and Public Policy: The Consequences

of Senate Apportionment for the Geographic Distribution of Federal Funds," *Journal of Politics* 60, no. 1 (February 1998), pp. 34–62.

112. Laura Schultz and Michelle Cummings, "Giving or Getting? New York's Balance of Payments with the Federal Government," Rockefeller Institute of Government, January 8, 2019, https://rockinst.org/issue-area/giving-getting-new-yorks-balance-payments-federal-government-2/.

113. David Altig, Alan Auerbach, Patrick Higgins, Darryl Koehler, Laurence Kotlikoff, Ellyn Terry, and Victor Ye, "Did the 2017 Tax Reform Discriminate against Blue State Voters?" Working Paper 2019-7, Federal Reserve Bank of Atlanta Working Paper Series, April 2019. Also see, Tata Golshan "4 Winners and Losers from the Republican Tax Bill," *Vox.com*, December 22, 2017, www.vox.com/2017/12/20/16790 040/gop-tax-bill-winners.

114. See Dye, "Malapportionment and Public Policy in the States"; and Hacker, *Congressional Districting, The Issue of Equal Representation*.

115. Scott Allard, Nancy Burns, and Gerald Gamm, "Representing Urban Interests: The Local Politics of State Legislatures," *Studies in American Political Development* 12, no. 2 (Fall 1998), pp. 267–302; Nancy Burns, Laura Evans, Gerald Gamm, and Corrine McConnaughy, "Urban Politics in the State Arena," *Studies in American Political Development* 23, no. 1 (Winter 2009), pp. 1–22; Gerald Gamm and Thad Kousser, "No Strength in Numbers: The Failure of Big-City Bills in American State Legislatures, 1880–2000," *American Political Science Review* 104, no. 1 (November 2010), pp. 2–20; and Gerald Gamm and Thad Kousser, "Broad Bills or Particularistic Policy? Historical Patterns in American State Legislatures," *American Political Science Review* 107, no. 4 (January 2010), pp. 663–78.

116. Allard, Burns, and Gamm, "Representing Urban Interests."

117. V. O. Key, *American State Politics: An Introduction* (New York: Knopf, 1956), p. 230.

118. Gamm and Kousser, "No Strength in Numbers," p. 670.

119. Boris Shor and Nolan McCarty, "The Ideological Mapping of American Legislatures," *American Political Science Review* 105, no. 3 (August 2011), pp. 530–51.

120. Alan Rosenthal, *Governors and Legislatures: Contending Powers* (Washington: CQ Press, 1990); and Alan Rosenthal, *The Best Job in Politics: Exploring How Governors Succeed as Policy Leaders* (Washington: CQ Press, 2012).

121. Charles Barrilleaux and Michael Berkman, "Do Governors Matter? Budgeting Rules and the Politics of State Policymaking," *Political Research Quarterly* 56, no. 4 (December 2003), pp. 409–17; and Thad Kousser and Justin H. Phillips, *The Power of American Governors: Winning on Budgets and Losing on Policy* (Cambridge University Press, 2012).

122. Gamm and Kousser, "Broad Bills or Particularistic Policy?"

123. While serving as a justice on the Iowa Supreme Court, in *Clinton v. Cedar Rapids and the Missouri River Railroad* (24 Iowa 455; 1868), Dillon articulated what would become known as Dillon's Rule establishing the premise of state supremacy over local governments: "Municipal corporations owe their origin to, and derive

their powers and rights wholly from, the legislature. It breathes into them the breath of life, without which they cannot exist. As it creates, so may it destroy. If it may destroy, it may abridge and control. Unless there is some constitutional limitation on the right, the legislature might, by single act, if we can suppose it capable of so great a folly and so great a wrong, sweep from existence all of the municipal corporations in the state."

124. See Benjamin Baker, "Municipal Autonomy: Its Relationship to Metropolitan Government," *Western Political Quarterly* 13, no. 1 (March 1960), pp. 83–98; and Jesse J. Richardson, "Is Home Rule the Answer? Clarifying the Influence of Dillon's Rule on Growth Management," Brookings Institution, Center on Urban and Metropolitan Policy, Discussion Paper, January 2003, www.brookings.edu/wp-content/uploads /2016/06/dillonsrule.pdf.

125. James DeHaven, "Raiders Practice Facility May Be Headed to Henderson, Chafing Northern Nevada Lawmakers," *Reno Gazette Journal*, December 1, 2017, www.rgj.com/story/news/politics/2017/12/01/raiders-practice-facility-may -headed-henderson-chafing-northern-nevada-lawmakers/910058001/.

126. Nicole DuPuis, Trevor Langan, Christina McFarland, Angelina Panettieri, and Brooks Rainwater, "City Rights in an Era of Preemption: A State-by-State Analysis, 2018 Update," *National League of Cities*, April 2, 2018, www.nlc.org/re source/city-rights-in-an-era-of-preemption-a-state-by-state-analysis.

127. These are also known historically as "Ripper Laws"; see Graham, "Red State, Blue City" and "Red State, Blue City: How the Urban-Rural Divide is Splitting America."

128. Filipe R. Campante and Quoc-Anh Do, "Isolated Capital Cities, Accountability, and Corruption: Evidence from US States," *American Economic Review* 104, no. 8 (August 2014), pp. 2456–81.

129. Thomas K. Ogorzalek, *The Cities on the Hill: How Urban Institutions Transformed National Politics* (Oxford University Press, 2018).

130. For a broader discussion of the effects of shifting policy agendas on patterns of regional partisan support, see Bensel, *Sectionalism and American Political Development*.

131. Bruce Katz and Jennifer Bradley, *The Metropolitan Revolution: How Cities and Metros Are Fixing Our Broken Politics and Fragile Economy* (Washington: Brookings Institution Press, 2013).

132. Katz and Bradley, *The Metropolitan Revolution*, p. 7.

133. Garrett Dash Nelson and Alasdair Rae, "An Economic Geography of the United States: From Communities to Megaregions," *PLoS ONE* 11, no. 11 (November 2016), pp. 1–23, https://journals.plos.org/plosone/article?id=10.1371/journal.pone.01 66083.

134. See Zoltan L. Hajnal and Paul G. Lewis, "Municipal Institutions and Voter Turnout in Local Elections," *Urban Affairs Review* 38, no. 5 (May 2003), pp. 645–88; and Zoltan L. Hajnal and Jessica Trounstine, "Where Turnout Matters: The Conse-

quences of Uneven Turnout in City Politics," *Journal of Politics* 67, no. 2 (April 2005), pp. 515–35.

135. Caroline Bleakley, "Unincorporated Clark County's Population Exceeds 1 Million," *8newsnow.com*, February 27, 2018, www.8newsnow.com/news/unincorpor ated-clark-county-population-exceeds-1-million/995745552/.

136. For an analysis of how local land use regulation and the provision of local public goods shape urban inequality and segregation, see Jessica Troustine, *Segregation by Design: Local Politics and Inequality in American Cities* (Cambridge University Press, 2018).

137. Ronald Brownstein, "The Prosperity Paradox Is Dividing the Country in Two," CNN, January 23, 2018, www.cnn.com/2018/01/23/politics/economy-prosper ity-paradox-divide-country-voters/index.html.

3

MID-ATLANTIC: PENNSYLVANIA AND VIRGINIA

Robert E. Lang

Pennsylvania and Virginia are swing (or even Democratic-leaning) states because their largest urban areas lie within the Northeast Corridor, and more particularly the Mid-Atlantic region. The Mid-Atlantic now comprises, along with the West Coast, perhaps the most reliably liberal section of the United States. In fact, every state north of the Carolinas that has an Atlantic coastline voted for Democratic presidential candidates in the past three elections.[1] The eastern part of Pennsylvania and the northern section of Virginia fall within this common sociocultural and economic space, and are, thus, competitive for Democrats.[2] Pennsylvania minus metro Philadelphia, or Virginia minus suburban Washington, D.C., would not be blue-leaning or even swing states, but part of red America.

It is easy to see Pennsylvania as part of the Mid-Atlantic, but Virginia was once associated with a very different political region. Throughout the twentieth century and, indeed, back to the founding of the British North American colonies, Virginia maintained a Southern identity.[3] That was true even for much of Northern Virginia, except for places such as Arlington and Alexandria, which were part of the state's original territorial concession to create Washington, D.C.[4]

The first observer to place a major section of Virginia inside a Northern economic zone was geographer Jean Gottmann in his 1961 book

Megalopolis: The Urbanized Northeastern Seaboard of the United States.[5] Gottmann argued that Virginia was now part of a linear urban system extending along America's East Coast from southern New Hampshire to Northern Virginia. Virginia's Washington, D.C., suburbs form the southern-most section of the Northeast Seaboard, which is sometimes called the Acela Corridor in reference to the high-speed rail that links the region.[6] In an update on *Megalopolis*, Arthur C. Nelson and Robert E. Lang show a "Chesapeake Megapolitan Area" that captures much of eastern Virginia, including Richmond and Hampton Roads (Virginia Beach) as part of an increasingly integrated economic zone that, in turn, links to a larger "Megalopolis Megapolitan Cluster" that now reaches north to southern Maine.[7]

Geographer Wilbur Zelinsky saw the relationship between Pennsylvania and Virginia in more sociocultural terms.[8] Zelinsky looks at origins and identities of places. He developed a "doctrine of first effective settlement" to account for enduring social norms that remain long after an initial population has been displaced.[9] For instance, while not a single structure remains in New York City from when it was New Amsterdam, the Dutch habits of religious tolerance, embracing diversity, and hyper-focus on commerce remain part of Gotham's ethos to this day.

Because Northern Virginia was proximate to a planned national capital that began its existence as a blank space, it was heavily influenced by a more centrist national culture, what Zelinsky identifies as "The Midland."[10] Southeast Pennsylvania (the old Quaker settlements) lies at the heart of The Midland, and so, by extension, does Washington, D.C., and its suburbs in Maryland and Virginia, which are more an extension of Pennsylvania than part of either the North or South. Thus, greater Washington, D.C., is a more national, or neutral, space than say Boston, Massachusetts, or Richmond, Virginia, which are strongly identified with the North and with the South, respectively.

STATE OF PLAY: PENNSYLVANIA

Pennsylvania has—as many states do—a split political personality. In this instance, the moderate Pittsburgh in the western part of the state and the politically liberal Philadelphia in the east are divided by a mostly conservative center—with notable exceptions, such as State College, home to Penn State. It is, in essence, much like rural America in political attitude.

Political consultant James Carville said, while working on the 1986 campaign for gubernatorial candidate Robert Casey Sr.: "Between Paoli and Penn Hills, Pennsylvania is Alabama without the blacks. They didn't film the *Deer Hunter* here for nothing—the state has the second-highest concentration of NRA members behind Texas."[11]

Liz Spikol, in the magazine *Philadelphia*, describes a journey through Pennsylvania's Appalachian Uplands[12] as a lifelong Philadelphia resident. The map that accompanies the article shows an area she labels pejoratively as "Pennsyltucky,"[13] which combines the state names Pennsylvania and Kentucky and is meant to convey the fact that, from the viewpoint of a Philadelphian, the middle of the Keystone State seems more like the rural South than the Northeast.

Pennsylvania is a complicated state that contains six political sections (see figure 3-1). Pennsylvania's nickname, the Keystone State, refers to the fact that it was the middle British colony and played a pivotal role linking key sections of the United States—the north, south, and Midwest (or what were the "Northwest Territories").[14] Thus, Pennsylvania's connectivity to these sections produces a microcosm of U.S. sectional interests within the state. It also makes Pennsylvania a key swing state in that it contains several competing political cultures.

Pennsylvania is also a big state, ranking fifth in population, just behind New York and ahead of Illinois. The state, however, lags in growth and could lose one of its eighteen seats in the U.S. House of Representatives by 2022 after a reapportionment based on the 2020 census. Losing a congressional seat would likewise reduce Pennsylvania's Electoral College votes from twenty to nineteen in the 2024 presidential election. Pennsylvania proved a pivotal state in the 2016 election, handing its Electoral College votes to Republican Donald Trump after voting for the Democratic presidential candidate in every election after 1988.

FIGURE 3-1. Pennsylvania

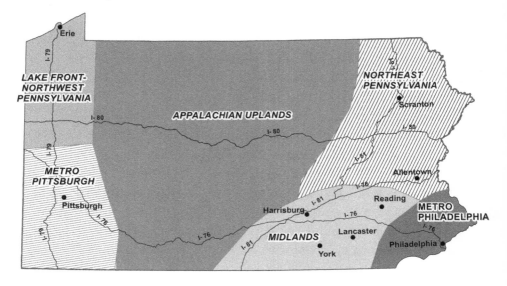

Metro Philadelphia

Philadelphia and its suburbs (a large share of which are located in southern New Jersey) form part of Gottman's *Megalopolis*. The city of Philadelphia and its inner suburbs represent the bluest part of the Keystone State. Table 3-1 shows the region contains nearly a third (32.2 percent) of Pennsylvania's 12.8 million residents.[15] Metro Philadelphia is also diverse in that it accounts for nearly two-thirds of the state's African American population, over 61 percent of Asians, and over half (54.3 percent) of foreign-born residents.

Philadelphia is by far Pennsylvania's largest metropolitan area (accounting for over a third of the state's total vote) and Democratic-dominated political region (see table 3-2). Democrats routinely win Philadelphia by wide margins. For instance, consider the 2018 U.S. Senate and gubernatorial contests. Democratic Senator Bob Casey Jr. won the region by a 41 percent margin over Republican challenger Lou

TABLE 3-1. Demographic and Economic Comparison between Pennsylvania and Metros

	Pennsylvania	Share in Philadelphia* [%]	Share in Pittsburgh [%]
Population	12,805,537	32.2	18.2
White	76.4%	25.4	20.4
Black	10.7%	65.6	13.4
Asian	7.3%	61.1	12.5
Latino	3.5%	39.8	4.3
Foreign-Born	7.0%	54.3	9.9
College Educated	31.4%	39.8	21.1
Jobs	6,110,556	32.2	18.7
GDP	$677,973	42.0	19.7

*Excludes counties outside of MSA primary state.

Sources: 2017 American Community Survey 1-Year estimates as aggregated by censusreporter.org, Department of Commerce, Bureau of Economic Analysis, 2015 Real GDP (millions of chained 2012 dollars) County Level Data, U.S. Department of Labor, Bureau of Labor Statistics 2017 County Level Data.

Barletta on his way to being elected to a third term. Meanwhile, Democratic gubernatorial candidate Tom Wolf won metro Philadelphia by a whopping 43.9 percent as he easily defeated Republican Scott Wagner to become Pennsylvania's forty-seventh governor. In 2016, Democratic presidential candidate Hillary Clinton won the region by 33.6 percent, but still lost the Keystone State to Donald Trump by less than 1 percent of the vote.

Like much of the Northeast, the Philadelphia metropolitan area is politically fragmented (see tables 3-3 and 3-4) in that it maintains over 240 local jurisdictions. The political divide between central city Philadelphia and its more remote suburbs reduces the region's influence in statewide elections and at the capital in Harrisburg. Philadelphia metro is becoming more isolated politically as a distinct region that is now far more integrated in the Northeast—in, for example, economic

TABLE 3-2. Comparison of Electoral Outcomes between Pennsylvania and Metros

| | Pennsylvania | Philadelphia | | Pittsburgh | |
Election	Outcome	Vote Share [%]	Outcome	Vote Share [%]	Outcome
2018 U.S. Senate	+13.1 Dem	34.3	+41.0 Dem	19.6	+14.3 Dem
2018 Gubernatorial	+17.1 Dem	34.3	+43.9 Dem	19.6	+17.4 Dem
2016 Presidential	+0.7 Rep	33.6	+32.3 Dem	19.6	+4.9 Rep
2016 U.S. Senate	+1.4 Rep	33.4	+24.9 Dem	19.7	+2.7 Rep
2014 Gubernatorial	+9.9 Dem	33.6	+33.5 Dem	19.3	+4.1 Dem
2012 Presidential	+5.4 Dem	34.2	+31.4 Dem	19.8	+1.2 Rep
2012 U.S. Senate	+9.1 Dem	33.7	+33.7 Dem	19.9	+5.7 Dem

Source: Data from Pennsylvania secretary of state's website.

TABLE 3-3. Partisan Composition of Pennsylvania State Government and Federal Delegation

| | | State Government | | | | Federal Delegation | | | |
| | | Upper House | | Lower House | | U.S. Senate | | U.S. House | |
	Governor	Dems	Reps	Dems	Reps	Dems	Reps	Dems	Reps
2019–20	Dem	22	28	93	110	1	1	9	9
2017–18	Dem	16	34	80	122*	1	1	8	10
2015–16	Dem	20	30	84	119	1	1	5	13
2013–14	Rep	23	27	93	110	1	1	5	13

*One vacancy.

Sources: Data from National Conference of State Legislatures, "State and Legislative Partisan Composition," for various years, and Pennsylvania secretary of state's website.

TABLE 3-4. Metro Governance Fragmentation and Autonomy in Pennsylvania

Governance Fragmentation

Metro	Number of Counties in Metro	Number of General Purposes Governments in Metro
Philadelphia*	5	242
Pittsburgh	7	463

Governance Autonomy

Local Government Autonomy Score	−0.336
Local Government Autonomy Ranking	43

*Excludes counties outside of MSA primary state.

Source: Data for Governance Fragmentation from 2017 Census of Governments. Data for Governance Autonomy from Harold Wolman, Robert McManmon, Michael Bell, and David Brunori, "Comparing Local Government Autonomy Across States," in *The Property Tax and Local Autonomy*, edited by Michael Bell, David Brunori, and Joan Youngman (Lincoln Institute of Land Policy Press, 2010), pp. 69–114.

sectors such as chemicals and pharmaceuticals—than connected to the rest of the Keystone State.

Metro Pittsburgh

Pittsburgh, in western Pennsylvania, lies in a different cultural and economic zone from Philadelphia. To geographers, Pittsburgh is the eastern-most part of the Midwest.[16] Pittsburgh was one of the most important trans-Appalachian cities to emerge in early nineteenth-century America. Pittsburgh's location at the origin of the Ohio River oriented its original connectivity to the Ohio and Mississippi watersheds. Thus, early nineteenth-century Pittsburgh had better transportation access to other river cities, such as Cincinnati, Ohio, and Saint Louis, Missouri, than it did overland to Philadelphia.

Pittsburgh industrialized and unionized in the late nineteenth and early twentieth centuries, and its politics reflected the working class interests of its residents, thus establishing a voting pattern that one would now recognize as Democratic-leaning. Pittsburgh has since undergone one of the most successful deindustrialization transitions to a new economy among so called "Rustbelt Cities."[17] Notably, its tech sector, anchored by Carnegie Mellon University, helped the city land such national-branded tech assets as Disney's Research Lab.[18] Pittsburgh also maintains well-established service and healthcare sectors, with the latter being supported by the University of Pittsburgh School of Medicine.

Pittsburgh's post-industrial success has been so dramatic that it has remade the region's politics, as well. Pittsburgh is now a less reliably blue-voting metro. This is especially true of the region's more distant suburbs, which are often solid red. The change has had the effect of making Pennsylvania more of a toss-up state than it has been in recent elections, where it formed part of the "Blue Wall" that Democrats could count on in presidential elections.[19]

The Pittsburgh metropolitan area casts about one in five votes in Pennsylvania's statewide races (see table 3-2). Metro Pittsburgh's politics are more contested than Philadelphia, and it is common for either party to win the region depending on the year. The 2018 midterm was a wave election for the Democrats as they gained the majority of seats in the U.S. House of Representatives, held off large losses in the U.S. Senate (despite having many more seats up than Republicans), and picked up several governorships across the country. In 2018, the Democratic candidates for the U.S. Senate and the governor in Pennsylvania both scored double-digit wins, 14.3 percent and 17.4 percent, respectively. But just two years earlier, in 2016, Democratic presidential candidate Hillary Clinton lost the region to Republican Donald Trump by 4.9 percent. In 2012, President Obama lost metro Pittsburgh by just 1.2 percent in his reelection bid and won the state by 5.4 percent.

Finally, Pittsburgh is one of the most municipally fragmented metropolitan areas in the United States.[20] Table 3-4 shows that it maintains 463 local jurisdictions, which, like Philadelphia, reduces the region's effectiveness in Harrisburg. Metro Pittsburgh is also mostly white, with minority shares that only slightly exceed the state as a whole (see table 3-1). Most minorities live in the city of Pittsburgh or its close-in suburbs, while the more distant suburbs are overwhelmingly white. The urban/suburban racial divide combined with municipal fragmentation further divides metro Pittsburgh politically and weakens its hand in the state legislature.

Appalachian Uplands

The Kentucky-like rural Appalachian Uplands section of Pennsylvania is also changing. The region is following the pattern seen in much of Appalachia, which extends all the way south to Georgia and through such states as West Virginia, where a mostly white population that has been cut off from the emerging tech and service economy in the nation's major metros is turning increasingly conservative.[21] It is notable that in the 2008 presidential election, where a large share of U.S. counties shifted blue in comparison to 2004 and 2000, Appalachia turned more red than before.[22] In the case of Pennsylvania, the red shift was most noticeable in the counties southwest of Pittsburgh in 2008. In the next two national elections, the shift registered more strongly in central Pennsylvania.

The recent surge in nativism has had an oversized impact on places like Appalachia, extending even into Upstate New York. The net effect is that it has made Pennsylvania's Appalachian Uplands more conservative and Republican-dominated than in past years. These effects can be seen in the politics of state government and the outcome in presidential elections as expressed via the Electoral College. Changes in Pittsburgh's politics, which now trend more moderate, and the deep red Appalachian parts of Pennsylvania put the state as a whole in play and reduce its reliability as part of the Democratic Blue Wall.

Northeast Pennsylvania

There is a part of Pennsylvania not often discussed as essential to the state's political dynamic that is emerging as one of the faster-growing and more politically dynamic sections of the Keystone State. The area lies in eastern Pennsylvania north of Philadelphia.

Pennsylvania counties that border on New Jersey and are increasingly part of the distant commuter sheds that connect to the New York metropolitan area economy and central New Jersey industries around Princeton to form part of the Northeast Corridor.[23] Farther west in this region, the city of Scranton remains almost as liberal as Philadelphia.

Just north of Philadelphia, Bucks County is close enough to central New Jersey that it now links to the tech and pharmaceutical sectors located from New Brunswick in the north to Princeton in the south and anchored by Rutgers and Princeton Universities as drivers of applied technology. Commuters from Pennsylvania now reflect the politics and values of New Jersey and are politically transforming communities in the eastern part of the state. The blue and moderate-red political attitudes from the Garden State now spill into Pennsylvania as the Northeast's high-wage and well-credentialed residences seek lower taxes and cheaper housing in the Keystone State.

The U.S. census includes the Lehigh Valley and places such as Pike County, Pennsylvania, as part of New York's combined statistical area due to commuting patterns. The original heavy industrial area in the Lehigh Valley, with its famous Bethlehem Steel Mill, has deindustrialized, but unlike Pittsburgh, the region has been less successful at replacing its old economy with a new one.[24] However, like Bucks County and Pikes County, the Lehigh Valley falls within greater New York's orbit via New Jersey. In fact, residents of the New York region, including many Latinos, have migrated to the Lehigh Valley seeking lower housing costs while remaining connected to family and jobs in the Northeast Corridor.

Politically, much of eastern Pennsylvania is either moderate-red or solidly blue. To an extent, this countervails some of the red-shifting change found in the rest of the Keystone State. In terms of overall state composition, Pennsylvania is quite complex: the east is now part of the Northeast Corridor, from Philadelphia to Pike County; the central part of the state is as red in sections as West Virginia or Kentucky; and, finally, western Pennsylvania is more moderate (but trending Republican) and driven by the new politics of greater Pittsburgh.

Midlands

It is easy to think of Pennsylvania as being comprised of three sections, as James Carville posited in 1986. But as noted, Pennsylvania's geopolitics are more complicated than that. For example, there is a string of cities lying west of Philadelphia, deep in the region's exurban hinterlands. This section of southeast Pennsylvania includes the state capital at Harrisburg and cities such as Lancaster, Reading, and York. The area contains Amish country and many farming communities. While less liberal than metro Philadelphia, the region overall leans Democratic. Southeast Pennsylvania now forms the far western fringe of the Northeast Corridor. The Midlands links to Maryland and Washington, D.C., by the Chesapeake Watershed, which includes the Susquehanna River.[25]

Lake Front–Northwest Pennsylvania

Finally, there is a part of Pennsylvania that is nearly forgotten in political discussions. It is an area that has more in common with northeast Ohio than the rest of Pennsylvania and includes frontage on Lake Erie. The region remains mostly small-town conservative, with the major exception being Erie County, which includes the Democratic-leaning city of Erie.[26]

Northwest Pennsylvania's emergence as a key swing area recently caught the attention of the *New York Times*.[27] Reporter Trip Gabriel notes that Erie County has many of what he calls "conflicted voters" who gave their votes to Obama in 2008 and 2012 and then to Trump in 2016.[28] According to Gabriel, many conflicted voters in this key swing county are reconsidering Trump, and a large share of them will likely back the Democratic presidential candidate in 2020.

Conclusion: Pennsylvania State of Play

Pennsylvania's politics is dominated by the dynamic between its million-plus metros and the rest of the state. The state of geopolitical play is made complex by a deeply conservative rural core, whose Republican-dominated politics are partly mitigated by other sections of Pennsylvania that are politically moderate and, in select instances, liberal.

Despite the fact that Pennsylvania remains a toss-up state and has been closely contested in recent election cycles, it has also seen considerable gerrymandering that skewed the U.S. House delegation to the Republicans. Even as Democrat Barack Obama won Pennsylvania in 2012 with 52 percent of the vote, the U.S. House delegation split five Democratic seats and thirteen Republican seats (see tables 3-2 and 3-3). The gerrymander also created a pro-GOP bias in the Pennsylvania statehouse. However, the 2011 Republican-drawn maps were thrown out by the Pennsylvania Supreme Court and replaced with maps overseen by the court. Under these maps, which were in place for the 2018 elections, the Democrats' gained parity with the Republicans within Pennsylvania's congressional delegation and gained nearly twenty seats in the state legislature.

The formula for winning statewide in Pennsylvania means running up big margins in metro Philadelphia of up to 40 percent or more while nearly breaking even in the Pittsburgh region. Together, the Philadelphia and Pittsburgh metros account for well over half the votes cast in Pennsylvania. The rural and smaller metros mostly break to the Republican candidate, with the notable exception of places such as Scranton and commuter counties in eastern Pennsylvania.

Not only are metros such as Philadelphia and Pittsburgh politically fragmented, the local governments have little autonomy to act on their own. Table 3-4 shows that Pennsylvania's "local government autonomy score" ranks the state at forty-three, meaning only seven states afford their localities less autonomy than the Keystone State.

In November 2019, Pennsylvania held an off-year election for municipal and county offices. In the last test for President Trump ahead of the 2020 election, Democrats scored major victories in eastern Pennsylvania, especially suburban Philadelphia. Democrats made similar gains throughout much of suburban America in 2019—in places such as Kentucky, Mississippi, and Virginia.[29] In Pennsylvania, the headlines tells the story: *Politico* led with "Pennsylvania Suburbs Revolt against Trump," while *Business Insider* ran with "Forget Kentucky and Virginia, the Worst Election News for Republicans Came Out of

Suburban Pennsylvania," and the local *Philadelphia Inquirer* declared "The Blue Wave Crashed Down on Pennsylvania Again, as Voters from Philly to Delaware County Turn Left."[30]

Democratic candidates swept county commission seats in suburban Delaware County, Pennsylvania, to the southwest of Philadelphia. As Eliza Relman at *Business Insider* notes: "Democrats flipped suburban Delaware County, which has been controlled by Republicans since the Civil War. The county's five-member council, which was filled by Republicans a few years ago, will now be occupied by Democrats."[31] Delaware County featured a well-oiled and legendary GOP political machine that kept electing Republicans to its board of supervisors for 150 years despite the fact that Democrats often maintained a registered voter advantage for much of the time. Democrats also took control of commissions in Chester and Bucks, two other major suburban counties outside of Philadelphia.

What sparked the dramatic changes in suburban Philadelphia? Maria Panaritis, an opinion writer for *The Inquirer*, argues that Trump shook Democratic suburban voters out of a deep, apathetic slumber:

> Democratic organizing and voter engagement had been pathetic to nonexistent in many communities before Trump came along. Republican incumbents would face weak or no challengers. Democratic voters were like self-satisfied zombies who trotted their half-conscious selves out to polling places only in sexy presidential election years. . . . Then came Trump in 2016. Talk about smelling salts.[32]

Holly Otterbine from *Politico* noted that, in contrast to Philadelphia, it was the Republicans that made political gains in suburban Pittsburgh. In fact, "The GOP took the majority in Washington County for the first time in a century."[33] She finds that "a political realignment has been underway for years in Pennsylvania: The GOP has bled college-educated voters in southeast suburbs at the same time that working-class white people have abandoned the Democrats in the west."[34]

Pennsylvania's red versus blue politics are in flux. An east/west divide is emerging that splits the state between the Democratic-voting

Northeast Corridor and the Republican-leaning Midwest. The Keystone State seems likely to return to its Blue Wall roots in 2020 given that the size of the 2019 Democratic gains in the east vastly outweigh its losses in the west.

EXPERT ANALYSIS: PENNSYLVANIA

William Frey is a senior fellow in the Metropolitan Policy Program at the Brookings Institution in Washington, D.C. He is also affiliated with the University of Michigan's Institute for Social Research and Population Studies Center. Dr. Frey is one of the leading demographers in the United States, with a special focus on how the nation's changing demographics affect its voting patterns. His recent work includes the book *Diversity Explosion: How New Racial Demographics are Remaking America*.[35] This interview was conducted on May 6, 2019. Note that interview responses may include minor edits to provide continuity and clarify language. Endnotes are also added to verify key facts.

Intrastate Political Dynamics

Dr. Frey was asked: "What is the political dynamic between Pennsylvania's major metropolitan areas and the rest of the state?" He answered:

Traditionally, Philadelphia and Pittsburgh have been much more Democratic, but more recently, in the 2016 presidential election, the western part of the state became more Republican. . . . The Democratic support had been much more around the Philadelphia area, but even in the eastern part of Pennsylvania, you talk about areas outside of Philadelphia and outside of Pittsburgh. The suburbs of Pittsburgh are not as Democratic as they used to be. The suburbs of Philadelphia still are a little more Democratic but did not do as well for the Democrats in 2016. The rest of the state is much more heavily Republican. James Carville once said Pennsylvania was Philadelphia and Pittsburgh—and they went Democratic—and the middle of the state was like Alabama.[36] That's not exactly right, but I think that's the general view people had. In the 2016 election, many more non-Philadelphia urban parts of the state and the smaller cities and suburban towns went for Trump.

In the 2018 congressional election, Pennsylvania Democrats picked up seats.... A good number of counties moved more toward the Democrats, especially in the eastern part of the state, where there was a surprising vote for the Republicans, for Trump, in 2016. These same places went back to voting for Democrats in 2018. Interesting for Pennsylvania, for the 2018 congressional election, the Pennsylvania Supreme Court prior to the election said the districts were far too gerrymandered in the Republican's favor, and they made the state redistrict all the congressional districts prior to the 2018 election, which has also benefited the Democrats because some of those gerrymandered districts incorporated more Republicans when there should have been more Democrats. Nonetheless, I think the voting patterns in Pennsylvania in the recent congressional elections are much more in favor of the Democrats, going back to the way things were before Trump.

And, of course, the governor and U.S. Senate races have been going Democratic. The Democratic governor won this time [in 2018], and the Democratic Senator who was up this time, Mr. Casey, won. Pennsylvania does have a Republican Senator but he wasn't up for reelection [in 2018]. The [current] Republican Senator Pat Toomey did win in 2016. The 2016 election was much more favorable to Republicans in Pennsylvania than any election, and any presidential election since 1988, which is the last time a Republican won the presidential vote in Pennsylvania.

Pennsylvania, I think of it as half like New Jersey and half like Ohio. [The New Jersey] part of the state tends to go a lot more Democratic—and [that includes] areas outside of Philadelphia that have a lot of urban concentrations, including the Lehigh Valley, including Scranton/Wilkes-Barre, and even Harrisburg, which is sort of more in the central part of the state. The western part of the state, for a long time, has been trending more Republican, and was much more dominated by Republicans in the 2016 presidential election than it had been before.... Some counties in that part of the state have moved a little more Democratic voting in the 2018 congressional election.

Expert Summary and Analysis

As noted in the State of Play section, Frey sees Pennsylvania as more divided east and west, rather than the notion posited by political consultant James Carville that the state is comprised of Pittsburgh and Philadelphia with Alabama jammed between. Frey also sees the east/west divide in Pennsylvania in larger sectional terms. He understands it to be a regional sociopolitical split between the east (New Jersey) and the Midwest (Ohio). Finally, Frey notes that Pennsylvania is likely to emerge as a blue state in 2020. The results of the 2019 county and city elections further support this conclusion. By all evidence from election results since the 2016 election, Pennsylvania should return to the Democratic Blue Wall in 2020.

Cultural Divisions

Dr. Frey was asked: "Is Pennsylvania culturally divided?" He answered:

[Pennsylvania] is probably like a lot of other states where a lot of demographic characteristics cluster together. In other words there are people who tend to be more conservative on social issues—whatever they are: abortion, immigration—tend to be living in smaller places, tend to be people we call blue-collar people, more whites than minorities. Pennsylvania has a very large rural, sort of small-town suburban population that lies outside Philadelphia and Pittsburgh. I think there probably is a sharp divide. I haven't looked at the survey data and so forth, [but] I think there is probably a sharp divide on those kinds of issues. Maybe [the divide is] not as sharp perhaps as in some other states. Maybe the conservative social issues raised by these more rural, small-town folks in Pennsylvania are not as conservative as those maybe in other parts of the country . . . in parts of the south, perhaps, parts of the Midwest. There's still a divide between them and the people who live in urban areas. From what I've seen in the polling data [related to] the last presidential election, immigration was an issue. Pennsylvania is not a big immigrant state, at least outside of Philadelphia. Nonetheless, you know that's an issue that tended to divide people in different parts of the state [as] it did nationally. That's probably one of the reasons Donald Trump won Pennsylvania. Again, I say it's a generally blue state overall.

Pennsylvania is probably less conservative as a whole on a lot of those issues as some other states that might be in the Midwest, and it's not just because it has a big large, urban population. Probably if you did a survey, you'd see some of the rural folks in Pennsylvania are a little bit less socially conservative than those in other parts of the United States. That's my own feeling from looking at some of the surveys and so forth over the years.

Expert Summary and Analysis

Frey argues, as does Bill Bishop in *The Big Sort*,[37] that the United States is seeing a rise of communities based on cultural habits and shared economic interests. The sorting also concerns political attitudes. Frey sees evidence in the stark splits in Pennsylvania's voting patterns. He also notes that residents of rural Pennsylvania tend not to be as conservative as rural populations in most Midwestern states. Damore and Lang argue that rural areas in the north, outside of Appalachia, tend to be less conservative than their southern counterparts.[38] The finding confirms Frey's observation regarding Pennsylvania, which unlike states such as Ohio, Indiana, and Illinois (in the lower Midwest), does not have a southern part of state. Pennsylvania's southern boundary forms the Mason-Dixon Line that once divided free and slave states, whereas the Ohio River served that role in Ohio, Indiana, and Illinois. Yet the southern parts of the lower Midwest reached into what geographer Wilbur Zelinsky defined as the cultural South based on settlement patterns.[39]

Demographic Change

Dr. Frey was asked: "How will Pennsylvania's demographic changes impact the political dynamic between the major metropolitan areas and the rest of the state?" He answered:

I think Pennsylvania continues to grow more rapidly in the eastern part of the state than in the western part of the state. People move from eastern New Jersey and New York inward. I mean, we've seen a lot of that—we're now going back like twenty, fifteen years prior to the Great Recession [of 2008]. There was a lot of rapid growth in eastern Pennsylvania. The Allentown-Lehigh Valley area grew quite rapidly up until about 2008 or 2009. There's this kind of outward flow from the New York region. That included people intending to vote Democratic, as well as many racial minorities, but also more highly educated folks just wanting to move further outward because they could get [lower] housing costs and so forth. Then [migration] generally just kind of spread inward from the greater New York metropolitan area. That helped make Pennsylvania more Democratic in general in that part of the state.

During the Great Recession, that [migration] had eased off a little bit. A lot of those areas didn't grow as rapidly. But I see that's going to continue again as the economy picks up. I think there's going to be more outward spread into the eastern parts of Pennsylvania by people who tend to vote more Democratic. Since that's still going to be the fastest-growing part of Pennsylvania—not just Philadelphia, but the Lehigh Valley, maybe even Scranton/Wilkes-Barre, maybe even moving over to Harrisburg. . . . That's a part of the state that is going to grow most rapidly over time—and it's the part of the state that's, therefore, I think going to become more Democratic in its voting patterns.

Expert Summary and Analysis

Pennsylvania is a slow-growing state. But as Frey observes, there is some moderate growth (especially before the Great Recession) in parts of eastern Pennsylvania, north of the Philadelphia metropolitan area. The fact that much of eastern Pennsylvania's population growth originates in the New York metropolitan area (with most of it coming from New Jersey) means the demographic profile is more diverse, urban, and educated than is found in areas of Pennsylvania outside greater Philadelphia. The new migrants from New Jersey to Pennsylvania are roughly equivalent of those who move from California into interior Mountain States such as Arizona and Nevada who then alter the social attitudes and politics of those states.

STATE OF PLAY: VIRGINIA

Virginia is quickly transitioning from a swing state to a blue-leaning one. In fact, the *Washington Post* recently noted that "in presidential elections, Virginia has moved so swiftly to the left in recent contests that it barely paused to be a swing state."[40] Old Dominion may prove a harbinger of a broader shift along the East Coast, where states such as North Carolina and even Georgia become more competitive for Democrats.[41] With 8.5 million residents, Virginia is the only state that currently has thirteen electoral votes and eleven seats in the U.S. House of Representatives. Over this past decade, Virginia's population growth has kept pace with the United States as a whole and, thus, it should maintain its current representation in Congress and the Electoral College following reapportionment based on the 2020 census.

As Virginia was turning from red to purple during the last decade, Robert Lang and Dawn Dhavale looked at the governor's race, where Democrat Timothy Kaine defeated Republican Jerry Kilgore. They suggested dividing the state into "four Virginias"[42]—or four distinct sociopolitical areas (see figure 3-2).[43] Robert Lang and Jared Lang used the same geographic frame to analyze the results of Virginia's 2008 presidential vote results where Democratic candidate Barack Obama defeated Republican John McCain and found similar results.[44]

Lang noted that without Northern Virginia, Old Dominion was akin to South Carolina in its political profile.[45] South Carolina has three political sections: Coastal (including Charleston); Capital Region (including Columbia); and Upstate (including Greensboro-Spartanburg). Virginia has political sections that mostly parallel these three areas. But what South Carolina lacks is a Northern Virginia equivalent—or a large, liberal, fast-growing urban-suburban zone that can turn a red state blue.[46]

Northern Virginia

Virginia's suburbs of Washington, D.C., (or Northern Virginia) comprise the state's bluest political section. Northern Virginia has its own culture and political identity within the state. As Robert Lang notes,

FIGURE 3-2. Virginia

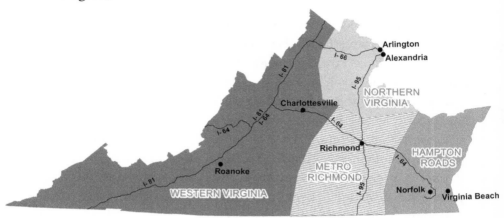

"The region is so different than the rest of Virginia, it's as though the New Jersey suburbs were grafted onto South Carolina."[47]

Northern Virginia is by far the most affluent, educated, and diverse section of the state (see table 3-5). The region maintains Virginia's largest share of Latinos, Asians, and foreign-born residents. It also produces nearly half (45.3 percent) Virginia's GDP, despite having just over a third of the state's population (35.3 percent). Half (49.7 percent) of all Virginia's college-educated residents live in Northern Virginia.

The closer-in suburbs of Arlington and Alexandria are really city-like extensions of Washington, D.C., and are highly diverse and densely built. Arlington's main commercial corridor (Wilson Avenue) was planned around mixed-use, high-rise neighborhoods built along Metro stops along Washington's mass-transit system.[48]

The slightly farther out suburb—but still mostly urbanized—Fairfax County contains over 1 million residents and is among the most diverse and wealthy large suburban counties in the United States.[49] Once home to a rock-rib Republicanism centered out of places such as McLean and Langley (home to the CIA headquarters), Fairfax has undergone one of the most dramatic switches from red to blue in

TABLE 3-5. Demographic and Economic Comparison between Virginia and Metros

	Virginia	Share in Northern Virginia* [%]	Share in Richmond [%]	Share in Virginia Beach* [%]
Population	8,470,020	35.3	15.4	19.9
White	61.7%	30.9	14.3	17.6
Black	18.8%	22.8	24.2	32.2
Asian	6.4%	71.9	14.6	12.0
Latino	9.3%	62.0	6.2	14.7
Foreign-Born	12.5%	70.3	9.1	10.4
College Educated	38.7%	49.7	14.8	16.3
Jobs	4,150,133	37.7	15.6	19.2
GDP	$454,098	45.3	15.9	18.9

*Excludes counties outside of MSA primary state.

Sources: Data derived from 2017 American Community Survey 1-Year estimates as aggregated by censusreporter.org, Department of Commerce, Bureau of Economic Analysis, 2015 Real GDP (millions of chained 2012 dollars) County Level Data, U.S. Department of Labor, Bureau of Labor Statistics 2017 County Level Data.

the United States, and this movement is likely to solidify, if not accelerate, in the future.

Interestingly, even the more distant D.C. suburbs of Prince William, Loudoun, and even exurban Fauquier County have all seen a blue shift. As Fairfax has grown, its economic influence and building practices have spilled into adjacent counties, such as the eastern sections of Loudoun County around Dulles International Airport. The Silver Metro Line is about to be completed to Dulles within eastern Loudoun County, yet many citizens in the western half of the county remain staunchly anti-growth. To quote a western Loudoun County resident:

The battle lines being drawn now are as old as America itself. Developers want restrictions loosened and transition boundaries pushed west, while those of us in the country want things to stay the same. There is a saying here that sums the fight up pretty well: "Don't Fairfax Loudoun." And there is a derisive acronym for those of us who love that Costco down in Leesburg but scream when a convenience store is proposed for the nearest corner: We're NIMBYs, the "Not in My Back Yard" set.[50]

The political battle line between residents who resist the kind of quasi-urban development that Fairfax County represents often form the Republican-voting line that prevents the density (especially around rail stops) and diversity (among residents) from spreading Democratic-friendly built environments deeper into the more conservative and conventional suburbs. Loudoun County is a prime example of such conflict.

Northern Virginia (and Fairfax County in particular) was used as a model by Robert Lang, Thomas Sanchez, and Alan Berube to track changes in suburban national voting patterns at the county and precinct level.[51] Beginning in 2006, with the Democratic takeover of the U.S. House and Senate, it was obvious that the main fault line for American politics lay in the suburbs.[52] To be specific, the tipping point in the red/blue divide pits urbanizing suburbs, which maintain many elements of cities but in a new urban form, against lower-density, larger-lot, and single-family home–dominated communities. Lang and Sanchez developed a predictive model for statewide races that showed if the Democratic-voting line (a 50 percent or more Democratic vote) pushed past Dulles Airport near the Fairfax/Loudoun County border, then the Democrats were likely to win statewide races in Virginia.

Collectively, Northern Virginia, with its urban core at Alexandria and Arlington and its far-flung exurbs in communities such as Winchester and Fredericksburg, now exceeds 3 million residents in a state with 8.5 million people. Were Northern Virginia a state on its own, it would be as Democratic-dominated as Connecticut, which has approximately the same population. Northern Virginia actually surpasses Connecticut in terms of affluence, education, and diversity. The main reason Virginia appears to be turning more solidly Democratic-leaning with each election cycle since 2005 is that Northern Virginia is large-scale (big enough to tip the state), growing faster than the rest of Old Dominion, and continues to diversify/urbanize in terms of people and places.

The evidence of Northern Virginia's blue shift is clearly seen in table 3-6. Consider 2018 and 2017, when the state had a U.S. Senate race and a gubernatorial contest (Virginia, along with New Jersey, hold off-year elections for their state legislative and governors' offices). In 2018, U.S. Senate candidate Tim Kaine won Northern Virginia with a 35.6 percent margin and was reelected by 16 percent statewide. Similarly, in 2017 Democratic gubernatorial candidate Ralph Northam won his race by 28.6 percentage points in Northern Virginia and 8.9 percentage points statewide.

In 2016, Democratic presidential candidate Hillary Clinton needed a big win in Northern Virginia to offset a surge in rural margins in Western Virginia. Clinton won the region with a 25.8 percent margin and won the state with a 5.3 percent edge over Republican Donald Trump. To put Clinton's Northern Virginia win in perspective, consider that President Obama won the region with a significantly smaller 15.8 percent of the vote as he went on to win the state by 5.9 percent. Clinton's higher margin in Northern Virginia saved the state for her in 2016. Also, Northern Virginia is gaining voting share, capturing 36.2 percent of ballots cast in 2016 versus 34.1 percent in 2012. Thus, Northern Virginia is not only becoming more liberal, it is also gaining vote share and turning all Virginia blue in the process.

Metro Richmond

Metro Richmond is the state's capital region, which includes the city of Richmond and its surrounding suburbs and exurbs. Richmond metro now contains nearly 1.3 million residents and forms the third-largest urban concentration in the state, after Northern Virginia and Virginia Beach. Nelson and Lang see Richmond as an extension of greater Washington, in that the southern exurbs of Northern Virginia actually reach the northern exurbs of metropolitan Richmond.[53]

Yet Richmond remains a Southern city and has not lost its regional identity in a way that Northern Virginia has, where decades of domestic and foreign migration to the region have all but effaced vestiges of the Old South. Thus, metropolitan Richmond is not nearly as blue as Northern Virginia. Rather, it is a purple-to-blue metro that serves as a key swing area for the state. At the center of the metropolis, the cities

TABLE 3-6. Comparison of Electoral Outcomes between Virginia and Metros

| Election | Virginia | Northern Virginia | | Richmond | | Virginia Beach | |
	Outcome	Vote Share [%]	Outcome	Vote Share [%]	Outcome	Vote Share [%]	Outcome
2018 U.S. Senate	+16.0 Dem	36.2	+35.6 Dem	16.7	+18.9 Dem	18.6	+20.4 Dem
2017 Gubernatorial	+8.9 Dem	35.3	+28.6 Dem	14.2	+0.3 Dem	18.9	+15.6 Dem
2016 Presidential	+5.3 Dem	35.1	+25.8 Dem	16.3	+9.0 Dem	19.1	+9.1 Dem
2014 U.S. Senate	+0.8 Dem	34.2	+10.7 Dem	17.0	+3.3 Dem	18.3	+4.7 Dem
2013 Gubernatorial	+2.5 Dem	33.3	+15.6 Dem	17.5	+4.9 Dem	19.2	+11.6 Dem
2012 Presidential	+3.9 Dem	34.1	+15.8 Dem	16.4	+3.9 Dem	19.8	+11.8 Dem
2012 U.S. Senate	+5.9 Dem	34.1	+5.9 Dem	16.4	+8.7 Dem	19.7	+13.6 Dem

Source: Data from Virginia secretary of state's website.

of Richmond and Petersburg have substantial African American populations and a strong Democratic lean (see table 3-5).

Metro Richmond has a small Latino community for an eastern urban area with more than a million residents (see table 3-5). Yet many nonminority voters in the city of Richmond vote for Democratic candidates more often than not. This is partly attributed to the fact that even Richmond (once the capital of the Confederate States of America) has seen some white Northern migration.

Outer suburban Richmond, especially the most distant exurbs where the Old South still thrives, remains deeply Republican. The balance between Richmond and its close-in suburbs versus its outer suburbs and exurbs produces, in most statewide and national election cycles, a region that may have a slight red tint or a deep blue one depending on the candidate.

Along with Northern Virginia, metro Richmond is turning bluer in recent years (see table 3-6). This is evident when contrasting the 2012 and 2016 presidential elections. In 2012, President Obama won metro Richmond by just 3.9 percent. Democratic candidate Hillary Clinton won the region by 9 percent in 2016, helping her secure Virginia's Electoral College votes that year. Democratic U.S. Senate candidate Tim Kaine (Richmond's former mayor), won metro Richmond with 8.7 percent of the vote in 2012 and then more than doubled that margin in 2018 with a 18.9 percent win.

Hampton Roads

The Virginia Beach Metro, known locally as Hampton Roads,[54] in southeast Virginia includes such cities as Virginia Beach, Chesapeake, and Norfolk. Home to over 1.7 million residents, this region features the world's largest naval base (Naval Station Norfolk). Hampton Roads has a split personality when it comes to politics. The cities of Norfolk and Virginia Beach, which are heavily African American, are Democratic dominated, while much of the rest of the region votes Republican. Hampton Roads has by far the largest share of African Americans in the state and accounts for nearly a third (32.2 percent) of all Blacks living in Virginia (see table 3-5). There are plenty of military retirees in the area as well, and they tend to be Republican voters.

Overall, Hampton Roads is a reliably Democratic-leaning region (see table 3-6). Other than a close race for the U.S. Senate in 2014, when incumbent Mark Warner eked out a statewide win of less than 1 percent in face of a Republican-wave election, all margins have been double-digit wins for the Democrats.

Western Virginia

Virginia is not just split north/south but also exhibits a noticeable political divide east/west. The eastern part of the state contains Northern Virginia, greater Richmond, and Hampton Roads. The western half of the state is a large, extended mountainous region that is part of Appalachia, and like the upland areas in the rest of the South, it is deeply Republican. A notable exception to this pattern is Charlottesville, home to the University of Virginia, which is as liberal as Arlington and Alexandria. While Western Virginia is the slowest-growing part of the state, it is, nonetheless, so red that it keeps the state in a swing state status (for now). But Western Virginia's power is fading with each election cycle, as all three of Virginia's million-plus metros either lean blue or are so strongly Democratic that even big rural winning margins and high voter turnout cannot overcome the state's urban vote.

There does not appear to be enough votes in Western Virginia, throughout the Blue Ridge Mountains or the Shenandoah Valley, to hold much promise that the state will vote Republican in the future. However, had Virginia not been forced by the Union in 1863 at the height of the Civil War to cede what is now the state of West Virginia as a separate legal entity within the United States, it is likely there would be enough of the western part of the original Virginia to keep the state as a political toss-up for some time. That is due to the fact that West Virginia is now a deep red state and has enough voters (at 1.8 million) to counterbalance blue Northern Virginia. But Virginia, as currently comprised, is a swing state trending Democratic, and new immigrants, foreign and domestic, that add to Northern Virginia's voter-eligible base enhance the movement.

Conclusion: Virginia State of Play

After centuries as a Southern state, Virginia has been politically remade by decades of migration to and growth in the Washington, D.C., suburbs. The new residents added considerable wealth, skills, and energy to Old Dominion, but in the process transformed Northern Virginia into an extension of the urbanized Northeast. The so-called Acela Corridor now extends deep into Virginia—and perhaps will move into Richmond within a few years.

Table 3-6 shows that Virginia became increasingly Democratic-voting over the past several election cycles. The U.S. Senate and gubernatorial races, in particular, indicate that pattern. Democrat Hillary Clinton just slightly underperformed Barack Obama in 2016 versus 2012, which means Virginia is likely to remain Democratic-leaning at the presidential level going forward.

Despite the gains Democrats made in statewide races, Virginia was so badly gerrymandered in the wake of the 2010 census that the Lower House in the general assembly was split sixty-seven seats for Republicans and just thirty-two seats for Democrats in 2013 (the split in 2015 was 33-67 and 2017 was 34-66). The Democrats gained almost enough seats for the 2018–19 session (based on the November 2017 election) to take the majority in the Lower House. That required an act of the courts that forced the state to redraw district maps.[55] The same is true in the U.S. House of Representative seats (see table 3-7), where the Democrats now hold the majority of congressional districts (six versus five for Republicans) based on altered district maps.

Republicans lost their Virginia Lower House supermajority by 2016–17 session. For the 2018–19 session, Democrats picked up fifteen seats, and almost gained a sixteenth seat after a tie, but lost the race based on tiebreaker.[56] As a result, Republicans retained control over Virginia's Lower House in 2018 with just fifty-one seats. The Democratic wins in the 2017 election, due in part to court-mandated redrawn district maps, set the party up for winning both houses of Virginia's general assembly in the 2019 election. Indeed, Democrats now control both the Upper and Lower Houses of the general assembly for the 2020–21 legislative session. The party split is 21-19 in the Upper House and 55-45 in the Lower (see table 3-7).

TABLE 3-7. Partisan Composition of Virginia State Government and Federal Delegation

| | | State Government | | | | Federal Delegation | | | |
| | | Upper House | | Lower House* | | U.S. Senate | | U.S. House | |
	Governor	Dems	Reps	Dems	Reps	Dems	Reps	Dems	Reps
2020–21	Dem	21	19	55	45				
2019–20						2	0	6	5
2018–19	Dem	19	21	49	51				
2017–18						2	0	4	7
2016–17	Dem	19	21	34	66				
2015–16						2	0	3	8
2014–15	Dem	20	20	33	67				
2013–14						2	0	3	8
2012–13	Rep	20	20	32	67				

*One independent was elected to serve in the lower house of the Virginia legislature in 2013.

Sources: National Conference of State Legislatures, "State and Legislative Partisan Composition" for various years, and Virginia secretary of state's website.

Like Pennsylvania's 2019 local elections, Virginia's legislative races were widely analyzed for handicapping the 2020 presidential race. The *Washington Post*, reporting on the outcome, ran the headline "In Virginia, Republicans Confront a Fearful Electoral Future."[57] The story quotes political demographer Ruy Teixeira on what the Virginia results mean for 2020 and beyond: "This is a nightmare scenario for a lot of people in the Republican Party. . . . Virginia is an example of a possible future for some of the states that are now part of the Republican Coalition."[58] *Washington Post* reporters Gregory Schneider and Michael Scherer conclude: "Virginia now stands as a fearful avatar for Republicans of what the nation's unrelenting demographic and cultural changes mean for the party, as moderate-to-liberal urban and suburban areas grow and more conservative rural areas lose ground. Similar shifts are starting to hit such states as North Carolina, Arizona, Georgia, and Texas, as minority populations increase and white, college-educated voters continue to turn away from the Republican brand."[59]

Finally, due to a limitation in the number of "independent cities," most Virginians live in unincorporated counties.[60] There are a limited number of local jurisdictions and, therefore, little municipal fragmentation (see table 3-8). This is a common pattern for the South and the West, where Dillon's Rule of state supremacy is the norm. As noted in chapter 1 and explored more fully in chapter 10, most Virginia suburbs are census designated places (CDPs). The census uses CDPs to indicate that a high concentration of people and commerce exists outside an incorporated place. Virtually every major commercial asset in Northern Virginia—including Tysons Corner and Reston Town Center—lies in a CDP. Even Arlington, Virginia, is a county rather than a city and, thus, the entire jurisdiction is assigned to a CDP.

TABLE 3-8. Metro Governance Fragmentation and Autonomy in Virginia

Governance Fragmentation

Metro	Number of Counties in Metro	Number of General Purposes Governments in Metro
Northern Virginia*	17	40
Richmond	17	25
Virginia Beach*	14	16

Governance Autonomy

Local Government Autonomy Score	0.151
Local Government Autonomy Ranking	20

*Excludes counties outside of MSA primary state.

Sources: Data for Governance Fragmentation from 2017 Census of Governments. Data for Governance Autonomy from Harold Wolman, Robert McManmon, Michael Bell, and David Brunori, "Comparing Local Government Autonomy Across States," in *The Property Tax and Local Autonomy*, edited by Michael Bell, David Brunori, and Joan Youngman (Lincoln Institute of Land Policy Press, 2010), pp. 69–114.

EXPERT ANALYSIS: VIRGINIA

Three scholars were interviewed for their expert opinion on Virginia politics. The first is Thomas Sanchez, a professor of urban affairs and planning at Virginia Tech. Dr. Sanchez was interviewed on April 17, 2018. Also interviewed was Geoffrey Skelley, the head of media relations and an associate editor at *Sabato's Crystal Ball* at the University of Virginia. Finally, William Antholis, director and CEO of the Miller Center for Public Affairs at the University of Virginia, was interviewed. Both Mr. Skelley and Dr. Antholis were interviewed on May 31, 2018. Note that interview responses may include minor edits to provide continuity and clarify language. Endnotes are also added to verify key facts.

Intrastate Political Dynamics

The political experts were asked: "What is the political dynamic between Virginia's major metropolitan areas and the rest of the state?" They answered:

Sanchez: The state is often considered as Northern Virginia, Richmond/Tidewater, and the rest of the state of Virginia. It's easy to see a blue blob in Northern Virginia and down south, and red elsewhere.

This would be reflected in national politics and a statewide pattern, too, is relatively similar. The red/blue makeup is evident in national and state representation. There is a little island around Charlottesville [home to the University of Virginia] and the Shenandoah Valley, which is, relatively speaking, fairly conservative.

Skelley: The main driver in Virginia politics, when you're looking a presidential election, has to be Northern Virginia—the Washington, D.C., metropolitan area. If you look over time, the state was historically Republican in presidential elections, at least in the modern era. It went back and forth a bit before that, when it was for, and then against, then for a Democrat again until 2008. It had even been Democratic when Jimmy Carter sought the South in 1976, in what was really a weird election.[61] I think politically the country has more of an east/west divide, but in Virginia it has historically been a north/south divide. Virginia actually went for Gerald Ford, unlike the rest of the historic Confederacy,[62] so it has been a Republican state, but as Virginia grew, it became more politically competitive and even Democratic-leaning.... John Kerry narrowly won what I would call the northern suburbs and outskirts of D.C. in Virginia in 2004. It went even more sharply in the Democratic direction when Barack Obama carried the state in 2008.

I think it's important that one remembers . . . [Northern Virginia has] been changing, and there are numerous reasons why. Its change comes down to the people who moved into Northern Virginia. Also, white, college-educated voters have trended more in the Democratic direction. [College-educated voters] . . . went fifty-fifty, roughly, in the last presidential election, according to national statistics. According to findings on the data sorted, that used to be a much more Republican-leaning constituent. . . . In Virginia, a pretty highly educated state, Northern Virginia is an area that is a very high-income, [and is] very well-educated. . . . It is actually very racially diverse [as well]. . . . For instance, Prince William County, which is now the [state's] second biggest locality after Fairfax, is majority nonwhite. Twenty years ago, that was far from the case.

The population of Northern Virginia has grown precipitously. As of 2016, population estimates show that the constituency for the Washington, D.C., area of Virginia made up 35 percent of the state's population. If you go back to the 1950s, it was only 18 percent. So, it's grown a lot. Some places, like Loudoun County for instance, which is part of the suburbs and one of the largest localities in the state now, have grown massively in the last couple of decades. I mean, you go from 1990 to 2016 and it basically [more than] doubled in size. I mean it grew 170 percent in that timeframe. These are pretty drastic changes to the population. It's become more diverse, it's well-educated, and that's the main thing about Northern Virginia and why it became such a major player. It is really a main reason that a state will go Democratic in a presidential election.

Antholis: Northern Virginia is the biggest in that regard. Increasingly, Richmond and the Richmond suburbs are, and the other blue cities are, Charlottesville, parts of Virginia Beach, but not all of Virginia Beach, and Norfolk, and other few blue dots. I mean, they're not really big blue circles; they're more tiny blue dots. . . . I would say that Virginia is no longer a red state, though; it is very much a purple state that probably leans blue. Since Obama in 2008, all three of the [presidential] elections have gone Democratic. After Obama was elected in 2008, Bob McDonnell was elected [Virginia's governor], which follows the historic pattern, which is the gubernatorial election [shifts parties] in the year after the presidential election. . . . That was a sign of Virginia being a purple state. It would go back and forth, depending on how it went at the presidential level. Now, this time Trump won, and it [the governorship] reverted back, but it was not a close election this time. It was a Democratic landslide as a result of Trump, which is a combination of two things, I think. One is that the response to Trump was quite large, but more important than that, I think, there is a longstanding trend where Virginia is increasingly becoming a Democratic state.

Expert Summary and Analysis

All three experts note the difference between Northern Virginia and the rest of the state. They also, secondarily, recognize an east/west split in Old Dominion. The urbanized eastern Virginia, including the metros Richmond and Virginia Beach (Hampton Roads), vote more often for Democrats, while Western Virginia clearly sides with the Republican Party. The experts also note that the growth and scale of eastern and Northern Virginia are transforming the state's politics from a swing or purple state to one that now leans Democratic. As major suburbs around Washington, D.C., such as Loudoun County, rapidly urbanize, this trend becomes especially pronounced.

Structural Features of State Government

The political experts were asked: "What is the structure of governance in Virginia?" They answered:

Skelley: Virginia is a state that historically has a fairly decent governorship. Governors cannot themselves nominate judges for state judge positions. If there's a vacancy at a state-level court and the general assembly is not in session, the governor can appoint someone, and the general assembly will sign off later. If the general assembly is in session, they appoint the judge. They can take the person out of office or put someone in their place. Historically, the governorship has been weak. It is still not among the strongest [in the United States].

Just yesterday [May 30, 2018], Virginia passed Medicaid expansion.[63] This was momentous because it's been a political debate in the state. [Governor] Northam's predecessor worked hard to make this happen.[64] Maybe it was possible before, but it never seemed likely. Much of that came down to the fact that the General Assembly was overwhelmingly Republican. There was no way [former Governor] McAuliffe was going to overcome the dominant control the GOP had of the [Lower] House. Maybe there was opportunity for majority vote for Medicaid expansion, but there was no way for the governor to do that unilaterally. In Ohio, [Republican] John Kasich went around the state legislature to expand Medicaid with Republicans opposing it. He had a means of doing that, but in Virginia that option did not exist.

Northam was able to do it because he was backing the deal. What made Medicaid expansion possible in 2018 was when Democrats won fifteen [more] seats in the [2017] House of Delegates [the Lower House] election. The fact it was a 51-49 [Republican-controlled] chamber in the House of Delegates made Republicans in the House say, "Let's make Medicaid expansion happen on our terms." They got a work requirement that Democrats might not have backed if they were leading the chamber. In the State Senate, they passed it, as well. It took a major [election] result in the General Assembly to make that change. Northam, with narrowly divided chambers, helped make that happen. The General Assembly was the lead actor here. The governor did not have a lot of unilateral power.

[On Dillon's Rule], there is an issue of confederate monuments and naming of buildings after confederates. Where I am in Charlottesville it was a focus of a Neo-Nazi rally and counter-rally in August 2017. There's a large statute of General Lee in downtown Charlottesville. There's a debate about whether or not the municipality can keep it because of state law and because Virginia is a Dillon's Rule state. I know that a lot of times they'll have a legislator backing a bill that a municipality wants to make a change about a policy, be it taxes or tax issues that localities have to prove in the [Virginia] General Assembly to make changes. The statue issue was on my mind and remains highly charged.

Antholis: The governor has fairly high constitutional standing in the state to do certain things, mostly to set the budget and oversee most of the cabinet agencies, but not all of the cabinet agencies. So, the governor does not appoint the lieutenant governor or the attorney general, but appoints pretty much everybody else. It is a one-term governor, and that weakens the governor's hand but also strengthens the governor's hand in that what usually happens is the governor comes in [and] accepts the budget that had been prepared by his predecessor, can make a few changes on the margin, and then tries to get it passed. But two years later, when they have their first full budget, they have quite a lot of autonomy in establishing and setting their budget. They do have to negotiate with both houses [of the Virginia legislature], but it's generally seen as the governor having a fairly high, much higher than say in the state of Texas, level of discretion in designing and building a budget. And then when [the governor is] a lame duck, they essentially design and build the budget for their successor because it's a very short window after the successor is elected when they can submit a budget to be passed.

[On Dillon's Rule], what I will say is the municipal authorities here have been inspired by Bruce Katz at Brookings.[65] . . . Well first of all, one, they're much more aware of how their jurisdictional divisions at the very local level have been inhibiting them from local cooperation; say at the local county and city level. I can give you an example here in Charlottesville, we have a city . . . and then we have unincorporated counties, or unincorporated cities in the county.[66] And the city and the county were not particularly good at coordinating what they asked for from the state government. That has improved pretty dramatically in the last ten year across the state.

Expert Summary and Analysis

Both Skelley and Antholis note that Virginia lacks a strong governor as opposed to a state such as Ohio, but that the position is stronger than a state such as Texas. Antholis observes that the Virginia governor does have power over budgets, as the state's chief executive has elsewhere, such as Nevada. Both Antholis and Skelley comment on Dillon's Rule. Skelley points out that the state of Virginia exercises so much power over a locality they can even force a community to keep an unwanted and controversial Confederate monument. Antholis, by contrast, finds that many of Virginia's localities are seeking greater autonomy and being proactive around their local interests due to the influence of Bruce Katz, who until recently was at the Brookings Institution.

Metro Power in State Government

The political experts were asked: "How much power do the metropolitan areas exert in state politics?" They answered:

Sanchez: Interesting question; there is a concentration of population in Northern Virginia and down south near Tidewater. Investments, or resources decisionmaking are related to economic activity. [The] … vast majority of the state is represented by another political party so that power becomes balanced out. Given that so much of the population, even geographically, is outside that area, there are tensions. Not everything flows to the Northern Virginia/D.C. region despite how productive or economically viable it is.

Skelley: They [the state legislature] meet at the start of every year and budget cycles. In even years, the length of the session is longer. Sometimes they can't figure out the budget. They might need a special session to deal with that. The legislature does meet at the start of the year, every year. Budget sessions are longer than non-budget ones. That's the basic set-up. Thinking about how power is distributed, things have changed in recent times because of the 2017 Democratic election. Because of the nature in the House of Delegates, it was biased toward more rural interests. It was drawn with the idea of cementing Republican control. Most Democrats come from urban-suburban areas, and Republicans come from suburban-rural areas. If Republicans come from rural areas, it favors them and Virginia.

A good example is transportation. In Virginia, this has been a never-ending debate. In the 1980s, they [the state legislature] passed a gas tax to fund improvements. It took nearly thirty more years to get another agreement to encourage transportation funding. I don't remember how they structured that. I think the urban areas still argue they're not getting enough transportation funding based on their requirements. The more eastward you go in the state the more Democratic voters become. Democrats are concentrated in that area of the state. Now that the House [of Delegates] is evenly divided, there are no Democrats from west of Charlottesville. In the state senate, there are just two. Meanwhile, if you think about Republicans, there is just one left in the Northern Virginia [caucus of the] House of Delegates. There's a partisan split with divides over lifestyle and where they [delegates] come from, which has the potential to exacerbate things further because it's becoming more partisan.

Antholis: There's actually a fairly healthy balance of power where the cities recognize that the poorer southwest [Virginia] and the poorer deep south of the state require some support, and they tend to get it to them through the kinds of things that are pretty typical: roads and bridges, community colleges, and state universities. But not through things that people in those places might want and need, like hospitals.

Expert Summary and Analysis

All three experts agree that, despite the economic and demographic power of Northern Virginia, there is a balance of interests and Virginia's urban areas do not simply overpower the state and receive all the resources or necessarily prevail on most social issues. In this regard, Virginia remains a purple or swing state. In fact, as Skelley finds, if anything, Virginia had a rural bias before the 2017 election, when new district maps more fairly represented urban Democratic interests. Since 2017, the state has grown more fractured, as there are no longer any Republicans west of Charlottesville and only one Republican left in Northern Virginia; thus the state is now more divided than ever. In the current legislative session, where Democrats are now fully in control of both houses and working with a Democratic governor, there is a clear policy shift to the left. The *Washington Post* reports that the "change roils Virginia Republicans."[67]

Cultural Divisions

The political experts were asked: "Is Virginia culturally divided?" They answered:

Sanchez: Yes, the state is culturally divided, and, again, that comes back to the 2016 [election] map, the presidential election. There is a pretty stark contrast [between] Northern Virginia/Tidewater versus the rest of the state—fairly distinct, other than a couple of little specks/islands [of blue outside this area]. The flag, gun control, marijuana legislation—the split you would expect among conservatives and progressives, that pattern plays out across all these issues. Although, in the last state legislature, [the state elected the first] trans representative [Danica Roem][68] in the state house who won over a very conservative incumbent [Delegate Robert Marshall]. This is a very dramatic shift and change for Virginia politics. Midterm elections will be very interesting; what shifts/changes take place statewide. [There are] potentially some very big changes statewide given some of the national trends. There is common thought, culturally and politically, that there's Northern Virginia and the rest of the state, and that cuts across all of those issues and themes you mentioned. It's pretty predictable.

Skelley: One of the convenient things for Virginia is that it was close to the national outcome in 2016. On gun control, the country is evenly divided. Liberal urban Democrats want more gun control; rural Republicans want more gun rights. The suburbs are caught in the middle. On the gun control issue, if trends continue and suburbs become more Democratic, it will be bad for the GOP. [Democrats] . . . have looked for ways to limit gun rights when they're in power, and when Republicans have been in control [Democrats still] . . . tried to create restrictions on gun rights. Going back to [Douglass] Wilder's governorship,[69] Virginia had a ban called a "one-gun-a-month rule" that limited the number of guns one could buy in a month. In McAuliffe's governorship, they [Democrats] created a stronger background check system, but they were controlled by the [GOP] legislature. Reciprocity was part of that deal. Virginia's Democratic Attorney General said that Virginia would not recognize reciprocity on gun permits. So that deal [background checks] was part of addressing that issue.

Marijuana is brought up every year. Recently, medical marijuana got the "OK" in Virginia, but we're not Colorado yet in terms of legalization. Across the country, you'll find more voters in favor of legalization instead of keeping it illegal. Maybe a policy like medical marijuana is going to be a better option.

[On abortion] . . . it's certainly a partisan issue. It's what you would expect. There was a famous incident in recent times in Virginia when [Republican Bob] McDonnell[70] was governor. The state legislature tried to pass a law that a woman would have to get a trans-vaginal ultrasound before getting an abortion. Yeah, a lot of people think it actually rode on McDonnell's [failed] presidential campaign. You saw Republicans trying to restrict abortion rights. They also tried to require a person providing abortion services to have hospital-level treatment facilities. Democrats say they don't need to be on that level and it's just trying to put abortion services places out of business because they can't meet those standards.

It's been a big deal in Virginia and in other southern states, [to give] restoration of [voting] rights for people convicted of felonies who are now out of jail. Virginia is one of the states that have no route to restoration of rights aside from the governor. When McAuliffe was governor, it became an issue because he tried to restore all rights, most specifically voting rights, of every eligible felon in the state. Initially, he tried to assign everyone's rights back. But the state's court ruled that the constitution said he had to do it individually. So he did. That was a big deal that affected about 200,000 people. Virginia still has no procedure for dealing with this outside of a governor [individually] addressing it.

Expert Summary and Analysis

Sanchez and Skelley find that Virginia is culturally divided, especially over such hot-button issues as marijuana, gun rights, abortion, and voter rights. As expected, urban areas seek to legalize marijuana (and have succeeded in doing so for medical uses), limit gun rights (with some success), maintain abortion rights, and enfranchise more voters, in particular those who lost such rights due to imprisonment. In the last instance, Democratic governor Terry McAuliffe actually used a good deal of his time in office restoring the voting rights of 200,000 felons on a case-by-case basis (which is the only way to enfranchise an ex-inmate in Virginia). Sanchez observes that Virginia has grown so culturally progressive that, in 2017, it voted in its first transgender member to the House of Delegates, and she beat a social conservative while attaining the seat. It appears that in Virginia, Democrats are winning the so-called culture war.

Demographic Change

The political experts were asked: "How will Virginia's demographic changes impact the political dynamic between the major metropolitan areas and the rest of the state?" They answered:

Sanchez: Particularly southwest Virginia—some of the more rural areas—if population continues to age and they continue to lose young people, if they move out/go to school and are not returning. . . . Reinforcing some of these distinctions and cultural issues that already exist, skilled labor [is] moving into two main metros, reinforcing that growth on the other end. I don't see any change in the political dynamic, absent of any investment in rural areas. I don't know what form, or what industry, would be attracted to these areas. Southwest Virginia had tobacco, furniture assembly, [but] those jobs are [now] mechanized or moved out of Virginia or even out of United States. There hasn't been a follow-up to attract [new] industry.

Skelley: Overall, Virginia's growth rate, population-wise, has thawed a bit in the last few years. There was a thought that maybe Virginia would get another congressional district after the 2020 census. That doesn't seem likely, but it's still possible. In the areas of the state that are still changing and growing, like Hampton Roads and the Greater Richmond area, they are in metro areas. For the most part, in the other parts of the state, the population is not growing. The outer edges [of Northern Virginia], like Loudoun County or Prince William County and down in the Tidewater area, which is part of Hampton Roads, have grown in recent times. These are places that are growing rapidly. The south side, [the] southwestern part of Virginia, those areas are either not growing or are shrinking. If you think about the economics of the state, the drivers are the urban areas and major metropolitan parts of the state and some of the college towns, like Charlottesville or [Harrisonburg] where James Madison University is or down in Blacksburg, in Montgomery County where Virginia Tech is [located]. Those are islands to some degree, though, in those parts of the state.

If you go further south and west [in Virginia], it tends to be very [white and] rural and [many] areas are struggling. In the southwest, Coal Country, there's not a lot of opportunity and young people are moving away. Rural hospitals are a concern because they're closing, and there's not one nearby for people who need them. The south side used to be textile and industrial towns. They had woodworking and clothes manufacturing. Now, the unemployment rate in those areas is 20 to 25 percent. Those areas are struggling economically, and it's not obvious where the next opportunity is going to come from.

There are all sorts of efforts for reinvestment [in south side Virginia]. A few years ago, there was a tobacco case where Virginia had a commission that had to pay a settlement to move beyond tobacco-growing investment. There's always talk about needing more rural broadband to energize those areas, because it's not obvious what the next opportunity to make them grow will be. There's talk of building a new four-year university in south side Virginia, which hasn't come to pass yet.

These are all concerns that the northern part of Virginia doesn't face. The 10th Congressional District, which includes Loudoun County, has the highest income, and it's one of the most well-educated [places in the country]. The 8th and 11th Congressional Districts [in Northern Virginia] are also highly educated and have high incomes. . . . A lot of people work in government and government contracting. The government has been a major driver, as have military bases. Both McAuliffe and Northam tried to diversify the economy to avoid potential drawbacks [overreliance on federal jobs and contracts].

Expert Summary and Analysis

Both Sanchez and Skelley note that rural parts of Virginia are experiencing population loss. By contrast, although Virginia's growth has cooled this decade, the areas that remain developing include the suburban fringes around major metropolitan areas. Both note that efforts have been made to invest in rural areas, but so far it has not stimulated a broader economic expansion and these places continue to struggle.

CONCLUSION: THE MID-ATLANTIC

Both Virginia and Pennsylvania are in a state of flux due to economic and demographic shifts. From results of the 2016 presidential election, it would appear that Virginia is growing bluer, while Pennsylvania is getting redder. Yet both states saw a Democratic wave sweep away Republicans in the 2018 midterm election. The 2019 city and county races in Pennsylvania and the legislative election in Virginia were major victories for Democrats and predict that both states will be blue come November 2020.

In 2020, Pennsylvania would seem more up for grabs than Virginia. At this point, Virginia leans blue enough that virtually any path the Democrats have to the 270 electoral votes run through Old Dominion. But Democrats can ill afford to lose Pennsylvania. Perhaps a loss in the Keystone State may be compensated for by wins in emerging blue or purple states such as Arizona, North Carolina, or Georgia. But the Democrats cannot count on these places if they lose Pennsylvania. It is more likely that a purple state such as Georgia would be swept up in a wave election where the Democrats correspondingly pull out a solid win in Pennsylvania.

NOTES

1. Most of these states have voted Democratic in every presidential election since 1992. The only states not to follow this pattern are New Hampshire, Pennsylvania (just once), and Virginia.

2. The U.S. Bureau of Labor Statistics (BLS) includes both Pennsylvania and Virginia in the Mid-Atlantic region. Delaware, Maryland, West Virginia, and Washington, D.C., are also included in the Mid-Atlantic. See www.bls.gov/regions/mid-atlantic/home.htm.

3. For example, during the American Civil War (1861–65), General Robert E. Lee from Virginia led the Army of Northern Virginia in armed conflict with the North. Lee, in fact, led an invasion of Pennsylvania in 1863 and only retreated after a loss at Gettysburg, Pennsylvania.

4. Virginia retroceded the city of Alexandria (Old Town) and Arlington back to Virginia in 1847.

5. Jean Gottmann, *Megalopolis: The Urbanized Northeastern Seaboard of the United States* (New York: The 20th Century Fund, 1961).

6. The term is often used by conservatives who see the region as peopled by elitists along the East Coast, who live in large urban complexes and support mass transit. Sam Stein, "Sorry Acela Elites, This Budget Deal Is Not for You," *HuffPost,* January 16, 2014, www.huffpost.com/entry/high-speed-rail-budget_n_4611853.

7. Arthur C. Nelson and Robert E. Lang, *Megapolitan America: A New Vision for Understanding America's Metropolitan Geography* (Chicago: American Planning Association Press, 2011).

8. Wilbur Zelinsky, *The Cultural Geography of the United States* (Englewood Cliffs, NJ: Prentice Hall, 1973).

9. Ibid.

10. Ibid., p. 119.

11. Carrie Budoff Brown, "Extreme Make Over: Pennsylvania Edition," *Politico,* April 1, 2008, www.politico.com/story/2008/04/extreme-makeover-pennsylvania-edition-009323.

12. Liz Spikol, "I May Live in Pennsylvania, But I Am No Pennsylvanian," *Philadelphia Magazine,* January 31, 2016, www.phillymag.com/news/2016/01/31/pennsyl

vania-pennsyltucky-philadelphia/. Technically, much of Pennsylvania outside the southeastern section of the state is included as part of Appalachia, based on the definition by the Appalachian Regional Commission (ARC). President Donald Trump proposed to scrap this agency, but given that much of Kentucky lies within the ARC's designated area, Republican Senate Majority Leader Mitch McConnell fought to retain its federal funding. Elaine Godfrey, "Trump's Proposal to Scrap the Agency Devoted to Developing Appalachia," *The Atlantic*, March 16, 2017, www .theatlantic.com/politics/archive/2017/03/why-the-appalachian-regional-commis sion-matters/519876/.

13. The term "Pennsyltucky" is a common identifier for the Appalachian uplands of central Pennsylvania. Pennsyltucky is commonly enough used that there is even a Wikipedia entry that covers the term: https://en.wikipedia.org/wiki/Pennsyltucky.

14. Pennsylvania's southern boundary forms the Mason-Dixon Line that once divided free and slave states.

15. Note that this calculation includes only the Pennsylvania share of Phila-delphia's metropolitan population and omits residents living in New Jersey and Delaware.

16. Zelinsky, *The Cultural Geography of the United States.*

17. Nicole C. Brambila, "Pittsburgh Ranked as Third Best Rustbelt Comeback Story in the Nation," *Pittsburgh Tribune*, September 11, 2019, www.commercialcafe. com/blog/rust-belt-cities-comeback-stories/.

18. Note that the Disney Research Lab recently left Pittsburgh after ending a collaborative agreement with Carnegie Mellon University. See Courtney Linder, "As CMU's Disney Lab Closes its Door, the Research Carries On," *Pittsburgh Post-Gazette*, February 8, 2018, www.post-gazette.com/business/tech-news/2018/02/08/cmu-dis ney-lab-closes-collaborative-innovation-center-pittsburgh/stories/201802080159.

19. Robert E. Lang and David F. Damore, "The End of the Democratic Blue Wall?" Brookings Mountain West Brief, December 2016, https://digitalscholarship.unlv. edu/cgi/viewcontent.cgi?article=1045&context=brookings_pubs.

20. Myron Orfield, *American Metropolitics: The New Suburban Reality* (Washing-ton: Brookings Institution Press, 2002).

21. Mark Muro and Jacob Whiton, "America Has Two Economies—And They Are Diverging Fast," *The Avenue*, Brookings Metropolitan Policy Program, September 10, 2019, www.brookings.edu/blog/the-avenue/2019/09/10/america-has-two-econo mies-and-theyre-diverging-fast/.

22. "Presidential 2008 Election Map (by State and County)," *New York Times*, December 9, 2008, www.nytimes.com/elections/2008/results/president/map.html.

23. Nelson and Lang, *Megapolitan America.*

24. Jason Margolis, "A Pennsylvania Reinvents Itself with a Future Beyond Steel," PRI's The World (Public Radio International, July 25, 2018, www.pri.org/stories /2018-07-25/pennsylvania-steel-town-reinvents-itself-future-beyond-steel.

25. Maryland even once claimed this portion of Pennsylvania under its original

royal charter in 1632. Mark Stein, *How the States Got Their Shapes* (New York: Harper-Collins, 2008), p. 127.

26. A notable exception was the 2016 presidential election when Republican candidate Donald Trump beat Hillary Clinton in Erie County by nearly 2,000 votes out of 123,679 ballots cast. For a description of the social and economic forces that swung Erie to the Republicans in 2016, see Trip Gabriel, "How Erie Went Red: The Economy Sank and Trump Rose," *New York Times*, November 13, 2016, www.nytimes.com/2016/11/13/us/politics/pennsylvania-trump-votes.html.

27. Trip Gabriel, "I Gave the Other Guy a Shot," *New York Times*, October 7, 2019, www.nytimes.com/2019/10/07/us/politics/trump-democrats-pennsylvania-.html.

28. Ibid.

29. William H. Frey, "This Week's Election and Last Year's Midterm Bear Good News for Democrats in 2020," Brookings Institution Report, November 7, 2019, www.brookings.edu/research/recent-elections-bear-good-news-for-democrats-2020/. Also see David Montgomery, "The Urban-Rural Political Divide is Growing: Votes in Virginia, Kentucky, and Mississippi All Show How the Suburbs Are Getting More Democratic While Rural Areas Get More Republican," *CityLab*, November 6, 2019, www.citylab.com/equity/2019/11/election-results-surburban-voters-rural-urban-density-index/601585/.

30. Holly Otterbine, "Pennsylvania Suburbs Revolt Against Trump," *Politico*, November 6, 2019, www.politico.com/news/2019/11/06/pennsylvania-suburbs-trump-067078; Eliza Relman, "Forget Kentucky and Virginia, the Worst Election News for Republicans Came out of Suburban Pennsylvania," *Business Insider*, November 6, 2019, www.businessinsider.com/trump-should-worry-about-swing-state-suburbs-in-2020-2019-11; and Julia Terruso, "The Blue Wave Crashed Down on Pennsylvania Again, as Voters from Philly to Delaware County Turned Left," *Philadelphia Inquirer*, November 6, 2020, www.inquirer.com/news/pennsylvania-2019-election-results-2019 1106.html.

31. Relman, "Forget Kentucky and Virginia."

32. Maria Panaritism, "Trump on Borrowed Time after Democratic Election Massacres in Battleground Pennsylvania Suburbs," *Philadelphia Inquirer*, November 6, 2019, www.inquirer.com/news/columnists/pennsylvania-2019-election-results-suburban-massacre-democrats-trump-maria-panaritis-20191106.html.

33. Otterbine, "Pennsylvania Suburbs Revolt Against Trump."

34. Ibid.

35. William Frey, *Diversity Explosion: How New Racial Demographics Are Remaking America* (Brookings Institution Press, 2018).

36. As noted, political consultant James Carville said this in 1984. See Brown, "Extreme Make Over: Pennsylvania Edition."

37. Bill Bishop, *The Big Sort: Why the Clustering of Like-Minded Americans Is Tearing Us Apart* (New York: Mariner Books, 2009).

38. Damore and Lang, "Beyond Density & Diversity."

39. Zelinsky, *The Cultural Geography of the United States*.

40. Gregory S. Schneider and Michael Scherer, "In Virginia, Republicans Confront a Fearful Electoral Future," *Washington Post*, November 9, 2019, www.washingtonpost.com/politics/in-virginia-republicans-confront-a-fearful-electoral-future/2019/11/09/2bbdc7aa-026b-11ea-8bab-0fc209e065a8_story.html.

41. In the 2008 presidential election, Democrat Barack Obama won every state with an Atlantic Ocean coastline except Georgia and South Carolina. In total, fourteen states form the East Coast of the United States.

42. Robert E. Lang and Dawn Dhavale, "The 2005 Governor's Race: A Geographic Analysis of the 'Four Virginias,'" Metropolitan Institute at Virginia Tech Election Report 05:01, November 2005 (Metropolitan Institute at Virginia Tech). Publication available from author.

43. Teixeria and Frey divide Virginia into four political sections, as well, that nearly match the "Four Virginias." William H. Frey and Ruy Teixeira, "The Political Geography of Virginia and Florida: Bookends of the New South," Brookings Metropolitan Policy Program Report, October 10, 2008, www.brookings.edu/research/the-political-geography-of-virginia-and-florida-bookends-of-the-new-south/.

44. Robert E. Lang and Jared M. Lang, "The 2008 Presidential Race: A Geographic Analysis of the 'Four Virginias,'" Metropolitan Institute at Virginia Tech Election Brief 01:09, April 2009. Publication available from author.

45. Drew Lindsay, "Will Northern Virginia Become the 51st State?" *Washingtonian*, November 1, 2008, www.washingtonian.com/2008/11/01/will-northern-virginia-become-the-51st-state/, pp. 48–59.

46. A key element in this book is the notion that if one were to pull a big blue metro out of a state, the state often would be left red. For instance, without the Las Vegas metropolitan area (Clark County), the rest of Nevada would essentially be a Dakota in its politics, economy, density, and size.

47. Lindsay, "Will Northern Virginia Become the 51st State?"

48. Robert E. Lang and Jennifer B. LeFurgy, *Boomburbs: The Rise of America's Accidental Cities* (Washington: Brookings Institution Press, 2007). The Arlington plan is so well regarded that many fast-growing suburban cities throughout the United States seek to emulate its planning practices. Lang and LeFurgy note that Lakewood, Colorado, for example, used Arlington as the model to plan development around its light rail stops.

49. Robert E. Lang, Edward J. Blakely, and Meghan Z. Gough, "Keys to the New Metropolis: America's Big, Fast-Growing Suburban Counties," *Journal of the American Planning Association* 71, no. 4 (Autumn 2005), pp. 381–91.

50. Robert Nelson, "A Tale of Two Counties: Battle Lines Drawn in Loudoun," *Virginia Living*, April 27, 2017, www.virginialiving.com/culture/a-tale-of-two-counties/.

51. Robert E. Lang, Thomas W. Sanchez, and Alan Berube, "The New Suburban Politics: A County-Based Analysis of Metropolitan Voting Trends since 2000," in *The Future of Red, Blue, and Purple America: Election Demographics, 2008 and Beyond*, edited by Ruy Teixeira (Washington: Brookings Institution Press, 2008), pp. 1–38.

52. Robert E. Lang and Thomas W. Sanchez, "Suburban Blues: The 2006 Demo-

cratic Sweep to the Metropolitan Edge," Metropolitan Institute at Virginia Tech Election Report 06:01, December 2006, www.china-up.com:8080/internationalcase /case291.pdf; and Robert E. Lang, Thomas W. Sanchez, Lawrence Levy, and Rebecca Sohmer, "The New Suburban Swingers: How America's Most Contested Suburban Counties Could Decide the Next President," Metropolitan Institute at Virginia Tech Election Report 08:02, September 2008, www.hofstra.edu/pdf/academics/css/the -new-suburban-swingers.pdf.

53. Nelson and Lang, *Megapolitan America.*

54. Hampton Roads is the common local name for what the census identifies as the Virginia Beach-Norfolk-Newport News, VA-NC MSA.

55. Ariane de Vogue, Ryan Nobles, and Devin Cole, "Supreme Court Hands Democrats a Win in Racial Gerrymander Case," CNN, June 17, 2019, www.cnn. com/2019/06/17/politics/supreme-court-racial-virginia-gerrymandering-case/ index.html. The Supreme Court upheld the lower court's requirement that Virginia redraw its maps ahead of the state's 2017 legislative election.

56. John Bacon, "And the winner is . . . Republican Wins after Name Drawn from Bowl in Virginia House Race," *USA Today*, January 4, 2018, www.usatoday.com/story/ news/nation/2018/01/04/drawing-today-decide-virginia-state-house-race-major ity-party/1002910001/.

57. Schneider and Scherer, "In Virginia, Republicans Confront a Fearful Electoral Future."

58. Ibid.

59. Ibid.

60. Much of the South (such as Georgia) shares the same jurisdictional pattern of counties serving as local governments in the absence of cities. Given the legacy of large plantations that once dominated their economies, the county worked as a better functional economic unit than smaller townships and cities.

61. The election is weird in the current context because, in the late twentieth century, Democratic presidential candidates from the South, such as Lyndon Johnson. Jimmy Carter, and Bill Clinton, often won southern states. That pattern shifted dramatically in the 2000 election when Democratic presidential candidate Al Gore Jr. lost every southern state, including his home state of Tennessee.

62. In the 1976 presidential election, Democratic candidate Jimmy Carter won every state that was once part of the Confederate States of America, with the exception of Virginia. Carter also won every border state from the Civil War. Republican President Gerald Ford won California, including such current liberal strongholds as Marin County north of San Francisco. Ford also won such now solid blue states as New Jersey, Illinois, and Connecticut.

63. For an analysis of Virginia's Medicaid expansion, see Laura Vozzella and Gregory S. Schneider, "Virginia General Assembly Approves Medicaid Expansion to 400,000 Low-Income Residents," *Washington Post*, May 30, 2018, www.washington post.com/local/virginia-politics/virginia-senate-approves-medicaid-expansion-to-

400000-low-income-residents/2018/05/30/5df5e304-640d-11e8-a768-ed043e33f1dc
_story.html.

64. Democrat Ralph Northam is Virginia's current and seventy-third governor. Virginia's seventy-second governor, Democrat Terry McAuliffe (2014–18), worked to pass Medicaid expansion throughout his term in office, but he never had the votes in the state legislature to do so.

65. Bruce Katz and Jennifer Bradley, *The Metropolitan Revolution: How Cities and Metros are Fixing Our Broken Politics and Fragile Economy* (Washington: Brookings Institution Press, 2013).

66. Virginia has independent cities that are not part of counties. The counties include no cities and, thus, all of their land is unincorporated.

67. Gregory S. Schneider, "This Is What a Blue State Looks Like: Rapid Change Roils Virginia Republicans," *Washington Post*, January 27, 2020, www.washingtonpost.com/local/virginia-politics/this-is-what-a-blue-state-looks-like-rapid-change-roils-virginia-republicans/2020/01/26/de8aa188-3d75-11ea-b90d-5652806c3b3a_story.html.

68. Danica Roem currently serves in the Virginia House of Delegates from the 13th District. She was reelected to the office in November 2019.

69. Douglass Wilder was Virginia's sixty-sixth governor, serving from 1990 to 1994. Wilder was the first African American to serve as the governor of a southern state since Reconstruction.

70. Republican Bob McDonnell was Virginia's seventy-first governor, serving from 2010 to 2014.

4

SOUTH ATLANTIC:
GEORGIA AND NORTH CAROLINA

Robert E. Lang

Georgia and North Carolina are now the most popu-
lous states in the South besides Texas and Florida.[1] Both states are
on track to gain almost 1 million new residents this decade, based on
their growth from 2000 to 2018.[2] North Carolina is likely to add a seat
in the U.S. House of Representatives after the post-2020 census reapportionment. At the moment, the Tar Heel State has thirteen House
seats, while Georgia has fourteen. In the 2020s, North Carolina should
match Georgia in both congressional delegation size and electoral
votes, with sixteen each.[3]

Not only is the South Atlantic populous and outpacing the nation's
growth rate as a whole, it is also becoming a politically competitive
region. North Carolina has been a swing state since the 2008 presidential election, when Democratic candidate Barack Obama won it
by 0.32 percent.[4] Georgia recently emerged as contested state, which
Republican presidential candidate Donald Trump won by 5.2 percent
in 2016, making Georgia one of just eleven states to vote more Democratic in 2016 compared with 2012.[5]

The South Atlantic has become a far more globally connected,
technology-driven, and cosmopolitan space in the past thirty years. It
maintains two major hub airports: Atlanta (Delta Airlines) and Char-

lotte (American Airlines). The airports include direct flights to Europe, Latin America, and Asia. The South Atlantic is far more diverse than it was just a generation ago—and now includes substantial Latino and Asian communities. The region is home to several leading public and private universities, including the University of North Carolina-Chapel Hill, Georgia Tech (Atlanta), Duke University (Durham), and Emory University (Atlanta).[6] From financial services in Charlotte to media and logistics in Atlanta, the South Atlantic has gained commercial assets that draw it into a global system of world cities.[7]

STATE OF PLAY: GEORGIA

Georgia, with more than 10.5 million residents as of 2018, now ranks eighth in population, recently overtaking northern states such as Michigan and New Jersey.[8] The Peach State is booming with immigrants from both the United States and abroad (see table 4-1), and the new residents are changing the state's political dynamics, especially in metropolitan Atlanta. Georgia has been a reliable red state for the past thirty years, but Democrats now see opportunity due to the state's rapidly shifting demographics and massive urbanization.[9]

Georgia maintains a complex political geography that makes it hard to read in terms of statewide races. The state features five political sections (see figure 4-1).[10] The main dynamic is an increasingly Democratic-dominated Atlanta balanced against deeply conservative small town and rural parts of the state. Georgia and its South Atlantic neighbor North Carolina are politically in about the place Virginia was two decades ago—a tempting target for Democrats with a big Electoral College payoff but not quite blue enough to count on in a presidential election.

Metro Atlanta

Any discussion of Georgia's political geography must begin with metropolitan Atlanta, which comprises over 56 percent of the state's population. Atlanta is a booming metropolis that has nearly 6 million residents and twenty-nine counties, and sprawls over 8,000 square miles (about the physical size of New Jersey).[11] If urban geography were

TABLE 4-1. Demographic and Economic Comparison
between Georgia and Atlanta

	Georgia	Share in Atlanta (%)
Population	10,429,379	56.4
White	52.6%	50.4
Black	31.1%	60.6
Asian	3.9%	83.7
Latino	9.6%	63.3
Foreign-Born	10.2%	77.5
College Educated	30.9%	69.1
Jobs	4,822,268	60.1
GDP	$479,242	68.7

Sources: 2017 American Community Survey 1-Year estimates as aggregated by censusreporter.org, Department of Commerce, Bureau of Economic Analysis, 2015 Real GDP (millions of chained 2012 dollars) County Level Data, U.S. Department of Labor, Bureau of Labor Statistics 2017 County Level Data.

FIGURE 4-1. Georgia

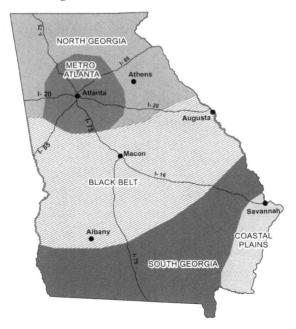

a horror film, then the title for Atlanta would be something like *The Blob that Ate North Georgia.*

Metro Atlanta and its rapidly shifting politics and demographics is the main reason the Democratic Party is competitive in Georgia's statewide races. Consider the last contest for governor in 2018 between Republican Brian Kemp and Democratic candidate Stacey Abrams. As Kemp campaigned, he retained his position as secretary of state (a controversial move given that the office oversees elections), while Abrams was the minority leader for the Georgia House of Representatives from 2011 to 2017. Abrams was also the first Black female major-party nominee for governor in U.S. history.[12]

Kemp won the 2018 Georgia governor's race by a slim margin—50.2 percent versus 48.8 percent (or 1.4 percent)—in a high turnout election (at 70 percent) that featured 1.5 million more votes cast compared to 2014. Thus, the Kemp/Abrams contest is the most current gauge on the state of Georgia's geopolitics now available. The results show an evenly divided state, with suburban Atlanta as the major battleground. Table 4-2 also shows that Atlanta accounts for nearly 60 percent of the vote total in statewide races since 2014. That figure should grow in coming years as the region outpaces the rest of Georgia in population gains and voter turnout.

Abrams ran up big margins in the dense and diverse parts of metro

TABLE 4-2. Comparison of Electoral Outcomes between Georgia and Atlanta

Election	Georgia Outcome	Atlanta Vote Share (%)	Atlanta Outcome
2018 Gubernatorial	+1.4 Rep	59.0	+14.0 Dem
2016 Presidential	+5.2 Rep	58.4	+8.1 Dem
2016 U.S. Senate	+13.8 Rep	59.0	+2.6 Rep
2014 U.S. Senate	+7.7 Rep	59.1	+1.4 Dem
2014 Gubernatorial	+7.9 Rep	59.2	+0.4 Dem
2012 Presidential	+7.8 Rep	57.4	+0.4 Dem

Source: Data from Georgia secretary of state's website.

Atlanta, such as in the central city of Atlanta and nearby suburban communities located mostly on the eastern and southern sides of the metropolitan area in places such as DeKalb County. Fortunately for the Democrats, the revitalization of Atlanta's urban core over the past two decades added thousands of new densely built housing units to the Atlanta metropolitan area to curb suburban sprawl and comply with environmental protection agency mandates that the region lower auto emissions.[13] If density plus diversity drive Democratic voting, as was posited in chapter 2, then Atlanta is gaining in both categories.

The recent gains Democrats made in Atlanta are demonstrated by comparing the 2014 and 2018 governor's races and the 2012 and 2016 presidential contests (see table 4-2). In the 2012 and 2014 presidential and governor's races, Democrats won metro Atlanta by just a 0.4 percent margin. Hillary Clinton won the region in the 2016 presidential election by an 8.1 percent margin, while Stacey Abrams won Atlanta by a 14 percent margin in the 2018 governor's contest. At this trajectory, the Atlanta metropolitan area could very well determine Georgia's winner in the 2020 Electoral College.

Table 4-1 shows that Atlanta maintains substantial African American, Latino, and Asian populations. The region accounts more than 60 percent of the state's Black residents, nearly 84 percent of all Asians, and over 63 percent of Latinos (see table 4-1). Most of Georgia's foreign-born population (77.5 percent) also lives in metropolitan Atlanta. The region produces nearly 69 percent of the state's GDP and contains over 69 percent of Georgia's college graduates.

For much of the late nineteenth and well into the twentieth century, Atlanta was a midsize southern city, along with other regional centers such as Birmingham, Alabama. Beginning in the Civil Rights era, Atlanta made a conscious effort to remake itself as *the* dominant city of the "New South"—a New York of the South.[14] Atlanta's dynamic and long-serving Mayor William Hartsfield (for whom Atlanta's airport—the busiest in the nation—is named) served as an essential figure in positioning Atlanta as the center of a new post-war and economically revitalized South.[15]

With the passage of the 1956 National Interstate and Defense Highway Act, the South acquired transportation infrastructure that matched the North.[16] Many Northern businesses looked to expand in the South, attracted by a business-friendly environment that included "right-to-work" laws. Yet, Northern business leaders feared that violence associated with suppressing the civil rights of African Americans could damage their companies' reputations.

Mayor Hartsfield devised an outreach campaign and slogan to demonstrate that Atlanta was, indeed, prepared to move past civil rights conflict and accept the kind of tolerance for diversity that is the hallmark of progressive world cities. Hartsfield famously proclaimed: "Atlanta was a city too busy to hate."[17] By contrast, consider the social conditions during the 1960s of Atlanta's chief southern urban rival—Birmingham.

At the start of the 1960s, Atlanta and Birmingham were similarly-sized, fast-growing metros and similarly positioned to attract branch facilities of Northern businesses. Unlike Atlanta, Birmingham proved to be a city that was not too busy to hate. For example, while Dr. Martin Luther King preached at the Ebenezer Baptist Church in Atlanta, he was thrown in jail in Birmingham, where he penned his famous "Letter from a Birmingham Jail."[18] Suffice to say, Mayor Hartsfield succeeded in his efforts to promote a prosperous, hard-working, and more tolerant Atlanta in contrast to Birmingham, and Atlanta has far outpaced Birmingham as a major metropolis. Birmingham now ranks as the forty-ninth most populous U.S. metropolitan area, while Atlanta ranks ninth.

Atlanta is now a world city, and its politics increasingly reveal a demographic shift. For decades, greater Atlanta attracted waves of immigrants, especially small-town, in-state movers seeking opportunity in the "Big Peach" (a play on New York's "Big Apple" moniker). Most out-of-state migrants to Atlanta before 2000 were from other southern states.[19] But since the 1990s, Atlanta has become a true national and international destination for migrants.[20] Culturally, Atlanta is now a global space that does not fear new people and ideas—and its lack of xenophobia helps Democrats.[21]

Atlanta's media boom, beginning with Ted Turner's Superstation and the 24-hour cable news network CNN, lifted the city's profile and helped Georgia later claim the status of "The Hollywood of the South."[22] Atlanta discovered the hard way that being a tolerant Hollywood-type place in what is still a southern red state carries risk. In 2007, the film industry spent $93 million on production projects in Georgia. By 2016, that figure grew to over $2 billion.[23] That boom came under threat when the Georgia state legislature passed among the most restrictive anti-abortion bills in the United States.[24] Hollywood immediately reacted to the legislation. Dozens of Hollywood stars and producers lined up and pledged never to work in Georgia again.[25]

Like Charlotte's fight with its state legislature over the so called "bathroom bill," Atlanta faced the consequences as a blue metro in a red state. Atlanta built a Hollywood in the South on a platform of tax incentives and a skilled workforce. Now the industry is threatened from a state legislature that seems to care little if it forfeits Atlanta's hard-won and long-cultivated competitive advantage in media and film production.

Suburban Atlanta, especially its affluent northern suburbs, is rapidly changing. Long a Republican bastion in an otherwise blue metropolis, these suburbs are growing more urban and diverse.[26] Atlanta's suburbs are seeing an influx of Northern, educated African American households, who are returning to the South after having fled the region in the early-to-mid-twentieth century as civil rights tensions mounted. And the white population in these districts is also growing more progressive—as is the case with many educated whites living in the nation's largest metro areas. The trend is especially true of educated white women voters who supported Abrams in 2018 in numbers not previously seen for a Democratic candidate.[27]

If the Democrats manage to flip or even gain parity in Atlanta's northern suburbs, there may not be enough votes left in the rest of the state to prevent metro Atlanta from handing Georgia's statewide elections to the Democrats. As *The Atlantic*'s Derek Thompson notes: "In Georgia, from the 2012 presidential election to the 2018 gubernatorial elections, the four counties constituting most of Atlanta and its suburbs—Fulton, DeKalb, Cobb, and Gwinnett—increased their Democratic margin by more than 250,000."[28] Given metro Atlanta's Democratic voter marginal growth trajectory (see table 4-2), combined with recent migration patterns, Georgia will likely become a true toss-up state in the 2020s. Atlanta's urbanizing suburbs now hold the balance of political power in Georgia.

North Georgia

North Georgia outside metro Atlanta remains solidly Republican, especially along the I-85 Corridor that connects to the hyper-conservative Upstate region of South Carolina (Greenville/Spartanburg).[29] North Georgia also forms part of Appalachia and follows the same conservative pattern as the mountainous areas in the rest of the east. The combination of high elevation in the south along with small-town and/or rural low socioeconomic status whites produces some of the most conservative voting areas in the United States—think West Virginia.[30]

A major outlier in the red conservative counties that ring metro Atlanta but lay beyond its economic, cultural, and political sphere of influence is Athens. Athens, named for the Greek city that in antiquity symbolized knowledge and culture, is home to the University of Georgia, the oldest public university in the United States. Like many other college towns in the former Confederacy, such as Chapel Hill, North Carolina, and Charlottesville, Virginia, it votes deep blue.

Black Belt

South of Atlanta is a region often referred to as the "Black Belt."[31] The section's name reflects the fact that it contains a significant African American rural population that dates back to pre–Civil War slavery. This condition is hardly unique to Georgia and remains apparent even now in large parts of the South.

At the start of the Civil War, the Lincoln administration commissioned a map of the slave population based on the results of the 1860 census in all southern counties.[32] To the surprise of the Census Bureau, the slave population was unevenly distributed across southern states. The environmental and soil conditions amenable to large-scale (or plantation) agriculture served as the key variable that produced large slave populations in any one county. Slave populations were concentrated from the tobacco-growing areas in eastern Virginia to the Cotton Belt in central Alabama. Nearly every southern county that bordered on the Mississippi River had a large concentration of slaves—because these places featured river frontage where slaves could easily load large quantities of agricultural goods directly onto barges.[33]

Georgia's Black Belt stretches through the central part of the state, from Augusta in the east to Columbus in the west, and includes cities such as Macon. While many counties in the Black Belt vote Republican, many rural areas and small cities reaching all the way down to southwest Georgia support Democrats. Sumter County, which includes the town of Plains (home to former Democratic President Jimmy Carter) lies in the region and cast its ballots for Democrat Stacey Abrams for Governor in 2018.

South Georgia

South of the Black Belt is Georgia's mostly rural southern section. This is a farming and agricultural processing region populated mainly by whites that mostly vote Republican. Some counties even approach North Georgia in their red voting pattern. In the past twenty years, increasing numbers of Latino immigrants have moved to this region to work labor-intensive jobs in food processing.[34] Many of these immigrants are not yet voter-eligible due to their citizenship status. However, their children born in the United States are voter-eligible upon their eighteenth birthday. That fact, combined with an older white population, means that over the next few election cycles this region may see some counties vote less Republican. The loss of white Republican voters due to population turnover and their replacement with minorities reduces the ability of rural Georgia voters to offset the power of increasingly Democratic-dominated Atlanta.

Coastal Plains

Finally, Georgia's Atlantic coastal counties form a distinct political section. To the north lies Savannah and its suburbs. Savannah was an eighteenth-century planned city by James Edward Oglethorpe. The Oglethorpe Plan of interspersing parks that break up the urban grid produced a livable and historically significant city that is loved by tourists and locals.[35] Savannah has an eccentric and Bohemian feel,[36] and is very much a blue-voting space based on demographics (including a substantial African American population) and tourist-driven urbanity. Yet the presence of Fort Benning, a large military base with army personnel, offsets metro Savannah's Democratic-voting power and results in a more contested region.

The counties down the coast from metro Savannah are far more conservative. These areas are seeing mostly white, older immigrants from the South who bring their Republican-leaning politics and mix with communities that once contained substantial Black populations.

Conclusion: Georgia State of Play

Georgia is a large, populous, globally connected yet Republican-leaning state for now. Based on recent demographic shifts and an increasingly energized educated (and particularly female) base in Atlanta, the state will continue to be more hospitable for the Democrats in the coming decade. Republicans still hold the upper hand in the statehouse, but the gap is closing so that the GOP no longer maintains super majorities (see table 4-3).

On the state level, Georgia is an exemplar of the blue metros, red states pattern documented in this book. Consider the example earlier noted of Atlanta having its film and media industries threatened by action taken by a conservative state legislature as a case in point.

TABLE 4-3. Partisan Composition of Georgia State Government and Federal Delegation

| | | State Government | | | | Federal Delegation | | | |
| | | Upper House | | Lower House* | | U.S. Senate | | U.S. House | |
	Governor	Dems	Reps	Dems	Reps	Dems	Reps	Dems	Reps
2019–20	Rep	21	35	75	105	0	2	5	9
2017–18	Rep	18	38	62	118	0	2	4	10
2015–16	Rep	18	38	59	120	0	2	4	10
2013–14	Rep	18	38	60	119	0	2	5	9

*One independent member served in the lower house of the Georgia Legislature during the 2013, 2015, and 2017 sessions.

Sources: Data from National Conference of State Legislatures, "State and Legislative Partisan Composition" for various years, and Georgia secretary of state's website.

Atlanta contains numerous counties and local jurisdictions that at times hamper its ability to act as a unified region in its own self-interest (see table 4-4). Yet the region is so large and wealthy relative to the rest of Georgia that it still controls most of the state's resource decisions.

EXPERT ANALYSIS: GEORGIA

Charles S. Bullock III, the Richard B. Russell Professor of Political Science at the University of Georgia, provided expert comments on politics in Georgia. Dr. Bullock is a scholar of Southern politics, elections, and legislative affairs. His recent work includes the book *Georgia Politics in a State of Change*.[37] This interview was conducted on May 7, 2019. Note that interview responses may include minor edits to provide continuity and clarify language. Endnotes are also added to verify key facts.

TABLE 4-4. Metro Governance Fragmentation and Autonomy in Georgia

Governance Fragmentation

Metro	Number of Counties in Metro	Number of General Purposes Governments in Metro
Atlanta	29	177

Governance Autonomy

Local Government Autonomy Score	19
Local Government Autonomy Ranking	0.166

Sources: Data for Governance Fragmentation from 2017 Census of Governments. Data for Governance Autonomy from Harold Wolman, Robert McManmon, Michael Bell, and David Brunori, "Comparing Local Government Autonomy Across States," in *The Property Tax and Local Autonomy*, edited by Michael Bell, David Brunori, and Joan Youngman (Lincoln Institute of Land Policy Press, 2010), pp. 69–114.

Intrastate Political Dynamics

Dr. Bullock was asked: "What is the political dynamic between Atlanta and the rest of the state?" He answered:

Atlanta has had different politics from the rest of the state going back most of the century. Go all the way back to the campaign of Gene Talmadge[38] back in the 1930s and 1940s, Atlanta was seen at that point as being more liberal than the rest of the state. It's maintained that differentiation ever since. Now, what's happened, of course, in the last seventy-five years is that Atlanta has become much larger . . . so when we talk about [metro] Atlanta, there is the city of Atlanta, which is a very small share of that—it's about 500,000 people—while the Atlanta metro area is well over 5 million, maybe closer to 6 million people.[39] The bulk of Georgia's population lives within metro Atlanta. Well, as one would expect, the closer one gets to the core of Atlanta, what is the physical confines of the city of Atlanta, the more likely you are to find Democrats.

Now what we've seen happen over the last fifteen years is the Democratic footprint in metro Atlanta expanded. So if [you] to go back to 2004, what was then twenty-seven or twenty-eight counties, only three of them were Democratic. That would have been Fulton, which is the most populous county in the state, DeKalb, which at that time was the second most populous, and Clayton County. . . . Barack Obama added three counties to the Democratic side and these were moving out east and west of the I-20, which is the east/west interstate [highway] that goes through Atlanta, so moving to the east added Rockdale and Newton County. And on the west side, Obama picked up Douglas County. In 2014, another county on the south side adjacent to Clayton County, Henry County, voted Democratic, for the first time in probably twenty years or so. And then Hillary Clinton managed to narrowly win/flip what by this point were the second and third most populous counties of the state, and that would be Gwinnett, which is on the northeast side, and Cobb, which is on the northwest side. Her margin in Gwinnett County as I recall was around 16,000 to 18,000 people/votes, where in Cobb it was closer to 6,000 or 7,000 votes. [2018 Democratic gubernatorial candidate] Stacey Abrams does even better. She wins both those counties by a fairly comfortable margin. It was like 57-43 probably in Gwinnett; it was like 55-45 in Cobb. So it looks like those counties have split. So to summarize, the four largest counties in the state, and in order would be Fulton, Gwinnett, Cobb, and DeKalb, all voted Democratic in 2018. Now, nine of the counties in metro Atlanta are Democratic; at least, we've seen them move Democratic in the most recent gubernatorial and presidential elections.

What we've also seen is an expanding Democratic footprint at the state legislative level. There were fourteen state house seats and two state senate seats that went from Republican to Democrat in the 2018 elections, and these were all metro Atlanta districts. Most of those districts, the two senate districts, and most of the house districts were on the north side of the city; so this would be Cobb, Gwinnett, and North Fulton area is where exclusively the bulk of them were. That also is the general area where Democrats picked up a congressional seat. That would be the victory of Democrat Lucy McBath in the 6th District of Georgia where she defeated Republican Karen Handel. The adjacent district to that would be the 7th District to the east of the 6th District. Democrats almost won that one. Democrat Carolyn Bourdeaux came within 433 votes of unseating Republican Congressman Rob Woodall.

Expert Summary and Analysis

As Bullock points out, metro Atlanta has grown massively over the past several decades in both population and land area. The region is now heavily influencing Georgia's politics. With each successive election, Democrats win more and more of metro Atlanta, putting the party in a competitive position in Georgia as a whole. The region is adding Democratic members to the state legislature and putting more statewide races in play. Atlanta is Georgia's future and, politically, Atlanta's future is blue.

Structural Features of State Government

Dr. Bullock was asked: "What is the structure of governance in Georgia?" He answered:

It's a strong governorship. Again, one might say it's not as strong as it was say sixty years ago when the governor named the Speaker of the House and a lot of the committee chairs. It's still a strong position. Governors generally get what they want, although I guess one could make the case that perhaps Brian Kemp[40] was less successful than Nathan Deal[41] had been in this particular year. But, yes, it is a strong governorship. And in part that's because our legislature is very much a part-time legislature. The Georgia constitution states the legislative session is only forty days of the year. Now, that's forty days in session, which gets spread out over about three months. Legislators are paid less than $18,000 a year. Many legislators, of course, spend the bulk of the rest of the year doing whatever their primary vocation is, so they're out of town—letting the governor do what he wants, he's in charge. The other thing that strengthens the hand of the governor is the governor sets the revenue estimates. The state budget cannot be for more than whatever the governor estimates the revenue for the state will be. . . . The appropriation process is to give money around underneath that estimate but it cannot exceed that estimate.

Expert Summary and Analysis

Bullock notes that Georgia has a strong governor, made even stronger by the fact that the state has a part-time legislature that cedes power to the chief executive when it vacates the state capitol. The governor also has power over the state budget via revenue estimates that the legislature cannot exceed.

Metro Power in State Government

Dr. Bullock was asked: "How much power does the Atlanta metropolitan area exert in state politics?" He answered:

The economic power—the large size—it's where the population is, so that's where the votes are. Georgia is a state which has always been very hospitable and interested in courting outside investments. And, therefore, like other states who are trying to attract new investments, one of the big successes the state has had in recent years has been in attracting the movie industry. You can get the precise figures on this, but what I've heard is there are more movies shot in Georgia than in Hollywood and more television shows shot in Georgia than in Great Britain. . . . So that has been one of the newest things the state has gone after.

What you see happening in parts of Georgia, especially rural areas, is the population is just emptying out. This is particularly true in the southwest quadrant of the state. But there's another area where a number of counties are losing population, which would be kind of a line between Athens and Augusta. . . . That line between the middle of those counties over there is losing people. And anecdotally, start driving around parts of rural Georgia; you'll see lots of cuts off the roads you're driving on and you know at some point there was at least one house if not multiple houses back wherever that cut was.

Rural Georgia is not succeeding in attracting investment. It is not succeeding in holding its population or holding its high school graduates. If you graduate and you're ambitious, you're going to move to Atlanta or maybe Savannah or maybe to Jacksonville, Florida, or Chattanooga, Tennessee, or somewhere because the opportunities simply aren't there. Now Georgia's had eight rural hospitals close in recent years. And at least what the planners tell us is that when a community loses its hospital it becomes more of a challenge for it to attract outsiders or outside investments.

Expert Summary and Analysis

Atlanta's booming and diversifying economy allows the region to dominate the state by targeting industries it chooses, such as television and film production. As noted, conservative forces within the state have jeopardized this expanding sector by passing among the most restrictive abortion laws in the United States. The less successful rural parts of Georgia seem to care little if they disrupt Atlanta's economy as they focus their legislative efforts on cultural wedge issues. Yet, the rural areas benefit by having so successful a metropolis as Atlanta within the state because there are resources available to be invested in initiatives throughout Georgia.

Cultural Divisions

Dr. Bullock was asked: "Is Georgia culturally divided?" He answered:

What I'd say about that is there is partially a partisan divide with Democrats not being as liberal as say California or New York Democrats, but well to the left of the Republicans within the state. So that on the state's refusal to join Obamacare, survey research shows most Georgians to be in favor of that. But the state has not expanded Medicaid because the governor and the legislature have been in Republican hands now for about a generation.

Probably the same thing is true on abortion. Again, this is an issue that inspires the Republican base. Brian Kemp, in the course of his campaign, promised to sign the most conservative, most restricting abortion bill in the nation. And, therefore, it's no surprise that he did sign this bill even though there were warnings that doing so might make Georgia less attractive as a place of investment. So then one might say that, in terms of personal ideology, Brian Kemp is more conservative than [former Republican governor] Nathan Deal.

So there's big cleavage between Democrats and Republicans with regard to the abortion bill, which was one of the most controversial items or maybe it was the most controversial item in the General Assembly this year—so these urban Republicans, those who survived, as a number of them got defeated, but those survivors kind of on the north side of Atlanta—some of them simply ducked out and didn't vote on that issue. So on the two critical votes on that abortion bill—in one instance it got ninety-two votes, the other time ninety-three votes. To pass legislation in Georgia requires a constitutional majority, and that's ninety-one votes. So it barely, barely got passed . . . so there were some Republicans who ducked out and there were a few who actually voted against it, and there's a widespread expectation that some share of those Republicans in the Atlanta metro area and maybe also one in Savannah and one down in Athens, by voting for that bill, they have ended their political career, or at least it will be harder to get reelected.

Expert Summary and Analysis

Cultural issues starkly divide Georgia as a conservative governor who was elected by running up big margins in rural Georgia counties imposes a controversial social agenda on the entire state, including metro Atlanta. Republicans from urban counties may face a backlash in the next election due to the abortion vote and their conservative record on social issues, which may not match the values and interests of many of their constituents. Atlanta is one of America's premier booster metros and it is highly likely that the business community will target state politicians who have worked to disrupt the region's commerce—even if a moral imperative led them to do so.

Demographic Change

Dr. Bullock was asked: "How will Georgia's demographic changes impact the political dynamic between Atlanta and the rest of the state?" He answered:

A take-off point for that is to say something more about the 2018 gubernatorial election. Brian Kemp's campaign focused on rural Georgia. He had a number of bus tours. He didn't spend much time in metro Atlanta. And he eked out a victory of slightly less than 55,000 votes. So it was very much an urban/rural split in that. Stacey Abrams carried nine of the counties in metro Atlanta. She also carried the main urban county and all the other urban centers—Athens, Augusta, Savannah, Macon, and Columbus. And that's about all she carried. . . . She did carry some of the very small rural Black Belt counties, which have a predominantly Black population. Kemp then swept most of rural Georgia. Some people's perspective is, "Yeah, ok, that worked in 2018. It will not work in 2022." There will not be enough rural votes at that point. So what we see happening in Georgia, you see this happening in some other southern states also, is that the youth vote is a Democratic vote. It has been so since 2014. Under-thirties are solidly Democratic and probably a 5-3 split roughly on that. And some of those who were in their upper-twenties four years ago are now moving into their thirties, and it looks like they're staying Democratic, and so the future of the young voters—young voters as they become young families and things like this—Democratic.

In Georgia, we know precisely how many Blacks, how many whites, how many Native Americans, how many Hispanics, and how many Asians voted. Now there is, of course, another census category—multiple race. There's no box for that category yet. But taking these ethnic figures—in 1996 between 77 and 78 percent were cast by white voters. Last year, that number was down to 59 percent. The Black vote, according to the exit poll, went about 92 percent for Stacey Abrams. When Obama ran, back in 2008, he got 98 percent of the vote. But then again, if you're a Democrat, you will get about 90 percent of the Black vote. When Black Democrats run, they do slightly better. Recent Democrats, this would be true for 2014, 2016, and 2018—get about 25 percent of the white vote. But given the kinds of trends that have been underway, such as the things I just mentioned, a Republican Party that relies pretty much exclusively on getting white voters, even though they may get 75 percent of them, sooner or later are going to run out of votes. There are going to be that many whites left. Sometime in the next decade, Georgia becomes a majority-minority state. . . . It's now 51 percent white. So the projections are that if the Republicans don't come up with a broader, more encompassing message, sooner or later they run out of voters.

Expert Summary and Analysis

Bullock, looking at the future, speculates that the model by which current Republican Governor Kemp won the state may not be workable in the 2020s. He notes that under-thirty voters are now solidly for the Democrats and appear to keep those politics as they age. The bottom line, Bullock argues, is that relying on oversized margins by white voters may cost Republican candidates in the long term as they simply run out of constituents when the state of Georgia—led by Atlanta—transitions to majority-minority status in the next several years.

STATE OF PLAY: NORTH CAROLINA

Like Georgia, North Carolina is a populous and politically complex state. With more than 10.4 million residents as of 2018, North Carolina now ranks ninth among states in population.[42] North Carolina contains seven different political sections (see figure 4-2), the most divisions identified for any state in this book. North Carolina is also a geographically diverse state that has an extensive coastline with numerous sounds (or bays) in the east and the highest peak in the Appalachian Mountains (Mount Mitchell, elevation 6,684) in the west.[43] The varied physical terrain translates into equally different economic, political, and sociocultural spaces throughout the state.

Unlike Georgia, North Carolina lacks a single massive metropolitan area that dominates the state (for example, Atlanta). Rather, the Tar Heel state contains an elongated arc of semi-urbanized spaces that run along I-85 through the "Carolina Piedmont."[44] North Carolina's extended urban complex contains two million-plus metros and stretches from the northeast (at Raleigh) to the southwest (Charlotte) and sweeps in several mid-to-large-size regions in between. The Carolina Piedmont even reaches into Upstate South Carolina, including metros such Greenville and Spartanburg. According to Arthur C.

FIGURE 4-2. North Carolina

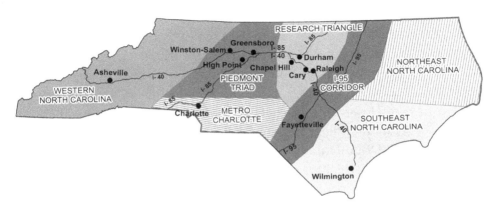

Nelson and Robert E. Lang, the Carolina and Atlanta Piedmont mega-politan areas form a nearly contiguous "countrified city" that runs from the border of southern Virginia south to eastern Alabama along I-85.[45] Only the centers of Atlanta and Charlotte maintain true high-rise, rail-accessible, and traditional city-like environments. Urbanized suburbs ring these cities and Raleigh, which are then surrounded by multiple lower-density suburban and exurban counties to form one of most-extended, semi-countrified urban complexes in the nation.

Research Triangle

As North Carolina boomed with population and employment in recent years, it has also grown even more politically complex. Its diversifying economic development has drawn migrants from especially the Northeast to work in its new industries in places such as the boomburb Cary, home to the statistical software firm SAS.[46] Cary has become so associated with outsiders, especially those from the North, that it is sometimes derisively referred to by the acronym "CARY, or Containment Area for Relocated Yankees."[47]

Cary lies inside North Carolina's Research Triangle (locally known as The Triangle), which lies between Raleigh (the state capital), Durham (home to Duke University), and Chapel Hill (home to the University of North Carolina). SAS was founded at North Carolina State University (located in Raleigh). The term *Research Triangle*, which is an industrial park located roughly equidistant between the Raleigh, Durham, and Chapel Hill, is also used to refer to the region as a whole.[48] Raleigh and Durham once manufactured cigarettes, furniture, and textiles, but have since transitioned into technology and service-driven economies. Note that Durham is a separate MSA from Raleigh and is not included in the million-plus metro data analysis that follows. However, Durham is part of a larger combined statistical area with Raleigh (CSAs are defined in text box 1-1), which in 2019 approached 2.3 million residents and roughly equates to the region identified here as the Research Triangle.[49]

Table 4-5 shows that the Raleigh metropolitan area contains 13 percent of North Carolina's current population (it exceeds 20 percent when combined with Durham). Raleigh has fewer African Americans and Latinos as a percentage of its residents than the rest of North Carolina. However, the metro has a large Asian community, accounting for over a quarter of all Asians within the state. Raleigh also has a significant number of foreign-born residents.

Raleigh is becoming a bluer-voting metropolitan area based on the data shown in table 4-6. The presidential and governor's races in 2012 compared to 2016 clearly show the change. In the 2012 North Carolina governor's race, the Democrat lost the Raleigh metropolitan area by 5 percent, while in 2016, Democratic candidate Roy Cooper won the region by 14.4 percent and eked out the win by a 0.2 percent margin statewide. President Obama lost North Carolina in 2012, but won the Raleigh metropolitan area by 5.6 percent that year. In 2016, Democratic presidential candidate Hillary Clinton improved on Obama's performance by gaining a 12 percent winning margin in metro Raleigh.

Given its rapid demographic change over the last several decades and the presence of three major research universities, the Research Triangle has seen its politics shift from red to blue. Even a city such as

TABLE 4-5. Demographic and Economic Comparison between North Carolina and Metros

	North Carolina	Share in Charlotte* (%)	Share in Raleigh (%)
Population	10,273,419	20.8	13.0
White	63.0%	19.7	12.6
Black	21.2%	22.1	11.8
Asian	2.9%	29.1	26.3
Latino	9.4%	24.8	11.8
Foreign-Born	8.1%	28.8	20.6
College Educated	31.3%	23.8	18.8
Jobs	4,717,237	22.8	14.2
GDP	$467,754	26.7	15.4

*Excludes counties outside of MSA primary state.

Sources: 2017 American Community Survey 1-Year estimates as aggregated by censusreporter.org, Department of Commerce, Bureau of Economic Analysis, 2015 Real GDP (millions of chained 2012 dollars) County Level Data, U.S. Department of Labor, Bureau of Labor Statistics 2017 County Level Data.

TABLE 4-6. Comparison of Electoral Outcomes
between North Carolina and Metros

	North Carolina	Charlotte		Raleigh	
Election	Outcome	Vote Share [%]	Outcome	Vote Share [%]	Outcome
2016 Presidential	+3.7 Rep	20.1	+1.5 Rep	13.6	+12.0 Dem
2016 U.S. Senate	+5.7 Rep	20.1	+5.3 Rep	13.6	+6.8 Dem
2016 Gubernatorial	+0.2 Dem	20.1	+0.8 Dem	13.6	+14.4 Dem
2014 U.S. Senate	+1.6 Rep	18.7	+3.6 Rep	13.6	+7.5 Dem
2012 Presidential	+2.0 Rep	19.8	+2.4 Rep	13.1	+5.6 Dem
2012 Gubernatorial	+11.4 Rep	19.8	+21.7 Rep	13.1	+5.0 Rep

Source: Data from North Carolina secretary of state's website.

Durham, which was home to J. B. Duke's American Tobacco Company and long a conservative bastion, has become Democratic-leaning as Duke University now dominates the city. The old American Tabacco campus has been turned into a historic shopping district, which symbolizes Durham's shift from a tobacco processor to a college town. In Chapel Hill, the campus is busy tearing down historic statuary associated with the Confederacy.[50] In short, the North Carolina Research Triangle may now be more Yankee in culture, economy, and politics than Southern—or at least it seems an extension of Northern Virginia and may soon share that region's politics.

Piedmont Triad

Just west of the Research Triangle along the I-85 Corridor lies the Piedmont Triad, which contains the Greensboro-High Point MSA (population 767,711 in 2018) and the Winston-Salem MSA (population 671,456 in 2018). The region contains a substantial African American population. Some of the African Americans now living in the Piedmont Triad, the Research Triangle, and Charlotte, are in fact Northern-born Blacks who have migrated back to the South.[51] African Americans from the north in particular are Democratic-leaning and have helped make the Piedmont Triad a mostly blue section of North Carolina.

No metropolitan area within the Piedmont Triad exceeds 1 million people and, thus, the region is not part of the demographic and political data analysis performed for this book. Yet the two Triad metros combine to form the Greensboro-Winston-Salem-High Point CSA, which had 1,677,551 residents in 2018.[52] If this book used CSAs instead of MSAs as the primary statistical unit of analysis, there would have been three separate million-plus metros in North Carolina rather than two, and the Raleigh region would have included Durham.[53] This fact is more proof as to the complex nature of North Carolina's extended urban system. North Carolina's three million-plus CSAs collectively contain nearly 6.7 million residents, which surpassed Atlanta's nearly 6 million people in 2018. North Carolina is as urban as Georgia, except it developed a far less centralized and cohesive urban form. The Piedmont Triad lies in the heart of North Carolina's I-85 urban corridor.

Metro Charlotte

South and west of the Piedmont Triad is found North Carolina's largest metropolitan area—Charlotte—with nearly 2.6 million residents.[54] Charlotte is a remarkably transformed metropolis when compared to just a few decades ago. The concentration of consumer banking headquarters, such as the Bank of America, and the construction of an international airport with direct connections to Europe and Latin America has made Charlotte the second-largest metropolitan area in the South Atlantic region, behind Atlanta.

Likewise, Charlotte's politics have changed, establishing the city as one of the most forward-thinking places in the New South. Thus, a conflict arose between Charlotte's city council, which tried to accommodate transgender residents by allowing them to decide their restroom of choice, and a conservative-dominated red state legislature that overrode the city's local ordinance. Charlotte is now a purple metropolitan area (see table 4-6), while Mecklenburg County (the urban core and home to the city of Charlotte) votes for Democrats.

Table 4-6 shows metro Charlotte's transition to more Democratic-friendly politics in recent years. Comparing the 2012 and 2016 gubernatorial and presidential races shows the change. In the 2012 North Carolina governor's race, the Democrat lost the Charlotte metropolitan area by a 21.7 percentage point margin, while in 2016, Democratic candidate Roy Cooper won the region by 0.8 percentage points. President Obama lost North Carolina in 2012 by 2 percentage points, and lost the Charlotte metropolitan area by 2.4 percentage points. Democratic presidential candidate Hillary Clinton improved on Obama's performance by losing metro Charlotte by just 1.5 percentage point. The political contrast within the Charlotte region is striking. The center city is deep blue, while the suburban fringe votes like rural North Carolina.

Arthur C. Nelson and Robert Lang made a case that the entire I-85 Corridor, or the Carolina Piedmont, is one extended urban region, which they define as a "megapolitan area."[55] Given its politics, a case can be made that, were the Carolina Piedmont a separate state, with over 7 million residents, it would be a Democratic-leaning one. Much of the geopolitical dynamic in North Carolina is the tension between the urban interests of the Carolina Piedmont versus rural and small-town North Carolina. The Carolina Piedmont is politically a pale blue, while much of rural North Carolina is a deep shade of red. That balance is what makes North Carolina a swing state.

Table 4-5 shows that the Charlotte metropolitan area represents one in five North Carolina residents. The metro contains the largest African American, Asian, Latino, and foreign-born communities in the state. Charlotte is a diverse and wealthy region that generates well over a quarter of North Carolina's GDP (see table 4-5).

Northeast North Carolina

East of the Carolina Piedmont is a complicated political landscape. Much of the area is Republican-leaning, but many rural North Carolina counties with significant African American populations vote for Democrats. That is especially true of the northeast part of the North Carolina east of the I-95 Corridor and west of the Atlantic coast. Interestingly, every North Carolina county with ocean frontage voted for President Trump in 2016, while most counties bordering the Atlantic Ocean from Virginia to Maine voted for Hillary Clinton.

I-95 Corridor

South along the I-95 Corridor is the midsized metro of Fayetteville, which was built in part to service the large military base of Fort Bragg to its immediate west. Fayetteville's development is also notable in that it was one of the last areas in which I-95, the U.S. interstate highway running from Holton, Maine, to Miami, Florida, was completed. Until the 1980s, all traffic travelling down this "main street of the East Coast" ran right through the city.[56] This, in turn, helped develop Fayetteville and expose many Yankee tourists to the city. For its size, Fayetteville is quite cosmopolitan, and like parts of northeast North Carolina, it has a substantial African American population. Thus, the Fayetteville metropolitan area leans Democratic, as does much of North Carolina's I-95 Corridor (especially along the border with Virginia).

Southeast North Carolina

In contrast to northeast North Carolina and metropolitan Fayetteville, virtually all of southeast North Carolina votes Republican. That even includes the Wilmington area—the region's largest metro. In the 2016 presidential race, every county in southeast North Carolinian voted for Republican candidate Donald Trump. However, in the 2016 governor's contest, Democratic candidate Roy Cooper won New Hanover County (which includes the city of Wilmington).

The Wilmington metropolitan area (or the Cape Fear region), which contains nearly 300,000 residents, is among the fastest-growing parts of North Carolina.[57] Wilmington trails only the Raleigh and Charlotte metropolitan areas in its growth rate since 2010.[58] The city of Wilmington, especially its historic downtown, is the most Democratic-friendly space in southeast North Carolina.

Western North Carolina

The large region west of the Carolina Piedmont is also Republican-leaning. This area includes the Appalachian parts of the state, which contains a section of the Great Smoky Mountains. A notable exception to this political pattern is Buncombe County, which includes the city of Asheville, an artsy and progressive place with a high quality of life that attracts many migrants from outside the state and contains a branch of the University of North Carolina.

There is an especially large retiree population in the region. Such retirees have been referred to as "halfbacks."[59] Many of these retirees originate in the Northeast and after they relocate to Florida, they may move halfway back to the Northeast by migrating to places such as Asheville and other smaller metros in the Appalachian Mountains of North Carolina, Georgia, and Tennessee. Thus, parts of even rural North Carolina are receiving Yankees, who, while not monolithically Democratic voting, are more liberal than most native residents of North Carolina's Appalachian region. Asheville, in particular, is a favored location for halfbacks.

Conclusion: North Carolina State of Play

North Carolina is a tipping point state. It has seen its Electoral College votes decided by 0.3 to 3 percentage points since 2008. Yet, demographically, the state is slowly beginning to shift blue. In fact, its transition appears similar in some ways to neighboring Virginia, where the move to an increasingly Democratic-voting state happened at least a decade ahead of North Carolina. Charlotte does not have quite the liberalism or sheer demographic punch of Northern Virginia. But along with the rest of the Carolina Piedmont metros, such as the Triad and the Research Triangle, the balance of political power in the Tar Heel State appears to be trending more urban and, thus, politically bluer.

Despite being a purple (or a competitive) state in recent presidential and governor's races, North Carolina's delegation to the U.S. House of Representatives currently has ten Republicans and just three Democrats (see table 4-7). Republicans hold an advantage in the statehouse as well; although the 2018 midterm election saw the gap significantly narrow (see table 4-7). North Carolina is among the most severely gerrymandered states in the nation, for both federal and state elections. In fact, the state legislative district maps have been so skewed to the Republicans they were tossed out by a North Carolina court in September 2019.[60] The court found that: "the state's legislative districts violated the North Carolina State Constitution through 'extreme partisan gerrymandering.' . . . The 2017 Enacted Maps, as drawn, do not permit voters to freely choose their representative, but rather representatives are choosing voters based upon sophisticated partisan sorting."[61]

Finally, although the Charlotte and Raleigh metropolitan areas do not exhibit excessive municipal fragmentation, North Carolina ranks below the midpoint in terms of "local government autonomy" (see table 4-8). That is why, for instance, the North Carolina legislature invoked state supremacy and passed a bill to reverse Charlotte's city ordinance allowing transgender residents to use the bathroom that matched their gender identity. While Charlotte has secured some resources, in meeting its needs for infrastructure improvements (such as enhancing its University of North Carolina branch campus), the city (along with Raleigh and even Asheville) must adhere to cultural standards set by a conservative-leaning and gerrymandered state legislature.

EXPERT ANALYSIS: NORTH CAROLINA

Mary Newsom, the director of Urban Policy Initiatives at the University of North Carolina, Charlotte, provided expert comments on politics in North Carolina. A lifelong newspaper journalist, Ms. Newsom completed a year-long Nieman Fellowship at Harvard University in 2007–08, and in 2005–06 was a Knight Fellow in Community

TABLE 4-7. Partisan Composition of North Carolina State Government and Federal Delegation

| | | State Government | | | | Federal Delegation | | | |
| | | Upper House | | Lower House | | U.S. Senate | | U.S. House | |
	Governor	Dems	Reps	Dems	Reps	Dems	Reps	Dems	Reps
2019–20	Dem	21	29	55	65	2	0	3	10
2017–18	Rep	15	35	46	74	2	0	3	10
2015–16	Rep	16	34	46	74	1	1	4	9
2013–14	Dem	18	32	43	77	1	1	4	9

Sources: Data from National Conference of State Legislatures, "State and Legislative Partisan Composition" for various years, and North Carolina secretary of state's website.

TABLE 4-8. Metro Governance Fragmentation and Autonomy in North Carolina

Governance Fragmentation

Metro	Number of Counties in Metro	Number of General Purposes Governments in Metro
Charlotte*	7	65
Raleigh	3	30

Governance Autonomy

Local Government Autonomy Score	−0.036
Local Government Autonomy Ranking	29

*Excludes counties outside of MSA primary state.

Sources: Data for Governance Fragmentation from 2017 Census of Governments. Data for Governance Autonomy from Harold Wolman, Robert McManmon, Michael Bell, and David Brunori, "Comparing Local Government Autonomy Across States," in *The Property Tax and Local Autonomy*, edited by Michael Bell, David Brunori, and Joan Youngman (Lincoln Institute of Land Policy Press, 2010), pp. 69–114.

Building at the University of Miami. This interview was conducted on May 23, 2018. Note that interview responses may include minor edits to provide continuity and clarify language. Endnotes are also added to verify key facts.

Intrastate Political Dynamics

Ms. Newsom was asked: "What is the political dynamic between the major metropolitan areas and the rest of the state?" She answered:

Well, in general, the cities are blue, just like the title of the book. The cities are blue, and the state [is] red. And within the metros, the same holds true. The cities tend to be much bluer, and the surrounding areas, including suburbs, and the rural areas within the metro are more like rural areas everywhere. In 2016, Hillary Clinton easily won [the city of] Charlotte. But Donald Trump won the state. And that's been fairly true for the last few elections.

In terms of [U.S.] House or Senate delegations, of course, we have extreme gerrymandering in North Carolina, so the congressional delegation is very unrepresentative of the state as a whole. . . . There are three Democrats and ten Republicans out of our thirteen house seats, and that's completely unrepresentative of the state. I mean, voters statewide are pretty closely divided, Republican versus Democrat. Our [U.S.] Senate seats are interesting in that two Republicans; both of them ran in years when there was a pretty strong Republican showing nationwide, one of them is from the Charlotte area, Tom Tillis. He's from a suburban area, and depending on the day of the week, he's either moderate Republican or extremely conservative Republican. Richard Burr is more consistently conservative, but not [an] extremist. He is from an urban area, also, Winston-Salem. So, I guess it shows that just because you live in a metro, it doesn't mean you are necessarily a Democratic politician.

The dynamic in state politics and gubernatorial races . . . [is] we have a Democratic governor, the cities tend to vote Democratic, and everybody else votes Republican. . . . As the cities, [and] as the metro areas grow larger and larger, it makes it possible for a moderate Democrat like Roy Cooper to win the state [in 2016].

Everybody has been predicting that the growth and the influx of newcomers will make the state more Democratic. I think that is happening to a lesser extent than people had predicted. But I'm not entirely sure why. I think it may . . . I was just going to speculate here . . . I have a friend who says, "Yes, a lot of New Yorkers are moving to the Charlotte area, but they're all from Long Island." That means we're not getting the more liberal Democrats from places like Manhattan, but we're getting the more suburban, more conservative voters from places like Long Island.

Expert Summary and Analysis

Newsom finds, as we see in other states, that cities and close-in suburbs vote blue while lower-density suburbs and rural areas tend to vote red. She also points to evidence of gerrymandering as the closely contested state of North Carolina sends just three Democrats to the U.S. House of Representatives as opposed to ten Republicans. Newsom recognizes that immigration to the state is changing its economy, culture, and voting patterns, yet it may not be making North Carolina as liberal as many observers predicted. She speculates that it may be that many of the Yankee transplants come from suburban areas of the Northeast (such as Long Island, New York) and may, therefore, be less inclined to vote for Democrats compared to immigrants from cities.

Structural Features of State Government

Ms. Newsom was asked: "What is the structure of governance in North Carolina?" She answered:

In terms of [the] government's powers, North Carolina historically has had a weak governor, while the legislature holds most of the power. I believe it was not until the early 1980s that the governor was even allowed to serve two terms.[62] And the governor finally acquired the veto power at some point in the 1980s. But the whole state government is essentially set up on the understanding that they didn't want tyrants; they didn't want strong people; they wanted power to the people, the legislature, to hold the bulk of the power.... Now in terms of personal political success, Governor Jim Hunt is probably the one that leaps to mind as the most successful. He is the one that got to serve two terms, and then he went away for two terms and came back for two terms. So, he served four terms and built a statewide political organization that is still in power in many places.... He was able to get beyond the limitations of the office by astute politics and by having a Democratic legislature to work with.

The governor before Roy Cooper [currently serving] was the former mayor of Charlotte, Pat McCrory, and I think a lot of people would view him as not particularly successful. Some of that was just due to his personal qualities. Some of it was due to—if you're from Charlotte, there are a lot of people in the state who aren't going to like you because of longstanding hostility to cities in general, and Charlotte in particular. And I think he had issues getting along with the state Republican Party apparatus, which is sort of irrespective of who voted for him and what his policies were. It was just that there were a lot of people in the Republican Party who didn't feel they were being respected, and I think that hurt him as well. So, some of his difficulties were due to him being from a city. And Charlotte is a weak-mayor city, and so he never really had to learn much about all kinds of things. The [Charlotte] mayor is kind of a figurehead. McCrory never had to learn anything about public education; the way they divvied up the powers here, he never had to learn anything about the environment. I mean those are pretty big chunks of government. McCrory didn't know anything about social services because our county government does that. So, there were large chunks of government expertise he did not pick up while he was mayor.

North Carolina is generally considered a Dillon's Rule state, although people who study local governments say no, it's a modified Dillon's Rule state. Frayda Bluestein[63] said, "If you're confused, you're not alone." That the state is a neither-or blend; if you were to ask one or the other, then the answer is none of the above. It's really kind of both. In my opinion, operationally North Carolina is a Dillon's Rule state. Professor Bluestein is really talking about court cases, and that may well be right, but in terms of the legislature being able to pretty much whip all the cities, yeah, North Carolina qualifies as a Dillon's Rule state.

Expert Summary and Analysis

North Carolina has a relatively weak governor that was limited to a single term until the 1980s. The governor's personal qualities help determine his or her success in the role. Also, a governor from Charlotte may be disadvantaged in that the city remains somewhat stigmatized at the state level, and the job of mayor is mostly ceremonial and may not prepare one adequately to be the chief executive of a state. Newsom observes that North Carolina is a Dillon's Rule state and that despite the fact that governance/legal experts technically define North Carolina as a home rule/Dillon's Rule-hybrid jurisdiction, the *de facto* reality is that the state legislature exerts enormous control over localities.

Metro Power in State Government

Ms. Newsom was asked: "How much power do major metropolitan areas exert in state politics?" She answered:

Historically the city of Charlotte and Mecklenburg County had seen a lot of turnover in their legislative delegations. There are a lot of reasons for that; the experts that I've heard from over the years have said . . . [that] in rural areas, if you can get to the state legislature, you have it made in the shade. And you can just keep that post forever. In cities, people are more mobile, people move in, they move out, [and] there are a lot of other job opportunities that pay better than being in the state legislature, and so the delegation never tended to build up the seniority that some of the rural legislatures had.

In addition, there is just kind of longstanding tension between the biggest city, Charlotte, and the rest of the state. There's a phrase here called "the great state of Mecklenburg,"[64] which everybody says, "Oh, no, that's not true anymore," but I think it does tend to come up again. And that's how Charlotte has the sense of a place apart. Some of that is just the civic DNA in Charlotte . . . [it] is very much a booster city; it's like Atlanta in that way. And if you're not the state capital and you're always bragging about how great your area is, it tends to make other areas of the state not quite friendly.

So, historically, Charlotte-Mecklenburg has not been a big powerhouse in state government. Raleigh is a smaller city; it's about half the size of Charlotte. So, they haven't bragged as much about how great they are because they didn't need to; they're the capital city. And also, I think just having legislators being there, they just have a better understanding of what it's like to be in Raleigh.

I think Durham—which is part of the Research Triangle area—I think Durham has become in some ways more and more like Charlotte in that they don't really give a hoot about Raleigh. I mean, Asheville has its own issues. It's like they're too liberal now; all those Wiccans hanging out.[65] So, all the metro areas have issues with the legislature, where a lot of the heft is from either rural areas or suburban areas.

And there's just hostility toward cities in America, which is deep-rooted; centuries old. I heard a wonderful speech years ago by Garry Wills, about how cities in America are viewed as places of sin. Unlike cities in Europe; that was the divine fete of the cathedral. America has this whole mythology about Western cities. You got out into the wilderness to be purified, and you don't go into the city to be purified. So, there's a thread of anti-city sentiment that exists today; even with all of the Millennial [generation] back-to-the-city hype, you can still pick up on this "cities are places of evil" thread. And I think that thread exists very strongly in North Carolina, especially in places that aren't cities. So, you have a lot of different threads that weave together to make Charlotte, in particular, disproportionately, I would say, disproportionately disempowered.

I also think there's some tension between Charlotte and Raleigh in terms of competition—although it mostly has to do with people in Raleigh more than Charlotte. (I am referring to the people who live in the city of Raleigh, not necessarily legislators who have gone there for the session.) But it's sort of a Raleigh civic establishment scorning Charlotte and the Charlotte civic establishment not even really thinking about Raleigh. Because people in Charlotte, they think about Nashville, they think about Atlanta, they think about Orlando. They don't think about Raleigh all that much. But there is some competition there, which is really too bad, because I think if the delegations from those two urban areas, and the others such as Greensboro, Winston-Salem, and Asheville, all got together, they would have more legislative heft.[66] But I don't think they do necessarily.

If you look at statewide transportation funding, we are so screwed in Charlotte. . . . There are no such things as county roads in North Carolina; they're either state roads or they're local municipal streets. So Charlotte's interstates don't get widened and [its] state roads are filled with potholes. [The roads are] . . . covered in trash, because not a lot of money is spent in Charlotte, proportionate to the population. . . . With that said, if you're in one of the rural counties where the economy is dead in the water and you see the city is comparatively economically healthy, if you look at the large numbers, you may say "holy cow, how dare the state spend money on anything in Charlotte when we're dying here."

So, there's a sense at the state level that we have to save our rural counties—because rural poverty can be horrifying. With that said, there are zip codes in Charlotte where the poverty is just as dire, if not more dire, than anywhere else in the state. But that doesn't get the attention of state government, because if you look at Mecklenburg County as a whole, it looks pretty good.

Expert Summary and Analysis

Newsom notes that Charlotte has relatively little power in state government. This is true for several reasons. One, the metropolitan area does not constitute a large share of North Carolina's total population. Data in this book (see tables 4-1 and 4-5) show that, compared to metro Atlanta, which contains 56.4 percent of Georgia's population, Charlotte's metropolitan area accounts for just over one in five North Carolina residents. In addition, Charlotte's legislative caucus experiences high turnover, especially compared to the state's rural areas, and, thus, its legislators do not accumulate power via seniority. Also, urban power in general in North Carolina is weaker than one might expect due to a metropolitan spatial form that scatters urban populations across multiple regions that have competing interests and cannot seem to align politically to advocate for common goals. Finally, Charlotte's perceived arrogance and an anti-urban bias tend to diminish its potential political power.

Demographic Change

Ms. Newsom was asked: "How will North Carolina's demographic changes impact the political dynamic between major metros and the rest of the state?" She answered:

I'm not the first one who has pointed out that the demographic changes are going to make the state bluer in the near future. I think this happens for several reasons. One is that more people are moving to the cities, into the metro areas, than to the surrounding areas for economic reasons, primarily, and the whole Millennial generation push to live in cities. I think there are a couple of other things that come into play here, and one is, I don't think you can capture it with data, but I think human beings . . . [are] social animals and we tend to imitate each other. And I do think if you're in a city and you're surrounded by people who have a certain political viewpoint; you're more likely to begin to adopt that viewpoint. The same way, if you're in a small town, you're going to be more likely to adopt the viewpoint of the people around you. So, I think if more people live in cities that are more and more blue, that's going to have an effect as well on people's political outlook.

There's another factor in Charlotte that is not true in Raleigh, and I don't know how it's going to play out; it's going to be really interesting to see. But that is that the political and governmental establishment is, all of a sudden, just in the last couple of years, almost 100 percent African American. We have an African American mayor, and an African American city manager, police chief, and planning director. The chair of the board of county commissioners is Black; two of the three at-large county commissioners are Black. The county manager is white. But you look around and you go, "Holy cow, this is a Black city." Which is very different, and probably you weren't paying attention, but former governor Pat McCrory, who has not been able to find a job, so he's now doing . . . a TV talk show on a local TV station, and he remarked, something about, "Oh, look at this, they're all Blacks." And he got a lot of . . . [heat] for that comment, because he made it sound as though this is a terrible thing. But I have been wondering how long it was going to take, especially with white Republicans, to notice that and start making that an issue.

The other thing that's happening within the city is a huge increase in African Americans and Latinos. And I think that is truer in the cities in North Carolina. There's a lot of Hispanics in rural areas, as well. North Carolina is an immigrant gateway, and Charlotte is an immigrant gateway city, but in the last fifteen to twenty years, a large number of those Hispanics have been undocumented. It's fairly difficult to get real numbers of undocumented versus documented, but I've seen estimates of maybe 50 percent. So, while you have Latino growth everywhere in the state; in the rural areas around chicken plants and farm workers who are, I think, more likely to not be voters.

Expert Summary and Analysis

Newsom contends that changing demographics will eventually make North Carolina a more competitive state for Democrats. She partly attributes the shift to a rise in urban living that will ultimately transform residents' social values and political inclinations. She also notes that there is a sharp rise in African American leadership in Charlotte. Newsom speculates that the city's image in the rest of the state may grow more complicated as North Carolinians outside of Charlotte take notice of the change.

CONCLUSION: THE SOUTH ATLANTIC

Georgia and North Carolina are two large-scaled booming Southern states that are now successfully linked to the global economy. The rise of the South Atlantic as a well-connected corporate space has transformed Georgia and North Carolina into demographic, economic, and urban powerhouses. Gone is the 1960s image of North Carolina being a state full of small-town "Mayberries,"[67] and in its place are banking, technology, logistics, and the sprawling I-85 urban corridor. Likewise, Georgia has shed its past imagery as the Southern backwater depicted historically in the film *Gone with the Wind* and in its place is the New York of the South and the busiest airport in the nation. Were *Gone with the Wind* remade today, chances are good it would be shot in the Hollywood of the South—Atlanta. Yet both Georgia and North Carolina are not fully transformed. Behind their sleek urban façades lies an Old South capable of highly restrictive abortion laws and a deep intolerance of the LGBTQ community.

NOTES

1. Georgia (with 57,906 square miles) and North Carolina (47,711 square miles) are also the largest states on America's Atlantic coast outside of Florida.

2. U.S. Census Bureau, "2018 National and State Population Estimates."

3. The combined thirty-two seats will be a major Electoral College prize and surpass every state except California and Texas.

4. Mitt Romney flipped North Carolina back to the Republicans in 2012, with a 2.04 percentage point victory.

5. Dave Leip, "2016 Presidential General Election Data – National," *Atlas of U.S. Elections*, 2018, https://uselectionatlas.org/.

6. Each state also has nationally ranked land grant universities: North Carolina State (Raleigh) and the University of Georgia (Athens). North Carolina and Georgia universities also lead the nation by the percentage share of industry-funded research. By this measure, North Carolina ranks first, with 12.1 percent of its university sponsored research coming from industry, while Georgia ranks second at 10.6 percent. The statistics show a high degree of integration between South Atlantic universities and major industries within the states, making the region a leader in many new technologies. Robert D. Atkinson, "Industry Funding of University Research: Which States Lead?" *Information Technology and Innovation Foundation Report*, January 8, 2018, www2.itif.org/2018-industry-funding-university-research.pdf?_ga=2.96484056.639605858.1586029662-1284264063.1585938709.

7. Peter J. Taylor and Robert E. Lang, "U.S. Cities in the World City Network," Brookings Metropolitan Policy Program Report, February 2005, www.brookings.edu/wp-content/uploads/2016/06/20050222_worldcities.pdf.

8. U.S. Census Bureau, "2018 National and State Population Estimates."

9. The last Democratic presidential candidate to win the state was Bill Clinton in 1992.

10. The Georgia sectional geography used in this chapter mostly concurs with the one depicted in Gimpel and Schuknecht's book *Patchwork Nation*. James G. Gimpel and Jason E. Schuknecht, *Patchwork Nation: Sectionalism and Political Change in American Politics* (University of Michigan Press, 2003). The key difference between the two political geographies is the area that is considered part of the Atlanta metropolitan area. The Atlanta metropolitan area grew considerably in population and scale since the early years of the last decade. The Atlanta metro is now ninth-ranked in the United States, having recently passed Boston, and will soon overtake Philadelphia. The Atlanta metropolitan area has nearly 6 million residents based on 2018 U.S. census estimates. The region covers 8,376 square miles (about the size of New Jersey) and contains 29 of Georgia's 159 counties. In the past two decades, Atlanta's population boom and physical expansion outpaced all top twenty-five ranked metropolitan areas outside those in the Texas Triangle.

11. Raisa Habersham and Jennifer Peebles, "Census: Atlanta Has the 4th Fastest Growing Population in the Nation," *Atlanta Journal Constitution*, April 18, 2019, www.ajc.com/news/local/census-metro-atlanta-has-4th-fastest-growing-population-nation/UvQfqt3mW8EQsJ5zI94ohP/.

12. Eric Bradner, "Stacey Abrams Wins the Democratic Primary in Georgia," CNN, May 22, 2018, www.cnn.com/2018/05/22/politics/georgia-governor-race-stacey-abrams/index.html.

13. James M. Shrouds, "Atlanta 'Conforms' to Clean Air Requirements," *Public Roads* 64 (September/October 2000), www.fhwa.dot.gov/publications/publicroads/00septoct/atlanta.cfm.

14. Numan V. Bartley, *The New South, 1945–1980: The Story of the South's Modernization* (Louisiana State University Press, 1996).

15. Atlanta's rapid usurpation of Birmingham was not due to Mayor Hartsfield alone. The city long included global brand companies, such as Coca-Cola.

16. John D. Toon, "Interstate Highway System," *New Georgia Encyclopedia*, June 8, 2017, www.georgiaencyclopedia.org/articles/business-economy/interstate-highway-system.

17. Virginia H. Hein, "The Image of 'A City Too Busy to Hate': Atlanta in the 1960s," *Phylon* 33 (September 1972), pp. 205–21.

18. Martin Luther King, "Letter from a Birmingham Jail," April 16, 1963, https://kinginstitute.stanford.edu/encyclopedia/letter-birmingham-jail.

19. Gimpel and Schuknecht, *Patchwork Nation*.

20. Audrey Singer, Susan Hardwick, and Caroline Brettell, "Twenty-First Century Gateways: Immigrants in Suburban America," *Migration Policy Institute Feature Article*, April 30, 2008, www.migrationpolicy.org/article/twenty-first-century-gateways-immigrants-suburban-america.

21. Taylor and Lang, "U.S. Cities in the World City Network," ranked Atlanta as the sixth most globally connected city in the United States, just behind San Francisco and Miami and just ahead of Washington, D.C., and Boston.

22. Eliana Dockterman, "How Georgia Became the Hollywood of the South," *Time*, July 31, 2019, https://time.com/longform/hollywood-in-georgia/.

23. Ibid.

24. Patricia Mazzei and Alan Blinder, "Georgia Governor Signs 'Fetal Heartbeat' Abortion Law," *New York Times*, May 7, 2019, www.nytimes.com/2019/05/07/us/heartbeat-bill-georgia.html.

25. Yohana Desta, "Hollywood Takes Strong Stand against Georgia's Controversial Heartbeat Bill," *Vanity Fair*, May 8, 2019, www.vanityfair.com/hollywood/2019/05/hollywood-response-georgia-heartbeat-bill-abortion.

26. Fentit Nirappil, "For Democrats, the Elusive Dream of a Blue Georgia Hinges on Rapidly Diversifying Atlanta Suburbs," *Washington Post*, July 30, 2018, www.washingtonpost.com/politics/for-democrats-the-elusive-dream-of-a-blue-georgia-hinges-on-rapidly-diversifying-atlanta-suburbs/2018/07/30/84802c2a-9025-11e8-b769-e3fff17f0689_story.html.

27. Ibid.

28. Derek Thompson, "American Migration Patterns Should Terrify the GOP," *The Atlantic*, September 17, 2019, www.theatlantic.com/ideas/archive/2019/09/american-migration-patterns-should-terrify-gop/598153/.

29. Gimpel and Schuknecht, *Patchwork Nation*.

30. Atlanta lies at a high elevation compared to most major American metropolitan areas. Atlanta is exceeded in elevation by only Mountain West major urban regions such as Denver. Atlanta has the highest median urban elevation among the ten most populous metropolitan areas in the United States.

31. Gimpel and Schuknecht, *Patchwork Nation.*

32. The official name of the map is "Map Showing the Distribution of the Slave Population of Southern States of the United States compiled by the Census of 1860." It was printed in Washington, D.C., in September 1861. Rebecca Onion, "The Map That Lincoln Used to See the Reach of Slavery," *Slate*, September 4, 2013, https://slate.com/human-interest/2013/09/abraham-lincoln-the-president-used-this-map-to-see-where-slavery-was-strongest.html.

33. This pattern of rural Black concentration along the southern Mississippi River is so pronounced into the late twentieth century that, in 1992, Bill Clinton won all counties along the Mississippi River based on Black turnout.

34. Manuel A. Vasquez, "Latino Immigration in the South: Emerging Trends and Critical Issues," *Just South Reports*, presented at Jesuit Social Research Institute People on the Move Conference Loyola University—New Orleans, Louisiana, November 9, 2009, www.loyno.edu/jsri/latino-immigration-south-emerging-trends-and-critical-issues.

35. Thomas D. Wilson, *The Oglethorpe Plan: Enlightenment and Design in Savannah and Beyond* (University of Virginia Press, 2015).

36. For a sense of Savannah's eccentricities, see John Berendt's 1994 book *Midnight in the Garden of Good and Evil.* John Berendt, *Midnight in the Garden of Good and Evil* (New York: Random House, 1994).

37. Charles S. Bullock and Ronald K. Gaddie, *Georgia Politics in a State of Change* (London: Pearson, 2009).

38. Democrat Eugene Talmadge was Georgia's sixty-seventh governor, serving from 1933 to 1937 and from 1941 to 1943.

39. Metropolitan Atlanta had 5,949,951 residents as of July 1, 2018, as estimated by the U.S. Census Bureau, "County and Metro Population Estimates."

40. Republican Brian Kemp is Georgia's current governor. He was elected in 2018.

41. Republican Nathan Deal was Georgia's eighty-second governor, serving from 2011 to 2019.

42. U.S. Census Bureau, "2018 National and State Population Estimates."

43. At 6,684 feet, Mount Mitchell is the highest point in the United States east of the Mississippi River.

44. Arthur C. Nelson and Robert E. Lang, *Megapolitan America: A New Vision for Understanding America's Metropolitan Geography* (Chicago: American Planning Association Press, 2011).

45. Ibid.

46. Robert E. Lang and Jennifer LeFurgy in their 2007 book *Boomburbs: The Rise of America's Accidental Cities* (Washington: Brookings Institution Press, 2007), identify Cary, North Carolina, as a boomburb. A boomburb is a large, urbanizing suburb that has seen its population grow by double digits in every census since 1950. Boomburbs are especially prominent in large metropolitan areas in California, Texas, Florida, and the Mountain West states.

47. Asma Khalid, "Newcomers to the South Mark Shift in Regional Politics," *National Public Radio*, August, 11, 2016, www.npr.org/2016/08/11/489661947/new comers-to-u-s-south-mark-shift-in-regional-politics.

48. David Kroll, "RTP: Research Triangle Primer," *Forbes*, October 22, 2012, www. forbes.com/sites/davidkroll/2012/10/22/rtp-research-triangle-primer/.

49. U.S. Bureau of the Census, *Metropolitan and Micropolitan Statistical Areas Population Totals and Components of Change* (U.S. Department of Commerce, March 26, 2020). The nine-county Raleigh-Durham-Cary CSA had a population of 2,079,687 as of July 1, 2019, based on county estimates.

50. Scott Jaschik, "Protestors Tear Down Silent Sam," *Inside Higher Education*, August 21, 2018, www.insidehighered.com/news/2018/08/21/protesters-tear-down -confederate-statue-unc-chapel-hill.

51. Greg Toppo and Paul Overberg, "After Nearly 100 Years, Great Migration Begins Reversal: College Grads and Retirees are Leading the Return of Blacks to the South," *USA Today*, February 2, 2015, www.usatoday.com/story/news/nation/2015 /02/02/census-great-migration-reversal/21818127/.

52. U.S. Bureau of the Census, *County and Metro Population Estimates*.

53. We use MSAs instead of CSAs for our major metro geography because combined statistical areas are not fully comparable to metropolitan statistical areas. For example, there are major metros such as Austin, Texas, where there is only an MSA and no CSA. Also, CSA county components are less stable than MSAs. The census's American Community Survey updates MSA and CSA components based on commuting patterns between counties as determined by the "employment-interchange measure" (see box 1-1). Counties at the CSA fringe often enter and leave the region with census updates, making CSA geography less fixed than MSAs. For example, the Las Vegas CSA earlier last decade included Mohave County, Arizona. Yet in the 2019 census "components of change" update, Mohave County was not included in the Las Vegas CSA. Had we selected CSAs as the metro unit of analysis and used the 1 million population threshold as the criterion for inclusion as a "major metro," there would be one more state and six more million-plus metros in the study. Because the Albuquerque-Santa Fe-Las Vegas, NM CSA exceeds a million residents (with 1,156,187 people in 2018), and New Mexico was decided by less than a ten-point margin in the 2016 presidential election, the Land of Enchantment would have been the fourteenth swing state using this criteria. The other CSAs that would have made the million-plus metro threshold in the other swing states (besides those in the Piedmont Triad) are: Cape Coral-Fort Myers-Naples, FL CSA (population 1,174,654); Dayton-Springfield-Kettering, OH CSA (population 1,079,837); El Paso-Las Cruces, TX-NM CSA (population 1,063,075); and North Port-Sarasota-Bradenton, FL CSA (population 1,044,060).

54. Ibid.

55. Nelson and Lang, *Megapolitan America*.

56. Plans stalled for years on the section of I-95 that would eventually become the Fayetteville Bypass. Despite the fact that the environmental review on the

project was completed in 1972, Fayetteville resisted completing the project until 1982. Matt Leclercq, "I-95 Near Fayetteville Will be Widened to Eight Lanes," *Fayetteville Observer*, June 5, 2018, www.fayobserver.com/news/20180605/i-95-near -fayetteville-will-be-widened-to-8-lanes.

57. Hunter Ingram and Renee Spencer, "Welcome to Boomtown: Wilmington, Region Continue to Grow," *Wilmington Star News*, April 19, 2019, www.starnewsonline. com/news/20190419/welcome-to-boomtown-wilmington-region-continue-rapid -growth.

58. U.S. Census Bureau, "County and Metro Population Estimates."

59. Cameron McWhirter, "Forget Florida: More Northern Retirees Head to Appalachia," *Wall Street Journal*, May 15, 2018, www.wsj.com/articles/forget-flor ida-more-northern-retirees-head-to-appalachia-1526388500.

60. Ella Nilsen and Tara Golshan, "A North Carolina Court Just Threw Out Republicans Gerrymandered State Legislative Maps," *Vox.com*, September 3, 2019, www.vox.com/policy-and-politics/2019/9/3/20848087/north-carolina-court -republican-gerrymander-state-legislature-map.

61. Ibid.

62. In 1971, North Carolina added an amendment to its state constitution to allow the governor to serve two terms. Until then, the state's governor was limited to a single term. In 1980, Democratic Governor Jim Hunt became North Carolina's first chief executive eligible to run for two terms. Hunt was the sixty-ninth and seventy-first governor of North Carolina, serving from 1977 to 1985 and from 1993 to 2001.

63. Frayda S. Bluestein is a Distinguished Professor of Public Law and Government at the University of North Carolina-Chapel Hill.

64. Charlotte is a city in Mecklenburg County.

65. Wiccans practice pagan witchcraft as a religion. For an interesting piece on the Wiccans in Ashville, see Tara I. Burton, "I spent the Eclipse with Ashville's Witches," *Vox.com*, August 21, 2017, www.vox.com/identities/2017/8/21/16178848/ eclipse-asheville-witches.

66. As noted in the State of Play section, North Carolina lacks a dominant metropolitan area, as in the case of Georgia, where the Atlanta region accounts for a majority of the state's population. The urbanized sections of North Carolina remain fragmented in a series of smaller metropolitan areas that lie along I-85 in the Carolina Piedmont. See Nelson and Lang, *Megapolitan America*.

67. Mayberry was the mythical town in the *Andy Griffith Show*, which aired on CBS Television from 1960 to 1968 and was based on Andy Griffith's hometown of Mount Airy, North Carolina. See Lynne Brandon, "Mount Airy: Mayberry and Memories," *1808 Greensboro New and Record*, June 29, 2018, www.greensboro. com/1808greensboro/mount-airy-mayberry-and-memories/article_70796a66-e9f4-5385-9eb1-5e168b6e6baa.html.

5

FLORIDA

Karen A. Danielsen

The place is geographically huge, almost prohibitively
expensive, exceptionally diverse in many ways, with huge
chunks of voters who cancel each other out. It is a place
that structurally wants to be hyper competitive. Take the
Senate race—I've argued for nearly a year that despite
what the polls say, both Bill Nelson and Rick Scott have
a floor of 47% or 48%. Both parties have huge and loyal
bases—neither has a clear base path to 50%. A handful
of voters decide every election—and within that cohort
one will find very few commonalties. The place is both
fascinating, and maddening.[1]

—*Steve Schale*

Florida is among the most politically interesting states in
the United States. It is, for the moment, the most populous and pivotal
swing state in the nation—having decided the contested 2000 presidential election between Republican George W. Bush and Democrat
Al Gore.[2] In the last three election cycles, a margin of less than 3 percentage points determined Florida's Electoral College votes. Barack
Obama won the state by narrow margins in 2008 and 2012.[3] Trump
won Florida by an equally close figure in 2016.[4] In 2018, the races for
Florida's U.S. Senate and governor's seats were so close that a recount
was needed to settle both contests.[5]

With over 21 million residents, Florida is now the third-largest
state in the United States, behind California and Texas (Florida passed
New York in 2014).[6] Florida currently has twenty-nine Electoral Col-

lege votes, and is on track to pick up two new seats in the U.S. House of Representatives based on reapportionment following the 2020 census.[7] To put that growth in perspective, consider that, in the 1980 election, Florida was tied with New Jersey with seventeen electoral votes. Thus, Florida is not only the biggest toss-up state; it is also growing so quickly that by the 2024 presidential election it may have as many as thirty-one Electoral College votes.

STATE OF PLAY: FLORIDA

Florida features five political divisions that are as culturally and politically different from one another as they are from the rest of the nation (see figure 5-1). James G. Gimpel and Jason E. Schuknecht also divide Florida into five political regions.[8] However, they show an "Atlantic Coast" region that extends from Jacksonville south to Palm Beach.[9] Ruy Teixeria and William H. Frey divide Florida into just four political sections—North Florida, I-4 Corridor, South Florida, and Miami Metro—and include Jacksonville in the north section.[10] Interestingly, researchers looking at Florida's political geography do not agree on the Jacksonville metropolitan area's location within the state's political sections. In this book, Jacksonville forms a distinct political region that borders on the Florida Panhandle to the west and the I-4 Corridor to the south.[11]

The Florida Peninsula qualifies as what cultural geographer Wilbur Zelinsky calls a "Voluntary Region."[12] According to Rex J. Rowley, "voluntary regions are places that attract individual, like-minded people away from long-standing 'traditional regions,' based on a desire for amenity and economic opportunity."[13] People moved to Florida mostly from the eastern half of the United States. The Northeast provides most migrants to southeast Florida, or greater Miami. There is a point along I-95 where one can travel so far south (in direction) that they have effectively left the South (as a cultural zone).[14] The Miami metropolitan area feels more a part of the Caribbean than the American South, given the region's climate and racial diversity (see table 5-1).[15]

A look at the Roosevelt-era *Works Progress Administration Guide to Florida* (*WPA Guide*) from 1940 shows how dramatically Florida has changed over the last eighty years.[16] In 1940, the state had less than a

FIGURE 5-1. Florida

TABLE 5-1. Demographic and Economic Comparison between Florida and Metros

	Florida	Share in Jacksonville (%)	Share in Miami (%)	Share in Orlando (%)	Share in Tampa (%)
Population	20,984,400	7.2	29.3	12.0	14.7
White	53.8%	8.4	16.5	10.4	17.2
Black	15.4%	9.8	38.6	11.9	11.1
Asian	2.8%	10.7	26.1	18.4	18.6
Latino	25.6%	2.5	51.9	14.2	11.2
Foreign-Born	20.9%	3.2	57.7	10.7	10.0
College Educated	29.7%	7.2	31.7	12.4	15.0
Jobs	9,669,230	7.5	30.9	13.0	15.0
GDP	$835,928	7.8	35.6	14.0	15.4

Sources: 2017 American Community Survey 1-Year estimates as aggregated by censusreporter.org, Department of Commerce, Bureau of Economic Analysis, 2015 Real GDP (millions of chained 2012 dollars) County Level Data, U.S. Department of Labor, Bureau of Labor Statistics 2017 County Level Data.

tenth its current population, with 1.9 million residents. Thus, modern Florida is a product of just one lifetime, where it transitioned from a sleepy southern outpost dependent on citrus and sunshine to become one of the three largest states in the Union and the eastern anchor of the booming American Sunbelt. Yet, the *WPA Guide* shows that even in 1940 Florida had already established a settlement pattern that would be reinforced significantly by future migration. As the *WPA Guide* notes:

> Politically and socially, Florida has its own North and South, but its northern area is strictly southern and its southern area definitely northern. In the summer the State is predominately southern by birth and adoptions, and in winter it is northern by invasion. At all seasons it is divided into Old and New Florida, separated by the Suwannee River. The political thought that controls it originates in a united minority above the Suwannee and reaches down into the more populated peninsula to impose the diminishing theory that Florida should be preserved for Floridians rather than exploited for visitors.[17]

Finally, Florida, like North Carolina, lacks a single large metropolitan area that politically dominates the state (although greater Miami on its own is an enormous region). Rather, Florida has four million-plus metros—Miami, Orlando, Tampa, and Jacksonville. Politically, this means that metropolitan areas must form coalitions if they seek, for instance, state funding for investment in infrastructure. A good example of metro-to-metro coalition building was the effort in the 2000s to establish new state-supported medical schools in Miami (at Florida International University) and Orlando (at the University of Central Florida). Karen Danielsen and Robert Lang report that the civic leadership in Orlando sought an alliance with those in Miami to show a united front when they lobbied the state legislature and the governor for new medical schools.[18] While Miami and Orlando combined do not constitute a majority of votes in the state legislature, they are just below that threshold. Tampa, which Arthur C. Nelson and Robert Lang include in an unified megapolitan area with Orlando, often supports Orlando on resource investments along the I-4 Corridor. The combo of the I-4 megapolitian area with Greater Miami does constitute a majority share of voters and representatives in the legislature.[19]

Panhandle

The Panhandle, which runs from west of metropolitan Jacksonville and stretches about 200 miles to the Alabama border, just east of Mobile Bay, is the most conservative part of Florida.[20] Parts of the Panhandle are so far west that they are in the Central Time Zone. The region developed early in the state's history because it was not swampland, unlike much of the Florida peninsula. It contains the state capital of Tallahassee, which is located at the Panhandle's midpoint and, thus, reflects a central location for much of Florida's original nineteenth-century population.

The Panhandle is the reddest section of the Sunshine State and the most Southern in social and cultural character, which is ironic given it is the most northern part of Florida. A surge in Panhandle voters in the 2018 presidential election helped deliver the state to Donald Trump.[21] Were the Panhandle not part of Florida but, instead, formed a Gulf of Mexico coast for Georgia and Alabama, Florida would almost certainly be a blue state.

I-4 Corridor

A key swing section in Florida politics is the so-called I-4 Corridor that connects metropolitan Orlando and Tampa. Much has been written about the I-4 Corridor because it is the major swing district in the most important swing state.[22] Therefore, understanding its politics is critical to securing the electoral votes needed to win a presidential election. And it is a key to understanding sectional and metropolitan political coalitions in state politics.

The I-4 Corridor is not monolithic in its culture, economy, or politics. Orlando and Tampa, while proximate to one another, represent very different political worlds.[23] Orlando is a booming, vibrant economy based largely on tourism. It is rapidly filling with immigrants, both foreign and domestic, that continue to swell its population. One of the most notable immigrant groups attracted to Orlando are Puerto Ricans. Residents of Puerto Rico are American citizens at birth. Thus, unlike other Latino immigrants to Florida, a move from Puerto Rico to the Sunshine State represents a domestic migration. Puerto Ricans, the leading Latino population in Central Florida, are eligible to vote by age eighteen once they move to Florida. Outside Miami, Orlando has the largest share of voter-eligible Latinos in Florida.[24] Puerto Ricans lean strongly Democratic, and their presence in the I-4 Corridor can swing Florida blue in statewide races.

Disasters in Puerto Rico, such as Hurricane Maria in 2018, can induce migration to mainland United States, with Central Florida serving as one of the leading destinations.[25] Hurricane Maria, a Category 5 storm, so disrupted commerce and infrastructure on the island that thousands of Puerto Ricans sought refuge, mostly in Florida. As the impact of the storm unfolded, a migratory stream began to the United States in general and Orlando in particular.[26]

The west side of the I-4 Corridor tends to be more moderate-to-conservative in character. Polk County, which lies between Tampa and Orlando, is the most conservative part of the I-4 Corridor, but that pattern is shifting as residents from Orange County (which includes Orlando) spill over into the eastern part of Polk County. Many of the new residents are minorities who work in the tourist sector in places such as Disney World and Universal Studios.

Table 5-2 shows the vote shares in the past several statewide elections for both Orlando and Tampa. Note that Orlando votes more consistently for the Democrats than Tampa. And Orlando appears to be turning a deeper blue when comparing the 2012 and 2016 presidential elections. In 2012, President Obama won the region by a 7.7 percent, while Hillary Clinton's margin in 2016 was 11.6 percent. Thus Clinton actually gained votes in metro Orlando compared to Obama in 2012, though she lost Florida while Obama won the state in 2012.

The demographic data from table 5-1 shows that both the Tampa and Orlando metropolitan areas, which anchor the I-4 Corridor, are both more diverse that the state of Florida as a whole. Both regions have significant Asian communities, while Orlando is home to more Latinos than Tampa. Neither metro has large foreign-born populations, especially when compared with Miami. This is in part because

TABLE 5-2. Comparison of Electoral Outcomes between Florida and Metros

Election	Florida Outcome	Jacksonville Vote Share [%]	Jacksonville Outcome	Miami Vote Share [%]	Miami Outcome	Orlando Vote Share [%]	Orlando Outcome	Tampa Vote Share [%]	Tampa Outcome
2018 U.S. Senate	+0.1 Rep	8.0	+14.8 Rep	25.3	+25.5 Dem	11.6	+11.0 Dem	15.3	+1.1 Dem
2018 Gubernatorial	+0.4 Rep	8.0	+12.7 Rep	25.4	+25.2 Dem	11.5	+12.4 Dem	15.2	+0.4 Dem
2016 Presidential	+1.2 Rep	7.9	+4.8 Rep	26.4	+27.5 Dem	11.6	+11.6 Dem	15.2	+3.0 Rep
2016 U.S. Senate	+7.7 Rep	7.9	+29.7 Rep	26.3	+17.0 Dem	11.6	+2.1 Dem	15.3	+5.3 Rep
2014 Gubernatorial	+1.1 Rep	7.8	+25.7 Rep	23.8	+25.9 Dem	10.7	+1.8 Dem	16.0	+4.7 Dem
2012 Presidential	+0.9 Dem	8.0	+19.0 Rep	26.5	+25.6 Dem	11.0	+7.7 Dem	15.3	+3.1 Dem
2012 U.S. Senate	+13.0 Dem	8.1	+2.4 Dem	26.4	+32.1 Dem	10.9	+20.2 Dem	15.4	+18.6 Dem

Source: Data from Florida secretary of state's website.

Latino migrants come mostly from Puerto Rico and are, therefore, American citizens at birth.

Metro Jacksonville

Another red-leaning political section of Florida is the Jacksonville metropolitan area. Jacksonville has a Southern feel in that it is Florida's largest northern metropolitan area (again, to find the South in Florida, one must go north). But with over 1 million residents, the city is large-scale and cosmopolitan enough to have a moderating effect on its Southern-influenced politics. The region also contains a substantial African American population, which also moderates its politics by offsetting conservative white voters. The liberal college town of Gainesville (home to the University of Florida) at the western edge of metro Jacksonville also provides a counterbalance to white conservative voters in suburban Jacksonville.

The demographic data in table 5-1 shows that Jacksonville is the least diverse million-plus metropolitan area in Florida. Jacksonville maintains sizable Asian (mostly Filipino) and Black communities. But the metro lacks Latino and foreign-born residents, although Puerto Ricans are beginning to migrate to Jacksonville as a lower-cost alternative to Orlando.

Table 5-2 shows that while Jacksonville remains a Republican-leaning section of Florida, Democrats have made gains in presidential years. In 2012, President Obama lost the Jacksonville metropolitan area to Republican Mitt Romney by a 19 percent margin. Yet in 2016, Democrat Hillary Clinton lost Jacksonville by only 4.8 percent. The metro's changing demographics are shifting the region to a swing district in presidential election years and bringing it roughly in line with the Tampa metropolitan area.

Jacksonville is also shifting economically as it transitions to a more tech-driven business environment. For example, Jacksonville led all U.S. metros in growth for technology jobs in a tech job survey by Burning Glass Technologies. Jacksonville had the most year-over-year growth for these jobs, adding 54 percent more job listings from 2018–19 in its core industries of banking and insurance.[27] Having a booming tech economy tends to draw on a diverse and educated workforce who vote more often for Democrats.[28]

South Florida

The largest, most diverse urban complex in the Sunshine State is South Florida, which runs from the area just south of Cape Canaveral in the north to Miami (Dade County) and the Florida Keys in the south. The region was mostly uninhabitable until the early twentieth century when the U.S. Army Corps of Engineers devised a way to drain the swampland along the coast.[29] South Florida's mild winters and rail connections to the Northeast sparked a real estate frenzy that resulted in boom-and-bust cycles that, nonetheless, ratcheted up the region's population to big metropolitan status by the mid- to late-twentieth century. As noted, South Florida today feels more a part of the Caribbean or Latin America than the rest of the United States. In fact, the region has positioned itself as the nation's gateway to Latin America—via trade and banking.[30]

Demographically, South Florida is a majority-minority region, with Latinos representing the largest minority group—comprising over half the total Latino population of the Sunshine State (see table 5-1). There is also a substantial Black population, with immigration from parts of the Caribbean such as Haiti and Jamaica that adds to the domestic African American population.[31] The white population of South Florida is also notable in that it is distinctly non-Southern in character. Many white residents in South Florida have county-at-birth origins in the Northeast, especially counties in New York and New Jersey.[32]

Despite being the southernmost part of the mainland United States, South Florida is among the least Southern places in America by culture and politics. South Florida as a whole is a solid blue metropolitan area and serves as a political counterweight to the deeply conservative Florida Panhandle. The most conservative subset of South Florida's population is not whites from the Northeast but, instead, a Cuban population that dates to the Cuban revolution in 1959. For sixty-plus years, the ex-pat Cuban community has opposed the communist regime in their homeland. Because of the Republican Party's historic strong anti-communist stance, many South Florida Cubans came to identify with and vote for the GOP.[33] This one minority group in one part of one state has driven Cuban American relations for decades and, in return, has handed Republican wins in statewide elections, including in 2000 when the Elián González case helped George W. Bush win the presidential election.[34]

Despite the Cuban Republican vote, South Florida (for example, Miami metro) remains the most liberal political section within the state. Table 5-2 shows that Democrats win the region on average by at least 25 percent (the exception being the 2016 U.S. Senate race). South Florida's vote share remains consistent over this decade (at just over a quarter) and, due to a large foreign-born population (see table 5-1), is a smaller figure than the region's total population share of the state (just under 30 percent).

Florida major metros, especially Miami, have a plethora of fast-growing, large-scale urbanizing suburbs with over 50,000 residents. Robert Lang and Jennifer LeFurgy label such places "boomburbs."[35] South Florida boomburbs include such municipalities as Coral Springs (population 133,507), Hialeah (population 238,942), and Pembroke Pines (population 173,374), along with eleven other examples.[36] The biggest boomburb in the I-4 Corridor is Clearwater (population 116,478) outside of Tampa. Florida's many boomburbs include a diverse array of places, many of which Lang and LeFurgy found to have such a large share of minority and foreign-born population that they labeled it, along with other such diverse places, as a "New Brooklyn."[37] With nearly 239,000 residents, Hialeah exceeds traditional cities such as Boise, Idaho (population 228,790), and Des Moines, Iowa (population 216, 853), in population and is far denser and diverse than either of those two cities.

Gulf Coast

Finally, the last key section of Florida to consider is the Gulf Coast—or the west coast of Florida. This area runs from the Tampa metropolitan area south to the Everglades. Cities such as Sarasota, Naples, and Fort Myers lie within the Gulf Coast. The Gulf Coast of Florida is far less urban and less diverse than South Florida. And the white population in this part of the Sunshine State mostly did not immigrate from the Northeast. Rather, they are often Midwestern in origin. There is a sorting or self-selection of more conservative immigrants to Florida who choose to live on the Gulf Coast. These migrants want beach-front communities but avoid the more urban and diverse Atlantic coast of Florida.[38] And the Midwesterners from small-town and suburban Ohio and Michigan who now call the Gulf Coast home are mostly conservative. The net effect is that the red Gulf Coast adds conservative ranks to the historically Republican Panhandle and makes Florida a nearly 50/50 Republican/Democratic state in the senate, gubernatorial, and presidential races.

Conclusion: Florida State of Play

The complex and ever-shifting balance between regions has kept Florida on a razor's edge politically for two decades. It is hard to predict when Florida may finally swing definitively one direction or another. But given the growth in the minority population and a trend among Cubans under thirty to vote for Democrats. Florida may turn blue, or pale blue, in a couple of election cycles. For now, the state remains up for grabs.

Table 5-3 shows that the current Florida delegation in the U.S. House of Representatives is nearly even, with thirteen Democrats and fourteen Republicans. In the 2018 midterm election, the Democrats picked up two U.S. House of Representatives seats, while losing a high-profile U.S. Senate race by a slender margin. Democrats also made gains in the statehouse in the 2018 midterm election, although they are still in the minority in both the Upper and Lower House within Florida's state legislature (see table 5-3).

Finally, table 5-4 indicates that Florida local governments have a high degree of autonomy from state government, ranking twelfth in the United States. That means that liberal metros such as Miami and Orlando are free to develop a good deal of local policy in areas such as economic development and infrastructure investment without having to constantly seek approval from Tallahassee. Given the diverse nature of Florida's politics and its strong regional identities that drive state sectionalism, having local autonomy mitigates some of the potential state-level conflict by allowing a measure of regional sovereignty.

TABLE 5-3. Partisan Composition of Florida State
Government and Federal Delegation

| | | State Government | | | | Federal Delegation | | | |
| | | Upper House | | Lower House | | U.S. Senate | | U.S. House | |
	Governor	Dems	Reps	Dems	Reps	Dems	Reps	Dems	Reps
2019–20	Rep	17	23	47	73	0	2	13	14
2017–18	Rep	15	25	41	79	1	1	11	16
2015–16	Rep	14	26	37	82	1	1	10	27
2013–14	Rep	14	26	46	74	1	1	10	17

Sources: Data from National Conference of State Legislatures, "State and Legislative Partisan
Composition" for various years, and Florida secretary of state's website.

TABLE 5-4. Metro Governance Fragmentation
and Autonomy in Florida

Governance Fragmentation

Metro	Number of Counties in Metro	Number of General Purposes Governments in Metro
Jacksonville	5	21
Miami	3	107
Orlando	4	40
Tampa	4	39

Governance Autonomy

Local Government Autonomy Score	0.247
Local Government Autonomy Ranking	12

Sources: Data for Governance Fragmentation from 2017 Census of Governments.
Data for Governance Autonomy from Harold Wolman, Robert McManmon, Michael
Bell, and David Brunori, "Comparing Local Government Autonomy Across States,"
in *The Property Tax and Local Autonomy*, edited by Michael Bell, David Brunori, and
Joan Youngman (Lincoln Institute of Land Policy Press, 2010), pp. 69–114.

EXPERT ANALYSIS: FLORIDA

Expert analysis was provided by four distinguished observers of Florida politics: Dr. Darryl Paulson, emeritus professor of government at the University of South Florida in Tampa, Florida, a specialist in U.S. political parties and elections, Florida, and Southern politics (interviewed May 3, 2018); Dr. Sean Foreman, chair of the Department of History and Political Science and professor of political science of Barry University in Miami Shores, Florida, whose research interests include U.S. politics and elections, state and local government, and the politics and economics of sports (interviewed May 8, 2018); Dr. Brian Fonseca, director of the Jack D. Gordon Institute for Public Policy at Florida International University in Miami, Florida, with a technical expertise in U.S. national security and foreign policy (interviewed May 15, 2018); and Dr. Richard Phillips, associate professor of sociology and religious studies at the University of North Florida in Jacksonville, Florida, whose expertise is the sociology of religion and the regional dynamics associated with place identity (interviewed May 16, 2018).[39] Note that all interviews were conducted ahead of the 2018 midterm election.[40] Remarkably, the experts were mostly accurate in their predictions, especially in the political dynamics and the outcomes of the House and Senate races in fall 2018.

Intrastate Political Dynamics

Florida, as all the experts agree, is an extremely complex state politically. Power has shifted in the last fifty to sixty years from a time where sparsely populated rural areas exerted more political clout in a political arena to where power is now distributed between rural and metropolitan areas. Tremendous population growth over this time period has taken Florida from the "least populated [southern] state east of the Mississippi River" in the middle of the twentieth century to the country's third-largest state and growing.[41]

Professor Paulson chronicled the scale of demographic change over the last century in terms of population and its immediate political impact. He noted that, around 1900, 75 percent of all the state's population lived in North Florida; now about 80 percent live within twenty to twenty-five miles of either the east or west coast. Furthermore, he continues: "about two-thirds of the population are not native to the state of Florida. Only the state of Nevada has more non-native residents." The percentage of non-native residents has a profound political impact on any state, particularly "if two-thirds of your citizens come from somewhere else, it's very difficult for politicians to put together majority coalitions and to find issues that are going to attract these people to support particular candidates or particular parties."

Changes in Florida's Congressional Delegation

Paulson also reported that population change has had a significant impact on state politics in general but more so on the size of the congressional representation in the state over the last half century. Florida had only one member of Congress when it gained statehood in 1845. As late as World War II, the state sent only six members to Washington, D.C. Currently, the Sunshine State's delegation is the third largest in Congress, with twenty-seven members, and is likely to increase to at least twenty-nine after the 2020 census and reapportionment, in Paulson's estimation.

He also traces the how the Republicans began to win federal and state offices:

You first had this presidential Republicanism, and then Republicans would start to win some of the Senate races and some of the congressional races. In my area here [Tampa] the first Republican congressional seat that the Republicans won was back in 1954 when Bill Kramer became the congressman for what was Pinellas and part of Hillsborough County, which is Tampa, and also Castro County at that time. He was the first Republican congressman since prior to the end of Reconstruction, some sixty-eighty years ago. But gradually, Republicans would pick up strength, in the Senate and the House and then it would filter down to the state legislature. Finally, in the 1990s, the Florida Senate went Republican.

Two years later, the Florida House went Republican, so it's very clearly a top-down process in terms of politics. But Barack Obama won a majority of the suburban vote in Florida in both 2008 and

2012. He narrowly won, but everyone thinks with suburbs being strong Republican territory but that wasn't the case

Republicans have done very well; they now completely control the state of Florida, but that's very much in jeopardy with the 2018 election. It's the first time, really, since they took political control in the 1990s that there's a serious threat to Republican Party domination. They control about 60 percent of both the Florida House and Senate. Of the twenty-seven congressional seats, Republicans now hold sixteen of those seats. Democrats hold eleven. Democrats are very likely going to pick up anywhere between two and four congressional seats, so they have the opportunity the first time in thirty years to take over political control of the Florida congressional delegation. I'm not saying it will happen, but they've got a great opportunity to do so.

Republicans dominate all the statewide elected offices, but the only one they don't hold is Bill Nelson's Senate seat. That's why there's so much interest in this [race]. Rick Scott is really the first serious candidate that Bill Nelson has faced. It's oftentimes been said that there's no luckier politician in America than Bill Nelson. The first time he ran for the senate in 2000, he ran against Bill McCollum, who was not exactly known as "Mr. Charisma." Nelson was able to easily defeat him. Six years later, he ran against Katherine Harris, who had been the [Florida] secretary of state during the George Bush election in the 2000 election. Even though she won the Republican primary, she got creamed by Bill Nelson. That was just a devastating blow for the Republicans because many Republicans thought they should have won, except for the fact that Harris was their candidate. In 2012, Nelson ran against Connie Mack IV, who was going through a very messy divorce at that time, and had arrests for several fist fights and drunkenness. Bill Nelson has faced three easy candidates. He's had the good luck of facing them in past campaigns.

Now, for the first time, he's facing a well-funded candidate. But he's still won in two races that everyone thought he was going to lose; that's why so much attention is going to be focused in on this Senate race in Florida. It will probably be the Senate race of the year.

The congressional delegation growth reflects the degree to which the state has accumulated population over the last half century. The experts commented extensively on not just the population growth but how specific groups have changed the political landscape of the state at all levels, congressional, state, and metropolitan areas. The population changes have exerted the strongest influence on the congressional delegation, particularly in South Florida. For instance, both Foreman and Fonseca mention specific changes in the 26th and 27th Congressional Districts. They both focus on Ileana Ros-Lehtinen, the former representative from the 27th District,[42] as an indication of how an already moderate Republican had to swing even more to the left. She was able to keep her seat for thirty years in what was considered a safe, Republican-leaning district. She, according to Foreman, had been able to run uncontested in a couple of the past election cycles and was able to win comfortably "because the value of incumbency that she had built up over the thirty years." But that is changing now, as Fonseca observes:

Take a seat like Ileana Ros-Lehtinen, for example, [in] District 27 [that] has been held by a Republican for a very, very long time. It is now the Democrats' seat to lose because Ileana has opted to bow out. She will not run for reelection, and she says she's not really running for reelection for one reason, but the reality is the data tells us she's not running for reelection because she's now beatable. She was never as vulnerable as she is now because her district has moved so far toward the Democratic side, and she's also shifted in terms of her views to align with [progressive issues] where she could. But now, it's getting so pronounced that someone like [Scott] Fuhrman jumped in the race. He's a young guy in his late twenties or early thirties, has three recent DUIs on his record, including one where he ran away from a police officer. He was able to get within ten points of Ileana. . . . That was the writing on the wall for Ileana. She decided she wasn't going to run for reelection. So now that seat is up[43] and in the big ticket [race] there now is Donna Shalala. Even though it has become a festival with dozens of names thrown in the hat, it's now largely argued that it's a Democrat's seat to lose.[44]

Foreman forecasts a similar Republican turnover for the 27th District:

Ileana Ros-Lehtinen, who is retiring from Congress this year, is a moderate Republican. She won her district . . . [one] that Hillary Clinton won by a large amount, but Republican candidate Ros-Lehtinen also won by a significant amount. I think [it was] the biggest red [win] in the country. She's retiring, so that district is a wide-open competition with competitive primaries on each side. And the reason Ros-Lehtinen was able to win by such comfortable margins, even in the environment where she was vocally anti-Donald Trump's candidacy . . . [was because] . . . of the value of incumbency she had built up over thirty years, the personal relationships, the likability, the reputation for strong constituent service. That is a seat that could potentially flip to [a] Democrat based on the numbers, but we're going to have to see who the personalities are, who will win the primary.

Another important South Florida U.S. House seat that is shifting away from the Republicans is the 26th District (which it did in the 2018 midterm election). Fonseca observes that the 26th District is politically changing, much like the 27th:

It's the same thing with, for example, Carlos Curbelo's congressional seat . . . his time is up.[45] He's not going to run much going forward because that district is also moving quickly blue. So Broward in South Florida is pivoting away toward the blue.

Foreman concurs with Fonseca but again illustrates that South Florida Republicans are trying to adapt to the current political arena by moderating their views on more progressive issues, such as climate change and LGBTQ (lesbian, gay, bisexual, transgender, queer) rights:

Carlos Curbelo, who's an incumbent [in District 26], is also being targeted because that's a swing district. He has been successful so far in his couple of terms in Congress by taking more moderate stances on climate change and on LGBTQ rights and, at least in rhetoric, being in line with his district on healthcare and affordable housing issues. I think that [it is true] at least [for] the Republicans in Congress in South Florida . . . and you can put Mario Díaz-Balart in the category but to a lesser extent. He's more conservative in his work in serving along these issues than the other two. These top Florida Republicans [have had to] moderate as their views on these issues [since] they are critical to South Florida voters.

Phillips sees Senator Rick Scott, Florida's governor in 2018, also moderating to accommodate Puerto Ricans interests in the Jacksonville area:

The Puerto Rican influence is going to be massive in statewide politics. Everything you see is that the typical Republican has tacked to the center to make sure they're palatable in statewide politics. I don't even recognize Rick Scott these days; I don't even know who Rick Scott is anymore. Because the Rick Scott who's running for the Senate against Bill Nelson[46] is nothing like the Rick Scott that ran for governor. One thing about that guy is he's good at sticking his finger in the wind to see which way it's blowing. The closer we get to the election, the less tied to Trump he is. I haven't heard him utter Trump's name in a long time and he's acting pretty moderate these days. If you just listen to the way Rick Scott behaves, I think that's a good bellwether. Rick Scott's in an excellent position to win the Senate race because he just benefits from the housing market destroyed [and] the recession [that] destroyed Florida's economy. Lucky for Rick Scott, he has been presiding over an economic recovery that's been going on now for the past eight years. I don't know how much credit for that he deserves—probably none. But the fact is that he was in office when things have been progressively getting better and better. Bill Nelson is an old guy; he's been there forever. I would probably give Rick Scott the edge when it comes to who's going to take the Senate seat.[47]

He further observes that:

Since the [2016] election, you've seen Marco Rubio positioning himself [to] where he really is—pulling back from the Tea Party fire-breather [to] more the Marco Rubio we all recognized when he was in the state legislature here. The purple state ends up with purple politicians.

Paulson also recognizes Rick Scott's move toward the center, saying:

The governor [is] coming out in support of many of these changes and coming out in part certainly for political reasons. He's running for the U.S. Senate. Politicians often try to position themselves on the right side of the political issue, and the right side may not necessarily be how they truly feel about a political issue but how they perceive what the popular sentiment is at this point in time. Governor Scott's position is partly reflective of that. He realizes that if [he is] going to have a chance of defeating Bill Nelson, he's got to appeal especially to [all] individuals in the state of Florida, not necessarily to the Democrats but those of no party affiliation and those who are Independents. One way to do that was by coming out and supporting stronger gun control measures, because this is so overwhelmingly popular among the residents of Florida. That's just one of a number of issues where politicians are constantly looking at certain factors that might influence political changes. In the case of Florida, nobody could have anticipated the Parkland situation and that's profoundly changed Florida.

Demographic Resorting: Changes and Immigration
All four of the experts spent a considerable amount of time speaking about the role of demographic changes and immigration in the state's politics.

Paulson's comments on demographic changes:

What had been a state mostly inhabited by native Floridians, most of whom lived in North Florida and were fairly equally divided between whites and Blacks, over a period of fifty to seventy-five years became the third largest state in the country, reflective of a massive demographic shift. The Black population went from essentially a majority Black population around 1900 to the point today where

Blacks are about 16 percent of Florida's population and very close to what the national numbers are there.

That created cultural issues, too, demographically [speaking], because the Hispanic population about ten years ago surpassed the African American population as the largest minority population in the state of Florida. That's created a cultural divide between those two different groups. If you look at the numbers there right now, Florida is about [55] percent white, [26] percent Hispanic, and only [16] percent Black in population, so Hispanics have just surpassed Blacks as the largest minority segment, and you get that tension between Hispanics and the African American population.[48]

It's also reflective of what's going to be a growing political divide in the state of Florida—that the white population is rapidly decreasing, like it is in a number of states. It's now 78 percent white, but that's going to go down substantially (actually in terms of the overall population, the white population is at about 60 percent). By 2020, 40 percent of Florida's population is going to be white and African American. [The state is] getting closer to the situation that California passed a number of years ago, when the minority population is no longer a minority but is now the majority in that state. That's going to create all sorts of new cultural and political tensions for the state to address.

Paulson continues on immigration:

Immigration is one of those issues [in Florida] that has been greatly affected by [demographic] changes. Forty percent of our population is minority—a lot of that is Hispanic. People used to think of Hispanics in Florida as being Cuban Hispanics, but Cuban Hispanics are now less than a third of the Hispanic population in the state of Florida. You've got such an influx of Puerto Ricans and South American and Central American Hispanics coming into Florida that Hispanics today means something fundamentally different than it did just a few short years ago. You're likely to get cultural disputes between Central and South American Hispanics and

Cuban Americans, as they're vying for their own political clout. In terms of what happens with respect to that immigration, it really has profoundly changed the politics of Florida and not just with minority populations.

One example I often cite about an area that has had tremendous immigration and for the past couple of years has been the fastest-growing metropolitan area in the United States is The Villages in the Ocala area. It is an overwhelmingly white community, a very small minority population, [that] is very Republican and very conservative. It voted for Donald Trump by 39 percent. He not only won that area, he completely dominated the politics of The Villages. People often look at immigration as a one-sided aspect that is going to have profound impact and advantage only to the Democratic party, but The Villages is just testimony to the other side of that coin, where many of the white immigrants coming from other states into Florida have completely different political viewpoints and orientations than many of the ethnic immigrants who have moved into the state of Florida.

Phillips remarks on immigration and population change in the Jacksonville area:

[Jacksonville] is a surprisingly tolerant city with respect to immigration. One of the things I see in my part of town is the city has been used to resettle a lot of refugees from Afghanistan and from parts of the Middle East. There's a very large mosque, and it's overflowing; they need to build another one. The Baptist church across the street lets the worshippers at the mosque park there on Friday. I think those people go out of their way to be as good neighbors as they could possibly be. There's a large influx of Filipinos, and I don't know why that is, but that's been a huge stream of immigration into the city [on the] south side. I think there has been, in general, tolerance for immigration. When you talk about bad ethnic relations in the city, it's really the divide between Black and white that's problematic, and it gets all the press. I think the rest of the city is doing a decent job with respect to immigration.

Fonseca remarks on immigration and Hispanics in South and Central Florida:

[In] Miami, the [Latin American] line keeps moving further north. So now the argument is that anything south of West Palm Beach is considered Latin America and anything north is the United States. But that's changing again because of the Central Florida corridor that's now becoming very Hispanic.

The Hispanic population is growing incredibly fast, and now the Hispanic population is unique in that it is comprised of a variety of different cultures, whether you're from Central America ... from the Caribbean, or ... from Venezuela or Colombia in the South American portion. Those are all very distinctly different cultures, but there's a lot of divisions within Hispanics.

The biggest fight is between Hispanics, Blacks, and white non-Hispanics. Those are really the three dominant communities you have in Florida. They represent really distinct values; they have very distinct cultures. If you go up into some of the rural parts of Florida, off over toward, let's say, the coastal sides, so the west coast or the east coast from Naples up is a lot of largely white non-Hispanic community. If you go on the east coast and you go Miami up to Orlando, there are a lot of Hispanic communities; you go north of Orlando, a lot of white, non-Hispanic communities. Within the major urban centers, that's where your strong Black communities lie. And then there are a lot of small Black communities throughout the state in small pockets in rural areas like Clearwater, Florida.

Broward in South Florida [is] pivoting away toward the blue, and that's what makes immigration such an important public policy issue in Florida. [In] these major urban centers, that's one of the top issues on their mind, aside from [the] economy and some of the other traditional [issues like] healthcare. But, immigration is really passionate down here in these largely Hispanic-populated communities.

Miami [has] not always been favoring the Democrats [in] the last few cycles of national general elections. President Obama was one of the first times that Miami went for a Democratic presidential candidate. That was a product of the fact that you had a lot of first- and second-generation Americans that were distinct from what their immigrant parents (the Cubans) are. You see that divide between [the] first and second generation and those that had migrated in and were foreign-born in South Florida but still had voting rights.

Foreman discusses the influence of Cuban Americans in the Miami-Dade Region:

Locally, the influence of Cuban Americans in Miami-Dade politics has reached [a] critical mass. Starting in the 1980s, you had Hispanic, and particularly Cuban Americans, getting elected to various levels of office, and they now really dominate the mayor, county commission, local elections, and elections at the state and national level. The Cuban Americans, in general, [are] registered to vote as Republicans, and of course the older generation maintains that party affiliation more strongly than the younger voters, [who] are up for grabs.

When they [the presidential candidates] come to Miami-Dade County, what might [be] different than when they visit the rest of the state, Orlando or Jacksonville, will be [that they have] to talk about international politics, and most specifically U.S. policy toward Cuba. If you can find differences in how candidates approach Florida, that would be one of the most prominent ones that a candidate must talk about their positions on Cuba when they're in South Florida and to win favor with Cuban Americans. Typically, they'll take the position of hardline, pro-embargo and continuing frosty relations with Cuba. In more recent years, some Democrats have expressed more popular messages of easing the embargo and having more favorable relations with Cuba, similar to the policies laid out by President Obama in 2014.

The Influence of the Puerto Rican Migration
Although Latino immigration in general has had a tremendous impact on politics in Florida in the last several election cycles, all the experts specifically pointed to the vast influx of Puerto Ricans to Florida in the wake of Hurricane Maria. Their influence, in the opinion of

the experts (as just noted), though just showing up on the political radar of most candidates in the past election cycles, is sure to become a significant bloc of voters to be courted by both the Republican and Democratic parties going forward.

Paulson sees that:

> The growth of Hispanics, in particular, has been one of the notable factors, especially spurred on by Hurricane Maria, which brought some 300,000 additional Puerto Ricans to the Orlando area and has completely transformed the politics of that area. Back in 2000, Republicans held all three congressional seats from the Orlando area. Today, we see demographic changes, predominantly the growth in the Hispanic population. You now have a Vietnamese Democrat, a Black Democrat, and a Hispanic Democrat holding those three congressional seats in a bid for Orlando. They've had a tremendous impact politically.

Foreman remarks not only on the growth of Puerto Ricans in the state but their impact in terms of their immediate voter eligibility:

> One dynamic is the arrival of poor people from Puerto Rico to Florida. Of course, Puerto Rico is an [American] territory, so Puerto Ricans come to Florida and automatically register to vote [and can] participate in Florida elections. We're not sure of the total number of people who will have relocated since Hurricane Maria in 2017 and will register to vote in 2018, but you would think it would be a significant group of voters and that they will largely register with Democrats. I believe some data came out recently that showed that the party identification of newly registering Puerto Ricans is more evenly split than people thought it would be. And there's a lingering doubt about whether newly arrived Puerto Ricans will really be motivated to vote and make much of a difference in upcoming elections. But Governor Scott, who is running for the Senate, is talking about Puerto Rico and the efforts of the state of Florida to help with recovery after the storm. I think Scott made a recent visit there, as well. He did have the resident commissioner, the representative in Congress from Puerto Rico, come to Florida and endorse his candi-

dacy. There will be competition for the newly arriving or newly registering Puerto Rican voters who are already in Florida. But there is a question about the significance of those numbers.

Phillips shows us that although the Puerto Rican migrants originally established themselves in Orlando, they are starting to see Jacksonville as a more economically suitable place to settle:

You have a lot of equity migrants, particularly Puerto Ricans, who have found that it's cheaper to live in Jacksonville than it is to live in any of the other metros. The cultural influence of South Florida is moving north, and you see that with a rising Hispanic population. The city is at a crossroads, and it's rapidly morphing from a Southern city into a more of a multicultural city—becoming more and more like Orlando every day.

If you're familiar with Florida, the old saying in Florida is that the further south you go, the further North you are. People joke that the state is divided at Gainesville into two states: north Georgia and south New York. So the Panhandle, if you cut the peninsula off, the peninsula is more diverse. The Hispanic influence is large and getting larger. One of the things, probably the most important dynamic for the 2020 election in Florida—maybe even the midterms—is the massive influx of Puerto Ricans.

There was already a massive influx of Puerto Ricans before Hurricane Maria. But the hurricane has literally—you're talking about hundreds of thousands of Puerto Ricans just over the past four or five years. That has really changed, tipped the balance in a state that was already pretty evenly divided. So one of the things you see is that Hispanic influence—a lot of those people settled in metro Atlanta. I always joke that Orlando is the new capital of Puerto Rico, and that's really not a joke. But so many have moved in there that you start to see them look for cheaper rents and cheaper homes in Jacksonville. And one of the things I do gauge [is the] penetration into this city, which is more wide and evangelical, the increase in sort of ethnic eateries and food trucks and things like that. That kind of thing dominated down in Orlando, but we're getting more and more of it up here. So I think the cultural divide is the northern part of the state, which is white and Southern, and the increasing Latino influence, and then the cosmopolitan urban dwellers that constitute the Democratic base. The Puerto Rican influence is going to be massive in statewide politics.

Finally, Fonseca covers the influence of all the Latino migrants to various parts of the state, including the Puerto Ricans:

A lot of Puerto Ricans have moved into the Orlando area. South Florida is dominated by a lot of Cubans and now the Venezuelan community and Central American communities that have replaced old Cuban communities. Up in Central Florida, there are really robust Puerto Rican communities, which are voting constituencies for the most part.

The other one we thought was unique was the Latino vote. We had a project under my institute called the Latino Public Opinion Project, which was essentially looking at Latinos in the state. We did focus groups [in] Orlando with Puerto Ricans and in Miami with Cubans and Venezuelans. We went just north to talk to Central Americans, and then we had a working group in Central Florida with Mexicans. Our focus groups indicated that the overwhelming, at least in that election, a big percentage supported the Democratic candidate because of the rhetoric Trump had at the time. But [when] the data came out, the data was not as overwhelming as we expected it to be. They were still pretty interesting. All the polls . . . favored the Democratic candidate, but the turnout wasn't as overwhelming.

The second- and third-generation communities are more refined as a constituency and rallied around a particular side or the other. The rest are still in the middle. I'm not seeing that the demographic change right now will overwhelmingly impact the presidential election, but you may see the Democrats pick up a few seats in Florida, with Ileana Ros-Lehtinen leaving her seat being one of them. There's a seat in Tampa that could be picked up, because Tampa, particularly the St. Petersburg area, tended to poll blue.

Structural Features of State Government

All the commenters noted that Florida, like many southern states, historically had "extraordinarily weak governors" until the late 1990s. According to Paulson, "power was diffused" away from the governor to the state legislature, whose strength came from the lack of term limits. The resulting incumbency allowed for some legislators to rack up twenty-five- to thirty-year reigns against governors who were permitted only a "single, four-year term" until a 1968 constitutional amendment changed that to two possible terms.[49] The governors who won two terms were then able to exert "more clout."[50] Foreman notes that there were mostly Democratic governors from 1968 until 1998, when "Jeb Bush was elected."[51]

Jeb Bush became a stronger governor because he won during a time when the legislature was weakened by term limits. Florida voters approved a constitutional amendment by ballot popularly called "Eight is Enough" in the early 1990s that went into effect in the middle of the decade.[52] Paulson remarks that "it completely altered the power structure in the state of Florida."[53] Since senators and house members now faced an "eight year [term] limitation along with now an eight-year gubernatorial tenure," the end result was to "essentially put legislators and governors on equal footing."[54] Term limits, with the resulting turnover in the legislature, tends to favor the governor.

Both Foreman and Paulson characterize Jeb Bush's win in 1998 as a crossroads in state politics because, as Paulson notes, "the power of the governor has really been enhanced and it all comes into effect during the Bush administration." Yet, Foreman says that "since 1968, there's been a movement for more power for governors," albeit, as Foreman says, more like a "semi-strong governor." Paulson notes that the legislature also has been granting more power to the Republican governors since Bush's tenure because the Republicans also controlled the statehouse. For instance, the governor "pretty much completely dominates the appointment of the state supreme court judges, appellate judges." Paulson emphasizes the power shift embodied in the Jeb Bush administration by calling Bush "the conservative activist" because he was able to "institute numerous fundamental changes in public policy in Florida, many of which were controversial," such as "ending affirmative action as it existed" in Florida. Foreman notes that although additional powers were given to the governor, they were reeled back somewhat by the legislature to allow for powers like the line item veto to be overridden by the legislature.

However, the strong governors resulting from legislative term limits might not be the only reason Florida's governors are so politically powerful. Foreman suggests that the Republican governors since 1998—Jeb Bush, Charlie Crist, and Rick Scott—were able to "have policy successes as a result of their personal influence." But the ability of the governor to have two terms has been critical to shaping a strong governor since, as Foreman notes, Scott needed the first term to develop relationships with the legislative leaders but, "by the second term, things were more in harmony."

Recently, there has been some movement toward reducing the partisan politics that have pervaded the governor's races. Fonseca says that although Republican candidates were polling well for the most recent race, former Democratic congressman Patrick Murphy and former Republican representative David Jolly floated the idea that they would run on a joint ticket with Murphy as the governor and Jolly as the lieutenant governor, and polls showed some support for that combination.[55] He notes that "Democrats seem to be favoring the more moderate candidate" and that "there's an appetite, particularly on the Democratic side, for a moderate bipartisan candidate . . ." Republicans are still on the fence with regard to bipartisanship, and as Fonseca says, support for bipartisanship is "still kind of scattered on that scale from conservative to moderate."

Another Democratic candidate[56] for governor in 2018, Gwen Graham, did something similar by originally supporting David Jolly as a running mate, but as Foreman tells us:

> She backpedaled by essentially claiming . . . that she would entertain or she would select a Democrat for lieutenant governor that essentially supported her progressive views. . . . So there is this emotional temperature right now that's really evaluating the partisanship . . . in our state. The Republicans and Democrats have been really dug in on their respective sides and the Republicans have been able to outcompete for the most part [and] for quite some

time but there may be a shift, or at least there's a consciousness to it now, with the constituents.

Paulson also argues that the size of the state is also having an impact on the legislature. Although the legislature convenes annually, it meets for only sixty days. There have been calls to extend the time and to put a full-time legislature in place since policies in such a big and growing state "need to have sufficient time to develop." As a consequence, the state is left with a legislature of "wealthy individuals who can afford to take out the sixty days during the period when the legislature meets" and who "do not mirror the demographics of the constituents they represent" because the "the salary is quite low . . . in the low $20,000 range for both members of the Florida house and senate."[57]

Local Municipal Authority
Paulson observed that although Republicans run on smaller government and more local control that that has never really been acted on by governors or the state legislature despite the state having some measure of "home rule" since 1968. Governors and the legislature also impose more unfunded mandates to localities and school boards. To Paulson:

One of the strange things in the state of Florida, to me, is that Republican governors have long touted giving local governments far greater discretion over their own political activities, since they were elected by local people back home and knew the situation best. Republicans have always touted, at all levels of government, [more] local control, yet what we have seen in Florida is that, time after time, Republicans have violated this notion and imposed all sorts of restrictions on local government. The state is now dictating policy to both municipalities and county governments. This has had a profound effect with respect to tax issues, as the state legislature has oftentimes cut back funding for cities and counties and school boards in Florida and then imposed more duties and obligations for these local governments to perform. It's a no-win situation for local governments. They're told that you have to do more things that previously were the responsibility of the state, but we're going to take away much of your money to accomplish those things. So local governments have been in quite an uproar and feel somewhat betrayed by the Republican Party for not following through on their own political philosophy of allowing local control and letting local governments define what is in their [own] best interest instead of having policies dictated from Tallahassee. It continues to be a source of great controversy, especially among school boards, but also county governments as well.

Foreman comments on how local governments, particularly small cities, feel constrained and somewhat abandoned by the state because they have no influence in the state government.

I can only speculate, really, that [small cities] are trying to gain influence with their state representatives or state senators. There are different organizations, Leagues of Cities and so forth, that do collective advocacy work. But I have seen stories about this over the years, [that] these smaller cities just try to make do on their own. They realize it's not their game to spend money to go to Tallahassee and to lobby. They try to have influence directly through their state representatives. Otherwise, I think they get involved in [more specific] issues. [Those] issues are ones that are going to impact city finances, like red light cameras or high-speed rail lines across the state, FPL (Florida Power and Light, the main utility in the state) policies dealing with their rates or where their lines or facilities are located. It's probably more like [cities] get involved when they need to and hope, otherwise, that the state doesn't interfere too much. Because, with Republicans in the majority since the 1990s, it has been more of an ideology of rolling back government, rolling back regulations, giving local governments more local control. Of course, it depends on the issue.

Metro Power in State Government

There has been considerable change in the power distribution from rural to large metropolitan areas in the state. About power distribution, Paulson says:

It is much better today than it used to be in the 1960s. Florida in the 1960s had the most poorly apportioned legislature of the fifty states. You had approximately 12 percent of the population of Florida that could elect a majority of the Florida house and senate. For a good period of time, they used a county system of representation, where every county was guaranteed a representative in the legislature. Many of those were rural counties in North Florida that had very few people in them, while the metropolitan counties such as Tampa and Miami, Jacksonville, and, increasingly, Orlando would have hundreds of thousands of people but they would get one representative and some North Florida counties with few people would get one representative. Eventually this all changed with the Supreme Court decision *Baker v. Carr*,[58] which calls for the one person one vote decision to be instituted because it's much more equitable today in terms of representation than it used to be. In terms of geographical diversity, the Florida legislature is in a much better position today than it was about a half century ago. The metropolitan areas are [better] represented, but you're always going to have lingering effects of prior policies.

And according to Foreman, the Miami-Dade legislative delegation has gained more power in the last generation:

The Miami-Dade's legislative delegation used to be relatively weak through the 1980s and 1990s. Due to population shifts, they gained more seats in the House and Senate [and] the size of the delegation grew. Then in 2006, Marco Rubio was a state representative from Miami selected as the Florida House speaker, and that helped bring more influence to South Florida. His colleague, David Rivera, was the budget committee chair. Very prominent budget committee chairs can steer more funding and programs to their home area. South Florida's home influence increased a bit, but we still have a very topical competition between South Central and South Florida in terms of regional influence in Tallahassee. There's a lot of resentment against South Florida. Some people think it's too different, too crazy, too international, not like old Florida. That also plays a role in what policies make the top of the agenda.

The experts could not agree on whether the geographic distance between Miami and Tallassee was a problem for large metros (or even smaller cities) to gain access to their representatives in the state legislature. As Foreman describes:

> The geographic distance from Miami to Tallahassee is a huge challenge for local leaders to try to gain access in Tallahassee. Literally, there are very few flights from Miami to Tallahassee, and they're very expensive. The drive is a solid eight hours. People do it all the time, but it's taxing. One of the criticisms of the Miami-Dade County mayor and commissioners is that they are not as visible or present in Tallahassee as maybe they could be. They certainly do make trips and they hire well-connected lobbyists in Tallahassee, and that probably makes a difference. But the more you're visible, the more you're able to meet with leaders in their offices, the more you can push your agenda. That's a concern and even more so for the leaders of the municipalities that are small city mayors or council members. It's hard for them to get there. And there are so many cities and sixty-seven counties in Florida, so it's hard to get attention from state leaders."

Fonseca is uncertain as how the geographic distances in the state actually impact legislators or even voters:

> It is fascinating because we're a long state to begin with and, like most of the other states, [the] capital is probably just a few short hours away from wherever you are in the state. For us, having the robust influence that South Florida has in terms of population proportionality [or] in terms of significant members of our legislators coming out of South Florida, representing the state, even on the federal side, I don't know how much of a challenge it proposes. It's evident that many have houses out there in Tallahassee where they'll go during session. They'll stay in their homes or in their condo. It doesn't make for a very easy transition up and down routinely, but it is something that makes Florida a little unique in the scheme in that there is a big geographic gap between South Florida

and Tallahassee. You're talking about a seven-hour drive, roughly. It's an hour-and-a-half flight, an hour flight or so. I'm not sure if it has a major impact. I haven't heard [about] it. It hasn't really manifested as something that's being hugely important. Now the other question is whether or not there's distance between what goes on in Tallahassee in the consciousness of our voters in South Florida. You're not getting pulsed maybe in the consciousness of voters of what goes on in Tallahassee, unless it has a direct impact to the South Florida community. There could be some challenges there to just inform voters when it comes to broader state politics. Instead, what you get is just the issues that play . . . into those really big ticket items. Outside of that, you don't get a whole lot of information coming this way. I don't know if that's a product of geographic proximity or not.

Paulson describes some of the problems associated with vast geographic expanses between the population centers in the state:

If you go to North Florida, it's almost like you're in a different political entity, or the old maxim of Florida politics, the further north you go in Florida, the further South you get. North Florida, the "Redneck Riviera," so to speak, the area from Tallahassee to Pensacola, is much closer to Alabama and Mississippi politics than it is to the politics of the rest of the state. Part of this is a reflection, not only of the large population but also of Florida's diversity in terms of geographical area, which oftentimes gets ignored in terms of the political process.

One of the things that many people point out with respect to Florida politics is that there is a greater distance from Key West to Pensacola than there is from Pensacola to Chicago. That reflects the geographic diversity of Florida. It's an enormously large state. You have a number of major metropolitan areas, and you've got a large percentage of rural residents and two-thirds of whom are not native to Florida. That's going to create all sorts of cultural pressure points in the state. Florida certainly exhibited those cultural pressure points throughout much of history.

The state sought to alleviate this problem, according, to Paulson, when there was a proposal in the 1970s to move the state capital to Orlando:

> Everything seems to have shifted to the Orlando area, and it probably makes some sense. . . . That was actually put to a vote and defeated based on . . . [the] costs already in the building in Tallahassee. What in the world's going to happen to all these facilities in Tallahassee? How can we relocate all of these government workers who are now in Tallahassee? So, we [Florida] just figured it wasn't going to work, so inertia is oftentimes the thing that stymies government changes that many people believe are needed, and that's what happened here, inertia. You just leave things as they are.

Economic Power and Political Power

Another important question raised with the experts was how economic power translates into political power in Florida. Paulson starts off with the overall sense of how dramatically the state's economy has changed in Florida since the 1960s. Next, the commenters focus on the influence wielded by some of Florida's major metropolitan areas because of the strength of their economies and specific industries that exert more political influence.

Paulson begins by detailing the growth of economic power and its influence in Florida since the 1960s:

> Economic powers have long dominated the politics of every state; even when Florida was a much more rural environment, it was completely controlled by the rural north Florida politicians. Prior to the gerrymandering decision from the 1960s, a small number of individuals and corporations dominated public policy in the state of Florida. Ed Ball of Jacksonville was notorious. Giant books have been written about Ed Ball, who was a member of the DuPont Organization (the chemical interest in the state of Florida). [He] was considered by many to be the most powerful person in the state of Florida for decades because of his wealth and influence with respect to the legislature. As Florida has grown tremendously in population, moving now to where we've got over, I can't remember the

most recent population figures, but something like I think we're up to about 22 million people or thereabouts, the third largest state. The economic interests have been diversified, but economic powers are always going to have a profound influence over the legislature because in many cases that economic power is reflected in such things as campaign contributions [from] these large corporate entities. They're prohibited from on their own making certain contributions, but all the individuals who work for these corporations are free as individuals to make campaign contributions and so they have a profound effect on influencing legislative outcomes simply by their campaign contributions.

Orlando

As noted in the previous State of Play section, the Orlando metro area is booming. The experts comment how this metropolitan powerhouse has changed and is able to exercise more influence in state and national politics.

According to Paulson:

Everyone in recent elections refers to the I-4 Corridor, stretching across the central part of the state from Tampa through Orlando over to Florida's east coast. Clearly, that's an important area because, of all the metro areas in the state, that's the area that has experienced the most rapid rate of growth, and one of the factors [that] distinguished Florida from almost all the other states is its rapid population growth.

The Orlando area is the fastest growing of the metro areas [and] has about 4 million people. They are 20 percent of Florida's electorate. The growth of Hispanics, in particular, has been one of the notable factors, especially spurred on by Hurricane Maria, which brought some 300,000 additional Puerto Ricans to the Orlando area, which has completely transformed the politics of that area. Back in 2000, Republicans held all three congressional seats from the Orlando area. Today, we see demographic changes, predominantly the growth in the Hispanic population. They've had a tremendous impact politically. Then you have Tampa and southwest Florida, stretching down the southwest coast down to Fort

Myers. You have about 6 million who live in this area. Essentially, if you drive south from Tampa, the area becomes wealthier and more hospitable to the Republican Party and its candidates. This is an area that Romney won by about 4 percent four years ago, and Donald Trump did extraordinarily well in in the 2016 election.

Fonseca explores those industries beyond tourism that exert the most clout in Tallahassee based on the scale of Orlando's population growth:

The two specific industries I can think of that do wield power, driven largely by very influential private sectors, are the agricultural sector and aviation and aerospace competing in Orlando. This is why you're seeing a boom in influence in Orlando. One, the population is growing incredibly fast and it's becoming a really important voting bloc for national elections and statewide elections. Orlando is growing in terms of its utility in the electoral process. Toward the center part of Orlando, where Disney and Universal [are], the predominant [industry] is tourism. But then if you move slightly north and more out to the coast, you're talking about really robot aviation and aerospace industries that have really important research clusters, and they do hold some value. Then you can see exponential growth in the influence of many academic institutions. The two other really large institutions are University of South Florida and University of Central Florida. Tourism is there, and it's strong, but I've heard more about the impact and influence of the aviation and aerospace industries up there, these multibillion-dollar organizations that are defense contractors and the influence that they wield.

Jacksonville

Phillips observes, Jacksonville "is the most conservative of [all] the metros in the state. It's trending blue but it's still kind of red. I guess you would call it a purple city." But not when it comes to state politics. According to Phillips, even though Jacksonville:

Is the closest to the state capital, it is still really far from the state capital. So when it comes to resources and things like that, the primary battle, our arch-nemesis is not Tallahassee; it's Orlando. The battle is over the St. John's River. The St. John's River is the central battleground in intrastate politics in Jacksonville because we live at the mouth of the St. John's River and metro Orlando is at the headwaters of the St. John's River. So there's a constant battle over water rights. As Orlando gets bigger and bigger, they want to pull more and more of that water, and the salinity of the St. John's River backs up deeper and deeper into downtown, and so the fight is always over resources . . . with Central Florida.

South Florida, Tampa, Miami, they're doing their own thing. Politically, we're more in line with Tallahassee. The powers that be look favorably on Jacksonville, but the incredible growth in Orlando trumps all political machinations, and the way it manifests itself in this town is water.

Asked how Jacksonville translates the political tension between Orlando and Tallahassee into political power, Phillips continues:

We don't. We lose. Let me just give you an illustration of how we lose. Both the University of Central Florida in Orlando and the University of North Florida in Jacksonville started off as commuter finishing schools within the state university system. Over time, University of Central Florida has morphed into a major research university with a full complement of doctoral programs. It's now one of the largest universities in the nation. The University of North Florida looks like the kind of university you'd find—and it's a good school—but it's the kind of university you'd find in a city of 250,000, not a city of a million. . . . Jacksonville feels much smaller in terms of its libraries, public transportation, things like that. It just feels like a smaller city because it's not the darling of the state. Orlando has a huge tourist infrastructure, and so how do we compete? We don't, really, so things get better here as the pie gets bigger. The rising tide appears to float all boats, but in interstate competition, Jacksonville almost always loses out.

In terms of innovation, what they want to do is dredge the river and make the port deeper. That's how they think they're going to compete; they're going to increase the traffic into the port. So to me, that's not the same as saying, "Oh, we're going to lure in engineering firms and high-tech and innovation."[59]

I think that as the state grows generally and Jacksonville grows, Jacksonville is trending more toward . . . to the extent that the city becomes more diverse, will probably tend to vote more like the rest of the state. Jacksonvillers [are] becoming more diverse, so I think that Jacksonville will become more like Orlando than like Birmingham. Right now, it's more like Birmingham than Orlando, but I think it's definitely trending in that direction. And it's the Latino influence causing it.

South Florida

According to Fonseca, South Florida has a big impact on the state legislature due to the sheer size of the region:

South Florida legislators have a lot of influence because they do have a really big constituency and they represent a significant voting bloc when it comes to the gubernatorial elections. [And] . . . the next speaker of the house is from Miami, from Hialeah. . . . I think that elevates the status of South Florida when the majority speaker is from a small Cuban-centric district here in Miami.

Florida's Non-Metropolitan Area Political Clout

The experts were also asked to talk about the political influence of nonmetro areas (that is, the more rural areas) and how that has changed over time. When asked, "How do the non-biggest metro parts of the state exert power?" Paulson responded:

Well, it's very difficult. It's almost like a turnaround from the situation that existed fifty or sixty years ago in the state of Florida where these rural areas completely dominated the state even though they didn't have the numbers to justify that political clout. Now they're fighting to exert their political influence because to a great extent their power is more equally reflected in the legislature today. In terms of the political distribution of power, it's more equally distributed between urban and rural areas today. But the only way, one of the few ways, that rural areas can exert greater influence obviously is to form their own coalitions, which is the most common way in politics of trying to exert political influence. You can't do it by yourself. So [they] organize and put together political entities that can represent [their] interests, whether that's county government associations or associations of local government or local communities in a particular area of the state of Florida that might have a common economic interest. They have to form alliances and coalitions to try to exert that influence and to win over the support of legislators of the rural areas as well as the metropolitan areas. This is in the best interest of our region of the state but also in the best interest of the state of Florida overall. It's not an easy thing to do, but there aren't many alternatives for these rural areas. For most of Florida's history, they completely dominated the state, and now they're on the other end of the political spectrum, seeing their power wane substantially, and there aren't many effective ways to put them back in the glory days that used to exist for them.

Fonseca emphasizes that the agricultural sector still maintains a significant power base and political favor in the state legislature:

The more rural environments are led by Republicans that are in favor in Tallahassee. . . . Then going more into the rural areas, particularly up along Central Florida, the importance of the agricultural sector, whether it's juice production or fruit, and that's also really robust because they say that Florida is the breadbasket of the United States. We do have really strong agricultural production, or [an] agricultural sector in the state of Florida. That's another really important influence.

Phillips remarks on the traditional Southern influence of North Florida's nonmetropolitan area and the Panhandle:

In the northern part of the state and the Panhandle, the people are indistinguishable from their counterparts in neighboring Georgia and Alabama, and they pull the state hard to the right. So that is the Republican influence on the state, and they are increasingly monolithic and vote as a bloc.

Closeness of Election Outcomes

As noted in the chapter's epigraph, most candidates for office in Florida typically do not have an easy path to winning over 50 percent of the vote (unless, of course, they are the incumbent). The experts confirm that observation and note that there are two main drivers that impact the outcomes of elections. The first category is voter turnout, which mostly benefits the Republican candidates, and party registration drives, which have boosted Democratic election outcomes in recent election cycles. The second category that influences election outcomes includes the wedge or cultural issues that rise up and gain public attention during any given election. The experts will comment first on voter registration and turnout and then will consider various wedge or cultural issues that have become important in Florida's most recent election cycles.

Voter Turnout and Registration

The experts note that voter turnout can be the key advantage to either party during elections. Indeed, Foreman suggests there is a delicate balance of advantage for or against Democratic candidates depending on the turnout of Republican voters. Foreman and Fonseca both see that voter mobilization of younger voters would give the edge to the Democrats. Demographic changes, according to Fonseca, will be important in the future but he does not foresee that having an immediate impact in the upcoming 2020 general election. Part of the problem, he argues, is that Democratic candidates have not been able to depend on all their traditional voters for every election. African Americans, in particular, have been somewhat fickle in their support for Democrats and in turnout in the last few election cycles.

According to Foreman, voter turnout is key in future election cycles for both parties, albeit for different reasons:

> I think if they [voters] come out in significant numbers in 2018 and 2020, they could continue to help the Republican candidate. If they don't come out, it might be just enough of a difference for Democrats

who, in general, registered more of the younger voters, more of the diverse voters. [They] do have a voter registration advantage state-wide unless the Democratic Party can win over rural, white voters in Florida or until they're disinterested and they don't vote or they die off, then that's where the Republican advantage still is with those voters. That might be what we watch in the upcoming election.

Fonseca asserts that voter mobilization is necessary to improve turnout. But he suggests that voters, in particular African American voters, need a strong motivation to come out to the polls in Florida. An energized Democratic electorate, he argues, would decidedly shift the state blue:

I don't think there will be any type of demographic change that would maybe shift it overwhelmingly by the time you get to 2020. What it comes down to is [the] mobilization of voters. That's usually the case. You're getting voters out, but you saw, from what I recall, a pretty significant decline in the Black voter turnout than the Democrats were expecting. President Obama came down ("Souls to the Polls"[60]) trying to get the Black vote out there because it would support the Democratic side, but that turnout wasn't there. If that turnout was there, could Florida have changed? I think the answer is yes, it could have changed.

The other one that we thought was unique was the Latino vote. All the polls [showed them going to] favor the Democratic candidate, but the turnout wasn't as overwhelming.

Wedge Issues

Earlier, the experts commented on how Florida's Republican politicians have adapted to a more moderate stance on many issues to appeal to the state's blue-leaning voters. They were also queried on how certain so called "wedge" or "cultural issues" may influence elections outcomes. They were asked to select one or all hot-button issues, such as gun control, abortion, LGBTQ rights, climate change, and marijuana, and consider how these fights are playing out in Florida elections. Their comments demonstrate that there are stark urban/rural differences, metro/nonmetro splits, and upstate and downstate divides on many of these issues. However, given the state's growing diversity, some of these issues are moderating candidates' positions while other issues still persist in their expected geographic regions. The experts declared that in addition to voter registration and turnout, how a particular candidate stands on hot button issues may predict an election's winning margin.

Foreman first discusses how wedge issues influence the state's politics and the importance of these issues in Florida's characteristically close elections:

> Yes, there [are] wedge issues that matter in Florida and probably do make up the difference at the margin of close races. Interestingly, on gay marriage in 2008, we had an initiative on the ballot, a statewide constitutional amendment that year to regulate marriage as being only between one man and one woman. That passed pretty overwhelmingly. At the same time, Barack Obama won pretty significantly in Florida in 2008. If we're looking at the numbers on that, we would see that African American voters, which did come out in near-record numbers in 2008, supporting Obama overwhelmingly, voted Democrat, but then voted for that amendment. That's a cultural issue, in particular in African American communities, that they feel stronger about, but of course the statewide amendment was eventually overturned by the Supreme Court decision, banning all of those things.

The experts next consider how LGBTQ issues and rights have changed over time. They find that significant changes in attitudes have occurred over the last few election cycles, particularly in the state's large metros.

Foreman finds that LGBTQ issues have more support at the local level and have little traction at the state level:

> Many counties and municipalities have passed ordinances to protect the rights of gay people, but it's very hard to find that support at the state level because you've got conservative leadership in both the House and Senate over the past two decades.
>
> Gay adoption was also another issue that was not permitted

by the legislature. But the state court ultimately, a few years ago, permitted gay couples to adopt. These issues are working themselves out in Florida, maybe quicker than nationally. You do a have large and prominent gay community in Miami. Many of them are wealthy and influential donors in both parties. You have David Richardson, who is a state representative from Miami Beach, who I believe they say was the first openly gay person elected to the Florida legislature. Now, he is running for that congressional seat, [District] 27, held by Ileana Ros-Lehtinen. He has emerged as the main challenger to Donna Shalala, who was the former president of the University of Miami and was secretary of health and human services for eight years under the Clinton administration. [She] has a long reservoir [of] support among Democrats, but a criticism of Donna Shalala is that early in her career she said or wrote things that were not supportive of protecting the rights of gays and lesbians. I think that is going to become an issue in that race, and again, the gay community is mobilized and concerned about the statewide lack of protection for workers.

Phillips again notes the changing and mixed attitudes toward LGBTQ rights present in Jacksonville:

Although I will say that the gay issue is settled in terms of gay marriage and a broad acceptance of homosexuality into society. I think they win and that's settled. I think if you were on Jacksonville Beach and there'd be two guys who were holding hands walking down the beach in 2018, they'd be just fine. While the city is as pro-life is it has ever been since I lived here, there's been a massive shift on tolerance of gay rights and alternative sexualities.

Fonseca highlights the stark urban/rural divide in Florida on LGBTQ issues:

It's geographic, and the main [regions] LGBTQ is really going to play itself out [is] in places like Miami in Broward County and Key West. The rest of the state is maybe less inclined to support that social issue, for example. When you go out into the rural areas, it's probably still highly contentious, but in a place like Miami, it's pretty common and pretty open. You go to a place like Tampa, Naples, or further north into Florida, maybe not so much.

Gun Control

As one of the experts notes, Florida is considered NRA (National Rifle Association) country. But according to the experts' comments on this issue, it is evident that this (and abortion) clearly remain an urban/rural preference. Yet, the Parkland shooting of February 14, 2018, at the Marjory Stoneman Douglas High School has, surprisingly, shifted some of the hardline political attitudes about guns toward enacting a modest measure of gun control.

As Foreman tells us, gun control is becoming a very important issue to voters since the Parkland shooting:

> The gun issue varies significantly, but leaders realize it. After the shooting in Parkland, Florida, at Marjory Stoneman Douglas High School on February 14, we're having very real conversations about what's appropriate policy moving forward. You have legislators from urban areas acknowledging that guns are culturally important in rural parts of Florida and hunting is important. I think Senator Bill Nelson is a good an example on the Senate floor. Some people are talking about how he grew up hunting. He still hunts now with his son, but an AR-15 is not for hunting. I think we're trying to talk through the issue and realize that guns in urban areas [like] Liberty City, an area with a lot of crime, in Miami there's very real, palpable sense that you need to do something to gain control of the amount of weapons that are on the street. That one [issue] will most likely be more visible during the 2018 elections for both governor and for the congressional offices.

Fonseca maintains that someone's position on gun control still depends on whether they live in the urban or rural areas of the state, but age is becoming just as important, particularly in urban areas:

> In terms of the gun debate, that is probably pretty evenly rural versus urban. Even looking at Miami, for example, my area, [with]

the younger communities, there is also the distinction with this particular public policy issue. The younger population tends to be more for some form of control. The older Hispanic population tends to lean away from that and be more pro-gun, for example. But even then, it's still a good mix. You go out to the rural areas of Florida, up and down Florida, and it's pretty heavily favoring the pro-gun position.

While heading toward more progressive values on some issues, Phillips suggests that the gun issue reflects whatever remains of the Southern traditional attitudes in Jacksonville:

There's a strong Southern component to Jacksonville. I would think that's a pretty pro-gun state [and] this is NRA country. I'm sure most of my neighbors are armed, so there's going to be much more tolerance for guns here than there would be in, say, Miami.

When asked if the Parkland episode changed the conversation about gun control, Paulson replied:

Well it has, and nobody would have expected it. If you went back just a year ago and asked anybody if the legislature would pass the provisions that were just passed by this year's legislature with respect to gun control, 90 percent of the people would have said there is no chance this is going to happen.

Parkland changed everything nationally. It changed everything in the state, and here you have Republicans who had long opposed any kind of gun control measures who are coming out and supporting these controls. One can argue that they [the gun control measures] weren't enough, but they were profound changes given where Florida has been in the past and given what Florida politicians said they would or would not support with respect to gun control. You have the governor coming out in support of many of these changes and coming out in part certainly for political reasons. . . . Nobody could have anticipated the Parkland situation, and that's profoundly changed Florida.

Abortion

Unlike the recent changes in the gun control debate, abortion is one of those issues the experts observed to be a cultural value where voters remain steadfast to their respective positions. As expected, the experts find that the more rural parts of the state reflect more pro-life attitudes.

Fonseca starts by talking about how the abortion issue sorts out geographically and generationally:

> The abortion issue is [a] contentious issue [in] Florida. If you start to move toward Central Florida, if you're driving, for example, the turnpike between West Palm Beach in Orlando, you're going to see a barrage of anti-abortion signs sitting on the highway that have been there for years, and they're not going anywhere. But you're not going to see them south of West Palm Beach. You're going to see them north of West Palm Beach between North Palm Beach and the northern part of Orlando to the central northern-central Florida area. I drive that stretch pretty often, and [there is] a barrage of them. So you can see where that issue may be more openly accessible versus down here it's probably less so. It's less the younger populations and probably more with older populations because you are seeing that kind of turnover.

Phillips highlights the surprising contrast of changing attitudes toward the LGBTQ population and the strong religious culture that still persists in Jacksonville:

> The evangelical culture is powerful here; there are lots of mega-churches, and it's mostly pro-life. I see a lot of anti-abortion bumper stickers. While the city is as pro-life is it has ever been since I lived here, there's been a massive shift on tolerance of gay rights and alternative sexualities.

Marijuana

Marijuana may be the bellwether issue that illustrates the extent to which the state is turning purple. Both Foreman and Fonseca talk about the legislative fight over marijuana policy and how attitudes changed significantly from 2014 to 2016. Although, as they note, the issue remains an urban/rural preference split, the legislative passage of medical marijuana use and opinion polls that support recreational use signal a substantial blue shift. Phillips comments on the uneasy balance that marijuana represents in Jacksonville where there is still a significant conservative presence.

Foreman remarks on the difference between public sentiment in favor of marijuana legalization and the conservative legislative leaders' reluctance to enact a recently passed constitutional amendment allowing medical marijuana use:

> In 2014, we voted on the statewide initiative constitutional amendment for medical marijuana. It didn't pass. We have a 60 percent threshold that has to be met for constitutional amendments to be approved. It got 58.5 percent the first time. The question was put on the 2016 ballot, essentially the same language, and it did pass. There's popular support for medical marijuana. Opinion polls show majority support for recreational marijuana in Florida. But the legislative leaders, particularly from the conservative wing of the Republican Party, slow-walked the implementation of the amendment. There are concerns about how it's being implemented overall. I don't know [if] that's one that's going to gain electoral traction, but it is one that is in the policy arena. We do see a cultural divide in support for and how to implement medical marijuana policy in the state.

Fonseca too highlights the conservative/liberal divide on the issue and sees the issue as reflecting urban and rural cultural clashes:

> In terms of marijuana usage, [the state] passed medical marijuana in the state. I would tend to see [it] again [as] conservative versus the more liberal. The urban areas [are] going to be the more liberal and to tend to favor the exceptions for marijuana usage, whereas the rural areas (which still are significantly populated) tend to be more conservative in their views and tend to shy away from it.

Once more, Phillips comments on the cultural/political clashes that are unfolding in Jacksonville, where open marijuana use may foreshadow a massive cultural shift in the city but that still remains in flux:

> The marijuana thing is settled. I just noticed the other day on Beach Boulevard [that] there's a medical marijuana clinic. I have been here since the fall of 2000, so to the extent that student opinions are indicative of the future of the city, I'd say an outright marijuana legalization bill will probably pass in 2020. So they're going to cling to their god and their guns, but they will let go on gay rights and weed.

CONCLUSION: FLORIDA

Florida is a big, contested, and complicated state. All the political experts interviewed for this chapter concur on that fact. They also note that there remains political turbulence in the state born of both foreign and domestic migration. Florida's demographic shifts are evident to all observers, but the question remains as to when the eventual weight of diversity may dramatically shift the Sunshine State's politics to the Democrats. It was noted that Florida's growing urban cosmopolitanism allowed the Democrats to gain enough traction in recent years to make the state purple. But it seems, as new urban coalitions emerge, places such as the Florida Panhandle counter by voting, as one expert noted, in a solid Republican bloc. For now, Florida works as almost a political equivalent of Isaac Newton's Third Law of Motion, where each political action produces an opposite and equal reaction. But there are hints that a new, bluer Florida is emerging, as seen in even a rock-ribbed Republican city like Jacksonville, which is now turning purple. When the full effects of Florida's demographic transition take hold, there may simply not be enough Panhandle Republicanism to offset the blue rise. Florida would need a Panhandle that reached Texas to hold back the powerful demographic change that is coming and may arrive sooner than anyone is prepared for.

NOTES

1. Steve Schale, "Everything You've Ever Wanted to Know about Florida, But Were Afraid to Ask—V.2018," Blog, October 13, 2018, http://steveschale.squarespace.com/blog/2018/10/3/everything-youve-ever-wanted-to-know-about-florida-but-were.html.

2. NBC Political Commentator Tim Russert famously held up a small whiteboard while covering the 2000 election in the early morning hours of November 8, 2000, that read "Florida, Florida, Florida," thus indicating that the national election had come down to a single state. Russert's whiteboard was later given to the Smithsonian Institution in Washington, D.C., because it was deemed to be of national significance. Jonathan Storm, "Tim Russert, Giant of D.C. Journalism, Dies," *Philadelphia Inquirer*, June 14, 2008, www.inquirer.com/philly/obituaries/20080614_Tim_Russert__giant_of_D_C__journalism__dies.html.

3. Obama won Florida by 2.8 percent in 2008 and by 0.9 percent in 2012.

4. Trump won Florida by 2.1 percent in 2016.

5. Jacob Pramuk, "More Drama in Florida: Senate Race Heads toward a Recount as Gubernatorial Race Tightens," *CNBC.com*, November 8, 2018, www.cnbc.com/2018/11/08/florida-election-results-senate-and-governor-races-could-go-to-recount.html.

6. Paul Overberg and Gregg Toppo, "Florida's Population Overtakes New York," *USA Today*, December 23, 2014, www.usatoday.com/story/news/nation/2014/12/23/census-florida-new-york-population/20812473/.

7. U.S. census estimates show that Florida grew 13.3 percent from 2010 to 2018, which translates into a gain of nearly 2.5 million new residents.

8. James G. Gimpel and Jason E. Schuknecht, *Patchwork Nation: Sectionalism and Political Change in American Politics* (University of Michigan Press, 2003), p. 88.

9. Palm Beach County is clearly part of South Florida in that it forms part of the Miami metropolitan area.

10. William H. Frey and Ruy Teixeira, "The Political Geography of Virginia and Florida: Bookends of the New South," Brookings Report, October 10, 2008, www.brookings.edu/wp-content/uploads/2016/06/10_southeast_frey_teixeira.pdf; for map, see www.brookings.edu/wp-content/uploads/2016/06/maps_figures_2.pdf.

11. One of the experts interviewed for this chapter is a sociologist based at the University of North Florida in Jacksonville. We specifically selected a sociologist to report out of the region because Jacksonville is a hard-to-locate metropolitan area in terms of its sociocultural and regional characteristics.

12. Wilbur Zelinsky, *The Cultural Geography of the United States* (Englewood Cliffs, NJ: Prentice Hall, 1973), p. 135.

13. Rex J. Rowley, "Voluntary Regions and the Case of Las Vegas," *Journal of Cultural Geography* 35, no. 1 (January 2, 2018), pp. 102–32, 102. Other examples of voluntary regions include Orlando and Southern California.

14. A car traveling south on I-95 enters the South (as a cultural zone) around Fredericksburg, Virginia, just south of Washington, D.C. The vehicle would exit the South on I-95 somewhere along the Central Florida coast.

15. Jason Fitzroy Jeffers and Nathaniel Sandlers, "Is Miami the Caribbean?" *Miami Rail*, June 21, 2106, https://miamirail.org/summer-2016/is-miami-the-caribbean/.

16. Works Progress Administration, *Guide to Florida* (New York: Pantheon Books 1984, original 1940).

17. Ibid., p. 3.

18. Karen A. Danielsen and Robert E. Lang, "Comparing Orlando and Las Vegas," *Opolis* 3, no. 1 (forthcoming).

19. Arthur C. Nelson and Robert E. Lang, *Megapolitan America: A New Vision for Understanding America's Metropolitan Geography* (Chicago: Planners Press, 2011).

20. Tom McCloughlin, "NW Florida Dominates 'Most Conservative Cities' Rankings," *North West Florida Daily News*, March 26, 2018, www.nwfdailynews.com/news/20180326/nw-florida-dominates-most-conservative-cities-ranking.

21. Kelly Humphrey, "Panhandle Carries Trump to State Win," *North West Florida Daily News*, November 9, 2018, www.nwfdailynews.com/news/20161109/panhandle-carries-trump-to-state-win.

22. Adam C. Smith, "Florida's I-4 Corridor: Where Presidents Get Picked," *Miami Herald*, November 4, 2016, www.tampabay.com/news/politics/stateroundup/floridas-i-4-corridor-where-presidents-get-picked/2301429/.

23. Note that one of the more conservative parts of Florida is The Villages, which is a large-scale, age-restricted community. It is home to affluent retirees, many of whom come from conservative communities in the Midwest. The area is just north of the I-4 Corridor.

24. Florida has among the most diverse Latino populations in the United States. Historically, Cubans dominated South Florida, while Puerto Ricans located in Central Florida. In recent years, Latino and non-Latino immigrants have moved to Florida, including Mexicans and multiple Caribbean Islanders and South Americans—some from non-Spanish-speaking countries.

25. Martín Echenique and Luis Melgar, "Mapping Puerto Rico's Hurricane Migration with Mobile Phone Data," *City Lab*, May 11, 2018, www.citylab.com/environment/2018/05/watch-puerto-ricos-hurricane-migration-via-mobile-phone-data/559889/.

26. Lizette Alvarez, "A Great Migration from Puerto Rico Is Set to Transform Orlando," *New York Times*, November 17, 2017, www.nytimes.com/2017/11/17/us/puerto-ricans-orlando.html.

27. Dice Tech and Burning Glass Technologies, *Dice Tech Job Report: The Fastest Growing Hubs, Roles and Skills,* Issue #1: Q1 2020, p. 8, http://marketing.dice.com/pdf/2020/Dice_2020_Tech_Job_Report.pdf.

28. Richard Florida, "How the Creative Class Is Reshaping America's Electoral Map," *CityLab*, September 24, 2012, www.citylab.com/equity/2012/09/how-creative-class-reshaping-americas-electoral-map/3346/. For an empirical consideration of

the creative class's more liberal political leanings, see Jeffrey M. Berry and Kent E. Portney, "A Creative Class Theory of City Sustainability Policies," Conference Paper Presented at American Political Science Association, Philadelphia, PA, September 1–4, 2016, https://as.tufts.edu/politicalscience/sites/all/themes/asbase/assets/docu ments/berry/creativeClass.pdf.

29. Cynthia Barnett, *Mirage: Florida and the Vanishing Water of the Eastern U.S.* (University of Michigan Press, 2007).

30. Tom Groenfeldt, "Miami—The Operational and Financial Center for a Growing Latin American Market," *Forbes*, March 13, 2015, www.forbes.com/sites/ tomgroenfeldt/2015/03/13/miami-latin-americas-financial-center/#1571ecd93342.

31. Franco Ordoñez, "As Caribbean Immigration Rises, Miami's Black Population Becomes More Foreign," *Miami Herald*, April 10, 2015, www.miamiherald.com/arti cle18228377.html.

32. Mike Maciag, "Why Are So Many People Moving out of the Northeast?" *Governing*, December 12, 2018, www.governing.com/topics/urban/gov-migration -northeast-population-trend.html.

33. Note that this pattern has shifted in recent years as, especially, younger Cubans are no longer reliable Republican voters. See Francisco Navas, "In Miami, Cuban Americans have the Power to Push the State to the Left," *The Guardian*, November 4, 2018.

34. Elián González was a six-year-old (in 1999) Cuban citizen in the center of a bitter custody battle between his Cuban father, who wanted to take him back to Cuba, and his Cuban American relatives in Miami. This custody battle famously involved both the U.S. and Cuban governments. González was eventually returned to the custody of his father in an April 2000 raid by Clinton's U.S. Department of Justice. The dramatic event caused a massive voter backlash (termed "*el voto castigo*" or the punishment vote) against the Democrats, who had been gaining ground with Cuban Americans since the 1960s. Al Gore was perceived to be pandering to the Cuban American vote when he urged Congress to give Elián González permanent residency status and then changed his mind to match the Clinton administration's position. Gore's flipflop is what got him in trouble. In addition, most Americans, including Cuban Americans, wanted Elián to be reunited with his father. Bush got 25,000 more Cuban American votes than Al Gore and 15 percent less votes than Clinton got in the previous election. William Schneider, "Elián González Defeated Al Gore," *The Atlantic*, May 1, 2001, www.theatlantic.com/politics/archive/2001/05/elian-gonza lez-defeated-al-gore/377714/; and Adam Clymer, "While Conservatives and Liberals React, Gore and George Bush Hedge on Ruling," *New York Times*, June 2, 2000, https:// archive.nytimes.com/www.nytimes.com/library/national/060200cuba-boy-react .html.

35. Robert E. Lang and Jennifer B. LeFurgy, *Boomburbs: The Rise of America's Accidental Cities* (Washington: Brookings Institution Press, 2007).

36. Population estimates are for 2018 and come from the U.S. census's American Community Survey.

37. Lang and LeFurgy, *Boomburbs*. By "New Brooklyns," Lang and LeFurgy are making reference to Brooklyn, New York, having once been the leading gateway for immigrants. Other examples of New Brooklyns include Santa Ana, California, North Las Vegas, Nevada, and Irving, Texas.

38. Jeff Howells, *Where to Retire: America's Best and Affordable Places* (Guilford, CT: Globe Pequot Press, 2011), p. 45. "The state's [Florida's] west coast seems to draw an unusual number of emigrants from the Midwest, whereas newcomers from New York and New England seem to prefer the Atlantic side of the peninsula."

39. Quotes from interview transcripts were edited for clarity.

40. Because all these experts were interviewed in 2018, their comments about the then impending midterm elections in 2018 are reported as relayed to the interviewer. Relevant elections details and outcomes are provided in the endnotes.

41. Darryl Paulson, interview with Elaine Silverstone, UNLV, May 3, 2018.

42. Ilena Ros-Lehtinen served in the House from 1989 to 2017. She originally represented the 18th District until reapportionment after the 2010 census changed it to the 27th District for the 2012 election. She ran unopposed in the 1998 and 2000 general elections and in 2014 (both general and primary elections), and generally won nearly 20 percent more of the vote than her opponents until 2016, where the spread was less than ten points. She retired in 2017.

43. In 2018.

44. Donna Shalala won the 27th Congressional District seat in 2018.

45. Carlos Curbelo won the 26th Congressional District seat in 2014 but was defeated in 2018 by Democrat Debbie Mucarsel-Powell.

46. Scott ran against Nelson in the 2018 General Election.

47. Rick Scott won the 2018 Senatorial election with 50.1 percent of the vote.

48. Population percents updated to reflect U.S. census 2018 estimates. Stefan Rayer and Ying Wang, "Population Projections by Age, Sex, Race, and Hispanic Origin for Florida and Its Counties, 2020–2045 with Estimates for 2018," University of Florida Bureau of Economic and Business Research, *Florida Population Series BEBR Bulletin 184,* June 2019, www.bebr.ufl.edu/sites/default/files/Research%20 Reports/projections_2019_asrh.pdf.

49. Paulson interview with Elaine Silverstone, 2018.

50. Ibid.

51. Sean Foreman, interview with Elaine Silverstone, UNLV, May 8, 2018.

52. The Florida Term Limit amendment, Amendment 9, limiting terms was added to the Florida constitution in 1992 with the approval of 77 percent of the voters. There have been recent efforts to increase term limits again. Mary Ellen Klas, "Florida Legislators Propose Increasing Term Limits," *Miami Herald*, November 22, 2015, www.miamiherald.com/news/politics-government/state-politics/article4562 1033.html.

53. Paulson interview with Elaine Silverstone, 2018.

54. Ibid.

55. There is some question as to whether it would be legal in Florida to have

different parties on the ticket. See Lawrence Mower, "Graham Says She Would Not Pick Republican David Jolly as Running Mate," *Tampa Bay Times*, May 14, 2018, www.tampabay.com/florida-politics/buzz/2018/05/14/graham-says-she-would-not-pick-republican-david-jolly-as-running-mate/.

56. Alex Leary, "Patrick Murphy and David Jolly Making an Unprecedented Bipartisan Run for Florida Governor?" *Tampa Bay Times*, April 23, 2018, www.tampabay.com/florida-politics/buzz/2018/04/23/patrick-murphy-and-david-jolly-making-an-unprecedented-bipartisan-run-for-florida-governor/; and Mower, "Graham Says She Would Not Pick Republican David Jolly as Running Mate."

57. State senators make $29,657 per year plus expenses; a Florida house of representative member makes $18,000 plus expenses.

58. *Baker v. Carr*, 369 U.S. 186 (1962).

59. Ironically, since this interview, Jacksonville has been fairly successful in attracting more technology jobs, as noted in the State of Play section of this chapter. See also, Dice Tech and Burning Glass Technologies, *Dice Tech Job Report: The Fastest Growing Hubs, Roles and Skills, Issue #1: Q1 2020*, p. 8, http://marketing.dice.com/pdf/2020/Dice_2020_Tech_Job_Report.pdf.

60. "Souls to the Polls" refers to a recent African American voting tradition where on "the last Sunday of in-person early voting," "efforts to spur turnout started in past elections with pastors at Black churches encouraging parishioners to go directly from Sunday services to early voting sites." Anthony Man and Ryan Van Velzer, "Souls to Polls Efforts Aimed at Increasing Black Turnout for Hillary Clinton," *Sun Sentinel*, November 6, 2016, www.sun-sentinel.com/news/politics/fl-souls-polls-black-vote-20161106-story.html.

6

MIDWEST: MICHIGAN AND OHIO

John J. Hudak
Karen A. Danielsen

During much of the twentieth century, Michigan and Ohio helped form the core of American manufacturing. Bustling factories making a variety of products for domestic and international markets and military and civilian consumption powered the economies of these states. Employing tens of thousands of people, American manufacturing was the envy of the world, and its heart was the Midwest.

Advances in transportation and waterway infrastructure grew towns into global cities that became hubs for commerce, innovation, and education. Although cities like Detroit and Cleveland became famous for building cars and automobile parts, those industries were just part of the manufacturing sector that exploded in these two states and their metros. While differences existed across the two states, a shared economic experience that depended on work on both sides of their border drove similar population growth, demographic change, and public policy decisions.

However, industry is just one part of Michigan and Ohio's economic and political history. As geographically large states (for those east of the Mississippi), metropolitan areas compose a relatively small part of their land area. Vast swaths of rural areas and small cities stretch for thousands of square miles between metropolitan areas. The rural areas maintain significant agricultural production, and in southeastern Ohio, coal mining towns dot the map. Both states were diverse and attractive to workers from a variety of backgrounds, and their success was driven largely by industrial manufacturing for much of the twentieth century.

However, within these diverse geographic and economic spaces grew political divides that have lasted generations. Michigan and Ohio have been swing states in presidential elections, shifting support to candidates of both parties. In the fifteen presidential elections since 1960, Michigan voted Democratic nine times and Republican six times; Ohio supported a Democrat six times and a Republican nine times. That variation in party support extended to governors' races, as well. Since 1960, Michigan has had four Democratic and four Republican governors; Ohio has elected four Democratic and six Republican governors.

Although voting blocs within the state changed over time and continue to do so today, the recent history of these two Midwestern states is that of stiff political competition that allows either party to do well depending on the candidate and the moment. And the basis for these divided electorates, in large part, harkens back to the diversity within the state and divisions between urban areas and the rest of their respective states. Both states have multiple metropolitan areas. Historically, one metro in each state—Detroit and Cleveland—were each economic and population powerhouses and generated significant shares of the Democratic vote locally and in statewide elections. However, shifts in populations and differences within each state have caused different political outcomes and set each state on different tracks into the future. Evaluating the demographics and politics of each state is important to understanding their shared history and political trajectory.

Although the states are similar in that both were carved out of the old Northwest Territory and share the same Midwestern regional identity, Michigan and Ohio have also been bitter rivals at times. In 1835, the states fought what became known as the "Toledo War."[1] The dispute was over land that both states claimed—the Toledo Strip—which included the newly founded city of Toledo (then part of the Michigan Territory). According to Mark Stein, the war "resulted in the capture of nine surveyors working for Ohio and the stabbing of a Michigan Sheriff."[2] Ohio prevailed and Toledo was reincorporated in 1837 as part of the Buckeye State.[3] There is also a long-standing college football rivalry between the University of Michigan and Ohio State University.[4] The rivalry is so intense that HBO Sports did a documentary on the enduring bitterness between the two schools at the 99th anniversary of their first game.[5]

STATE OF PLAY: MICHIGAN

Michigan has a long history of a diverse economy and population. It is a state with nearly 10 million residents, of whom more than half (54 percent) live in the state's two million-plus metros: Detroit and Grand Rapids. But Michigan is about more than its metros (see table 6-1). Michigan has grown just 1.1 percent since the 2010 census.[6] By 2018, faster-growing North Carolina and Georgia actually bumped Michigan from the eighth to the tenth most populous state.[7]

Michigan can be divided into five general regions (see figure 6-1): Southeastern Michigan, Central Michigan, Western Michigan, Northern Michigan, and the Upper Peninsula (or U.P.)[8]

Southeastern Michigan

Southeastern Michigan is home to the city of Detroit, its extensive suburbs, and the college town of Ann Arbor. It is the liberal and Democratic-voting core of the state. Table 6-2 shows that in the Detroit metropolitan area, the Democratic Senate candidate, Gary Peters, won by a 17.1 percent margin in 2018 and the Democratic gubernatorial candidate by 19.9 percent. Democrat Senator Debbie Stabenow[9] was reelected, and Democratic gubernatorial candidate Gretchen Whitmer won because of the large margins posted in the Detroit metropolitan area. In 2012, President Obama won the region with a 20 percent margin and carried Michigan, while in 2016, Democratic presidential candidate Hillary Clinton won metro Detroit by only 10.7 percent and lost the state to Republican Donald Trump by a razor-thin 10,704 vote margin.

Detroit has become a global city and serves as a jumping off

FIGURE 6-1. Michigan

point for destinations all across the world via the Detroit Metropolitan Wayne County Airport—the seventeenth busiest airport in the United States.[10] It is home to major corporations, most notably General Motors, Ford Motor Company, and Fiat Chrysler Automobiles. In the suburbs west of Detroit, Ann Arbor is home to the state's flagship university, the University of Michigan, with nearly 50,000 students.

The Detroit metro is home to 43.3 percent of the state's population (see table 6-1). It is remarkably diverse, with a significant foreign-born population and large numbers of Black, Latino, and Asian residents. In fact, over 70 percent of Michigan's Black population, more than 60 percent of Michigan's Asian population, and over a third of the state's Latino population live in the Detroit metropolitan area.

A portion of the population that identifies as white comes from a

TABLE 6-1. Demographic and Economic Comparison
between Michigan and Metros

	Michigan	Share in Detroit (%)	Share in Grand Rapids (%)
Population	9,962,311	43.3	10.6
White	75.1%	38.3	11.2
Black	13.6%	70.3	4.8
Asian	3.1%	61.0	32.7
Latino	5.1%	37.9	5.5
Foreign-Born	7.1%	62.9	10.5
College Educated	29.1%	46.8	11.8
Jobs	4,660,716	43.3	11.9
GDP	$440,310	52.5	12.1

*Excludes counties outside of MSA primary state.

Sources: 2017 American Community Survey 1-Year estimates as aggregated by censusreporter.org, Department of Commerce, Bureau of Economic Analysis, 2015 Real GDP (millions of chained 2012 dollars) County Level Data, U.S. Department of Labor, Bureau of Labor Statistics 2017 County Level Data.

significant number of Arab immigrants and Arab Americans living in Detroit and its suburbs.[11] To highlight this point, there is a large number of Iraqi ex-patriots in the area, such that during Iraqi parliamentary elections, they are still voting for Iraqi candidates back home.

Western Michigan

Western Michigan also boasts a diverse economy, and is dominated by the Grand Rapids metropolitan area. The region is home to 10.6 percent of the state's population and generates 12.1 percent of the state's GDP. Although it is home to 32.7 percent of the state's Asian population, the Grand Rapids metropolitan area is much less racially and ethnically diverse than Detroit. For example, less than 5 percent of Michigan's African American population and just 5.5 percent of the state's Latino residents live in metro Grand Rapids.

Western Michigan's coastline along Lake Michigan provides a significant tourism economy from within the state and for Chicagoans seeking summer getaways. The region includes a mix of agricultural and industrial areas. In some ways, the Grand Rapids economy features the perfect analogy for the Western Michigan region and the state as a whole—the intersection of agriculture and industry, as the city and its suburbs are and were home to some of the largest cereal processing companies in the country, including Kellogg and Post.

In addition to being less demographically diverse than Western Michigan, it is also more conservative. Kalamazoo County tends to vote Democratic, but Kent County, home to Grand Rapids, leans Republican. The remainder of Western Michigan leans or is solidly Republican. Grand Rapids is one of the most conservative million-plus metros in the United States. For instance, in 2016, the Grand Rapids metropolitan area voted in favor of Donald Trump by a 14.2 percent margin (see table 6-2).[12] In 2012, Republican presidential candidate Mitt Romney won Grand Rapids by 15.7 percent over President Obama. In 2018, the margin was much closer, as Democrat Gretchen Whitmer lost the region by just 6.2 percent.

TABLE 6-2. Comparison of Electoral Outcomes between Michigan and Metros

Election	Michigan Outcome	Detroit Vote Share (%)	Detroit Outcome	Grand Rapids Vote Share (%)	Grand Rapids Outcome
2018 U.S. Senate	+6.5 Dem	43.1	+17.1 Dem	10.8	+9.9 Rep
2018 Gubernatorial	+9.6 Dem	43.0	+19.9 Dem	10.8	+6.2 Rep
2016 Presidential	+0.2 Rep	43.6	+10.7 Dem	10.6	+14.2 Rep
2014 U.S. Senate	+13.3 Dem	43.4	+23.9 Dem	10.0	+15.3 Rep
2014 Gubernatorial	+4.1 Rep	43.5	+1.8 Dem	10.0	+32.6 Rep
2012 Presidential	+9.5 Dem	44.1	+20.0 Dem	10.1	+15.7 Rep
2012 U.S. Senate	+20.8 Dem	44.0	+31.6 Dem	10.2	+10.7 Rep

Source: Data from Michigan secretary of state's website.

Central Michigan

Central Michigan includes a combination of liberal and conservative areas, while blending agricultural productivity with manufacturing, among other industries. Areas like Flint are home to automotive manufacturing and parts plants. Central Michigan also includes Ingham County, home to the state capital, Lansing, and the state's largest university, Michigan State.

The influence of the manufacturing strength of Detroit clearly impacts portions of Central Michigan. Yet substantial portions of the region make up the agricultural core of the state. Clinton and Gratiot Counties, north of Lansing, and Huron and Sanilac Counties, northeast of Flint, employ significant numbers of farm workers and produce millions of dollars in agriculture yearly. Culturally and politically, the areas further north of Lansing look more like North Michigan. Generally, as one moves further north through Central Michigan, residents are more conservative and Republican. The same conservatism is true for the eastern section of the region along Lake Huron—or Michigan's "thumb."

Northern Michigan and Upper Peninsula (U.P.)

The state's two northern regions—Northern Michigan and the Upper Peninsula, or U.P.—make up the rural center of the state. They are far less populated than the rest of the state. Tourism remains a major driver of the economy in both northern regions, and natural gas extraction is an important industry. The harsh climate in Northern Michigan and in the U.P. limits the opportunities for agricultural production, although exceptions exist, particularly for timber in the U.P.

The U.P. includes nearly 1,700 miles of coastline, dozens of protected areas, including some of the most unique natural sites in the United States. While the U.P. is, in many ways, culturally unique from the rest of Michigan, it is largely politically conservative like Northern Michigan. Exceptions exist, like the more Democratic Marquette County, home to Northern Michigan University. The U.P. and Northern Michigan are also much less racially and ethnically diverse when compared to the rest of the state, and both lack metros but contain micropolitan areas. The largest city in Northern Michigan is Traverse

City, with fewer than 15,000 people, and the largest U.P. city is Marquette, with around 20,000 people.

Conclusion: Michigan State of Play

The cultural, economic, and political divisions within the state have produced a divided electorate that shows itself most potently in presidential elections. For some time, Michigan has been considered a swing state and, in the 2016 presidential election, Michigan's electoral votes were decided by the narrowest of margins. Donald Trump bested Hillary Clinton by fewer than 11,000 votes statewide. And the political division between urban and nonurban areas is quite pronounced. Clinton won only eight of the state's eighty-three counties. Among the seventy-five counties Trump won, he received more than 60 percent of the vote in forty-four of them.

And while the governorship of Michigan has bounced between the parties for some time, the legislature has been shaped by more conservative small towns and rural areas. The ability to draw district lines to benefit Republicans has allowed outsized GOP control within the state legislature. The Democratic governor, Gretchen Whitmer, won in 2018 by nearly ten points, and Democrats had significant success in state legislative races, given the national political environment, yet Democrats still fell short of controlling the legislature. Republicans hold 58 percent of state senate and 53 percent of state house seats. The U.S. House delegation is now split evenly at seven seats for each party (see table 6-3).

And that increase is a dramatic improvement from just a few years ago. After Republican governor Rick Snyder was reelected in 2014 by a slim four points, the GOP held 71 percent of the state senate seats and 57 percent of the state house seats. The GOP also held nine of the state's fourteen U.S. House seats. It is also notable that the GOP governor likely underperformed in 2014; he won by nearly twenty points four years prior. Yet, in the open seat Senate race that same year, as Republicans won huge numbers of state legislative seats, the Democratic nominee, Gary Peters, won by over thirteen points.

Much of the Democrats' success in the state comes from Detroit, Lansing, Oakland, Kalamazoo, and Ann Arbor. Without those cities

TABLE 6-3. Partisan Composition of Michigan State
Government and Federal Delegation

		State Government				Federal Delegation			
		Upper House		Lower House		U.S. Senate		U.S. House	
	Governor	Dems	Reps	Dems	Reps	Dems	Reps	Dems	Reps
2019–20	Dem	16	22	52	58	2	0	7	7
2017–18	Rep	11	27	47	63	2	0	5	9
2015–16	Rep	11	27	47	63	2	0	5	9
2013–14	Rep	12	26	51	59	2	0	5	9

Sources: Data from National Conference of State Legislatures, "State and Legislative Partisan Composition" for various years, and Michigan secretary of state's website.

and the counties within which they sit, Michigan would not be a swing state like Ohio or Florida or Wisconsin. Its voting patterns would look at lot more like Indiana.

Finally, table 6-4 shows that Michigan has a "local government autonomy score" that places it in the bottom eleven U.S. states in terms of municipal independence from state government. Governor Rick Snyder was empowered to appoint emergency managers for many of Michigan's most distressed cities. The "takeover of local governments" was controversial from the start.[13] It proved especially contentious in the case of Flint, where a state-appointed emergency manager made the decision to switch the city's water supply from Lake Michigan to the Flint River. The polluted Flint River poisoned local drinking water with lead. The situation was so serious that criminal charges were considered against the emergency manager, although they were later dropped.[14]

EXPERT ANALYSIS: MICHIGAN

To better contextually understand Michigan's politics, we interviewed Tom Ivacko, associate director of the Center for Local, State, and Urban Policy at the Gerald R. Ford School of Public Policy at the University of Michigan.[15]

TABLE 6-4. Metro Governance Fragmentation and Autonomy in Michigan

Governance Fragmentation

Metro	Number of Counties in Metro	Number of General Purposes Governments in Metro
Detroit	6	213
Grand Rapids	4	112

Governance Autonomy

Local Government Autonomy Score	−0.273
Local Government Autonomy Ranking	39

Sources: Data for Governance Fragmentation from 2017 Census of Governments. Data for Governance Autonomy from Harold Wolman, Robert McManmon, Michael Bell, and David Brunori, "Comparing Local Government Autonomy Across States," in *The Property Tax and Local Autonomy*, edited by Michael Bell, David Brunori, and Joan Youngman (Lincoln Institute of Land Policy Press, 2010), pp. 69–114.

Intrastate Political Dynamics

Michigan has lost population in recent years, and nowhere is that more pronounced than in the city of Detroit. In the 1950s, the city of Detroit had nearly 2 million residents. Today, the city has just 672,669 residents, while the Detroit metropolitan is home to over 4.3 million people. By contrast, Grand Rapids is only a quarter that size, with nearly 1.1 million people. Grand Rapids has seen some fluctuations over time, but generally has maintained stable growth. However, population stasis or decline in Michigan is not just a Detroit phenomenon. There has been significant exodus from rural areas, as Ivacko notes, particularly among young people, as job opportunities waned in those regions and people sought careers in other fields. A transitioning economy and the decline of the manufacturing sector has had effects on the population base in Michigan, as has a shift away from agricultural work in rural areas.

Changes to Michigan's Congressional Delegation

Population changes have also affected the size and composition of the state's congressional delegation. After the 1960 and 1970 censuses, Michigan had nineteen seats in the U.S. House. Today, the number has dropped to fourteen, and it is expected that Michigan will lose another seat after the 2020 census. That would mean that in the course of forty years, Michigan lost 27.8 percent of its representation in Congress.

But as in the rest of the country, the 2018 election brought change to Michigan's House delegation.[16] Before the 2018 election, Republicans dominated the congressional delegation, controlling nine of the fourteen districts. The 2018 election notably ousted two Republican House members, which evened out the number of representatives for both parties, as Ivacko recounted:

> Two congressional seats flipped from Republican to Democrat and both have at least portions of their districts in the broader South-eastern Michigan region. At least one of them also stretches to areas dominated by rural parts of the state that I would classify as outside of the core part of Southeastern Michigan. And so the fact that it was [Mike Bishop's] seat that flipped Democrat, I think was pretty remarkable.[17]

Yet, the Republicans lost an additional member when Justin Amash from Michigan's third district changed parties in July 2019 to Independent. This has changed the congressional delegation to being majority Democrat. Ivacko does not find Amash's party change particularly unusual. He chalks up this behavior as somewhat typical of Michiganders:

> I think that in a weird way that fits a pattern about Michigan. We . . . sometimes find a way to break the mold. . . . Jesse Jackson beating Dukakis in the 1988 primaries, Bernie Sanders beating Clinton in 2016, the Reagan Democrats in Macomb County, Justin Amash bucking the Republican Party, and so on. Michigan has this history of breaking the mold at various times. I think the conversion of Justin Amash . . . I mean, he hasn't converted but the party has moved away from him. . . . His willingness to break from the party

in some ways is surprising but in other ways not necessarily so much.

Structural Features of State Government

State government in Michigan is headed by a powerful governor. The state always had a powerful governor's office, and Ivacko suggests that while Michigan no longer ranks among the country's most powerful governors, that has not happened because of a weakening of the state's office (he adds that the governor's strength slipped from around fifth in the 1960s to thirty-fifth in the nation). He argues this change can be attributed to *other* states strengthening the powers of their chief executive in the intervening time. Ironically, Ivacko goes on to say that after Michigan implemented legislative term limits in the 1990s, more power has been sent back to the executive branch (in particular, state agencies), further enhancing the influence a governor has over state policy. He further notes that this power shift includes more lobbyist influence in the executive branch but also the legislative branch as well.[18]

The governor's office has been dominated over the last half century by Republicans in terms of the total number of years they have served. The strength of the governor's office in the 1960s undoubtedly was partly a result of no term limits. Republican William Milliken, who was a beneficiary of that policy, served the longest term as governor (from 1969 to 1982). Republican John Engler served nearly three terms because he was elected before term limit legislation passed.[19] Republican governors, according to Ivacko, often enjoy unitary party control over the state government. When Democrats win the governorship, Ivacko observes, they usually contend with a "split state" legislature.

Yet, governors "over the last number of years have wielded significant power in the state," according to Ivacko, particularly if the legislature and the governor's office are controlled by the Republican Party. He offers the example of Republican Rick Snyder's contentious and controversial use of the emergency manager law:

Governor Rick Snyder, the current governor's predecessor, institute[ed] the emergency manager law in the State of Michigan, which is one of the most extreme, I think, state level policy actions in quite a long time. [The law] allowed him to appoint emergency managers to go into cities and school districts in the state that were in financial distress and really remove all power from local elected officials and have the local authority being run by the governor's appointee. That was a bold policy action very much supported by the Republican legislature. The entire time that Governor Snyder was in office, he had unified state control with [a] Republican legislature.

Ivacko argues that even the most recently elected governor, Democrat Gretchen Whitmer, is following suit with some bold actions herself in responding the COVID-19 crisis:

Governor Whitmer is, I think, today also showing some bold action, certainly in her response to the COVID crisis, [by] putting the state into a state of emergency pretty early in the process. Just in the last couple of days, the business community in Michigan, led by the Michigan Chamber of Commerce, were lobbying her to not set a shelter in place order. She held off a couple of extra days, but she's gone ahead and done that despite that pressure from the business community. And she, unlike the most previous Democratic governors during either divided statehouse with some Republicans some Democrats . . . Governor Whitmer is taking some other bold actions. An example is that the state legislature had passed a budget she was not pleased with and she used [her] administrative powers to move the budget among [and] across departments. She faced a lot of pressure not to do that. In fact, the legislature . . . was trying to take that power away from the governor's office but she wielded that power anyway. So, my impression is that Michigan's governor is a pretty strong office.

The Michigan State Legislature is notable for the fact that it is one of the few full-time legislatures in the county. Ivacko notes, "it's one of only four in the nation [that] meets throughout the year."[20]

The relative power between Detroit and Grand Rapids in terms of influence . . . is that certainly Detroit in Southeastern Michigan and Detroit metro area in particular as an economic engine for the state; it is front and center, but Michigan's legislature has been heavily gerrymandered over the years and controlled by Republicans much more often than not. The state Senate has been in Republican hands since 1983 and unbroken in streak. And so again there's not much love lost between Republican leadership in the legislature and more liberal Democratic interests of the Detroit region.

Metro Power in State Government

A stagnating population in the state's largest metro, Detroit, has weakened that area's influence within the state legislature specifically and state government more broadly. Because metros tend to be sources of significant Democratic political power, and Detroit is no different, Republicans and areas outside of the Detroit metro have been the beneficiaries of the relative population decline in Southeastern Michigan. Ivacko describes these demographic changes in detail:

Well, I think the thing that is most on my mind there are these hints that we saw in [the] 2018 [election] about potential demographic changes in the Grand Rapids region in particular but also the Grand Traverse region up north and that Ottawa County region. These regions have the fastest-growing populations within the state. Now that Detroit's population appears to have at least stopped declining; I don't know that we will see actual increases. I think one of the major goals of Mayor [Mike] Duggan was to see population growth by the 2020 census, and I'm not sure he will see that. So the population within Detroit, certainly Detroit proper, is not growing significantly. Whereas the other parts the state are growing faster and if, indeed, they are growing with younger populations that are leaning more Democratic than these regions have in the past, I think that has the potential to have significant impacts within state politics. I think that the biggest, to be honest, biggest factor in the state is going to be the new redistricting approach where Michigan for the 2020 census is going to be redistricted by an independent citizen's commission for the first time. And I think Michigan has been one of the most heavily gerrymandered states in the nation, both for congressional representation but also within the state legislature. And my expectation is that an independent citizens commission-led redistricting process is going to upend that. And probably the most important outcome from that will be increased Democratic representation within the state legislature, which has been dominated by the Republicans for quite a long time; the last decade plus has been quite conservative: anti-tax, anti-union, anti-environmental policies, and so on. So if, indeed, that does come to pass . . . if redistricting leads to better representation by Democrats in the legislature, I think that could really put Michigan on a different course going forward.

Ivacko adds how the "Independent Citizens Redistricting Commission" came about:

This was a remarkable movement that began with a single young person [posting on Facebook]. She wanted to do something about Michigan's extreme gerrymandering, and wanting to know if others would join her.[21] It turned into a nonprofit called Voters Not Politicians[22] that took off like wildfire. They organized to get a ballot initiative on the November 2018 ballot to take redistricting out of the legislature's hands and put the authority in the hands of an independent citizens redistricting committee. They had volunteers all over the state gather signatures to get the question on the ballot, and they did a truly remarkable job, gathering way more than the required number of signatures in a very short time period, the kind of thing most observers would have said could only be done by a professional signature-gathering organization with significant funding. They clearly tapped into a hunger for change among the citizens. The ballot initiative was approved by about 61 percent of the voters.[23] Going forward, this is likely to have a significant impact on Michigan's state house and senate [which has been controlled by the GOP since the early 1980s, despite Michigan clearly not being a red state].

Also, Michigan has seen declining union power. Republican legislators and governors, particularly during Rick Snyder's administration, passed laws further weakening unions. And as economic transitions happened in traditionally union-heavy industries, the percentage of unionized workers in the state dropped. In 1989, 26 percent of Michigan workers were union members.[24] By 2018, that number had dropped to 14.5 percent of workers.[25] As the population dropped in Michigan's most Democratic areas, a key tool for Democratic political organization faded as well.

Ivacko remarks that Michigan's population change also affected the state legislature. He explains that Detroit has less power than it once did within the state legislature due to population loss and gerrymandering that has pushed political power to suburbs and rural areas. Despite population shifts, Michigan remains a state with a significant share of people living in major metro areas, but a state legislature that does not reflect the state's urban dominance. Ivacko notes that, since 2000, there has been a dilution of power from Southeastern Michigan, despite the fact that it remains the most populous part of the state, containing about 43 percent of residents. Ivacko describes the political landscape of the state:

Detroit, Southeastern Michigan has been the core of the blue portion of the state of Michigan. The west side, all the rural areas, Northern Michigan up into the thumb, which is on the east side of the state, but not in Southeastern Michigan. Across the West Central and west parts of the state have been the more red parts. And now for the most part those patterns hold true even today, but there have been some, I think one of the other kind of significant things that we saw in 2018 in the November 2018 election are hints of potential demographic changes underway and a few parts of the state.

The Oakland County region, which is northwest of Detroit, has been shifting more toward Democratic power and Kent County, which is the home of Grand Rapids. Governor Whitmer won in Kent County. This is the first time a Democrat has won since 1986, I think, and she very nearly won also in Grand Traverse County up around the pinky area where Traverse City is. Democrats did better than they historically have in Ottawa County and the far west side of the state not too far from the Grand Rapids area.

Those regions, Kent County/Grand Rapids/Grand Traverse County/Traverse City and Ottawa County, are among the fastest-growing portions of the state. And so the fact that Democrats did quite well in those areas, I think, raises a lot of questions about whether there are some more fundamental changes underway in the state of Michigan.

Local Government Authority

The state government's relationship with local government is a complicated one. Ivacko explains that about 250 cities have home rule and about the same number of villages have the right to expand home rule. However, the vast majority of local governments—townships and counties—are subject to Dillon's Rule. This means that, geographically, state power over local government is strong in most of Michigan. However, given home rule rights in cities, a significant part of the population lives in jurisdictions with greater local power.

However, despite the formal powers of population-heavy home rule localities, the state has implemented extraordinary measures to enhance its authority. Ivacko explains that over the last decade, the state has acted to restrict local authority over a variety of policy areas via state preemption. The expanded state authority was seen most obviously during Governor Rick Snyder's administration. Under Snyder, the state exercised its preemption power in a variety of areas, including limiting local minimum wage increases,[26] labor laws around interviewing processes and background checks,[27] and banning taxes on plastic bags and junk food.[28] Ivacko cowrote a 2016 survey of local leaders' opinions on state preemption. According to the University of Michigan report, about 70 percent of local leaders think the state is taking too much control, and 49 percent of these leaders describe their relationship with the state as being "less than good."[29]

Ivacko also describes Michigan's system for funding local governments as "broken" and says that in some areas, such as transportation, the outsized power of Republicans helps rural areas and hurts major metros—even Grand Rapids. Using transportation as an example, Ivacko indicates that part of the problem for funding local governments, particularly in Detroit, is that there is a "lack of unity across the Detroit metro region." He continues:

> There is a lot of political infighting between Oakland County, Macomb County, both of which are on the northern borders of Detroit, and Wayne County (which is Detroit's county). Regional transit is a perfect example of that. We still do not have a unified regional transit system across this most important region of Michigan's economy. And they've tried a couple more times [since 2018 to do so]. There's an effort underway right now again to try to come up with a new system, and yet the infighting goes on [between] individual jurisdictions within Oakland and Macomb County trying to get the authority to opt out if a regional system is put in place by the voters. Individual jurisdictions want the ability to opt out, which would undermine the system. Maybe not make it irrelevant but make it less effective, for sure. And so the Detroit metro region hurts itself in terms of its overall potential state influence because of the infighting within the region.

Ivacko goes on to note that the state has failed to address a broken funding system while simultaneously diminishing local power through preemption, exacerbating problems at the municipal level, such as fiscal crises. On the other hand, Western Michigan and especially the Grand Rapids metro garners much more attention from the state legislature than Detroit partly because of Republicans' success in representing the region's interests. As Ivacko informs us:

> By comparison, Grand Rapids in the more western part of the state . . . I think it overperforms compared to Detroit. A lot of that is tied to the gerrymandering of the state legislature. The conservative forces in the state have very strong representation within the state legislature and have been more effective in getting their policies enacted than Democratic forces have within the state.

He suggests that Western Michigan exerts more power relative to Detroit due to the concentration of important business leaders in the state:

And economically Michigan is very much [a] divided state between still the progressive and labor forces primarily in Southeastern Michigan, the Detroit metro region, but also in other population centers around Saginaw Valley, and so on versus pretty conservative economic views represented by the DeVos family out of the Grand Rapids region, which has wielded a lot of power in the state.[30]

Cultural Divisions

Ivacko also notes that Michigan maintains a significant urban/rural divide, although he cautions against making a blanket statement. At the major metro level, Grand Rapids is more culturally conservative than Detroit. Ivacko ends with a discussion of "strong and significant" cultural issues facing the state. He focuses on four major issues that divide along ideological and geographic lines: LGBTQ[31] rights, marijuana legalization, gun rights, and abortion.

Progressives are making considerable strides in the state in terms of reforming gerrymandering, as noted earlier, but also on LGBTQ rights and marijuana legalization. All these efforts are taking place outside the legislature and are being fought via ballot initiative. A big win for progressives was the passage of the Proposal 1 ballot initiative in November 2018, legalizing recreational marijuana use that passed with 56 percent of the votes.

LGBTQ rights are in play now despite the state remaining conservative on the issue. Efforts are underway to change that through ballot initiative, as Ivacko notes:

Currently within the state of Michigan, the current law does not protect the LGBTQ community from employment discrimination; [someone can] be fired simply because they're gay. And there has been an effort within the state by progressives to amend the state constitution to prevent that and it has been an ongoing battle. I think there is an effort now to launch another ballot initiative for this coming November to get those protections written into state law. That absolutely has been a dividing point across the state.[32]

Gun rights form another key divide in the state between urban and rural areas. Rural Michigan is part of a larger movement of what is known as "Second Amendment Sanctuaries."[33] According to Ivacko:

> Gun rights, I think, mirror the urban/rural divisions across the nation. There has been a wave of efforts across the state just in recent months to establish Second Amendment sanctuary counties among counties in Northern Michigan and scattered across the state, and in rural portions as well. So the rural places see gun legislation as efforts to diminish Second Amendment rights, whereas I think the progressive forces in the state are looking at things like red flag laws, mental health considerations, and so on. So it's definitely a dividing line.

Abortion rights are also on the forefront of state issues. However, as Ivacko tells us, despite the fact that most people in Michigan want some form of abortion availability in the state, there is some troubling political maneuvering that may threaten abortion rights in Michigan:

> Abortion is an interesting issue, I think, where there certainly are going to be divisions, but the most recent poll I saw within the state is a number of years ago about abortion rights. I don't have it in front of me, but my recollection is that the residents within the state of Michigan are fairly similar to the overall views across America, which want to see *Roe v. Wade* protected and upheld but are still open to some additional restrictions.
>
> I think this is going to be a flashpoint in the state this year that probably will end up inflaming divisions more so than helping to build any kind of consensus because of the way it is going to be done. In Michigan, there's an effort to get an initiative onto the statewide ballot through signature gathering. If the effort gets enough signatures to get onto the ballot, the state legislature has the ability to simply enact that proposal and prevent it from even getting to the statewide ballot. And if they take that approach, the governor does not have the power to veto it. And so it looks like this is likely to happen in Michigan in the next few months. And I think if that happens, I think that process in particular will inflame a lot of division. People will feel that the legislature is preventing the will

of the people themselves from making a call on a really important issue. And this would be banning the D&E [dilation and evacuation] procedure. I think the policy reform that seems to be most likely is that the legislature would take this action on. I think if you did a town hall and could have a serious conversation with a range of Michiganders, I think you would probably find a fair amount of agreement on various aspects of abortion rights. But I think what we are going to see is this becoming a really high-profile and divisive topic in the state soon.[34]

STATE OF PLAY: OHIO

Ohio is sometimes referred to as the "bellwether state," given that it has voted for the successful presidential candidate in every election since 1964.[35] In fact, no Republican candidate has ever gained the presidency without winning Ohio.[36] It is a divided electorate that voted for George W. Bush twice, Barack Obama twice, and then Donald Trump. Although slightly whiter than Michigan, Ohio has a diverse economic and cultural history that helps shape its politics today.

Ohio is the most enduring swing state. Beginning in the post–Civil War era, Ohio has long been at the center of American politics. Seven U.S. presidents who served between the 1860s and the 1920s were born in Ohio: Ulysses S. Grant (1869–77); Rutherford B. Hayes (1877–81); James A. Garfield (1881); Benjamin Harrison (1889–93); William McKinley (1897–1901); William Howard Taft (1909–13); and Warren G. Harding (1921–23).

The Works Progress Administration's *Ohio Guide* (*WPA Ohio Guide*) from 1940 referred to Ohio as "The Barometer State."[37] A key reason Ohio remains a barometer of national tastes and trends is that it was settled by multiple migratory streams that represent the country as a whole. The *WPA Ohio Guide* notes: "In the early days, Ohio was favored with the best settlers from New England and the Southern colonies. Pioneers came from the mountains of Kentucky. Pennsylvania Dutch early settled Ohio in great numbers."[38]

Ohio has three different million-plus metros: Cleveland, Columbus, and Cincinnati, and large stretches of rural space and small towns in between. The state divides into four regions (see figure 6-2): Northeast

Ohio, West and Central Ohio, Southwest Ohio, and Coal Country (in the eastern and southeastern parts of the state).

Northeast Ohio

Historically, Northeast Ohio was a major population and economic engine in the state. Due largely to manufacturing and other industry, Cleveland (as well as the smaller Akron and Youngstown) became a major commercial hub, beginning in the nineteenth century. While manufacturing has diminished significantly, it remains an important part of the local economy. Bruce Katz and Jennifer Bradley cover Northeast Ohio in a chapter of their book on the metropolitan revolution, declaring the region a "post-hero economy."[39] The reference is to the fact that metro Cleveland's leadership is not seeking a miracle

FIGURE 6-2. Ohio

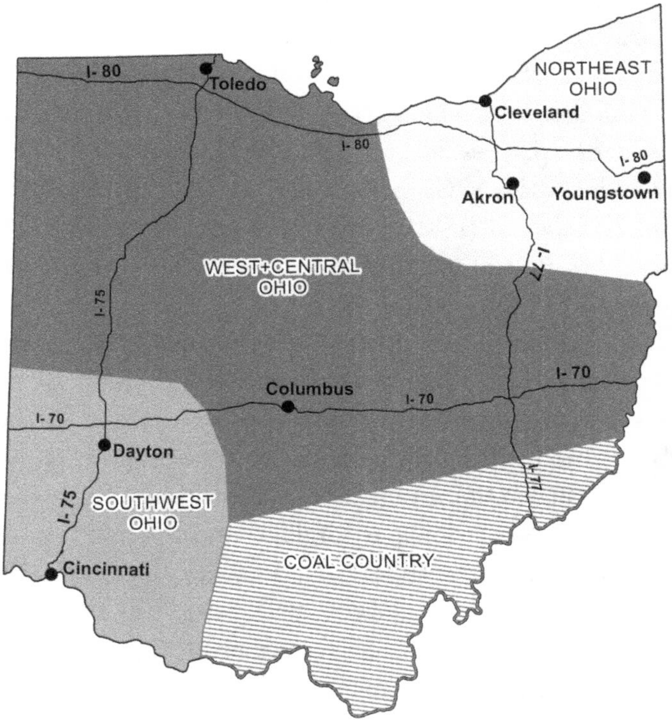

cure for its economic ills, but instead developed a series of support networks to incrementally improve and retain the region's competitiveness as a manufacturing center. They also note that parts of Northeast Ohio have revitalized, anchored by large employers like Progressive Insurance, the Cleveland Clinic, and Case Western Reserve University, which helped transform Cleveland into an innovation and learning region.[40]

The Cleveland metro remains significantly more diverse than the rest of Ohio. Cleveland is home to 17.7 percent of the state's more than 11.5 million residents and contains 28.2 percent of the state's Black population and 27.4 percent of the state's Latinos (see table 6-5). The region also punches above its weight economically, contributing more than one-fifth (21.3 percent) of Ohio's GDP. Northeast Ohio, driven by population centers in Cleveland, Akron, and Youngstown, tends to vote Democratic. Like Detroit, a history of union organizing has contributed to the continuing Democratic strength, but the area's diversity and focus on higher education also adds to the region's blue politics.

The Cleveland metropolitan area is the bluest part of Ohio. In 2018, the region gave the Democrats a bump in both the gubernatorial and U.S. Senate races (see table 6-6). The Democrats won metro Cleveland by a 17.7 percent margin for the governor and a 28.1 percent edge for the U.S. Senate. Cleveland helped easily reelect Democratic U.S. Senator Sherrod Brown to his third term and make the governor's race more competitive despite Republican candidate Mike DeWine winning on the strength of Ohio's rural vote. In 2012, President Obama won metro Cleveland by a 24.1 percent margin over Republican Mitt Romney, while Democratic presidential candidate Hillary Clinton managed only a 15.7 percent margin, which contributed to her losing Ohio to Republican Donald Trump.

West and Central Ohio

West and Central Ohio includes a significant portion of the state, running from the northwest corner west of Toledo diagonally across the state to just past Columbus. Much of this region is rural or exurban and, except for a few population centers, is less densely populated.

There are over 75,000 farms across Ohio, with the majority located in West and Central Ohio.[41] Agriculture, including soybeans, "corn for grain," and dairy is an essential part of the state's $10 billion agricultural economy. This region is generally more culturally conservative, except for two key population centers: Toledo and Columbus.

Toledo, a smaller city, is home to manufacturing, and historically leans more Democratic than other parts of the surrounding area. Columbus, located in the center of the state, is a major metro and Ohio's capital. It is home to the state's flagship university, The Ohio State University, and, in addition to the university and the state government, has major employers in health care and finance.

Columbus is growing rapidly (especially for Ohio), seeing a population increase over 50 percent since 1990. As Columbus has grown, and with it the university as a world class institution of higher education, the metro area has become more diverse. It has an outsized share of Black, Asian, Latino, and foreign-born Ohioans, and is now more populous than the Cleveland metro area (Columbus and Cleveland are the thirty-second and thirty-third largest metros in the United States, respectively) and nearly as diverse (see table 6-5). The rapid growth made Columbus the largest metropolitan area in the state. Despite passing Cleveland in population, Columbus maintains a slightly smaller metro GDP at 20.6 percent of the state.

Population diversity and the presence of a major university have also pushed Columbus in a more liberal direction in recent years. Table 6-6 indicates that in the 2018 election, Democrats performed much better in the U.S. Senate and governor's races than the party did in the 2012 and 2014 election cycles. If Columbus keeps growing and trending more liberal, it may help Ohio maintain its bellwether status.

Southwest Ohio

Southwest Ohio is anchored by Cincinnati, the state's third major city. Like Cleveland, Cincinnati was historically an industrial town that powered the economy of Southwest Ohio. Cincinnati was an iron production and meatpacking city, surrounded by suburbs, and the remainder of Southwest Ohio was and is more rural. Cincinnati was once so associated with hog butchering that in the mid-nineteenth

TABLE 6-5. Demographic and Economic Comparison
between Ohio and Metros

	Ohio	Share in Cincinnati* (%)	Share in Cleveland (%)	Share in Columbus (%)
Population	11,658,609	14.4	17.7	17.8
White	79.0%	13.9	15.6	16.5
Black	12.2%	17.3	28.2	22.5
Asian	2.2%	19.7	17.6	35.2
Latino	3.8%	13.1	27.4	19.5
Foreign-Born	4.5%	17.5	22.5	30.8
College Educated	27.9%	17.4	20.0	23.0
Jobs	5,483,140	14.7	17.9	18.8
GDP	$577,277	17.6	21.3	20.6

*Excludes counties outside of MSA primary state.

Sources: 2017 American Community Survey 1-Year estimates as aggregated by censusreporter.org, Department of Commerce, Bureau of Economic Analysis, 2015 Real GDP (millions of chained 2012 dollars) County Level Data, U.S. Department of Labor, Bureau of Labor Statistics 2017 County Level Data.

century it was dubbed, somewhat derisively, "Porkopolis."[42] Cincinnati has since become a modern regional center with metropolitan connections across the Ohio River in Kentucky. In fact, Cincinnati's main airport is located in Hebron, Kentucky.

The Cincinnati metro is home to major companies like Procter and Gamble, Kroger, and the formerly-named Fifth-Third Bank. The University of Cincinnati (a Carnegie R1 institution) provides a significant employment base for the metro as the state's second-largest research university.

As the third-largest metro in the state, Cincinnati, unlike Cleveland and Columbus, is much less diverse (see table 6-5). And Southwest Ohio outside of Cincinnati looks much more like the majority of West and Central Ohio: rural, white, and conservative. In fact, as a city, Cincinnati and its suburbs have been more conservative and Republican-leaning than Cleveland, despite having shared histories of being major industrial cities (see table 6-6). With Kentucky just

TABLE 6-6. Comparison of Electoral Outcomes between Ohio and Metros

Election	Ohio		Cincinnati		Cleveland		Columbus	
	Outcome		Vote Share [%]	Outcome	Vote Share [%]	Outcome	Vote Share [%]	Outcome
2018 U.S. Senate	+6.8 Dem		15.4	+2.8 Rep	18.7	+28.1 Dem	18.4	+17.1 Dem
2018 Gubernatorial	+3.7 Rep		15.3	+10.6 Rep	18.6	+17.7 Dem	18.3	+8.6 Dem
2016 Presidential	+8.1 Rep		15.2	+12.1 Rep	18.6	+15.7 Dem	17.7	+4.6 Dem
2016 U.S. Senate	+20.9 Rep		15.5	+29.6 Rep	19.1	+0.4 Dem	18.2	+11.3 Rep
2014 Gubernatorial	+30.6 Rep		15.0	+36.6 Rep	19.0	+18.4 Dem	16.8	+28.9 Rep
2012 Presidential	+3.0 Dem		14.6	+12.0 Rep	18.8	+24.1 Dem	16.7	+6.9 Dem
2012 U.S. Senate	+6.0 Dem		15.1	+7.5 Rep	19.4	+26.2 Dem	17.3	+9.0 Dem

Source: Data from Ohio secretary of state's website.

over the Ohio River, Cincinnati's politics tend to resemble Kentucky's southern orientation more than the state's other million-plus metros.

Coal Country

Coal Country covers a significant portion of eastern and southeastern Ohio. This section of the state lacks a metropolitan area—or even a good-sized city, with Athens being among the largest at just about 25,000 residents. Southeast Ohio blends rural farming communities with coal-mining towns. Ohio is the tenth-largest coal producing state in the country and the fourth-largest consumer.[43] The economic blend of coal mining and agriculture makes this part of the state more conservative. The only exception in this region is Athens County, where Ohio University is located.

Conclusion: Ohio State of Play

Much like Michigan, the drivers of political division in Ohio have much to do with regional economies. Agricultural and mining areas that occupy vast tracts of Ohio's geography are conservative and Republican-voting—many deeply so. The three major metros are more moderate to liberal and Democratic-voting. Those divisions have made Ohio a critical state in presidential elections. The 2004 presidential election was decided by the voters in this state, driving Republican George W. Bush to reelection[44]—after which it cast electoral votes for Barack Obama twice. In 2016, Ohio swung in the other direction, as Republican Donald Trump won the state by more than 8 percentage points.

The 2016 election showed some changing voting patterns within the state. Even as Clinton underperformed statewide, she won Columbus's Franklin County and Cincinnati's Hamilton County by margins similar to Obama's in 2012. Alternatively, the vast rural parts of Ohio became deeply Republican. Among Ohio's eighty-eight counties, Clinton won only seven. And of the eighty-one counties Trump won, he won sixty-six of them by over 60 percent.

Outside of the presidential race, Ohio's other statewide races highlight some of its political divisions. In 2018, Ohio's open governor's seat went to Republican Mike DeWine by 3.7 percentage points, while Democrat Sherrod Brown won reelection to the U.S. Senate by 6.8 percentage points. In those races, Democrats' support came most significantly from the Cleveland and Columbus metros. For example, Brown won the Columbus metro by 17.1 percent and the Cleveland metro by 28.1 percent, while his Republican opponent won in much of the rest of Ohio.

Ohio, like Michigan, has a state legislature that does not fully reflect the political divisions in the state (see table 6-7). In 2016, Donald Trump won 51.3 percent of the vote statewide, and in the legislative session beginning in 2017, Republicans controlled 73 percent of seats in the state senate and two-thirds of the state house seats. Even after the 2018 Democratic wave election in which Republicans narrowly won the governorship and a Democrat won reelection to the U.S. Senate, Republicans dominated the legislature. In the 2019 legislative session, the GOP held 70 percent of state senate seats and 62 percent of state house seats. In addition, Republicans have held twelve of the state's sixteen U.S. House seats since the 2012 elections.

One advantage major cities have in Ohio is a high "local government autonomy ranking" that places the state sixth highest in the United States (see table 6-8). Ohio has a strong tradition of home rule,

TABLE 6-7. Partisan Composition of Ohio State Government and Federal Delegation

| | State Government | | | | | Federal Delegation | | | |
| | | Upper House | | Lower House | | U.S. Senate | | U.S. House | |
	Governor	Dems	Reps	Dems	Reps	Dems	Reps	Dems	Reps
2019–20	Rep	10	23	38	61	1	1	4	12
2017–18	Rep	9	24	33	66	1	1	4	12
2015–16	Rep	10	23	34	65	1	1	4	12
2013–14	Rep	10	23	39	60	1	1	4	12

Sources: Data from National Conference of State Legislatures, "State and Legislative Partisan Composition" for various years, and Ohio secretary of state's website.

which allows a place such as Cleveland to innovate public-private solutions with very little interference from the state.[45] Still, as table 6-8 details, within each of the million-plus metro regions, there is a good deal of governmental fragmentation, particularly in Columbus, that may undercut the metros' abilities to develop and implement unified policy visions.

EXPERT ANALYSIS: OHIO

Expert analysis for Ohio was provided by Kyle Kondik, managing editor of *Sabato's Crystal Ball* and author of *The Bellwether: Why Ohio Picks the President* (interviewed May 18, 2018). We thank him for his willingness to assist with this project.

TABLE 6-8. Metro Governance Fragmentation and Autonomy in Ohio

Governance Fragmentation

Metro	Number of Counties in Metro	Number of General Purposes Governments in Metro
Cincinnati*	5	151
Cleveland	5	167
Columbus	10	266

Governance Autonomy

Local Government Autonomy Score	0.431
Local Government Autonomy Ranking	6

*Excludes counties outside of MSA primary state.

Sources: Data for Governance Fragmentation from 2017 Census of Governments. Data for Governance Autonomy from Harold Wolman, Robert McManmon, Michael Bell, and David Brunori, "Comparing Local Government Autonomy Across States," in *The Property Tax and Local Autonomy*, edited by Michael Bell, David Brunori, and Joan Youngman (Lincoln Institute of Land Policy Press, 2010), pp. 69–114.

Intrastate Political Dynamics

Modern politics in Ohio has been shaped by the original settlement patterns and various waves of immigration to the state. According to Kondik:

> There are certain settlement patterns that I think were important in determining the state politics. Really, from the time even before it became the state, Northeast Ohio was part of the Connecticut Western Reserve and was essentially owned by the New England states. People who settled in Northeast Ohio originally were also from New England. There are actually still some similarities between Connecticut and Northeast Ohio in terms of the way they vote. Part of the similarity is that a state like Connecticut and Northeast Ohio changed the same way over time. Northeast Ohio, just like Connecticut and a lot of New England, really got a significant amount of immigration through the decades. A second wave of immigration from Italy and Eastern Europe ended up being the major ethnic players in the politics of those areas. Also, a lot of people were attracted by the heavy industrial jobs that emerged in Connecticut, Cleveland, and Youngstown.
>
> Columbus and Cincinnati did not get nearly the amount of immigration in that time; their settlement patterns were different, too. The middle part of the state was settled by people from Pennsylvania, Maryland, and Mid-Atlantic places. A lot of Southwest Ohio was part of the Virginia Military District, so it was land that was set aside for veterans of the Revolutionary War from Virginia. So Southwest Ohio [has] a Southern character. More recently, the state developed its significant African American population, just like many Northern states did during the Great Migration. And a lot of African Americans headed up there, particularly in Cleveland, but also in Cincinnati.

Kondik makes a particularly important point about the lasting impact of these regional settlement patterns on the state's politics in terms of Ohio's "Americanness":

There is this old saying about Ohio . . . if you look at the *Ohio Guide* from the New Deal era of the federal Writer's Project,[46] they talked specifically about how Ohio was the seventeenth state to enter the union but in some ways was the first truly American state because of those settlement patterns from all across the original country [that] came into play in Ohio. There's still a regional divide in how the state votes: with Northeast Ohio generally being the most Democratic, Central Ohio Republican-leaning (but more of a battleground), Southwest Ohio being very Republican and very conservative outside of Cincinnati. I do think that there are those kinds of regional divides that have defined the state from the very beginning to this day.

Yet, in recent decades, Ohio has seen dramatic slowdowns in population growth, especially relative to the national average, and population change loss has happened in two of the state's three largest metros, and the cities themselves—Cleveland and Cincinnati—have seen significant declines. In the mid-twentieth century, Cleveland was a bustling city of nearly 1 million people. Today, that population has slipped under 400,000. Cincinnati was once a city of half a million people, and today, just over 300,000 call the place home. Deindustrialization, the outsourcing of manufacturing jobs to other parts of the country and abroad, had dramatic effects on the population bases of those metros.

Trends in Ohio's Congressional Delegation

Ohio's shrinking population also had political consequences. After the 1960 census, Ohio had twenty-four U.S. House seats. Today that number is sixteen, and like Michigan, the Buckeye State is expected to lose another seat after the 2020 census. If that happens, Ohio will have lost 37.5 percent of its House representation in half a century. The losses in representation happened not because Ohio's population declined over time but because the state failed to grow at the same pace as the nation. However, as Ohio's population was stable or grew slowly, some of its cities lost significant numbers of people. This dynamic caused meaningful political fallout within the state, as well.

Million-plus metros tend to be more liberal, especially the principal cities within these metros. Kondik explains that, over time, the Columbus metro has become significantly more liberal, particularly as the population has grown. Even Hamilton County, home to Cincinnati, though more conservative than the other two metros, remains more liberal than many other parts of the state:

> It used to be in Ohio politics that Cleveland was the dominant source of Democratic vote in the Cleveland area. If broadened out to Northeast Ohio to include places like Youngstown, Warren, and Akron in that group; that is the dominant source of the Democratic vote today. For many decades, Columbus and Cincinnati were pretty conservative and Republicans would routinely win Franklin and Hamilton Counties. In recent years, Franklin and Hamilton Counties have started to vote Democratic for president. In the 2016 [election], Hillary Clinton won in Cuyahoga, Franklin, and Hamilton Counties by roughly the same margin of votes as Obama did.

Yet because Republicans control most of Ohio's government, congressional districts have been manipulated to concentrate Democrats mostly in the urban areas of the state. Indeed, the Democratic congressional delegation, as Kondik relates, has been "rooted in Northeast Ohio." And he adds "[the Democrats] have a few other seats in the northern part of the state, mostly in Northeast Ohio [but] the Republicans control everything else in state politics." Despite Northeastern Ohio being the Democratic stronghold in the state, he argues that Republicans still maintain a significant political presence in the region:

> The collar counties[47] of those [Northeast Ohio] urban counties are almost all Republican, really, with the exception of Summit County, which is Akron, [and] Lorain County, which contains the cities of Lorain and Elyria. Even in the presidential election, Trump actually almost won Lorain County, which is a pretty bad performance for a Democrat there. Summit County voted for Clinton but not by the margins that I think a Democrat should have won.

He continues to explain that the Republicans who drew the state's most recent U.S. House district map created a Democratic district in

Columbus (Central Ohio), which "allowed them to build a bunch of relatively safe Republican seats around Joyce Beatty's district in Columbus. Now the same is probably true for Franklin County, but those urban areas, the cities and the closest suburbs, I think, are turning Democratic overall."

Yet, as the August 2018 special election in Ohio's 12th District (in the suburbs northeast of Columbus) to replace Republican Pat Tiberi indicated, the Democrats have still not secured the region's suburbs. Republican Troy Balderson won the 12th in a close race against Democrat Danny O'Connor as Kondik predicted. Balderson won with 51 percent of the vote after the "race was too close to call for nearly three weeks" according to the *New York Times*.[48] Kondik characterized the recent political tug-of-war in that district as:

Ohio's 12th [District], that is likely to be a highly contested special election this fall. It's a district that Trump won by about a dozen points that was Tiberi's seat. Prior to that, it was Governor Kasich who held that House seat for almost two full decades. That district is a very bedrock Republican territory including Delaware County, which is the fastest growing, most affluent, most educated county in the whole state. It has the longest unbroken string of voting Republican for president of any county in the state, going back a hundred years to 1916. But it's also one of the few places in the state where Clinton actually did a little bit better than Obama did in 2012. The demographics are the reason why, across the country, Trump underperformed in a lot of traditionally Republican, suburban counties that have high education levels. But he more than made up for that in Ohio by running up the score in more rural counties that have lower formal education levels. There are just more places in Ohio that looked like that as opposed to looking like Delaware County. Trump still won Delaware County by, I think, sixteen or seventeen points. But you usually expect a Republican to win that county by more like twenty or twenty-five [points]. So, Ohio 12 [is] the district you'd expect a Republican to hold. A district drawn to elect a Republican, but we've seen Democrats over-performing in special elections all over the country, so you expect it to be close and competitive in August [2018].

Kondik adds that Southwest Ohio is also Republican country despite Cincinnati having more of a Democratic influence. He explains any Democratic advantage at the local level in the Cincinnati metro has been muted by Republican gerrymandering in the region as exemplified by Ohio's 1st Congressional District:

> Cincinnati has occasionally elected Democrats to the U.S. House, but currently the one district in Southwest Ohio that's most competitive is Steve Chabot's seat, which is Ohio [Congressional District] 1. But it has been gerrymandered in such a way that it includes much of the city of Cincinnati and the western counties. It also includes all of Warren County, which is a pretty deeply Republican exurban county. So, I think that generally speaking, a place like Hamilton County might be a little bit better for Republicans down ballot than it is at the presidential level.

Kondik comments that nonmetro areas are becoming increasingly conservative and Republican voting. The key for a Democrat to win statewide is not necessarily winning rural areas. Kondik explains that the reason Hillary Clinton in 2016 underperformed Barack Obama in 2012 was not that Obama won rural areas but that he paired wins in metros with more moderate losses in rural counties:

> The problem for Clinton is that in the other eighty-five [nonmetro] counties in the state she did way worse than Obama did. Ohio is a state unlike, say, Illinois, for instance, where the big metro areas did not necessarily dominate the voting in the state. Even though the three big cities and their counties have become increasingly Democratic, all the changes in the other parts of the state have actually conspired to either keep the state as it was, which was a slightly Republican-leaning swing state to, in 2016, having a more significant Republican lean, and we'll see if that's how the state begins to perform in presidential elections going forward.

Kondik remarks that Clinton lost rural Ohio by a landslide, handing the state's eighteen electoral votes to Donald Trump. If that trend continues, the Democratic margins in Ohio's metros will not be significant enough to offset the Republican margins in rural areas. And that situation can shift Ohio away from being a swing state and toward being more reliably Republican:

> Hillary Clinton did really badly outside the three big urban counties. She even ran behind what a Democrat should get in Cuyahoga County although she kind of made up for that by doing better than a Democrat typically does in Franklin and Hamilton. Richard Cordray, the Democratic [gubernatorial] nominee . . . will have to put up big margins in Cuyahoga and Franklin, which are the two biggest sources of [Democratic] votes in the state. But he also will have to . . . build on what Clinton did in some of the typically Republican suburbs, particularly in the Columbus area where Cordray is from. And he'll also have to restore Democratic performance, particularly in the Appalachian eastern part of the state and in the Mahoning Valley, containing the cities of Youngstown and Warren. Those are places where Democrats should win . . . by twenty-plus points, like Mahoning County (Youngstown), Trumbull County (Warren). Clinton actually lost Trumbull County and only barely won Mahoning. In Ohio River places like Jefferson, Belmont, and Moreaux Counties (which had a Democratic lineage going back to the New Deal), these are places that have trended Republican over the last twenty years or so [but] that you'd expect the Democrats to at least be able to do better in those counties than Clinton did, which of course she lost those counties by a landslide.

But even if the Democrats make inroads into suburban and rural areas of the state, these efforts still may not be enough to help the party win statewide elections, particularly the presidential election. Kondik offers another reason why Democrats face an uphill battle in Ohio. The three big urban areas do not contain a significant enough share of the state's population and, in particular Democratic-leaning populations, to elect a Democrat as president:

> Ohio is the state where you do have three significant urban areas, but to put it in perspective, Cuyahoga, Franklin, and Hamilton [Counties] together cast a little less than 30 percent of the total

votes for president. If you look at Cook County, Illinois . . . I think Cook [County] itself is like 40 percent of the total statewide vote. So combined . . . Cook's cast a higher share of the total Illinois state vote than Cuyahoga and Hamilton and Franklin combined do in Ohio. And Cook is significantly more Democratic than Cuyahoga, Franklin, and Hamilton [Counties] combined. The fact that the three big urban counties in Ohio are not necessarily as Democratic as some of the urban areas across the country and that they cast a smaller proportion statewide vote than say a city like Chicago does in Illinois or New York City does in New York reduces the ability of those three big urban areas to dominate the state. In fact, I would argue that, particularly after 2016, the big urban areas, at least the closer you get to the cities, the political preferences in those places get swamped by the suburbs and the rural areas.

The Persistent Purple Senate Delegation

Still, it seems in U.S. senate races particularly, Ohio appears as a purple state. As Kondik relates, Ohio currently has both a Republican and a Democratic senator, which is historically quite common:

You've got a fairly conservative Republican in Rob Portman, a fairly liberal Democrat in Sherrod Brown. I think historically Ohio's a state that's elected all sorts of different people with different ideologies. It was home to Senator Robert Taft, who was known as "Mr. Republican." He was very much an ideological conservative in the forties and fifties in the Republican Party. But then you also have senators like Steven M. Young, Howard Metzenbaum, Sherrod Brown, who really are sort of on the liberal edge of their respective Senate caucuses. Portman, I think, is definitely a mainstream conservative. Mike DeWine and George Voinovich, when they were in the Senate, they'd be moderate on certain issues, but they also were fairly conservative on other ones. So, the state is historically closely divided among the two parties, divided enough that it's capable of electing anyone across the political spectrum in a given year. And Brown and Portman are great examples of that. Brown won the two Senate elections in 2012 and 2018, which were Democratic years in Ohio, and also nationally. Portman won in 2010 and 2016; 2010 was definitely a Republican year in Ohio and nationally. And 2016 was kind of a neutral year nationally, but certainly a Republican one in Ohio. The state is historically pretty closely divided. Sometimes, it just pays off to be with the right time and the right place running statewide in Ohio.

Kondik concludes by emphasizing that Democrats have to change their strategy of focusing solely on metro areas to perform better in presidential elections:

The thing about the three big urban areas winning through the big urban counties, it is not [an] efficient [way] to win the state. You need to do well in Toledo, do well in Dayton, and do well in Youngstown. If you're a Democrat, you need to do well in some of the college counties like Wood County [Bowling Green University], which is a swing county, Portage [County] in Northeast Ohio [Kent State], and Athens [County] in Southeast Ohio [Ohio University], a county Democrats should win in a landslide. And then also not necessarily win the some of the rural Appalachian counties, but not lose them in a landslides the way that Clinton did.

Structural Power in State Government

The Ohio governor is a powerful actor in state government. As Kondik reports, because Ohio has had extended stretches of Republican control of the governor's office and unified Republican control of the legislature, there have been limited checks on the governor's authority:

My understanding of the Ohio governorship has always been that it is a strong governorship. In terms of the history, at the end of governor Kasich's term (at the end of the calendar year [2018]), the Republicans will have helped the governorship for twenty-four of the last twenty-eight years.[49] They've held much of the rest of the machinery of state government for kind of a similar amount of time; a little bit less time in the state house, and some of the executive offices. But more often than not over the last three decades, the Republicans have had unified control of the government. So state politics have definitely had a distinctly Republican flavor for most of the last thirty years and for much of Ohio's history too, even though the state has generally been voting relatively close to the statewide or the national average for presidential elections for many decades now.

Compared to states with governors of different parties commonly or in states where the governor clashes with a legislature of the opposite party, Ohio has seen relative harmony, as Kondik describes:

Just like any other state, the three big urban areas send a lot of Democrats to state legislature. However, almost everywhere else in the rest of the state outside of Dayton, Toledo, and Youngstown send Republicans to the state legislature. The more rural areas, more rural parts of the state, have ended up exercising more [power] because they sent Republicans to the state legislature. And the Republicans again have had control of the state legislature for the lion's share of the last the last thirty years.

In addition, Ohio has a relatively well-paid full-time legislature, as Kondik observes:

The state legislature meets year-round. It is a full-time legislature, although they're not called in all the time. It's not like some states where they meet for a few months a year or something like that. My understanding is that the pay levels for legislators is pretty high compared to other states. I think the base salary is something like $60,000, but most members end up making significantly more than that because of leadership positions and committee assignments.[50]

Kondik maintains that, like in many states, the implementation of legislative term limits has naturally enhanced the power of the executive branch.[51] The change helped make an already powerful governor even more influential. The depth of Republican legislative control is consequential and enduring, even during times when national trends favor Democrats:

There are a lot of people in government and observers of state government who believe that legislative term limits enacted in Ohio in the nineties, just like they were in many other states, have essentially empowered both lobbyists and the executive branch. Vetoes can be overturned by a three-fifths vote in both the house and the state senate. That's obviously less of a threshold than the federal government, but it's more of a threshold than, say, West Virginia where vetoes can be overturned by a simple majority vote in the state assembly and the state senate.

Local Municipal Authority

The relationship between state and local governments is characterized by significant independence and periods of conflict, as Kondik explains. The Ohio constitution grants municipalities the power to exercise home rule. The constitutional provision generally offers local governments fairly strong protections from state government intervention.

But tension between state and local governments happens regularly, and the dynamic is more pronounced between liberal cities and million-plus metros and a conservative, Republican legislature and governor. Ohio's state government increasingly uses preemption power to disrupt home rule. Kondik recounts a recent example of state preemption involving gun regulation. Urban areas—most centrally Cleveland—enacted stricter gun regulations. This set up a clash between big cities that bear the brunt of gun violence and a conservative state government committed to protecting gun rights. Ultimately, the state stepped in and blocked local government's power to enforce additional gun regulation. Then Cleveland lost a lawsuit on the topic, so the preemption action remained.[52]

The state legislature has usurped home rule power on guns. So in some of the municipalities that wanted to enact harder rules on guns, the state legislature had weighed in on that. I think that the state municipalities generally do have some home rule powers, but the state legislature will sometimes intervene to prevent them [the cities] from doing anything on those [specific] matters.

However, that preemption power and the tension between state and local government over the boundaries of power did not begin recently, nor does it concern only controversial issues like gun control. Ohio has exercised preemption power on issues ranging from local fracking regulations[53] to minimum wage laws.[54] In fact, a 2019 *CityLab* article notes: "While both of the major political parties have a history of imposing state laws that override local ordinances, the preemption advantages of the past decade have tilted far more in favor of rural and conservative suburban legislative districts that typically vote Republican."[55]

Metro Powers in State Governments

Cincinnati and Cleveland, two of Ohio's three million-plus metro areas, have seen dramatic losses in population over the past half century that have reduced their representation in the state legislature. Not only has the population in these two metro areas decreased, but the percentage of the state population they encompass dropped significantly. Because the two cities lost seats in the state legislature, other regions are benefitting significantly by gaining legislative power. The Democratic dominance within big cities and in their metro areas translated to a weakening of Democrats' political strength in the wake of lost seats. Kondik noted that Cleveland was formerly the powerhouse in Ohio politics, but population trends have since diminished its power.

In addition to population shifts, the weakening of unions further diminished Democratic political power in Ohio. Unions served as a tool for organizing, and Democrats relied on them heavily throughout much of the twentieth century for political success in a variety of states. State policy changes stripped organizing rights and power, as manufacturing and other union-heavy industries began moving out of states like Ohio. In 1989, 21.3 percent of Ohio workers were in a union.[56] By 2018, that number fell to just 12.6 percent.[57] And although not every Ohio union member lives in a major metro, a significant proportion do.

While Cleveland and Cincinnati saw population declines, Columbus experienced the opposite. That growth has, in turn, helped Democrats turn metro Columbus more liberal than it once was, but not at a level to offset the party's losses elsewhere. Columbus's changes have a further complication, as Kondik notes. As the metro has grown in size and representation, it has also trended Democratic, but because the Democrats are the minority party in the state legislature, the political effects of the region's growth have been less than expected.

Demographic, economic, and migratory shifts in the past several decades resulted in a significant urban/rural divide within Ohio, although that phenomenon is not unique to the state. The same divide is happening in Michigan, Pennsylvania, and Wisconsin, as well as outside the industrial heartland in Sun Belt states like Arizona, Nevada, and Texas. What is different between the former group of states and the latter cases centers on where population growth happens within the urban/rural divide. In places like Ohio, some metros have seen population loss. In Arizona, Nevada, and Texas, major metros represent the largest population growth drivers. So, in a state like Nevada, the urban/rural divide continues, but Democratic strength is growing while rural political power continues to decline. In contrast, that same urban/rural divide in Ohio has largely benefitted Republicans—ditto Michigan and Wisconsin and to a lesser extent Pennsylvania.

The changes in power structures are seen most clearly in the Republican dominance of state legislative chambers in Ohio and Michigan. Although gerrymandering helped Republicans artificially boost their numbers (as Democrats often do in states where they are the dominant political party), there is a baseline strength of rural and Republican legislative power. Traditionally, Republicans were not the dominant force in all rural politics. However, as the two parties begin to divide not just ideologically but geographically, the GOP has become the party of rural and exurban voters, while Democrats have remained a party of urban and, to a lesser extent, more mature suburbs. As Kondik characterizes it:

> The political power of the state is Republican, and Republicans come from the rural areas and not really the big cities. Now there are some suburban Republicans from suburban Cleveland, suburban Columbus, suburban Cincinnati, particularly in the exurbs. There's kind of a suburban-rural Republican alliance verses the

urban Democratic alliance and the suburban rural component of the state because they're Republican.

Kondik asserts that partisan-geographic divisions also have distributive effects, especially in a state like Ohio.[58] As Republicans representing exurban and rural areas locked down control of state legislatures, it gave them significant, enduring control of policy agendas.[59] That power allowed Republicans to advance a bevy of ideological policies more consistent with the conservative values of the GOP. It also handed the party control over one of a state legislature's most important and valuable powers—the distribution of funding to localities.

Much has been written about the politicization of government funds. It happens at the federal, state, and local levels. Legislators do it; executives do it, and they do it to benefit key constituencies. State legislators can politicize funding by directing money for specific projects or by amending statutes to redesign formulas that allocate funding in policy areas such as transportation, education, and/or social services.

As Ohio Republicans became an exurban/rural party and as Democrats lost legislative power, funding was more easily steered to benefit nonmetro areas in disproportionate ways. Republicans rightly saw their base as being in outer suburban and rural places, and they used their legislative powers to assist those communities. This transition left many metro core areas, especially those dominated by Democratic politics, underfunded.

Conclusion: The Midwest

Changes in Michigan and Ohio may well send them in different directions. Although both states voted for Donald Trump in 2016, Michigan did so narrowly, while the president won Ohio by a comfortable margin. Republicans fared well in Ohio's 2018 election, winning all five statewide offices—even in a Democratic-dominated year. By contrast, in Michigan, Democrats won all statewide offices in 2018. The outcome could signify a trend. Both experts suggest that each state may be leaning toward one party and that the trend may continue.

Ivacko finds that Michigan is trending toward Democrats. He notes that there are far more Democrats in the state than Republicans. In fact, in recent Pew polling, 47 percent of Michiganders identify as Democrats, 34 percent as Republicans, and 19 percent as Independents. Ivacko notes that while reporting on Michigan's population changes often focuses on population loss in Detroit, that is not the whole story. There is also significant flight out of rural parts of Michigan, especially among younger residents. Those migration patterns, combined with indications that urban areas are beginning to see an inflow of people (especially diverse pools of people), could mark a trend in the Wolverine State. Thus, Trump's winning Michigan in 2016 could have been an aberration. He was the first Republican to win the state since 1988. It will likely take some time for pro-Democratic demographic changes to affect Republicans' success in the state legislature, but the implementation of an independent redistricting commission should expedite that process.

In Ohio, Kondik suggests a trend that favors Republicans. He reports that Ohio is whiter than most states, especially larger ones, and the number of college-educated voters in Ohio is below the national average. With that observation, Kondik predicts the end of Ohio as a bellwether state:

> I wrote that book [*The Bellwether: Why Ohio Picks the President*] before the 2016 election and I finished it before it was clear that Trump was going to be a nominee. I identified one reason why Ohio might not be as much of a bellwether going forward. Because Ohio is whiter than the national average and as the country becomes more diverse, then Ohio is becoming more diverse, too. But this is the other reason. [Ohio] is starting from a whiter place and it's not diversifying quite as fast. If America's politics continue to splinter on racial lines, you might naturally expect Ohio to get more Republican. The piece of it that I didn't identify because it wasn't as clear a political cleavage was that Ohio also is both whiter than the national average, but it also has a slightly lower level of four-year college attainment, so it has a definitely higher than average proportion of whites without a college degree. That group has been a Republican-leaning group for some time. But it's really becoming a *very* Republican-leaning group, particularly in the time of Trump.

Those two demographic characteristics, whiter than the national average and also less educated in terms of four-year college degree than the national average, would suggest that Ohio is probably going to be trending Republican over time.

Partisanship in Ohio looks very different than it does in Michigan. In recent Pew polling, 40 percent of Ohioans identify as Democrats, 42 percent as Republicans, and 18 percent as Independents. Those figures do not show a dominant Republican presence, but a stronger Republican position than in Michigan. Time will tell whether the 2016 presidential election and Republicans' subsequent statewide success in a Democratic year (2018) were real indications of a trend. As Kondik notes, part of the reason Hillary Clinton underperformed in Ohio relative to President Obama in 2008 and 2012 was not because of dramatic voting changes in metros but because she lost the rest of Ohio by dramatically larger margins. If the nonmetros are trending more Republican, Ohio will not hold the title of "swing state" much longer. According to Kondik:

> If trends continue as parties continue to split, it does seem like the three big urban counties are going to continue to be Democratic. In fact, Columbus in particular is becoming very Democratic, and Hamilton County might be heading that way, too. But much of the rest of the state outside of the three big urban counties seems to be heading the other way. There's more votes outside those three big urban counties than there are in those three big urban counties. It may be that the suburban and rural versus urban dynamic in the state may only intensify with the urban areas on the losing side of those battles because they just don't have quite as many people as the rural and suburban places have.

As major Midwestern states, Michigan and Ohio have large, diverse economies driven by vast stretches of rural, agricultural, and mining communities and million-plus metropolitan areas. The resulting urban/rural divide launched a competition over political power, economic influence, public policy, representation, and state funding. However, that split between cities and rural communities has not been a static one. Drastic changes in American economic order and the nature of industry within each state has motivated shifts in populations within the states and outside of them.

Since the 1960s, Midwestern population change shifted power within state governments and diminished the size of delegations to the U.S. Congress. As metro areas like Cincinnati, Cleveland, and Detroit lost residents, their political power and representation in their respective state legislatures diminished, and that power was transferred to other parts of their states—namely rural areas and the two growing million-plus metros, Columbus and Grand Rapids. In general, however, the population shifts combined with gerrymandering efforts allow Republicans, with a focus on rural and exurban constituencies, to gain outsized influence within the state legislature, often winning supermajorities. Over the past decade and a half, these Republican political successes helped deepen the urban/rural divide, shift disproportionate state aid away from major metros, and limit metros' abilities to enact policies that differ from the ideologies of the legislature's majority party.

Ohio and Michigan appear to be at a political crossroads in presidential politics. Ohio, traditionally the presidential bellwether state, and one that was frequently decided by just a few points in either direction, swung decisively to the Republican presidential nominee in 2016. The recent voting pattern reflects underlying trends that had been building in the state for some time. Michigan, meanwhile, though a competitive state, had been trending Democratic for nearly two decades, despite Donald Trump winning it in 2016. As demographic, economic, and political transitions continue, future elections will tell us whether 2016 was an anomaly for one or both states, or whether longer-term trends may take hold in the Buckeye State or the Wolverine State.

NOTES

1. Mark Stein, *How the States Got Their Shapes* (New York: HarperCollins, 2008), p. 144.

2. Ibid.

3. This dispute delayed the entrance of Michigan into the Union as Ohio demanded that Michigan prove that the territory exceeded the 60,000-person threshold required for statehood. The Michigan territorial legislature authorized a census

in 1834 that proved there were 82,273 inhabitants. Works Progress Administration, "Michigan: A Guide to the Wolverine State," American Guide Series (Oxford University Press, 1941), p. 48.

4. Greg Emmanuel, *The 100-Yard War: Inside the 100-Year-Old Michigan–Ohio State Football Rivalry* (New York: John Wiley & Sons, 2005).

5. Adam Jardy, "HBO to Show OSU-Michigan Rivalry Documentary," *Bucknuts /24hour sports.com*, October 30, 2007, https://247sports.com/college/ohio-state/Art icle/HBO-To-Show-OSU-Michigan-Rivalry-Documentary-104466019/.

6. U.S. Bureau of the Census, *County and Metro Population Estimates* (Washington: U.S. Department of Commerce, April 18, 2019).

7. U.S. Bureau of the Census, "Florida Passes New York and North Carolina Passes Michigan in Population," December 24, 2014, https://dilemma-x.net/2014/12/24/ florida-passes-new-york-and-north-carolina-passes-michigan-in-population/. Georgia passed Michigan in 2012.

8. The Michigan sectional geography used in this chapter mostly concurs with the one depicted in James G. Gimpel's and Jason E. Schuknecht's *Patchwork Nation: Sectionalism and Political Change in American Politics* (University of Michigan Press, 2003). The key difference between the two political geographies is that the Detroit metropolitan area is combined with the larger geography of Southeastern Michigan.

9. The state's U.S. Senate delegation is now Democratic, with both senators coming from Southeastern Michigan.

10. Detroit ranks sixteenth as a global city, according to Taylor and Lang. Peter J. Taylor and Robert E. Lang, *U.S. Cities in the World City Network*, (Washington: Brookings Metropolitan Policy Program, February 2005).

11. Note that the U.S. census classifies most immigrants whose ancestry originates in the Middle East as Caucasian (or white).

12. Republican President Gerald Ford was the U.S. House member from Western Michigan (then the 5th Congressional District) from 1949 to 1973, when he became vice president of the United States under Richard Nixon.

13. Richard Thompson Ford, "A State's Right: Why States, Like Michigan, Have the Power to Take over Local Governments," *Slate*, March 15, 2011.

14. Leonard N. Fleming and Beth LeBlanc, "Criminal Charges Dropped against Lyon, 7 Others in Flint Water Scandal," *Detroit News*, June 13, 2019, www.detroitnews. com/story/news/michigan/flint-water-crisis/2019/06/13/involuntary-man slaughter-charges-dropped-flint-water-scandal/1445870001/.

15. Tom Ivacko was interviewed April 28, 2018, and March 24, 2020. Comments were edited for clarity and corrections were made where necessary.

16. Ivacko also emphasizes the importance of the 2018 election in Michigan by noting that Democratic women won significant offices throughout the state. Women won the Governor's office (Gretchen Whitmer), Secretary of State (Jocelyn Benson), Attorney General (Dana Nessel, the second openly gay attorney general in the United States and first openly gay statewide office holder in Michigan). This trend contin-

ued the following year when Bridget McCormick was appointed Chief Justice of the Michigan State Supreme Court.

17. Democrat Elissa Slotkin narrowly won (50.6 percent) Michigan's 8th Congressional District over incumbent Mike Bishop (46.8 percent). The other upset was in Michigan's 11th Congressional District where Democrat Haley Stevens defeated (51.8 percent) Republican Lena Epstein (45.2 percent).

18. Research has born the trend of term limits shifting power away from state legislators to the executive branch, particularly to the professional executive branch workforce (that is, civil servants). See Graeme T. Boushey and Robert J. McGrath, "Experts, Amateurs and Bureaucratic Influence in the American States," *Journal of Public Administration Research and Theory* 27 (January 2017), pp. 83–103; and Thad Kousser, *Term Limits and the Dismantling of State Legislative Professionalism* (Cambridge University Press, 2005).

19. Rick Snyder (2011–18) was the first Republican governor subject to term limits since being implemented in 1992.

20. There have been several ballot initiatives attempted in the last decade (mostly by Tea Party members or supporters) to constitutionally change Michigan's full-time legislature to a part-time legislature, including one sponsored by the last lieutenant governor, Brian Calley. The initiative has failed repeatedly to qualify for the ballot because of insufficient signatures. See Up North Live Newsroom, "Lt. Governor Announces Ballot Drive to Make Michigan Legislature Part Time," *Up North Live*, May 30, 2017, https://upnorthlive.com/news/local/lt-governor-announces-ballot-drive-to-make-michigan-legislature-part-time.

21. Katie Fahey started the movement and was the executive director of "Voters not Politicians." She now is the executive director of a different 501(c) 3 called "The People," https://thepeople.org/our-team/.

22. "Voters Not Politicians" is a 501(c)4 organization started in Michigan in February 2017. See https://votersnotpoliticians.com/.

23. The success of Michigan's Proposal 2 (2018) ballot initiative has sparked similar movements around the country. The Brennan Center has set up a webpage that tracks these efforts. See www.brennancenter.org/our-work/analysis-opinion/citizen-and-legislative-efforts-reform-redistricting-2018. Virginia recently passed a constitutional amendment to set up a citizen commission, which is on the ballot in 2020. Graham Moomaw and Ned Oliver, "Virginia House Passes Redistricting Reform Measure, Sending Constitutional Amendment to Voters," *Virginia Mercury News*, March 6, 2020, www.virginiamercury.com/2020/03/06/virginia-house-passes-redistricting-reform-measure-sending-constitutional-amendment-to-voters/. In 2018, Ohio passed a constitutional amendment requiring districts to be drawn in a bipartisan manner by legislative members, not in a citizen committee. See Reid Wilson, "Ohio Voters Pass Redistricting Reform Initiative," *The Hill*, May 18, 2018, https://thehill.com/homenews/state-watch/386839-ohio-voters-pass-redistricting-reform-initiative.

24. U.S. Bureau of Labor Statistics, Midwest Information Office. "Union Membership Historical Table for Michigan, 1989–2019," www.bls.gov/regions/mid west/data/unionmembershiphistorical_michigan_table.htm.

25. U.S. Bureau of Labor Statistics, "Economic News Release: Table 5. Union Affiliation of Employed Wage and Salary Workers by State," January 18, 2019, www .bls.gov/news.release/union2.t05.htm.

26. Rick Pluta, "Snyder Signs Local Wage Preemption Law," *Michigan Radio (National Public Radio)*, June 30, 2015, www.michiganradio.org/post/snyder-signs -local-wage-preemption-law.

27. Jaclyn Giffen and Bill Vincent, "Michigan Expands Preemption Law to Cover Job Interview Limitation," Blog, *Society for Human Resource Management*, April 4, 2018, www.shrm.org/resourcesandtools/legal-and-compliance/state-and-local-up dates/pages/michigan-expands-preemption-law-to-cover-job-interview-limita tions.aspx.

28. National Federation of Independent Business, "Michigan Paves the Way to Preemption," Blog, October 31, 2017, www.nfib.com/content/news/michigan/michigan -paves-the-way-to-preemption/.

29. Debra Homer and Tom Ivacko, "Michigan Local Leaders' Views on State Preemption and How to Share Policy Authority," *Michigan Public Policy Survey*, Center for Local, State and Urban Policy, University of Michigan, June 2017, http:// closup.umich.edu/files/mpps-policy-authority-2016.pdf.

30. Grand Rapids is and has been home to very prominent conservative families, such as the Meijer (supermarkets), DeVos (Amway), and Van Andel (Amway) fami lies, not to mention President Gerald Ford.

31. LGBTQ is an abbreviation for lesbian, gay, bisexual, transgender, and ques tioning (or queer).

32. David Eggert, "Ballot Drive to Bar LGBTQ Discrimination Begins in Michigan," *U.S. News and World Report and the Associated Press*, January 7, 2020, www.usnews.com/news/politics/articles/2020-01-07/ballot-drive-to-bar-lgbtq -discrimination-begins-in-michigan.

33. According to Noah Shepardson, the phrase "Second Amendment sanctuary" is an umbrella term used to describe a jurisdiction that passes a resolution declaring that restrictive gun control laws another legislative body passes are unconstitutional and will not be enforced there." Noah Shepardson, "America's Second Amendment Sanctuary Movement Is Alive and Well," *Reason.com*, November 21, 2019, https:// reason.com/2019/11/21/americas-second-amendment-sanctuary-movement -is-alive-and-well/.

34. Kathleen Gray, "Right to Life Turns in Enough Signatures to Get Abortion Procedure Ban before Legislature," *Detroit Free Press*, December 23, 2019, www. freep.com/story/news/politics/2019/12/23/abortion-signatures/2735176001.

35. Kyle Kondik. *The Bellwether: Why Ohio Picks the President* (Ohio University Press, 2016).

36. Philip Bump, "The Two States that Almost Always Predict which Candidate is

Headed for Defeat," *Washington Post*, September 17, 2016, www.washingtonpost. com/news/the-fix/wp/2016/09/07/the-two-states-that-almost-always-predict -which-candidate-is-headed-for-defeat/.

37. Works Progress Administration, *The Ohio Guide*, American Guide Series (Oxford University Press, 1940), p. v.

38. Ibid.

39. Bruce Katz and Jennifer Bradley, *The Metropolitan Revolution: How Cities and Metros are Fixing Our Broken Politics and Fragile Economy* (Washington: Brookings Institution Press, 2013), pp. 64–87.

40. Ibid.

41. "Ohio Agriculture," *Farm Flavor*, Ohio Department of Agriculture, www.farm flavor.com/ohio-agriculture/.

42. Greg Hand, "Remember Cincinnati: 'Porkopolis' Was Not a Compliment," *Cincinnati Magazine*, November 14, 2016, www.cincinnatimagazine.com/citywise blog/remember-cincinnati-porkopolis-not-compliment/.

43. "Ohio Coal Quick Facts," Ohio Coal Association, www.ohiocoal.com/infor mation-library/quick-facts.php.

44. Robert Lang showed that it was the "micropolitan area" vote that gave Bush the ballot edge in 2004. See Jon Gertner, "The Micropolis," *New York Times 4th Annual: Year in Ideas*, December 12, 2004, Section 6, p. 83.

45. Michael E. Bell and Daniel Brunori, "Comparing Local Government Auton- omy Across States," in *The Property Tax and Local Autonomy*, edited by Michael E. Bell, Daniel Brunori, and Joan Youngman (Lincoln Institute of Land Policy Press, 2010), pp. 69–114.

46. See Works Progress Administration, *The Ohio Guide*, p. 16. Kondik is referring to this passage: "And when in 1803, having the requisite population, Ohio became a State, it could be said, as of no other State at that time, that it was typically Ameri- can. Throughout the nineteenth century Ohio continued to draw people from vari- ous sections of the Nation and from a variety of European countries. Ohio is still as typically American as any State in the Union; it is neither North nor South, neither East nor West; it lies where they all meet and has characteristics and habits of all of them."

47. Kondik is referring to the "Cuyahoga County collar" which he defines as Lake, Portage, Summit, Lorain, Geauga, and Medina Counties, the six counties that sur- round Cuyahoga County. See Kondik, *The Bellwether*, pp. 123–24.

48. Maggie Astor, "Ohio Special Election Results: 12th Congressional District" *New York Times*, September 24, 2018, www.nytimes.com/interactive/2018/08/07/us/ elections/results-ohio-special-house-election-district-12.html.

49. Since former Republican Senator Mike DeWine has been Ohio's governor since 2018, this figure is now twenty-six of the last thirty years.

50. The base pay of an Ohio legislator is $63,007 per year with additional stipends paid to committee chairs and party leaders, which ups the pay to about $65,000 per year. The House Speaker and the Senate President make $94,437 per year. See The

Council of State Governments, "State Legislative Branch," *Book of the States 2019*, http://knowledgecenter.csg.org/kc/system/files/3.9.2019.pdf.

51. Ohio house members are limited to four consecutive two-year terms. In the state senate, terms are limited to two consecutive four-year terms. See The Council of State Governments "State Legislative Branch."

52. NRA Institute of Legislative Action (ILA), "Cleveland Loses Firearm Preemption Case, Leaves Taxpayer to Foot the Bill," *Daily Caller*, February 2, 2018, https://dailycaller.com/2018/02/02/cleveland-loses-firearm-preemption-case-leaves-taxpayers-to-foot-the-bill/.

53. Noah Nadler, "Ohio Supreme Court Prohibits Municipality from Restricting Fracking," Practice Points Blog, *American Bar Association,* March 2, 2015, www.americanbar.org/groups/litigation/committees/environmental-energy/practice/2015/030215-energy-ohio-supreme-court-prohibits-municipality-from-restricting-fracking/.

54. Michael Griffaton, "New Ohio Law Will Preempt Local Wage-Hour Ordinances Aimed at Private Employers," Employment Law Blog, *Ohio Council of Retail Merchants*, January 6, 2017, www.ocrm.net/employment-law/new-ohio-law-will-preempt-local-wage-hour-ordinances-aimed-at-private-employers/.

55. Brentin Mock, "State Preemption of Local Legislation is Getting Worse," *CityLab*, August 9, 2019, www.citylab.com/equity/2019/08/states-gun-control-cities-preemption-laws-legislation/595759/.

56. U.S. Bureau of Labor Statistics, Midwest Information Office, "Union Membership Historical Table for Ohio 1989–2019," www.bls.gov/regions/midwest/data/unionmembershiphistorical_ohio_table.htm.

57. U.S. Bureau of Labor Statistics, "Economic News Release: Table 5. Union Affiliation of Employed Wage and Salary Workers by State," January 18, 2019, www.bls.gov/news.release/union2.t05.htm.

58. WOSU Radio (National Public Radio) All Sides Staff, "The Urban and Rural Divide in the Ohio General Assembly," *All Sides with Ann Fisher*, WOSU Radio, March 15, 2019, https://radio.wosu.org/post/urban-and-rural-divide-ohio-general-assembly#stream/0.

59. David Uberti, "A Divided Empire: What the Urban-Rural Split Means for the Future of America," *The Guardian*, January 9, 2017, www.theguardian.com/cities/2017/jan/09/donald-trump-divided-empire-urban-rural-america-future.

7

UPPER MIDWEST: MINNESOTA AND WISCONSIN

William E. Brown Jr.

But the Wisconsin tradition meant more than a simple
belief in the people. It also meant a faith in the application
of intelligence and reason to the problems of society.
It meant a deep conviction that the role of government
was not to stumble along like a drunkard in the dark,
but to light its way by the best torches of knowledge and
understanding it could find.[1]

—*Adlai Stevenson*

Minnesota has its own Mason Dixon line. I come from
the north and that's different from southern Minnesota;
if you're there you could be in Iowa or Georgia. Up north
the weather is more extreme—frostbite in the winter,
mosquito-ridden in the summer, no air conditioning when
I grew up, steam heat in the winter and you had to wear
a lot of clothes when you went outdoors. Your blood gets
thick. It's the land of 10,000 lakes—lot of hunting and
fishing. Indian country, Ojibwe, Chippewa, Lakota, birch
trees, open pit mines, bears and wolves—the air is raw.
Southern Minnesota is farming country, wheat fields and
hay stacks, lots of corn fields, horses and milk cows. In the
north it's more hardscrabble.[2]

—*Bob Dylan*

Minnesota and Wisconsin, two Upper Midwest states
with similar size populations, demographics, and climates, have long
been strongholds of the Democratic Party. Each has a million-plus

metro and extensive rural lands, and both states share a history of welcoming Scandinavian and German immigrants.[3] With histories of populism and progressivism and reputations for clean government and family-supporting policies, Minnesota and Wisconsin helped the Democratic Party create a long-standing Midwestern "Blue Wall."

But in 2010 this began to change. The Badger State elected Republican Scott Walker governor and gave control of the legislature to Republicans, while the Gopher State made Democrat Mark Dayton governor and, in 2012, elected a Democratic legislature. Since then, there has been a stark difference in economic policies between the two states,[4] and in 2016, for the first time since 1984, Wisconsin (Trump) and Minnesota (Clinton) separated their Electoral College votes.

Will the two states return to joint blue status in 2020, or did 2016 start a long-term transformation of the Upper Midwest? Certainly the two large million-plus metros of Minneapolis and Milwaukee will have much to say about this, as will other parts of these states. Yet, like the other swings states covered in this volume, suburban boomburbs such as Brooklyn Park, Minnesota, and Waukesha, Wisconsin, will determine which way these states tip. Each is home to large numbers of residents who commute to the Twin Cities and Milwaukee, respectively, but vote very differently. In 2016, Brooklyn Park delivered a 2-1 margin for Hillary Clinton, while Donald Trump won Waukesha by 4,000 votes. Thus, even in states with such strong urban/rural divisions, the balance of power rests with suburban voters.

STATE OF PLAY: MINNESOTA

In Minnesota, a coalition between the Democratic Party and the Farmer Labor Party created a populist movement that has delivered Minnesota's electoral votes to the Democratic Party in every election since 1972. In 1984, the state offered its Electoral College votes to Democratic candidate and native son Walter Mondale, giving the former vice president his lone state victory (along with Washington, D.C.) in a landslide loss to Republican Ronald Reagan. The continued growth of Minnesota's largest cities, led by Minneapolis and St. Paul (the Twin Cities), and the concurrent loss of population and economic downturn in rural Minnesota would appear to strengthen this coalition. However, the results of the 2016 presidential election, in which Hillary Clinton carried the state by approximately 45,000 votes, give Republicans hope to claim this formerly solid blue state. Republican opportunities in small town and rural Minnesota reflect the growing urban/rural divide that exists in many states across the nation.

For most observers, there are two Minnesotas. One Minnesota contains "lakes, farms, country roads and depending upon whom you ask, a lot of hardworking people who feel their needs aren't being met and their message isn't being heard, or misguided bumpkins who voted against their interests."[5] A second Minnesota, "a metropolis straddling the banks of the Mississippi River, is made up of two growing cities and their suburbs, with increased infrastructure demands and depending upon your thinking, a bunch of people trying to make a good life for themselves and others, or a den of liberal busybodies taking up state resources and pushing their agenda on people who live far away."[6]

The Minneapolis metro region, anchored by the Twin Cities of Minneapolis and St. Paul, is home to more than six of ten Minnesotans. In keeping with the national trend, Minnesota's metro areas are growing, and the less populated places are losing people. The rural areas of the state are also older, less diverse, and, on average, individuals earn less than their urban counterparts.[7] While Minnesota features a strong urban/rural divide, this volume identifies a third region, the Iron Range/Northeast Minnesota, a region linked with Wisconsin's Far North region, distinctly Democratic-voting areas that are distant from each state's major blue metro (see figure 7-1).

If one were to understand Minnesota, according to the 1938 Works Progress Administration (WPA) American Guide Series, one

must keep always in mind the fact that within the span of a single lifetime 54 million acres of forests, lakes, rivers, and untouched prairies have been converted into an organized area of industrial cities and rich farms, of colleges, art centers, golf clubs, and parks. The men and women who accomplished this were for the most part New Englanders, Germans, and Scandinavians probably as hardy as the world has produced and it is their children and their grandchildren who determine today the pattern of the contemporary scene.[8]

FIGURE 7-1. Minnesota

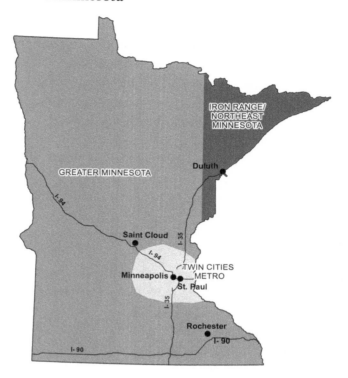

Authors of the *WPA Guide* also described Minneapolis: "Its largest city boasts of one of the finest park systems in the world, yet endures philosophically the dangers and irritations imposed by many railroad grade crossings. While remaining Republican in theory, county, city, or State will cheerfully try almost any variety of politics, whether Populist, Non-Partisan League, Farmer-Labor, or Socialist."[9] Later in the volume, the state's urban/rural divide is noted: "The population of Minnesota is divided almost equally between the cities and country. This numerical balance prevents urban domination, while increased facilities of transportation and communication in one generation have diminished appreciably not only the physical but the spiritual, economic, and social distances between city dweller and farmer."[10]

In their 2011 book, *Patchwork Nation: The Surprising Truth About the*

"Real" America, Dante Chinni and James Gimpel describe Minnesota as a relatively obscure state to non-Minnesotans, where "the Minneapolis and St. Paul suburbs have become political battlegrounds that divide along class or economic lines."[11] They also note that "the suburban counties surrounding Minneapolis and St. Paul have become critical turf for both parties."[12] Yet, this political competition takes place within a sociocultural context that has been shaped in large part by the largest Lutheran Church denomination in the United States. As a liberal, progressive church with a history of tolerance and openness to refugees, it is not surprising to see this view reflected in Minnesota politics, even in the Republican hinterlands.

Twin Cities Metro

Such is the divide in Minnesota that many people define the Twin Cities metro region as containing the seven counties of Anoka, Carver, Dakota, Ramsey, Hennepin, Scott, and Washington and refer to the remaining eighty counties in the state as "Greater Minnesota."[13] However, the Office of Management and Budget, which determines metropolitan statistical areas based on commuting patterns, includes selected Greater Minnesota and bordering Wisconsin counties in the Minneapolis MSA. Thus, while colloquial and statistical definitions of what is and is not Greater Minnesota may differ, the point is clear. When people refer to Greater Minnesota, or use the more pejorative "Outstate Minnesota," they mean outside the Minneapolis region, an expression of the alienation of rural residents from their urban counterparts.[14]

In a 2017 editorial series, ECM Publishers, a media distribution company operating in Minnesota and western Wisconsin, referred to the ongoing sectionalism in Minnesota in simple terms: "Outstate communities struggle as the younger population is drawn to metro areas and promises of better paying jobs." The editorial board added, "Lower home values as a result of declining populations has left a weakened tax base in outstate Minnesota. . . . Spending however, is split nearly 50-50. . . . But despite that economic sharing of wealth, it is not uncommon to hear in many outstate coffee shops or diners that 'our tax dollars go to all that development in the cities.'"[15]

Tables 7-1 and 7-2 capture the demographic, economic, and political differences that undergird the state's urban/rural divisions. In comparison to most of the twenty-seven million-plus metros represented in this volume, Minneapolis contains the fourth-highest percentage of white residents, at 74.9 percent (see table 2.1). However, as table 7-1 details, within Minnesota, the Minneapolis-St Paul MSA is home to the vast majority of the state's Asian, Black, and Latino populations, as well as more than eight-in-ten Minnesotans who were born abroad. The metro also contains the vast majority of the state's college-educated population and, consequently, generates nearly three-quarters of Minnesota's GDP despite accounting for less than two-thirds of population.

Consistent with these demographic differences, voters within the Twin Cities region are the basis for the Democrats' strength in the state. As table 7-2 summarizes, in 2016 Hillary Clinton won the state with 46.4 percent of the vote compared to 44.9 percent for Donald Trump. Clinton's 45,000 vote margin resulted from her 14-percentage-point advantage in the Minneapolis metro. Indeed, while Democratic candidates have won every statewide election during the decade, the rural parts of Minnesota have "grown progressively more 'red' with each presidential election" since 2008.[16] Trump won nineteen counties that Obama carried in both 2008 and 2012, and in total, he carried seventy-eight of the state's eighty-seven counties. While Clinton secured more votes in the state's more populous counties, Trump's significant margins in rural areas resulted in a close race.

Thus, while the state's limited diversity and extensive rural population makes Minnesota a 2020 Republican target, the political weight of the Twin Cities Metro, home to the bulk of Minnesota's minority and college-educated populations, remains a formidable Democratic stronghold. Among the metros covered in this book, only Las Vegas eclipses Minneapolis's potential electoral impact. These metros, because of their scale and Democratic-voter margins, are capable of offsetting the GOP's strong support outside the metro region to deliver statewide elections for the Democrats. Yet, as table 7-3 reveals, the Democrats metro-fueled dominance at the top of the ticket and in the U.S. House elections does not always extend down the ballot. The GOP controlled the majority in each chamber of the statehouse

TABLE 7-1. Demographic and Economic Comparison between Minnesota and Minneapolis

	Minnesota	Share in Minneapolis* [%]
Population	5,576,505	62.2
White	79.9%	58.3
Black	6.4%	86.1
Asian	4.9%	88.0
Latino	5.3%	70.6
Foreign-Born	7.1%	81.0
College Educated	36.0%	72.6
Jobs	2,952,963	62.7
GDP	$311,336	72.4

*Excludes counties outside of MSA primary state.

Sources: 2017 American Community Survey 1-Year estimates as aggregated by censusreporter.org, Department of Commerce, Bureau of Economic Analysis, 2015 Real GDP (millions of chained 2012 dollars) County Level Data, U.S. Department of Labor, Bureau of Labor Statistics 2017 County Level Data.

TABLE 7-2. Comparison of Electoral Outcomes between Minnesota and Minneapolis

	Minnesota	Minneapolis	
Election	Outcome	Vote Share [%]	Outcome
2018 U.S. Senate	+24.1 Dem	64.0	+32.8 Dem
2018 U.S. Senate (Special Election)	+10.6 Dem	64.0	+19.3 Dem
2018 Gubernatorial	+11.4 Dem	64.0	+20.3 Dem
2016 Presidential	+1.5 Dem	62.4	+13.6 Dem
2014 U.S. Senate	+10.2 Dem	61.2	+12.9 Dem
2014 Gubernatorial	+5.6 Dem	62.4	+9.1 Dem
2012 Presidential	+7.7 Dem	62.7	+12.4 Dem
2012 U.S. Senate	+34.7 Dem	62.8	+36.7 Dem

Source: Data from Minnesota secretary of state's website.

for part of the decade, including unified legislative control after the 2016 election.

Compared to other million-plus metro regions considered in this volume, Minneapolis also is better positioned to exert influence over state policy. To be sure, the fact that Minnesota's capital, St. Paul, is located within the million-plus metro benefits the region, as does the fact that Minneapolis is growing faster than the rest of the state. In addition, the metro's seven core counties are served by the Metropolitan Council, which is tasked with administering regional services, including transportation, sewage, and planning, and has the authority to supersede decisions made by local governments.

A governance body such as the Metropolitan Council helps overcome the region's extensive municipal fragmentation and ensure the flow of resources into the metro. As table 7-4 indicates, the Minneapolis MSA consists of fourteen counties and has a total of 352 general purpose governments. Also note that, despite a history of home rule, Minnesota ranks low in local government autonomy, reflecting the significant level of state or regional control over municipal matters. Historically, this was less of a concern. However, the tensions between state government and the Twin Cities region have been amplified recently with Republican majorities in the statehouse.

Greater Minnesota

The results of the 2016 presidential election foreshadowed the increased saliency of Minnesota's growing metro versus rest-of-state divide. With the GOP controlling both chambers of the state legislature, the 2017 legislative session considered bills to reduce or eliminate funding for infrastructure (light rail) and other programs for urban areas such as Minneapolis, St. Paul, and Duluth. During the 2018 gubernatorial campaign, one Republican candidate ran on a platform emphasizing "Minnesota values," not "Minneapolis or St. Paul values," while another proposed to abolish the Metropolitan Council.[17] Despite these efforts to assert the primacy of Greater Minnesota in state politics, 2018 was a Democratic year. The party's gubernatorial candidate Tim Walz (who previously represented the rural 1st U.S. House District that runs along the state's southern border) prevailed by double

TABLE 7-3. Partisan Composition of Minnesota State
Government and Federal Delegation

		State Government				Federal Delegation			
		Upper House		Lower House		U.S. Senate		U.S. House	
	Governor	Dems	Reps	Dems	Reps	Dems	Reps	Dems	Reps
2019–20	Dem	32	35	75	59	2	0	5	3
2017–18	Dem	33	34	57	77	2	0	5	3
2015–16	Dem	39	28	62	72	2	0	5	3
2013–14	Dem	39	28	73	61	2	0	5	3

Sources: Data from National Conference of State Legislatures, "State and Legislative Partisan Composition" for various years, and Minnesota secretary of state's websites.

TABLE 7-4. Metro Governance Fragmentation
and Autonomy in Minnesota

Governance Fragmentation

Metro	Number of Counties in Metro	Number of General Purposes Governments in Metro
Minneapolis*	14	352

Governance Autonomy

Local Government Autonomy Score	−0.201
Local Government Autonomy Ranking	36

*Excludes counties outside of MSA primary state.

Sources: Data for Governance Fragmentation from 2017 Census of Governments. Data for Governance Autonomy from Harold Wolman, Robert McManmon, Michael Bell, and David Brunori, "Comparing Local Government Autonomy Across States," in *The Property Tax and Local Autonomy*, edited by Michael Bell, David Brunori, and Joan Youngman (Lincoln Institute of Land Policy Press, 2010), pp. 69–114.

digits, as did both Democratic U.S. Senate candidates, Amy Klobuchar and Tina Smith (see table 7-2). The Democrats also gained eighteen seats in the lower chamber of the state legislature to regain the majority after four years of Republican control (see table 7-3). The GOP did, however, expand its majority in the upper house by one seat.

Perhaps more indications of the state's internal divisions can be gleaned from the outcomes of the U.S. House elections. In 2018, the Democrats lost the open 1st and 8th Districts, but knocked off two Republican incumbents in the 2nd and 3rd Districts. While the outcomes did not change the partisan composition of the state's House delegation (see table 7-3), it did reinforce the urban-rural divide. Minnesota's 1st and 8th House districts are outside of the Minneapolis MSA. In contrast, the 2nd and 3rd Districts are within the Minneapolis MSA.

It is no surprise that the counties that constitute Greater Minnesota are much more Republican-voting than metro Minneapolis. However, this does not mean that these counties are monolithic in their embrace of Trumpian politics. For instance, following the Trump administration's decision to give states and counties veto power over refugee settlements, an executive order subsequently blocked by the federal courts, Beltrami County voted to prohibit refugee settlements by a 3-2 vote of its County Board of Commissioners, one of the first in the nation to do so.[18] In contrast, Pope County, where Trump captured 60 percent of the vote, decided to welcome refugees in a unanimous vote, even though no refugees have been settled in the county for years and there were no immediate plans to do so.[19] For his part, President Trump sees this as a winning issue in the state. During an October 2019 Minnesota campaign rally, the president touted his executive order prohibiting refugee settlements. Prior to the 2016 election, Trump told Minnesotans that they had "suffered enough" from accepting refugees.[20]

Trump's messaging, and that of some Republican candidates competing in 2018, suggests that, like neighboring Wisconsin, there is a belief among rural voters that the state is run by its million-plus metro, with little or no concern for the rural parts of the state.

Iron Range/Northeast Minnesota

As bordering states, Minnesota and Wisconsin share an economic sector built on the mining and shipping industries centered around Duluth, Minnesota, and Superior, Wisconsin. These two inland port cities (the Twin Ports) on Lake Superior also are Democratic-voting places.

The Iron Range/Northeast region of Minnesota, with its extensive iron ore reserves, defies the conventional wisdom that all rural areas are conservative. The tradition of Minnesota's religious tolerance and the historical strength of blue-collar unions, created in response to the development of big mining operations, provide the social, economic, and political infrastructure for this region to remain blue.

While Northeast Minnesota's mining-based economy represents a challenge to Democrats, the Twin Ports metro now serves a bi-state region of nearly 300,000 people and functions as a regional center for education, healthcare, engineering, aquatic research, and tourism. Duluth, in northeastern Minnesota, and Superior, in northwestern Wisconsin, are both home to branches of their respective state universities and, as a consequence, tend to be more Democratic-voting than the region as a whole, despite limited demographic diversity and exposure to immigration.[21]

Conclusion: Minnesota State of Play

With regard to urban places and politics, it may be worth noting a great Minnesota experiment. In 1967, the Minnesota Experimental City, a brainchild of Athelstan Spilhaus, proposed a modern urban utopia—a self-sustaining metropolis complete with transportation, recycling, public transit, and computer technology (of the time)—for a population of 250,000 at a cost of $10 billion. A Minnesota Experimental City Authority went so far as to select a site—in Aitkin County, 105 miles north of Minneapolis. Fiscal realities and political practicalities soon ended any further consideration of this project.[22]

Today, Minnesotans continue to debate the role and place of urban areas in state politics, a debate that has become more complicated by the growing demographic diversity in its million-plus metro compared to the rest of the state. Most notably, the 2018 congressional election of Ilhan Omar saw her garner 78 percent of the vote to become the first Somali-American and first nonwhite women elected to Congress from Minnesota. Omar, who represents Minnesota's 5th U.S. House District, which includes the city of Minneapolis and a portion of its suburbs, received the largest percentage vote for a nonincumbent U.S. House candidate in state history.[23] Despite her impressive 2018 electoral margin, President Trump seems poised to continue his verbal assaults on Representative Omar, describing her as an "American hating socialist" and stating that she "is the big reason that I am going to win, and the Republican Party is going to win Minnesota."[24]

Also consider Congressmember Collin Peterson, a conservative Democrat representing the 7th Congressional District. His rural district supported Donald Trump in 2016 by thirty points. The Republican Party approached Peterson about switching parties as he debated whether to vote to impeach Donald Trump. Peterson voted as one of only two Democrats not to impeach Trump on both articles. Representative Jeff Van Drew of New Jersey, the second "no" vote, did switch his party affiliation. Peterson's tenuous hold on his district and the intense competition for Minnesota's electoral votes in 2020 gave him the leeway to diverge from his party on this heated issue.[25]

Befitting Minnesota's status as a toss-up state, both parties are working toward a 2020 election victory. Donald Trump, defying recent political trends, described winning Minnesota in 2020 as "really, really easy."[26] Vice President Joe Biden's 2020 primary victory in Minnesota, aided by home state U.S. Senator Amy Klobuchar's withdrawal from the race and subsequent endorsement days before the primary, encouraged Democrats to "try to add not only to gains they've made in suburbs and among women in cities, but to add votes to the Iron Range."[27]

Just how important is Minnesota? The Gopher State is mentioned in *The Mueller Report*, the investigative document that contributed to the impeachment of President Donald Trump. The report notes that Trump's former campaign chair Paul Manafort briefed Russian agents about polling data for Michigan, Wisconsin, Pennsylvania, and Minnesota.[28] During the campaign, Minnesota also experienced a high level of "Russian troll activity."[29] Adding to uncertainty about the state's direction is that in 2016, nearly 9 percent of the presidential vote went for a candidate other than Donald Trump or Hillary Clinton. As J. Patrick Coolican reported, "8.7 percent of Minnesota voters chose someone else in 2016. . . . Some people even left the presidential line blank. All told, that's about 277,000 votes up for grabs."[30] Still, given the Democrats' strong showing in 2018 (see tables 7-2 and 7-3) and the weight of its blue metro, Minnesota is likely to remain out of reach for the GOP in 2020.

EXPERT ANALYSIS: MINNESOTA

William Stancil, research fellow at the Institute of Metropolitan Opportunity, University of Minnesota Law School, offered his analysis of current and future political trends in Minnesota. This interview took place via telephone on October 2, 2019. Note that interview responses include minor edits to provide continuity and clarify language.

Intrastate Political Dynamics

What is the political dynamic between major metro(s) and the rest of the state?

As you probably expect, we have cities [that] tend to be much more Democratic—much bluer, more liberal. Then you have the rural areas that are traditionally pretty conservative, pretty Republican.

I believe Minnesota has some of the most conservative Democrats in the country. One sort of odd thing about Minnesota is you have the Iron Range, which is up north on the lake, and it's one of the longest running Democratic strongholds in the country—going back to, I want to say, Nixon versus McGovern when he pretty much won in a landslide. . . . It went blue; it's one of the very few places that didn't [shift].

But, it has shifted. It's also a very rural, white, working-class area. Industrial, it's mining. When that demographic shifted in the last election—that area has become much more Republican. And so, Minnesota, I believe is the only state in the country—so the Democrats lost two seats in 2018, they picked up everywhere, but they lost two. I believe both of them were in Minnesota. I know that two of them were in Minnesota. One was Walz's seat [when he won the election as governor]; that's in the southern part of the state, which is mostly rural farming. One was Rochester and the other was that Iron Range seat.

Metro Power in State Government

What is the political dynamic between the major metro and the rest of the state?

I think we might actually be the only state right now that has a divided legislature, when I think about it. So right now we are in a holding pattern, wait and see what happens in 2020.

If the Democrats pick up two seats in the (state) Senate [in 2020] there will be a trifecta and they will be able to push some of this stuff through. If they don't do that, we are in gridlock mode, going forward.

And what we have had the last couple of years is—because not everything has gotten done, it will be special sessions in the summer where they finish some additional business. A lot of that is the product of the divided legislature and the standoff between the legislature and the governor. By summer, they are done.

How much power does the biggest metro exert in state politics?

So, this is an interesting question because the Twin Cities region constitutes a majority of the state population and there's a constant tension—I'm sure it goes back and forth—I mean, it goes on in other states but I think it's probably more pronounced here between metro and I call it "out-state," a lot of people call it Greater Minnesota. I think people living not in the metro prefer Greater Minnesota to out-state. And so, there's a constant tension. One of things that is interesting here, and this has changed over time a little bit, traditionally both parties had significant strongholds in both sections, the Democrats have, obviously, the Twin Cities— some of the inner ring suburbs especially—and Republicans have the wealthier suburbs and the exurbs and some of the rural areas.

But then you have the Iron Range, which throws it off. It has been such a Democratic stronghold for such a long time. And so I think one of things that played out underneath all this is Democrats' give-away[s] to out-state interests [such as] money [for] funding programs [are] direct[ed] toward the Iron Range. As the Iron Range in particular has grown more Republican, there have been fewer incentives for Democrats to pay any attention to the rural area. And so I think, given that at the moment this is primarily a Democratic-controlled state, I think you have seen a commensurate increase in the influence of the cities. But my sense of it is that the metro has grown more powerful over time mostly because of that sorting business. The state as a whole has actually grown more Republican. And probably a point will come where Republicans do control a lot of the government here and then it will shift the other way.

The metro is growing relative to the rest of the state. So the imbalance is getting worse. The rural areas are shrinking; people are leaving and very often are moving to the metro. So the population imbalance is getting worse, which will tend to push the population of the metro up. One thing about Minnesota is the metro—it's explicitly carved out. You have the Metropolitan Council—a lot of people have separate geographies. The point is a lot of state law will explicitly say—this money to the metro, this money to the rest of the state. It is explicitly laid out.

Does economic power translate into political power?

I think not. The wealthiest communities in the state are the suburbs of the Twin Cities. And of course the central cities have a lot of industry and they have a lot of business. If anything, what's happened is that a lot of money [is] sent up to the Iron Range because it's been such a long-standing political stronghold for Democrats, and because they would like to hold onto it.

How do smaller metros in the state exert power?

They have a formidable bloc of legislators. You've got deep red outside the northeast part of the state. Those areas are mostly deep red. There's actually one exception to that. I'll get back to that. But they're deep red generally. There are enough votes to control at least the Republican caucus and certainly enough to have a closely divided legislature, which ours is, to really throw your weight around. So those places are not lacking for political power, although [they are] losing out to the metro. I guess over time the number of seats they hold will diminish, and that's one of the things I can't really speak to, unfortunately. I do metro stuff and not really rural stuff. I know they have farm politics, and I just don't know the issues very well. But anyone who aspires to, for statewide office in Minnesota really needs to be cognizant of this stuff. It's not a coincidence really.

Our current governor, Tim Walz, he was a state senator, did a pretty good job of it; he is definitely associated with the metro, or he didn't have a lot of rural connections. But part of the reason he won the primary, it was a good year for Democrats. He probably would have won anyway, but one thing that helped him out is that he was a former U.S. Representative from a primarily rural, or heavily rural, district. He can speak that language a little better than some of the other Democrats [in the city]. He talked a lot about veterans' issues, farms ... and while certainly he's a liberal, he is practiced at sort of framing that in the correct language.

The one thing I would say, though, as these rural areas lose population, one of the things you are seeing, and we don't see the political effects of this yet at all that I'm aware of, but one of the things you are seeing is that places like Worthington, which is a small town in southern Minnesota near the border with Iowa, they are farm towns—the farms are increasingly worked by immigrants and not just Hispanic immigrants—Somalian immigrants, Southeast Asian immigrants—Worthington [has] the largest share of non-U.S.-born population in the state. So that's fairly shocking— you think of these places as being entirely white, entirely rural, sort of traditionally Americana. You go to downtown Worthington and all the signs are in Indonesian. You don't really see the political effects of this yet because I don't think the population is quite large enough to swing the districts. These are very deeply red places. But I don't think it's inconceivable that over time this would start to muddy the politics.

STATE OF PLAY: WISCONSIN

Wisconsin, with a history of progressive and reactionary politics, embodied by figures such as U.S. Senators Robert La Follette and Joseph McCarthy, is home to a classic urban/rural divide. The million-plus metro region of Milwaukee e, buoyed by nearby Madison, the state capital and home to the historically liberal University of Wisconsin, are the core Democratic voting regions. These metros' relative density and diversity, particularly Milwaukee's (see table 7-5), contrasts with Wisconsin's older white exurbs and small towns. It is these tensions that underlie the state's political regions, depicted in figure 7-2, and it is the increased saliency of these divisions that has made Wisconsin a battleground state in presidential elections. Prior to 2016, the state voted for the Democratic presidential candidate in every election since 1984.

FIGURE 7-2. Wisconsin

TABLE 7-5. Demographic and Economic Comparison between Wisconsin and Milwaukee

	Wisconsin	Share in Milwaukee [%]
Population	5,795,483	27.2
White	81.2%	22.3
Black	6.3%	71.1
Asian	2.7%	37.2
Latino	6.9%	42.8
Foreign-Born	5.0%	40.1
College Educated	30.4%	31.8
Jobs	3,307,456	26.4
GDP	$254,595	37.1

Sources: 2017 American Community Survey 1-Year estimates as aggregated by censusreporter.org, Department of Commerce, Bureau of Economic Analysis, 2015 Real GDP (millions of chained 2012 dollars) County Level Data, U.S. Department of Labor, Bureau of Labor Statistics 2017 County Level Data.

In this regard, Donald Trump's narrow victory in 2016 capped Wisconsin's decade-long rightward shift. Facilitated in no small part by substantial investments by the conservative Koch brothers network,[31] the GOP held unified control of state government for much of the decade and a majority of Wisconsin's seats in the U.S. House of Representatives. In response, unions and affiliated groups have sought to remain relevant and keep Wisconsin blue. Dan Kaufman, author of *The Fall of Wisconsin: The Conservative Conquest of a Progressive Bastion and the Future of American Politics*, explained these countervailing forces by suggesting that there are "these deep channels of Wisconsin political culture that weave back and forth.... There's a tension, which has often been a healthy tension, between social responsibility and individual responsibility."[32]

Some of these tensions are a consequence of long-term economic displacement that shifted Wisconsin's economy from agriculture to manufacturing during the twentieth century. For instance, a 1941 *WPA Guide to Wisconsin* described this change by noting that, "Since

1900 the history of Wisconsin has been marked by the growth of large-scale industry and the concentration of population increases in industrial areas, especially in the southeastern and lakeshore counties and in the Fox River Valley. Accompanying this concentration there has been a shift from rural to urban population."[33] At the onset of the twentieth century, the *WPA Guide* noted, "Employment agents at New York met incoming Germans, Belgians, and Scandinavians and offered them two weeks' room and board and free transportation to the mills and factories in Wisconsin."[34] By the 1930 census, the effects of generations of foreign immigration were particularly notable in Madison[35] and Milwaukee.[36]

More recently, the ascendency of U.S. Congressman Paul Ryan to the Speakership of the House of Representative (2015–19) and the election and reelection of Governor Scott Walker in 2010 and 2014 brought the historical tensions within Wisconsin's political culture to the national stage. In an interview with conservative radio host Glenn Beck, when he was ranking minority member of the House Budget Committee, Ryan explained that his goal was to "indict the entire vision of progressivism," which he labeled a "cancer," as well as "the intellectual source for the big government problems that are plaguing us today."[37] Reflecting on the division in Wisconsin between Milwaukee and Madison on one side and the state's rural regions on the other, Ryan insisted that "this stuff [progressivism] comes from these German intellectuals to Madison, University of Wisconsin."[38]

Scott Walker's rise to political office can be traced to his virulent opposition to labor unions, public education, and other entities that conservatives associate with big government. Efforts to recall Governor Walker in 2012 further exacerbated political tensions within the state. In 2018, Walker ran for a third term against Democrat Tony Evers. Evers narrowly prevailed (see table 7-6). Yet despite the stronger showing at the top of the ticket, highlighted by a double-digit reelection victory for Democratic U.S. Senator Tammy Baldwin, the Democrats' down-ticket gains were blunted by a GOP gerrymander that yielded no gains in the congressional delegation and just one pickup in each chamber of the statehouse (see table 7-7).[39]

The 2018 election also did little to alleviate Wisconsin's urban/rural divisions. In defeat, Walker's allies were quick to dismiss Evers and his victory by characterizing the incoming governor "as a creature of the capital city, put there by people in the cities."[40] Robin Vos, the Republican speaker of the Wisconsin legislature, even went so far as to opine that "if you took Madison and Milwaukee out of the state election formula, we would have a clear majority," including "all five constitutional officers and we would probably have many more seats in the Legislature."[41] No doubt, contested partisan and geographic politics in Wisconsin will continue. 2020 will tell if the blue metro or the red state has the upper hand.

Southern Wisconsin (Milwaukee-Madison)

In Wisconsin, one million-plus metropolitan region, Milwaukee, located in the southeast corner of the state, and nearby Madison (home to the University of Wisconsin), contain the core of Democratic voters. The white Milwaukee suburbs and the remainder of the state provide the bulk of Republican voters. Milwaukee is by far the state's largest population center and is home to much of the state's minority and foreign-born populations (see tables 7-5 and 7-6). The region also delivers nearly 40 percent of the state's GDP despite constituting just more than a quarter of its population. The nearby

TABLE 7-6. Comparison of Electoral Outcomes between Wisconsin and Milwaukee

	Wisconsin	Milwaukee	
Election	Outcome	Vote Share [%]	Outcome
2018 U.S. Senate	+10.8 Dem	27.6	+11.5 Dem
2018 Gubernatorial	+1.1 Dem	27.6	+2.4 Dem
2016 Presidential	+0.8 Rep	27.2	+7.2 Dem
2016 U.S. Senate	+3.4 Rep	27.3	+1.8 Rep
2014 Gubernatorial	+5.7 Rep	28.4	+7.0 Rep
2012 Presidential	+6.9 Dem	28.4	+5.2 Dem
2012 U.S. Senate	+5.5 Dem	28.3	+3.0 Dem

Source: Data from Wisconsin secretary of state's website.

TABLE 7-7. Partisan Composition of Wisconsin State
Government and Federal Delegation

		State Government				Federal Delegation			
		Upper House		Lower House		U.S. Senate		U.S. House	
	Governor	Dems	Reps	Dems	Reps	Dems	Reps	Dems	Reps
2019–20	Dem	14	19	36	63	1	1	3	5
2017–18	Rep	13	20	35	64	1	1	3	5
2015–16	Rep	14	19	36	63	1	1	3	5
2013–14	Rep	15	18	39	60	1	1	3	5

Sources: Data from National Conference of State Legislatures, "State and Legislative Partisan Composition" for various years, and Wisconsin secretary of state's website.

Madison MSA has 660,000 residents, and in addition to state government and university employees who tend to vote Democratic, it is a growing center for digital service jobs.[42] Still, despite the fact that Milwaukee and Madison are the most densely populated parts of Wisconsin, when combined, the two MSAs are home to less than 40 percent of the state's residents.

Moreover, the region's Democratic tendencies are offset in part by rural southwestern counties that fall within Madison's MSA. Within the Milwaukee MSA, the suburban counties are home to a Republican, white population in comparison to the region's Democratic, more racially diverse urban center. Compared to 2012, in 2016, the region's core county, Milwaukee County, experienced a tremendous decline in the number of raw votes cast, and Hillary Clinton garnered 43,000 fewer votes than Barack Obama.

Needless to say, in an election decided by fewer than 23,000 votes, the failure of the Democrats to engage urban voters had as much to do with the outcome as did Trump's strong support in the exurbs and the state's hinterlands. In particular, Waukesha County, located on the western side of the Milwaukee MSA, produced more Republican votes in 2012 than any similar-size county in the nation.[43] Along with Ozaukee and Washington—collectively referred to as the "WOW counties" that ring much of the city of Milwaukee—these counties are primarily white and more Republican-voting, and serve to undercut the electoral impact of the state's blue metro. This is a notable contrast to the neighboring states of Illinois and Minnesota, where the large metro centers of Chicago and the Twin Cities dominate voting patterns.

Although the Wisconsin constitution allows local governments regulatory and policy authority in local matters, Milwaukee and all Wisconsin cities are subject to oversight from the legislative branch and the legal interpretation of the limits of home rule powers by state courts. In recent years, legislative actions and court decisions have weakened the power of municipal home rule in Wisconsin, and state government has increasingly preempted local governments. For instance, after previously prohibiting cities from setting their own minimum wages, in 2018, the state further weakened municipal governmental authority by preempting local regulation of any employment standards, including paid leave and other benefits, the information that can be collected on a job application, and overtime and scheduling.[44]

The imposition of such limitations on local governments is often a result of blue metros, red states politics, particularly in states such as Wisconsin where the Republican Party is in control of the legislative and, until 2019, the executive branches. As table 7-8 indicates, local governments in Wisconsin rank thirty-second in terms of their autonomy. Also note that while the Milwaukee MSA contains just four Wisconsin counties, there are ninety-four general purpose governments within the region. The fragmentation is further exacerbated by the partisan differences between Milwaukee and its suburbs and the Republican gerrymander of the state legislature, which reduced the number of districts contained within the city of Milwaukee.

Greater Wisconsin

As figure 7-2 suggests, the majority of Wisconsin's land area is contained within the Greater Wisconsin region, and it is within this region that rural alienation is most apparent. As Katherine Cramer detailed in her comprehensive work, *The Politics of Resentment: Rural Consciousness in Wisconsin and the Rise of Scott Walker*, "For many people in rural communities in Wisconsin, people understand public

TABLE 7-8. Metro Governance Fragmentation
and Autonomy in Wisconsin

Governance Fragmentation

Metro	Number of Counties in Metro	Number of General Purposes Governments in Metro
Milwaukee	4	94

Governance Autonomy

Local Government Autonomy Score	−0.091
Local Government Autonomy Ranking	32

Sources: Data for Governance Fragmentation from 2017 Census of Governments. Data for Governance Autonomy from Harold Wolman, Robert McManmon, Michael Bell, and David Brunori, "Comparing Local Government Autonomy Across States," in *The Property Tax and Local Autonomy*, edited by Michael Bell, David Brunori, and Joan Youngman (Lincoln Institute of Land Policy Press, 2010), pp. 69–114.

issues through a lens of rural consciousness. This is a perspective that encompasses a strong identity as rural resident, resentment toward the cities, and a belief that rural communities are not given their fair share of resources or respect."[45]

This perspective shifts the focus of what rural means, from descriptive terms relating to place and recognizing the political values and beliefs of individuals who reside in rural locations. As Cramer travelled throughout rural Wisconsin interviewing residents, she encountered this "rural consciousness."

It was this sense of, "We don't get our fair share, and all the stuff goes to Milwaukee and Madison—all the public money, all the attention and all the respect. The people in the cities are making all the decisions and communicating them out to us. They don't understand us; they don't know us; they don't value what we value. And they don't actually even like us: they think we're uneducated and unsophisticated and racist and the whole gambit."[46]

In fact, a large portion of northern Wisconsin is classified as "Frontier and Remote areas" Level 4 by the U.S. Department of Agriculture's zip code level system. Residents in these zip codes are "at least an hour's drive from a major city and fifteen minutes away from the nearest community of 2,500 people." Combined, these counties contain less than 2 percent of the state's population but are dispersed over nearly 16 percent of its land area. In total, thirty-two of Wisconsin's seventy-two counties are rural, comprising 49 percent of the state's land area, and home to 13 percent of the population.[47]

Against this backdrop, the results of the 2016 presidential election seem rather predictable. Donald Trump defeated Hillary Clinton in Wisconsin by 23,000 votes of more than 2.9 million votes cast by winning the red parts of the state that, ultimately, outvoted the blue metro regions. That no Republican had won Wisconsin since 1984 is significant, but also is the fact that voter turnout among the voting age population was the lowest since 2000,[48] with much of this decrease in key Democratic areas. Minor party and write-in candidates also played a role. Compared to 2012, the share of voters who did not support either the Democratic or Republican presidential candidates increased nearly fivefold.

From this perspective, the notion that Trump's Wisconsin victory was a consequence of an untapped surge of support among rural Wisconsinites is inaccurate. Trump ran nearly 75,000 votes behind Ron Johnson, who won reelection to the U.S. Senate by more than three points (see table 7-6), and he received slightly fewer votes than Mitt Romney in 2012. In contrast, Hillary Clinton received almost 240,000 fewer votes than Barack Obama.

Far North Wisconsin

Superior, Wisconsin, although much smaller in size than its cross-state neighbor, Duluth, joins that city via a shared port on the Great Lakes to form the Twin Ports MSA. As in neighboring Minnesota counties, this region has a history of voting Democratic, due in part to mining and shipping economies dominant in the region—with their strong union ties—as well as the presence of Native American communities in this region. In fact, in Scott Walker's 2014 gubernatorial campaign, the bluest part of Wisconsin was the community of Sanborn, located on Lake Superior. Walker received only 12 percent of the vote.[49] In 2016, Hillary Clinton carried Bayfield County, where Superior is located, by nearly ten points.

Conclusion: Wisconsin State of Play

Wisconsin continues to be a state in transition. With each passing year, the state is becoming more urbanized and more divided. U.S. census data from 2017 reveals that Wisconsin gained 108,195 residents from April 2010 to July 2017. Nearly two-thirds of this growth occurred in Wisconsin's most populous counties—Dane (48,341), Milwaukee (4,349), and Waukesha (10,685)—while many rural counties lost population.[50] The state's politics create an additional challenge to bridging the rural/urban divide even though the state's urban and rural economies are codependent. Rural areas produce important, valuable commodities such as cheese and other dairy products, cattle and hogs, and lumber that require urban infrastructure to process and distribute.

Even with these growing divisions, neither party is conceding the state. Most notably, the Democratic Party selected Milwaukee as the location for the 2020 Democratic National Convention. Political parties chose their convention city with great care, and it is no accident that Milwaukee will host the Democrats in 2020. While the Democrats' prospects are improving in the Sun Belt (see chapter 10), regaining the traditional Democratic-voting states of the Midwest and Pennsylvania will increase the number of paths by which the party's nominee can secure the 270 Electoral College votes needed to win the presidency. Yet, in comparison to Pennsylvania and Michigan, two other states that swung to the GOP in 2016, Wisconsin has the whitest population and the highest share of noncollege whites, and is the least urban of the three states.

Moreover, while Milwaukee will deliver the bulk of the expected Democratic vote, increasing Democratic turnout in the region will necessitate overcoming the state's aggressive voter identification requirements[51] and the potential removal of thousands from the voting rolls.[52] In 2016, Clinton won Milwaukee County by more than 162,000 votes, but Milwaukee's share of the statewide vote decreased by over a point compared to 2012 (see table 7-6). The Democratic presidential candidate also must perform better in the suburban counties within the Milwaukee MSA. Clinton lost the WOW counties by more than 104,000 votes, netting fewer than 60,000 votes from Wisconsin's million-plus blue metro.

EXPERT ANALYSIS: WISCONSIN

Katherine Cramer is a professor of political science and the Natalie C. Holton Chair of Letters and Science at the University of Wisconsin, Madison. Author of an award-winning book, *The Politics of Resentment: Rural Consciousness in Wisconsin and the Rise of Scott Walker*, Cramer redefined what it means to live in rural America and illuminated the contemporary urban/rural divide that exists throughout America. In researching her book, Cramer travelled throughout Wisconsin, to meet Wisconsin residents where they live and work and to listen to their observations on local, state, and national politics. She was interviewed on April 23, 2018. Note that interview responses may include minor edits to provide continuity and clarify language.

Intrastate Political Dynamics

When asked about Wisconsin's intrastate political dynamics, Cramer suggested that Wisconsin's status as a "purple state" is a function of the urban/rural, Democratic/Republican divide, as well as the fact that "the Milwaukee suburbs tend to be Republican." As a consequence, there "have been very closes races" in the state for most of the decade, with some of this stemming from the uneven urban turnout in nonpresidential election years. Reflecting the tensions within the state's political culture, Cramer noted that Wisconsin voters support strong conservatives, such as former governor Scott Walker, as well as liberals such as Tammy Baldwin, the first openly gay member of the U.S. Senate.

Cramer also suggested that broader economic changes are realigning the state's historical economic balance of power. In particular, Milwaukee's long-standing role as the economic engine for the state is changing. The growth in and around the Madison metro (Dane

County) due to the development of high-tech jobs, including health-care, innovation, and software development sectors, has amplified Madison's economic status.

Regarding the demographic differences between the urban and rural parts of Wisconsin, Cramer noted that how these differences will evolve in the future appears uncertain, but the national attention applied to Wisconsin since the 2016 presidential election has created "more awareness of our urban/rural split and the way it coincides with party leanings." This split is now a "prominent part of . . . campaigns and the kind of candidates that will be seen as viable."

Still, the Milwaukee-Madison relationship and this region's separation from Greater Wisconsin remains steadfast. Cramer noted, "Republican-leaning representatives from Milwaukee benefit from portraying themselves as in touch with the rest of that state," that is, they describe themselves by noting "they grew up on a farm, go deer hunting, [and are] a true Wisconsinite."

One issue that does not fall into the urban/rural divide neatly is that of gun control. Although "the suburbs are more Republican and conservative," and "hunting is such a common pastime," the divide on this topic is "not as stark a divide as you might expect" because "even people who own guns are not necessarily opposed to gun control." Cramer also suggested that attitudes toward same-sex marriage have evolved. In 2006, Wisconsin voters by a nearly 3-2 margin ratified a constitutional amendment that was referred by the state legislature recognizing only marriages between a man and women. Like similar provisions in other states, Wisconsin's ban on same-sex marriage was invalidated by the federal courts. Since the passage of the amendment, Cramer indicated that "people don't feel that way (as strongly) given rapidly changing views since then. Wisconsin is a very purple state—you don't always get conventional."

Structural Features of State Government

Cramer noted that even though the state legislature meets annually, the Wisconsin governorship has become much stronger. She pointed to former Republican governor Tommy Thompson, who served for three terms, from 1987 to 2001, as a key figure for increasing executive power. Cramer suggested that because Thompson was "very charismatic, very popular," he was able to leverage his personality to enhance the office. She also noted that much of former governor Scott Walker's success stemmed from inheriting an office that had been strengthened by his predecessors and by having a unified Republican legislature. This allowed Walker to push through a lot of conservative legislation, such as Wisconsin Act 10 (2011), which eliminated collective bargaining for public sector unions in the state. The legislation was the subject of years of litigation (it was ruled constitutional by the Wisconsin Supreme Court in 2014) and prompted a recall election of Walker in 2012, which he survived. Indeed, the fact that such legislation could be passed in a state with such historical union strength and that its main proponent could survive a recall is indicative of the state's changing politics.

Cramer also noted that despite being a purple state, the parties within the Wisconsin legislature are highly disciplined in large part because of the strength of the formal party caucuses. She characterized these organizations as "very powerful" and capable of "controlling the behavior" of legislators.

In terms of the autonomy granted to local government, Cramer indicated that "home rule is more powerful in Wisconsin than in other states. Local municipalities have a lot of say over their own business." However, as just discussed, through legislative preemption of localities and legal interpretations parsing where local control ends and state control begins, there has been an erosion of local control in the state.

Metro Power in State Government

Cramer suggested that the amount of power Milwaukee exerts in state policymaking is a matter of perception. By virtue of its population and economic clout within the state, Milwaukee "has a lot of say." This view certainly is shared by legislators representing part of Greater Wisconsin: "If you're not from Madison or Milwaukee you perceive most resources go there and that those regions have a disproportionate say." The opposite holds for the urban areas: "If you're from Madison or Milwaukee, you think that outstate has representation and more say because of geography and that the state is predominantly rural."

CONCLUSION

Minnesota and Wisconsin, partners in what some call the "Great Midwestern Divide,"[53] are two key states in the 2020 presidential election. They are among the small roster of states with the potential to flip their electoral votes and, thus, affect a close election. Minnesota has the potential to vote Republican in 2020 and Wisconsin could return to the Democratic Party. Either or both of those scenarios would have a major impact on the 2020 election. These two Midwestern states, with similar origins and history, have taken divergent political and economic paths in recent years, and the 2020 election will be a watershed moment for each traditional stronghold of Democratic politics.

Minnesota, with its Twin Cities metro region and a significant number of college-educated white voters, is more likely to remain with the Democratic Party. Wisconsin, should the election be a referendum on the performance of President Trump and the Democratic candidate generates only moderate voter enthusiasm, hangs in the balance. The ability of each party to generate voter turnout (or diminish voter turnout from the opposing side) will be critical.

NOTES

1. Goodreads, Wisconsin Idea Quotes, www.goodreads.com/quotes/tag/wisconsin-idea.

2. Lillian Speakman, "Bob Dylan Talks at Length about Minnesota in Rare interview," *The Current*, March 23, 2017, www.thecurrent.org/feature/2017/03/23/bob-dylan-interview-minnesota.

3. Nineteenth-century Wisconsin's largest minority was German-speaking, such that "Wisconsin German" refers to the dialects of the German language found in the Badger State. The 1910 census revealed that the German language remained widespread, and not until World War I and a wave of anti-German sentiment did some towns become English-speaking.

4. Phil Anderson, "A Tale of Two States," *Middle Wisconsin*, September 29, 2018, www.middlewisconsin.org/a-tale-of-two-states/.

5. Greta Kaul, "Politicians Love to Talk about the Urban-Rural Divide in Minnesota. But How Much of a Divide is There, Really?" *MinnPost*, September 1, 2017,

www.minnpost.com/politics-policy/2017/09/politicians-love-talk-about-urban-rural-divide-minnesota-how-much-divide-the/.

6. Ibid.

7. Ibid.

8. "Past and Present," *Minnesota. A State Guide,* compiled and written by the Federal Writers' Project of the Works Progress Administration, sponsored by the Executive Council, State of Minnesota (New York: Viking Press, 1938), p. 3.

9. Ibid., p. 4.

10. Ibid., p. 5.

11. Dante Chinni and James Gimpel, *Patchwork Nation: The Surprising Truth About the "Real" America* (New York: Avery, 2011), p. 171.

12. Ibid., p. 173.

13. Michael Peterson, "A Greater Understanding of 'Greater Minnesota' (and 'Metro' Areas)," *Minnesota State Demographic Center,* August 3, 2015, https://mn.gov/admin/demography/news/ada-to-zumbrota-blog/?id=36-245952.

14. Editorial Board, "Rural Minnesota Cannot be Left behind as State Changes," *Isanti County News,* December 13, 2017, www.hometownsource.com/isanti_county_news/free/rural-minnesota-cannot-be-left-behind-as-state-changes/article_2b05d364-e041-11e7-91ce-5b4e6716fc43.html.

15. Ibid.

16. Andrea Mayer-Brusette, "Hillary Wins Minnesota . . . Barely," *Alpha News,* November 9, 2016, https://alphanewsmn.com/hillary-wins-minnesota/.

17. Briana Bierschbach, "Get Ready," *MinnPost,* November 7, 2017, www.minnpost.com/politics-policy/2017/11/get-ready-hear-lot-more-about-urban-rural-divide-minnesota-politicians.

18. Jon Collins and John Enger, "Beltrami Co. becomes First in State to Reject Refugee Resettlement," MPR News, January 20, 2020, www.mprnews.org/story/2020/01/07/beltrami-co-rejects-refugee-resettlement.

19. Jennifer Brooks, "Minnesota's Pope County, in Trump Country, Votes Unanimously to Welcome Refugees," *Star Tribune,* February 1, 2020, www.startribune.com/minnesota-s-pope-county-in-trump-country-votes-unanimously-to-welcome-refugees/567494922/.

20. Tessa Berenson, "Donald Trump: Minnesota Has 'Suffered Enough' Accepting Refugees," *Time,* November 6, 2016, https://time.com/4560078/donald-trump-minnesota-somali-refugees/.

21. Alex Marshall, "How Much Diversity Does a Modern City Need?" *Governing,* March 3, 2020, www.governing.com/community/How-Much-Diversity-Does-a-Modern-City-Need.html.

22. Lorraine Boissoneault, "How a $10 Billion Experimental City Nearly Got Built in Rural Minnesota," *Smithsonian,* March 29, 2018, www.smithsonianmag.com/innovation/how-10-billion-experimental-city-nearly-got-built-rural-minnesota-180968617/#ak8xBWjmRKpci21I.99.

23. Eric Ostermeier, "Ilhan Omar Nearly Breaks Minnesota U.S. House Electoral Record," *Smart Politics*, November 13, 2018, https://editions.lib.umn.edu/smart politics/2018/11/13/ilhan-omar-nearly-breaks-minnesota-us-house-electoral -record/.

24. S. V. Date, "Minnesota Hasn't Gone Republican Since Nixon, But Trump is Pushing Hard Anyway," *HuffPost*, October 10, 2019, www.huffpost.com/entry/ trump-rally-minnesota-hardcore-base_n_5d9f7940e4b087efdbaa9cc5.

25. Patrick Condon, "Rep. Collin Peterson Votes against Impeaching Trump, " *Star Tribune*, December 18, 2019, www.startribune.com/rep-collin-peterson-votes -against-impeaching-trump/566328582/.

26. Judy Keen, "Will Minnesota be a Tossup State in 2020 Elections?" *Star Tribune*, www.startribune.com/will-minnesota-be-tossup-state-in-2020-elections/5007 57901/.

27. Editorial Board, "Trump Says Immigrants are Unwelcome in Minnesota. What's Unwelcome Is His Bigotry," *Washington Post*, October 12, 2019, www.wash ingtonpost.com/opinions/trump-says-immigrants-are-unwelcome-in-minnesota- whats-unwelcome-is-his-bigotry/2019/10/11/e607feba-ec62-11e9-9c6d-436a0d f4f31d_story.html.

28. Kerry Eleveld, "Minnesota Was Mentioned Just Once in *The Mueller Report*. Here's Why It Matters," *Daily Kos*, September 2, 2019, www.dailykos.com/stories /2019/9/2/1881870/-Minnesota-was-mentioned-just-once-in-the-Mueller-report- Here-s-why-it-matters.

29. Ibid.

30. J. Patrick Coolican, "Can President Donald Trump Really Win Minnesota?" *Star Tribune*, October 18, 2019, www.startribune.com/can-president-donald-trump -really-win-minnesota/562922092/.

31. Alexander Hertel-Fernandez, Caroline Tervo, and Theda Skocpol, "How the Koch Brothers Built the Most Powerful Rightwing Group You've Never Heard Of," *The Guardian*, September 26, 2018, www.theguardian.com/us-news/2018/sep/26/koch -brothers-americans-for-prosperity-rightwing-political-group.

32. Dan Kaufman, *The Fall of Wisconsin: The Conservative Conquest of a Progressive Bastion and the Future of American Politics* (New York: W. W. Norton & Company, 2018), p. 81.

33. *Wisconsin: A Guide to the Badger State, Illustrated American Guide Series*, compiled by Workers of the Writers' Program of the Work Projects Administration in the State of Wisconsin, Wisconsin Library Association (New York: Duell, Sloan, and Pearce, 1941), p. 45.

34. Ibid., p. 190.

35. Ibid., p. 217. "Though representatives of more than 20 different stocks are included in Madison's population, the foreign-born constitute less than 9.5 percent; natives of foreign parentage constitute 29.5 percent; nearly two-thirds of the people are descendants of native Americans. The largest national groups are German and

Norwegian, still retaining cultural and religious societies. Irish, English, and Italians comprise the next largest divisions. Italians and Negroes constitute the only distinct and homogeneous groups."

36. Ibid., p. 242. "18.9 per cent of Milwaukee's population is foreign-born. Germans form the largest group of foreign stock, though the percentage of German foreign-born has shrunk considerably in recent years. In 1880, thirty-five per cent of Milwaukee's population was made up of foreign-born Germans, and Germans comprised 68 per cent of the total foreign-born; in 1930, eight per cent of the total population was composed of foreign-born Germans, and Germans comprised 37 per cent of the total foreign-born. Of the entire population, foreign-born Germans and Germans of the first generation (including Austrians) comprise 29.7 per cent. Assimilation of the German elements has accompanied the decline of German immigration to the city. Milwaukee no longer seems a city transplanted from the Rhine to the banks of the Milwaukee River."

37. Kaufman, *The Fall of Wisconsin*, p. 45.

38. Ibid.

39. Soon after the 2016 presidential election, in the case *Gill v. Whitford*, a federal court ruled that the maps created by Wisconsin's Republican-led state legislature in 2011 created "an unconstitutional partisan gerrymander that violated both the Equal Protection Clause of the Fourteenth Amendment and the First Amendment's protection of freedom of association" (Kaufman, p. 217). However, after the U.S. Supreme Court ruled in June 2019 that such cases were outside the purview of the federal courts, the Wisconsin case was dismissed despite the fact that in 2018 the Democrats secured a mere thirty-six of ninety-nine seats in the State Assembly, yet garnered 54 percent of the vote (see table 7-7).

40. Emily Badger, "Are Rural Voters the 'Real' Voters? Wisconsin Republicans Seem to Think," *New York Times*, December 8, 2018, www.nytimes.com/2018/12/06/upshot/wisconsin-republicans-rural-urban-voters.html.

41. Ibid.

42. Zach Brandon, "Unlocking Greater Madison's infinite potential," *Wisconsin State Journal*, September 29, 2019, https://madison.com/wsj/business/technology/unlocking-greater-madison-s-infinite-potential/article_8ad199b5-bd74-5413-b34c-bbf8e283b26b.html.

43. Craig Gilbert, "Ultra-Red Wisconsin County Struggles with Trump," *USA Today*, September 7, 2016, www.usatoday.com/story/news/politics/elections/2016/09/07/trump-clinton-waukesha-wisconsin-republicans/89724308/.

44. Mike Gotzler, "Impacts of Wisconsin's Local Employment Preemption Bill," *Greater Madison InBusiness*, March 28, 2018, www.ibmadison.com/Blogger/Open-Mic/March-2018/Impacts-of-Wisconsins-local-employment-law-preemption-bill/.

45. Katherine Cramer, *The Politics of Resentment: Rural Consciousness in Wisconsin and the Rise of Scott Walker* (University of Chicago Press, 2016) p. 51.

46. Mark Sommerhauser, "In Donald Trump Era, UW Prof's Rural Wisconsin Insights Gain National Prominence," *Wisconsin State Journal*, February 20, 2017,

https://madison.com/wsj/news/local/govt-and-politics/in-donald-trump-era-uw-prof-s-rural-wisconsin-insights/article_69bb90cc-008b-5d30-912f-bf2019732b59.html.

47. Malia Jones and Mitchell Ewald, "Putting Rural Wisconsin on the Map: Understanding Rural-Urban Divides Requires a Complex Spectrum of Definitions," *WisContext*, May 17, 2017, https://www.wiscontext.org/putting-rural-wisconsin-map.

48. United States Elections Project, Voter Turnout Data, selected years, www.electproject.org.

49. Craig Gilbert, "The Reddest and Bluest Places in Wisconsin," *Journal Sentinel*, December 3, 2014, http://archive.jsonline.com/blogs/news/284675921.html.

50. Scott Gordon, "Wisconsin's Modest, Uneven Population Growth So Far In The 2010s: 2010–17 Census Numbers Capture Patterns Of Urban Growth and Rural Losses," *WisContext*, June 5, 2018, www.wiscontext.org/wisconsins-modest-uneven-population-growth-so-far-2010s.

51. Michael Wines, "Wisconsin Strict ID Law Discouraged Voters, Study Finds," *New York Times*, September 25, 2017, www.nytimes.com/2017/09/25/us/wisconsin-voters.html.

52. Patrick Marley, "Wisconsin Appeals Court Rules Voters Targeted for Purge Will Remain on the Rolls," *Milwaukee Journal Sentinel*, February 28, 2020, www.jsonline.com/story/news/politics/2020/02/28/wisconsin-appeals-court-friday-struck-down-ozaukee-county-judges-ruling-thousands-people-had-quickly/4903600002/.

53. Theo Anderson, "The Great Midwestern Divide: Why Minnesota and Wisconsin's Political Schism Matters," *Inthesetimes.com*, July 26, 2017, https://inthesetimes.com/article/20312/two-paths-diverged-in-the-midwest-scott-walker-mark-dayton_.

8

TEXAS

David F. Damore
Robert E. Lang

Perhaps no state is more challenging to appraise than Texas. Classified by the U.S. census as part of the West South Central Division, Texas connects the southeast to the southwest. North to south, Texas extends nearly as far south as Monterrey, Mexico, while the northern edge of the Texas panhandle has the same latitude as Nashville, Tennessee, and Las Vegas, Nevada. The one-time independent nation succeeded from the United States to join the Confederacy during the Civil War. Five years after the war ended, Texas was readmitted after ratifying the Thirteenth, Fourteenth, and Fifteenth Amendments. Today, Texas is a "super state" with a population, economy, and land mass exceeding those of most industrialized Western democracies. The only state with a larger physical footprint is Alaska, and Texas ranks second, behind only California, in population and economic output.

With a majority-minority and highly urbanized population (see table 8-1), Texas is home to four of the thirty largest metro regions in the country, including two of the top five, Dallas and Houston. The state's million-plus metros are magnets for young, highly-educated domestic migrants from Democratic states such as California, New York, and Illinois, who come seeking lower housing costs and jobs in energy, technology, and healthcare.[1] Because of its vast breadth, Texas's diversity includes Black urban and rural pockets in the east and significant shares of Latinos distributed across the state's western half and along the Mexican border. These characteristics of the state's demography suggest that Texas is moving from a Republican stronghold to an electorally competitive swing state.

Yet, as this analysis suggests, Texas also includes enormous swathes of rural spaces that are reliably Republican and exert outsized influence in the state legislature. In recent years, these interests have chipped away at local government autonomy across a range of policies and imposed restrictions on ballot access while pushing an agenda heavy on divisive social issues. Moreover, as newspaper editorials lament how transplants to Texas's million-plus metro regions are threatening to change the state's politics,[2] Texas Republicans are ramping up their efforts to keep the Lone Star State in the Republican column.[3] As a consequence of these countervailing forces, Texas optimizes the urban/rural, blue metros, red states divide.

TABLE 8-1. Demographic and Economic Comparison between Texas and Metros

	Texas	Share in Austin (%)	Share in Dallas (%)	Share in Houston (%)	Share in San Antonio (%)
Population	28,304,596	7.5	26.1	24.4	8.7
White	41.9%	9.3	28.9	21.0	7.1
Black	11.8%	4.3	34.1	34.9	4.8
Asian	4.8%	9.1	37.1	40.1	4.1
Latino	39.4%	6.2	19.1	23.0	12.3
Foreign-Born	17.2%	6.6	28.5	33.6	5.9
College Educated	29.6%	11.8	30.8	26.7	8.4
Jobs	13,002,846	8.4	28.2	24.4	8.7
GDP	$1,589,956	8.0	30.3	30.1	7.3

Sources: 2017 American Community Survey 1-Year estimates as aggregated by censusreporter.org, Department of Commerce, Bureau of Economic Analysis, 2015 Real GDP (millions of chained 2012 dollars) County Level Data, U.S. Department of Labor, Bureau of Labor Statistics 2017 County Level Data.

STATE OF PLAY: TEXAS

Despite Texas's large size and vast physical diversity—with some of the most humid and arid counties in the United States—Texas contains four major political divisions. Culturally and physically, Texas has many more regions than just the four political zones identified here (see figure 8-1).

For instance, consider an area such as the Texas Hill Country, the birthplace of Lyndon Johnson, former Democratic president, vice president, and U.S. Senate majority leader, which lies in the south-central part of the state, just west of Austin and San Antonio. Hill Country is a region distinct from the rest of Texas in both topography and settlement history.[4] Hill Country was mainly settled by immigrants from

FIGURE 8-1. Texas

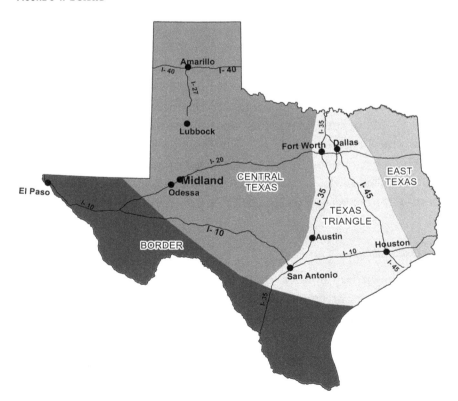

Germany and what is now the Czech Republic, as opposed to the Scots-Irish who peopled much of East Texas. At one point during the Civil War, the Hill Country's cultural and demographic distinctness from the rest of Texas gave the region an equally distinct politics. Hill Country German immigrants were so pro Union that they considered succeeding from the state of Texas and aligning with Northern interests.[5]

Today, Hill Country residents vote as reliably Republican as people living in most other parts of rural Texas. Hill Country remains culturally distinct in its foods and German beer festivals, but it has lost its political separateness from other rural districts in the Lone Star State.

Indeed, because rural Texas is so large and Republicans win most white-dominated rural counties by such large margins, the state has not elected a Democrat to statewide office in thirty years. Ann Richards, the last Democratic governor, lost her gubernatorial reelection bid to George W. Bush in 1994. More generally, the GOP maintains a stranglehold on the levers of power in state government, and Republicans dominate Texas's federal delegation.

Yet, there are cracks in the Republicans' dominance. In 2016, Hillary Clinton lost the state by nine points, the best showing for a Democratic presidential candidate since 1996. In 2018, Democrat Beto O'Rourke lost to incumbent Republican U.S. Senator Ted Cruz by less than three points (see table 8-2). The Democrats also picked up U.S. House seats in suburban Dallas and Houston and a handful of seats in the statehouse (see table 8-3). The Texas political divisions detailed in this chapter and in figure 8-1 are based in part on the results of the 2018 U.S. Senate election between Republican Ted Cruz and Democrat Beto O'Rourke, as well as the 2016 U.S. presidential election.

Texas Triangle

The key urban political district in Texas is an area known as the "Texas Triangle Megapolitan Cluster."[6] The region contains three megapolitan areas: Dallas-Fort Worth (at the top of the Triangle); Houston (to the east); and Central Texas—or Austin and San Antonio—(to the west).[7] The Texas Triangle contains the four most populous metropolitan areas in the state. In size rank terms, these are: Dallas (fourth in the United States); Houston (fifth in the United States); San Antonio

TABLE 8-2. Comparison of Electoral Outcomes between Texas and Metros

Election	Texas Outcome	Austin Vote Share [%]	Austin Outcome	Dallas Vote Share [%]	Dallas Outcome	Houston Vote Share [%]	Houston Outcome	San Antonio Vote Share [%]	San Antonio Outcome
2018 U.S. Senate	+2.6 Rep	9.2	+31.4 Dem	27.9	+1.7 Dem	23.2	+3.7 Dem	9.9	+4.4 Dem
2018 Gubernatorial	+13.3 Rep	9.7	+19.1 Dem	27.8	+10.3 Rep	23.3	+6.8 Rep	8.8	+8.0 Rep
2016 Presidential	+9.0 Rep	8.7	+19.5 Dem	27.1	+7.1 Rep	23.3	+1.0 Rep	8.8	+1.1 Rep
2014 U.S. Senate	+27.2 Rep	9.3	+1.5 Dem	25.0	+27.1 Rep	22.9	+22.9 Rep	8.8	+24.2 Rep
2014 Gubernatorial	+20.4 Rep	9.3	+11.5 Dem	27.1	+17.1 Rep	22.9	+15.7 Rep	8.7	+14.2 Rep
2012 Presidential	+15.8 Rep	8.1	+8.0 Dem	27.1	+14.9 Rep	23.3	+11.6 Rep	8.6	+8.0 Rep
2012 U.S. Senate	+15.8 Rep	8.1	+7.1 Dem	27.1	+15.2 Rep	23.5	+12.5 Rep	8.6	+8.0 Rep

Source: Data from Texas secretary of state's website.

TABLE 8-3. Partisan Composition of Texas State
Government and Federal Delegation

		State Government				Federal Delegation			
		Upper House		Lower House		U.S. Senate		U.S. House	
	Governor	Dems	Reps	Dems	Reps	Dems	Reps	Dems	Reps
2019–20	Rep	12	19	67	83	0	2	13	23
2017–18	Rep	11	20	56	94	0	2	11	25
2015–16	Rep	11	20	52	98	0	2	11	25
2013–14	Rep	12	19	55	95	0	2	12	24

Sources: Data from National Conference of State Legislatures, "State and Legislative Partisan Composition" for various years, and Texas secretary of state's website.

(twenty-fourth in the United States); and Austin (thirtieth in the United States). All four of the Texas million-plus metros are booming, with Austin growing the fastest, increasing by more than 25 percent between 2010 and 2018. The million-plus metros in the Texas Triangle together account for over two-thirds of Texas's total population (or 19.5 million out of 28.3 million).

While, as detailed in tables 8-1 and 8-2, there are regional demographic and political variations within the megapolitan areas of the Texas Triangle, all million-plus metros share a common set of demographics and voting patterns. All million-plus metro areas in the Texas Triangle are diverse[8] and growing more diverse each year; all have seen rapid growth this decade (and for many decades), and are gaining both foreign and domestic migrants. Finally, all are becoming more liberal in both their core areas and close-in suburbs.

As a consequence of this growth, Texas may pick up as many as three U.S. House seats after the 2020 census. Texas gained four seats after the 2010 reapportionment, but because of a GOP gerrymander, the state's U.S. House and state legislative districts were drawn with a strong rural Republican bias. In terms of Electoral College clout, between the 2008 and 2024 presidential elections, Texas will have added the equivalent of Democratic-voting Delaware and Rhode Island or Republican-voting Idaho and Wyoming.

Each Texas Triangle megapolitan area has a locally complex political geography, as one would expect given the large scale. And some parts of the Texas Triangle are new as major metros, so their current economic and political structure is more fluid than older large-scale regions in the east.

Consider the Dallas–Fort Worth Metroplex as an example of how radically transformed big Texas metros are from their recent past. Even the name *Metroplex* is a contrivance.[9] It was a name picked by business interests to label a place that until the 1970s simply did not exist as an organic region. As Robert Lang, Jaewon Lim, and Karen Danielsen explain, the federal government forced Dallas and Fort Worth into a common place:[10]

The cities of Dallas and Fort Worth today appear joined by a common history typical of other so called "twin cities," such as Minneapolis–Saint Paul in Minnesota or Tampa–Saint Petersburg in Florida, but historically Dallas and Fort Worth were distinct places with altogether separate identities—in fact, they were rivals. Dallas historically sought alliances with larger eastern metros, offering itself as being cosmopolitan enough to maintain branch offices of major national companies. Dallas had an early reputation for being snobbish, or as the Work Projects Administration (WPA) guide to Texas noted: "It came into existence as a serious community with citizens of a peaceable and cultured type."[11] By contrast, Fort Worth, which lies just one county over, remains proud to be a "Cowtown," or, as noted in the *WPA Guide*: "According to the masthead line in the *Star-Telegram*, Fort Worth is 'where the West begins.'"[12] In other words, Dallas and Fort Worth were separated by distance (about 35 miles), culture, taste, industry, and even the region of the United States that each one chose to identify with—East versus West. . . . What joined Dallas and Fort Worth at first was new modeling from the U.S. Census Bureau (in the 1960 census) that showed that despite their rivalry, there was substantial commuting occurring between the regions that was beginning to meld them into a unified metropolitan economy. Then, in the mid-1960s, Dallas and Fort Worth sought federal aid in improving their airports. The U.S. Federal Aviation Administration, seeing that the two cities were merging, insisted that Dallas and Fort Worth construct one large common international airport. The agreement was to have the main airport runways built literally at the county line between Dallas County and Tarrant County (Fort Worth).

Even though both Dallas and Tarrant (home to Fort Worth) Counties voted for Beto O'Rourke over Ted Cruz in the 2018 senate race, Dallas County did so by a much larger margin (66.1 percent versus 49.9 percent). In 2016, Donald Trump carried Tarrant County, while Hillary Clinton dominated Dallas County. The difference between the counties reflects both the larger African American population in Dallas County and its historic connectivity to the east and the fact that Tarrant County is home to Fort Worth (or America's largest "Cowtown"). Still, because of the size of the Dallas metro region, which encompasses thirteen of the state's 254 counties (see table 8-3), besides the 2018 U.S. Senate election, the metro votes Republican in large part because of strong GOP suburban support in the surrounding counties.

Texas is home to over a dozen fast-growing, large-scale urbanizing suburbs that Robert Lang and Jennifer LeFurgy label "boomburbs."[13] These are incorporated cities with more than 50,000 people that have seen double-digit growth each decade since 1970. The Dallas-Fort Worth Metroplex is home to most Texas boomburbs (although a few are located in Houston and Austin). Arlington, Texas (home to the NFL's Dallas Cowboys), just east of Fort Worth, is the state's largest boomburb, with 389,122 residents in 2018, making it more populous than New Orleans. Many boomburbs in the Metroplex are diverse and densely populated. Consider Irving, Texas (population 242,242 in 2018), which is served by the Dallas light rail system (DART) and supports mixed-use, mid-rise transit-oriented development. Irving is also home to a large foreign-born population (much of it Asian), which, according to Lang and LeFurgy, makes it a type of boomburb they call a "New Brooklyn" to signify its importance as an international gateway.[14] Moving forward, the dense and diverse boomburbs surrounding Dallas are more likely to vote for Democrats than the more sprawling and whiter suburbs at the metro fringe.

Austin also differs politically from its much more diverse (see table 8-1) megapolitan partner San Antonio. Clinton and O'Rourke won

Travis County (home to Austin) with nearly three-quarters and two-thirds of the vote, respectively, making it the most Democratic-voting county of any major urban county in Texas. By contrast, Clinton and O'Rourke won Bexar County (home to San Antonio, with 55 and 60 percent of the vote, respectively), but both Trump and Cruz carried the seven smaller counties within the San Antonio metro region. Models that link the percent of minority population to a higher turnout for Democrats would predict that Bexar, which is far more diverse than Travis County, would have a higher Democratic vote margin than Travis.

However, a closer look at Travis County and the city of Austin can explain why the region is so Democratic-friendly. To begin, Austin is the state capital, and as the second most populous state after California, Texas has a large state government with a significant number of public employees. Public employees tend to lean Democratic in their voting, as that party is seen as supporting government and its workers. The liberalism of the state's capital stands in notable contrast to the tenor of the policies pushed by the Republicans who control state government. The response from Governor Greg Abbott, who, after running afoul of Austin's tree removal policy, pushed legislation restricting local governments' regulatory authority over trees, encapsulates the friction between the state's Republican leadership and the host city for Texas's government. Austin also is home to one of the largest public universities in the United States—University of Texas, Austin. Finally, Austin is a Bohemian enclave[15] with an active music scene (Bohemian in Austin's case is semi-literal given that its settlement pattern is partly Czechoslovakian in origin and Bohemia is a region therein).[16] It is also a major technology hub that has received migration of people and firms from tech areas in California.[17] When Californians relocate, they tend to bring more liberal politics with them.[18]

Also note that compared to Texas's other million-plus metros, Austin is the most geographically concentrated region, covering just five counties (see table 8-4). As a consequence, with fifty-four general purpose governments within the metro region, Austin has less intrametro governmental fragmentation, particularly compared to Dallas and Houston, which feature 219 and 133 general purposes governments, respectively (see table 8-4). Still, as is the case in the state's other million-plus metro regions, the GOP tends to win the counties surrounding the core urban county (although in 2018, O'Rourke defeated Cruz in Williamson County, the second most populated county in the region, even as the Republican gubernatorial candidate, Greg Abbott, easily carried the county).

Harris County (home to Houston) also has shifted blue in recent election cycles. The county voted twice for Obama, once for Clinton, and went heavily for O'Rourke in 2018. In the 2018 midterm election, Democrat Lizzie Fletcher picked up Texas's 7th U.S. House District by defeating the Republican incumbent who had held the seat for almost two decades.[19] More telling, Fletcher did not run as a moderate Democrat. Rather, she ran as a progressive and an outsider in a district once held by former President George H. W. Bush.[20]

That Harris is now a reliably blue county is a big deal. It is the third most populated county in the country, trailing only Los Angeles County, California, and Cook County, Illinois, in population. If Dem-

TABLE 8-4. Metro Governance Fragmentation and Autonomy in Texas

Governance Fragmentation

Metro	Number of Counties in Metro	Number of General Purposes Governments in Metro
Austin	5	54
Dallas	13	219
Houston	9	133
San Antonio	8	62

Governance Autonomy

Local Government Autonomy Score	0.471
Local Government Autonomy Ranking	5

Sources: Data for Governance Fragmentation from 2017 Census of Governments. Data for Governance Autonomy from Harold Wolman, Robert McManmon, Michael Bell, and David Brunori, "Comparing Local Government Autonomy Across States," in *The Property Tax and Local Autonomy*, edited by Michael Bell, David Brunori, and Joan Youngman (Lincoln Institute of Land Policy Press, 2010), pp. 69–114.

ocratic support in Harris, with its 4.7 million residents, continues to increase, it will be more difficult for the Republicans to squeeze the requisite number of votes from the white rural Republican counties to offset the Democrats' urban support.

As is detailed in the following expert analysis, although Texas, in theory, extends a good deal of autonomy to local governments (the state's ranks fifth in this metric, see table 8-4), the state's constitution forbids localities from passing ordinances that contradict state law. Moreover, with the policy preferences of the state's million-plus blue metros continuing to diverge from the rest of Texas, in addition to tree removal authority, the Republican-dominated legislature has reined in local governments across a host of policy areas, such as fracking, ride-sharing, paid sick-leave, and plastic-bag bans. At one point, Texas Governor Greg Abbott went so far as to suggest a statewide prohibition on the ability of municipal governments to create any regulations, a step that would effectively eliminate any semblance of home rule in the Lone Star State.[21]

East Texas

East of the Texas Triangle lies the largely conservative political region of East Texas. East Texas can feel like an extension of Louisiana, especially southeast Texas.[22] The region is the most Southern-like in Texas. It is historically tied to the South in that a substantial slave population once lived in East Texas at the time of the Civil War. To this day, the region contains a large African American rural population, which makes the region a bit less conservative based on voting patterns when compared to Central Texas.

The bluest-leaning part of East Texas is found on the coast in Jefferson County (home to the cities of Beaumont and Port Arthur). The county voted for O'Rourke in the 2018 Texas U.S. Senate race and Hillary Clinton lost the county by just over 400 votes two years prior. Jefferson County is home to a large oil refining and chemical industry that employs a growing Latino population. Add to that a large Black community and it is easy to see how the Democrats can keep the county blue.

Central Texas

With few exceptions, Central Texas is a deep red political space. The region begins west of the Texas Triangle and extends through central Texas and up to the Texas panhandle. To the west, the political section borders eastern New Mexico. Outside of Texas Hill Country, most of Central Texas is flat, forming most of the Great Plains section of Texas.

Central Texas is energy rich and includes the productive Permian Basin. A major center for that industry is Ector County (home to Odessa, Texas). Odessa maintains a Latino community that often works in energy production, and their votes make Ector a slightly less Republican-voting county than the rest of Central Texas.

There is only one large university in the region—Texas Tech in Lubbock. The school may account for why Lubbock County is one of the few places that is a bit less Republican-voting than the rest of Central Texas. Another lighter red place is Potter County in the Texas panhandle. Its major city is Amarillo, home to a Latino community that works in the city's food processing industry.

The rest of Central Texas is ruby red and home to cattle ranches and small towns. Outside of the few select urban areas mentioned, Central Texas is among the most Republican-voting political regions in the United States.

Border

The most consistently blue-voting counties in Texas lie along the border with Mexico and have substantial rural and urban Latino populations. The region runs the entire length of the Rio Grande River, from Brownsville in the east to El Paso in the west. Except for Terrell County, which is a deep rural area just east of Big Bend National Park, Hudspeth County just east of El Paso, and sparsely populated Kinney County, every Texas county that shares a border with Mexico voted for O'Rourke in 2018 and Clinton in 2016. The southernmost part of the border region is the deepest blue region of Texas, especially the area south of the Nueces River.[23] That includes Nueces County and its county seat of Corpus Christi.

The blue areas of the border provide some political counterweight to red-voting East and Central Texas. If the Texas Triangle million-plus metros keep trending Democratic, then the vote from this region becomes even more significant in that, together, the two regions can turn Texas blue.

Conclusion: Texas State of Play

Texas is a big, complicated, nation-size state. Despite its complexity, its political state of play boils down to one key trend line—the demographically diversifying and politically shifting million-plus metros in the Texas Triangle. The future of Texas politics lies in how fast these places grow and how that growth shifts the state's political dynamic in favor of the Democrats. Still, because of lower levels of some Democratic voting constituencies, coupled with structural advantages, Republicans have ample resources, at least in the short term, to mitigate growing Democratic support in the state.

EXPERT ANALYSIS: TEXAS

Given Texas's size and complexity, interviews were conducted with three state experts, Bill Fulton, the director of the Kinder Institute for Urban Research at Rice University in Houston, who was interviewed on May 1, 2018; sociologist and founding director of the Kinder Institute, Stephen Klineberg, who was interviewed on May 24, 2018; and Cal Jillson, professor of political science at Southern Methodist University in Dallas, who was interviewed on May 2, 2018. All three have published widely on Texas demography, government, politics, and policy. In some instances, direct quotes provided by the experts were edited for clarity.

Intrastate Political Dynamics

In Texas, geographic differences reinforce partisan divisions, and the state provides a microcosm of the shifts occurring across the county. Klineberg sees the split in Texas as "between the people who live in the major multiethnic cities and are competing in the global economy, and rural and small-town folks, largely Anglos, in those rural areas where the world has changed on them." In Klineberg's telling, "the cities are the place where this new multi-America is taking shape, and the rural areas, in Texas and across the country, are the places where the jobs are being lost and the young people are leaving, and the sense of an America that's being taken away from me is powerful in those rural areas where it doesn't happen to the same degree in the cities where we have benefitted so much from all that integration."

A good deal of the urban/rural divergence is shaped by demographic differences. Jillson, for instance, suggested that "all of the major urban areas of Texas are seen as minority strongholds, which make them Democratic strongholds, and possessing a political culture that is more favorable to government and to government management of the economy and of social policy, higher taxes, those kinds of things. Lots of surveys show that Black and Hispanic citizens would prefer a wider range of government policies and to be involved in more things. Anglos tend to oppose those things."

Yet, despite the state's growing diversity and urbanization, the realization of urban preferences and increased Democratic support is hindered by greater conservatism among minority voters and lower levels of political participation among these voting blocs. Jillson explained that, compared to the rest of the country, polling suggests that Texas is "ten points more conservative than the country is generally, and even Texas Hispanics are about ten points more conservative, say, than California Hispanics. So, Texas attitudes shift conservative, not just among Anglos but among Blacks and Hispanics, who live within that sort of traditional political culture of Texas. So, Blacks and Hispanics are more progressive than our Texas Anglos but not as progressive as their counterparts are in the rest of the country."

Jillson also suggested that while Texas has been rapidly diversifying in the last twenty-plus years and "within the next couple of years, the number of Hispanics living in Texas will exceed the number of Anglos living in Texas," realizing the political consequences of these shifts may take "another fifteen years." This is the case because, in Jillson's estimation, "a third or more of Hispanics are not [citizens]" and, therefore, are ineligible to vote. In contrast, while "Anglos register to vote and turn out at numbers that do not match turnout in much of the rest of the country," they turn out at much higher rates than Hispanics in Texas. As a consequence, "Hispanics are approaching 40 percent of residents in Texas, but they cast only 20 percent of votes in statewide elections in Texas. . . . And Anglos, while they are about 40 percent of the population, just a little bit more than 40 percent, still cast about two-thirds of votes in statewide elections."

As a consequence of these dynamics, Jillson noted, "generally the Republican margin in presidential elections is in the mid-teens." Jillson suggested that Donald Trump's relatively poor showing in Texas in 2016 was a function of Trump being "an unusual candidate, and a relatively weak candidate," but Jillson expects if Trump "is the candidate in 2020, he'll actually carry Texas again." Fulton concurred, suggesting "it's hard to know how typical or atypical Trump is." Fulton also suggested that Beto O'Rourke's strong candidacy in the 2018 U.S. Senate election had a lot to do with the fact that "nobody likes Ted Cruz," and it was unclear what the race says "about the changing dynamics of the state as opposed to Ted Cruz's personality." Continuing, Fulton observed that "O'Rourke was the only serious Democrat who was taken as a challenge to anybody. None of the other Republicans [who ran in 2018] were at risk at all."

Still, even with these narrowing GOP margins, Jillson anticipates that it will not be until 2050 that "Hispanics will become part of the Democratic coalition that will govern Texas unless there are dramatic changes that take place." Continuing, Jillson observed that "as Hispanic noncitizens become citizens and become more comfortable with American political practices and register to vote and turn out at numbers, or proportions, closer to Anglo and Black turnout, they'll continue to vote 2-1 Democrat." Jillson also suggested that the continuing shift in the state's Democratic coalition will result in roughly 30 percent of the party's support coming from Anglos, who "as election results tighten up will be encouraged to wonder whether or not they want to remain in the minority-dominated Democratic Party, or maybe vote Republican. So, there will be dog whistle politics directed at Anglo Democrats."

To that end, Jillson expects that "when Texas politics begins to look like it's getting close to competitive in statewide elections, there will be an avalanche of conservative Republican money that now plays nationally that will come home to Texas to control state politics." Currently, "there's a lot of conservative Texas money, because it's not needed at home, that goes to play in senate races around the country, in presidential elections, and other kinds of elections that will come home to hold the line if it looks like Democrats are becoming competitive."

In the short term, Klineberg expects to see an intensification of the gap between public opinion and "politically effective opinion" that is caused by the lower levels of turnout among Latinos. Fulton refers to this as the "Democratic voter turnout problem." This gap is likely to deepen "the big divide in the legislature between urban representatives and rural representatives," particularly in terms of social issues. Klineberg observed that "the Republicans who represent the small rural areas are the ones who have this very deep-seated sort of commitment to the social agenda issues of abortion and gay rights and all those other divisions that, for people in the cities and borders, have basically been resolved." Continuing, Klineberg noted that "the overall support for gay rights in this country is increasing, but not in those pockets of rural poverty and conservatism." In contrast to the more homogenous demographics of rural Texas, Klineberg suggested that "growing up in the economically and ethnically diverse city inevitably leads you to interact with and come to know people who are not like oneself or people who are from other countries." He also noted that in "every question we ask in our surveys ["Kinder Houston Area Survey"] about comfort with diversity and support for immigration shows continual, increasingly positive views on the part of Houstonians as a whole, along with increasingly strong support for gay rights."

Fulton, too, suggested that "the politics in Austin are mainly focused on the more conservative, more rural, more red parts of the state" that magnify the "enormous cultural divide where the politically powerful Republicans are exactly where you'd expect the conservative Republicans to be, and the Democrats and the urban Democrats are exactly where you'd expect them to be." He noted that "a lot of time and effort and emotional effort has turned up in the legislature over extreme social issues." As an example, he noted that "the bathroom bill, as in North Carolina, was the major, major topic in the entire 2017 legislative session." Although the moderate Republican Speaker of the

House, who subsequently retired, killed the bill, Fulton characterized the polarization surrounding social issues as leading to "a very, very extreme divide" in the legislature.

In the long term, though, Klineberg anticipates that "ultimately, public opinion will win out," resulting in a "gradual and slow but unmistakable shift from a deep red state to a now only moderately red state, and eventually to a purple state, and some think even following California into a blue state, but it's going to take much longer than you would expect because Texas has one of the lowest rates of voter turnout of any of the states in the country."

Fulton suggested one potential wildcard in the state's politics: the growing unease in the business community resulting from the GOP's focus on divisive social issues. Fulton noted that "Texas was traditionally a conservative-Democratic business-oriented state," but "over the last forty or so years, most of those conservative business-minded Democrats have become Republicans, and there's increasingly a view that the business community's got no place to go in Texas because they can't imagine being Democrats, and it just drives them crazy to get caught up in the bathroom bill and gay marriage and all that stuff." Continuing, Fulton suggested that "there's an increasing level of discontent and concern on the part of the business leadership that they ... don't know how to get things done when everything is focused on these very, very divisive social issues." Fulton suggested that "Texas business leaders fall into pretty much the same place as the North Carolina business leaders stood: 'We don't want to do anything to drive business off.' The business community is pretty pro-immigration, and the conservative Republicans obviously are not."

Indeed, Fulton sees the "biggest political question is what does the business community do?" He noted a "tongue-in-cheek article" in *Texas Monthly* suggesting that the Texas business community should start backing Democrats "not because they think Democrats are going to win, but because that might force more moderate Republicans to run. . . . If you talk to business leaders in Texas, they understand where that's coming from. They are just totally flummoxed. They don't know what to do."[24]

Structural Features of State Government

By design, state government in Texas is weak. As Fulton explained, the Texas constitution intentionally tried "to keep the state government from getting too big." This is most evident by the relatively weak governorship and the fact that Texas remains one of four states where the legislature meets every other year.

In terms of limitations on gubernatorial power, Jillson noted that "the governor in Texas lacks the authority to draft the state budget. That is done by the legislative leaders through something called the legislative budget board. Almost every governor drafts the state's budget and then submits it to the legislature. That is not the case in Texas. The legislative leaders draft it and submit it to themselves, and the governor can comment if he wishes but does not control that process." Jillson also observed that "the governor does not appoint the other statewide leaders, doesn't select the lieutenant governor as a running mate, doesn't select the other cabinet-level officials, most of them are elected in their own right in a statewide vote." The end result according to Jillson is that "when you compare the fifty state governors, Texas will usually be among the ten or twelve weakest."

Jillson did suggest that Governor Rick Perry, who served as governor from 2000 to 2015, the longest tenure of any Texas governor, "showed that a weak governorship can be crafted into a powerful office through the broader appointment power, not cabinet-level appointments but there are other, I think it's about 1,800 offices in Texas, that are appointed by the governor, and he [Perry] appointed those multiple times over his fifteen years. And so everybody in Texas state government worked for the governor, had been appointed by him once, sometimes two or three times, and so Perry became a strong governor even though the institutional governorship of Texas is weak." Fulton suggested that because of the state's relatively weak governorship, there is "a widespread view that the lieutenant governor . . . is actually more powerful than the governor because of the way he controls the agenda in the legislature."

Jillson suggested that Texas's biannual legislative session is an outlier given that the other states with biannual legislatures—Montana, Nevada, and North Dakota—are much less populated. As a consequence, "Texas is really very unusual as a large, fairly complicated state in choosing to meet biannually. And the reason they do that is for the ideological sense that if the legislature's in session, it's going be making laws and regulations, and you've got too many of those already."

Both Fulton and Klineberg highlighted the effects of the GOP's control over redistricting on representation and on policy. Klineberg suggested that because of the large number of uncompetitive districts resulting from aggressive gerrymandering, "the primaries are the basic way by which you get elected, and people coming out in the primaries tend to be the most extreme from both parties," an arrangement that, in his view, leads to "a distortion of democracy." Fulton noted that because of redistricting, "the rural areas have much more power than they should . . . [even though] the rural areas of Texas are losing population, whereas big metros are growing," with the end result being that "you persistently see, particularly in the [state] senate, that the very, very conservative rural areas have a disproportionate amount of political power."

From Klineberg's perspective, the outsized influence of rural, conservative interests means that the legislature "has just spent so much of its effort energizing the Republican base." As evidence, he offered that "Texas has initiated more draconian measures to stop a woman's right to choose abortion than any of the other states, even though the majority of people in the state support a woman's right to choose." According to Klineberg, Texas also is "leading the country in its efforts at voter suppression" even though voter fraud "has never been a very serious problem in America, but the result is far more intimidation and discouragement of voting for those who vote rarely."

Klineberg also noted that because of the state's large size and multiple media markets, campaign costs in Texas are higher (note that Texas has fewer state senate seats than U.S. House seats). This, in turn, has implications for the state's policy agenda. "The whole way that the legislature operates, and the way it gets reelected, and who it listens to, and . . . who controls the agenda, who contributes to the campaigns, the whole donor class that is so, especially in a state like Texas, which is so expensive to run in because it is so enormous. . . . People in the East forget that the state of Texas is larger than the country of France.

... It's a gigantic state, costs a lot of money to run in, and wealthy folks have a lot more influence over government than poor folks."

Jillson observed that because of the state's preference for limited government, "Texas creates relatively weak counties and municipalities... and all counties in Texas are structured constitutionally. So all 254 Texas counties have the same constitutional governing structure of a county judge, which is the executive officer rather than a judicial office ... and then there are four county commissioners elected from geographical jurisdictions countywide, and the county judge and the four commissioners constitute the executive and legislative authority in Texas counties." As a consequence, "the county governments are limited by tight constitutional definitions of their institutions' powers." Similarly, "small municipalities have a mandated governing structure and larger municipalities can adopt one of several legislatively defined home rule charters."

Yet, even though in theory municipalities have "somewhat more autonomy" compared to other states, Jillson indicated that during "the last five years in particular and during Governor Abbott's term, the governor and the state legislature have been seeking to further limit municipal autonomy over things like property taxes and regulatory authority over the energy industry and ... even things like plastic bags, whether they [local governments] can limit plastic bags." Fulton concurred by noting that there has been "more and more conflict between the state and the locals as the state has attempted to preempt the locals on more topics, everything from fracking to plastic bags to Uber and Lyft."

Klineberg sees the tensions between the local autonomy and increasing state restraints as being driven by blue metros, red states politics:

> A blue city in a red state is a threat to the red state because the blue city is where the bulk of the population is. So, what we used to have in Texas was devolution out of the state to the local communities. That's a great ideology in Texas that local governments ought to make the decisions and not big federal or state governments, but now, increasingly, there's an effort to curtail the rights of the cities to make their own decisions, because they often counter what the state believes is in the interest of the state as a whole.

Klineberg noted that these tensions extend to issues such as local cooperation with ICE (Immigration and Customs Enforcement), particularly in Austin and Houston, where the cities' positions are "'We don't want to cooperate with ICE because we need to have good relations with the communities because that's how we prevent crime and build safety in the streets,' and the states are trying to curtail that right that cities have to make that determination."

Blue metros, red states politics also can underlie disputes about funding. After Hurricane Harvey devastated Houston in 2017, there was in Fulton's estimation a "lot of wrangling over the federal money flowing through the state and precisely where it goes." Jillson elaborated by suggesting:

> Both the federal government and Texas state government have expressed great concern for Houston's recovery, but both of those levels of the federal system have been slow in allocating resources to Houston, particularly Texas state government, which is sitting on a rainy-day fund with north of $12 billion in it. And the whole dilemma of Hurricane Harvey was there was sixty inches of rain over a short period of time that fell on Houston's Gulf Coast, and those rainy days did not lead Texas state government to draw substantially on the rainy-day fund to assist Houston. So, Houston has got some recovery funds, but not as much as it feels like it needs either from the federal government or the state government.

School funding provides another example. Jillson observed that San Antonio and Dallas have long struggled "with the state of Texas over education funding. I think that's probably the area in which the struggle between all the major metropolitan areas in Texas and the state, but particularly San Antonio. There had been a series of judicial cases, both federal and Texas court cases, out of San Antonio and its various school districts initiated to ensure that Hispanic students went to school with "Anglo kids," as we call them down here, and then later funding equalization lawsuits that have gone on for the last forty years. Most recently, one resulted in 2017, all of them are attempts to get the state of Texas to increase its contributions to public education and to improve funding of public education in general."

Metro Power in State Government

Given the animosity between Texas's million-plus metros and its Republican-led state government, metro power is closely watched. As Jillson explained, "because the cities are blue and the state is red, the state considers the major cities to be out of step with the Texas model of small government, low taxes, deregulation. And so cities need to be watched closely." Jillson also suggested that these tensions reflect different perspectives about why Texas's cities have been so successful:

> Texas state Republican political leaders consider the success of those cities to be a function of state policy for low taxes, small government, and deregulation. And they believe that the Democratic leadership of those cities would screw up the Texas economic miracle if allowed to do so by local regulations. And so, they, the state of Texas and its Republican leadership, know full well that those cities are the economic drivers of what they refer to as the "Texas Miracle," and what they tout to the rest of the country. But they believe that's because of their statewide legislative and regulatory policy, not because of what those cities have done themselves, and they further believe that the cities with their Democratic leaders would strangle themselves if permitted to do so.

Internal divisions also tend to weaken the influence of the large metro regions in state politics, with the end result being rural and suburban areas exerting, in Jillson's view, "a great deal more influence over state politics than the metroplex areas do, because the color spectrum of Texas state politics is blue in the metropolitan areas, purple in the inner-ring suburbs, going to red in the outer-ring suburbs, exurbs, and rural areas." Jillson observed that the inner-ring suburbs in Dallas and Houston are diversifying and are now performing "as more purple areas electorally," but the "second ring of suburbs, which would be the Planos and the Friscos in the Dallas area, the Woodlands north of Houston, are upscale, outer-ring suburban Republican strongholds, meaning 2-1 Republican electoral results." Although the rural areas occasionally vote for Democrats in local elections, particularly if the officials have been in office for a long time, in "presidential, gubernatorial, state legislative elections, those rural areas will vote Republican.'"

Fulton also suggested that intraregion cohesion can be illusory because of the fact that "the inner suburbs are blue and the outer suburbs are red." These partisan differences, in turn, make it difficult for the Democratic urban legislators and the Republican suburban representatives "to get together and agree on an agenda, a common agenda." He suggested that this affected the response to Hurricane Harvey. "The Republican and Democratic congressional members did a pretty bad job of working together to try to get money flowing to Houston." Fulton also sees a lack of cohesion in Dallas that is exacerbated by the fact that the Dallas-Fort Worth Metroplex has "by far the most decentralized local government structures: more cities, more counties, and even the City of Fort Worth is a mostly conservative city."

Fulton suggested "that the cohesion of the metro is better in Austin and San Antonio" because those metros "are more reliably Democratic and have more of their population in the central county." Still, there appears to be a special antipathy between Austin and the rest of the state. Jillson characterized it as "a palpable divide" resulting from the fact that "in the state capital of Austin, where you have Republican office holders from top to bottom, you've got almost 2-1 Republican majorities in both houses of the state legislature. And Austin is the bluest of blue dots in the middle of red Texas, long referred to as the 'People's Republic of Austin.' And you've got this sort of slogan, 'Keep Austin Weird.'" He continued by noting that Austin's culture, including its many music festivals, "drive the Republican office holders crazy" and suggested "that Texas is a red state but that Austin is a deep blue cultural area, is very much front of mind for everyone. And for Austin residents, it's a way to put a thumb in the eye of Republican officialdom."

Fulton offered that when Austin tries to assert its independence, the response is more constraints on local governments, exemplified by the tree removal episode. "The state passed a law limiting local governments' ability to regulate tree removal in large part because the governor himself got into a fight with the city of Austin over removing trees on his property. Austin was the center of a fight over Uber and Lyft. Looks like it's going to become the center of a legislative fight over motorized scooters."

CONCLUSION: TEXAS

Moving into the 2020 election cycle, there is a great deal of speculation that Texas will be competitive. Much of this thinking is based on Donald Trump's and Ted Cruz's relatively narrow margins of victory in 2016 and 2018. Yet, if Texas is to be competitive in 2020, it will require the Democrats and allied interests to substantially invest in voter registration and get out the vote efforts to boost turnout among Latinos and other Democratic voting constituencies and to continue making inroads into the suburbs, as the party did in 2018 when it picked up suburban U.S. House and state legislative districts.

At the same time, given Republican dominance of the state's politics, the Democrats lack a deep bench of quality candidates to contest statewide offices. The party's minority standing also means that unless the Democrats are able to flip enough seats to gain control of at least one chamber of the statehouse in 2020 (see table 8-3), then the GOP will again control the state's redistricting process after the 2020 U.S. census. In 2011, the GOP was not shy about using the process to maximize representation of rural, Republican interests. Moreover, as Jillson noted, once the Democrats' prospects in Texas appear to be improving, money from Texas sources that now funds campaigns elsewhere will stay in Texas to fortify the Republicans' position in the state.

The continuation of Republican control of state government is likely to have significant implications for the state's million-plus metro regions. In Fulton's estimation, "something like three-quarters of the economic power of the state is in the metros, and they do not have three-quarters of the political power; they have actually much, much less." In this regard, Texas's million-plus metros exemplify the mismatch between economic and political power underlying the "prosperity paradox" identified by Ron Brownstein (see chapter 2).[25] Not only are Texas's million-plus metro regions political lightweights, but the Republican-led state government, through aggressive preemption measures, is weakening the metros' abilities to chart their own courses across a range of policy areas. Thus, even as the Texas metros continue growing the state's economy and population, in the near term they will be governed according to the preferences and policies of legislators from the state's hinterlands.

However, as all three state experts suggested, the Democrats long-term prospects in Texas are much brighter. The state's aging, largely rural Anglo population is being replaced by younger minorities concentrated in the state's million-plus blue metros. Continued population replacement and growing Democratic support in the inner and outer suburbs, coupled with strong Democratic voting along the border, should tip the balance of power in the state to the Democrats. When this occurs depends on voter turnout and the continued movement of suburban voters into the Democratic fold. Data from the United States Elections Project overseen by University of Florida political scientist Michael McDonald reports that, in 2016, Texas had the fourth-lowest rate of voter turnout in the country, some 8 percentage points below the national average.[26] Even in 2018, when the state featured one of the most closely watched U.S. Senate contests of the cycle, voter turnout in Texas remained below the national average, and Texas only outperformed Washington, D.C., and nine other states, many of which had few if any competitive races.[27]

Since the interviews with the state experts were conducted in 2018, the political terrain in the Lone Star State has continued to shift. Increases in voter registration are outpacing population growth, and turnout for the state's March 2020 Democratic presidential primary surged, particularly in the suburbs. In response, the Democrats ramped up their candidate recruitment and fundraising efforts in hope that President Trump's lagging support in the suburbs, coupled with an infusion of new voters, will expedite Texas's blueward swing.

NOTES

1. Gregory Korte and Joe Carroll, "How a Booming Texas Economy May Help Democrats in 2020," Bloomberg.com, September 9, 2019, www.bloomberg.com/news/articles/2019-09-09/booming-texas-economy-may-usher-in-a-democratic-win-in-2020.

2. Arren Kimbel-Sannit, "See How Many Californians Moved to Dallas in Just 3 Months Las Year," *Dallas Morning News*, June 25, 2018, www.dallasnews.com/business/real-estate/2018/06/26/see-how-many-californians-moved-to-dallas-in-just-3-months-last-year/; and Dom DiFurio, "The West Coast Just Might Be Californiaing Your North Texas, According to a New Study," *Dallas Morning News*, April 4, 2019, www.dallasnews.com/business/2019/04/04/the-west-coast-just-might-be-californiaing-your-north-texas-according-to-a-new-study/.

3. Jonathan Easly, "Texas Republicans Sound Alarm about Rapidly Evolving State," *The Hill*, September 6, 2019, https://thehill.com/homenews/campaign/460 155-texas-republicans-sound-alarm-about-rapidly-evolving-state.

4. Wilbur Zelinsky, *The Cultural Geography of the United States* (Englewood Cliffs, NJ: Prentice Hall, 1973).

5. Tensions between the Germans in Hill Country and other Southern loyalist Texans resulted in several Hill Country residents being executed as traitors to the Southern cause. See Evan Andrews, "Six Unionist Strongholds During the Civil War," History.com, August 1, 2018, www.history.com/news/6-unionist-strongholds-in-the -south-during-the-civil-war.

6. See Robert E. Lang and Paul K. Knox, "The New Metropolis: Rethinking Mega-lopolis," *Regional Studies* 43, no. 6 (August 2009), pp. 789–802; and Arthur C. Nelson and Robert E. Lang, *Megapolitan America: A New Vision for Understanding America's Metropolitan Geography* (Chicago: American Planning Association Press, 2011), chapter 15.

7. A "megapolitan area" is a census-defined combined statistical area where the commuter connections between counties (based on the employment-interchange measure between counties) are projected to 2040. This produces a more expansive geography than the current combined statistical area. See Lang and Knox, "The New Metropolis: Rethinking Megalopolis."

8. For example, San Antonio has the largest share of Hispanics of any of the thirty largest metropolitan areas in the United States.

9. Robert E. Lang, Jaewon Lim, and Karen A. Danielsen, "The Origin, Evolution, and Application of the Megapolitan Area Concept," *International Journal of Urban Sciences* 24, no. 1 (January 2020), pp. 1–12.

10. Lang, Lim, and Danielsen, "The Origin, Evolution, and Application of the Megapolitan Area Concept," p. 4.

11. *Texas: A Guide to the Lone Star State,* compiled by Workers of the Writers' Program of the Work Projects Administration in the State of Texas. Sponsored by the Texas State Highway Commission (1940), p. 226.

12. Ibid., p. 259.

13. Robert E. Lang and Jennifer B. LeFurgy, *Boomburbs: The Rise of America's Accidental Cities* (Washington: Brookings Institution Press, 2007).

14. Ibid., p. 61.

15. Austin even plays up its Bohemian image in its tourist ads. For example, the tagline "Keep Austin Weird" was adopted by the Austin Business Alliance. *Weird* in this instance refers to Austin's off-beat and Bohemian reputation.

16. Jim Yardley, "Austin Journal: A Slogan Battle Keeps Austin Weird," *New York Times*, December 8, 2002, www.nytimes.com/2002/12/08/us/austin-journal-a-slo gan-battle-keeps-austin-weird.html.

17. See Maryann Castro, "Five Reasons Why So Many Californians Are Relocating to Austin, TX," JB Goodwin Realtors, May 21, 2019, www.jbgoodwin.com/blog/5-reasons-why-so-many-californians-are-relocating-to-austin-tx.html; and John Egan,

"How Many Californians Are Moving to Austin: The Numbers Will Surprise You," CultureMap.com, December 12, 2016, http://austin.culturemap.com/news/city-life/12-2-16-californians-moving-to-austin-census-data/. In fact, both Californians and New Yorkers are migrating to all of the major metros in the Texas Triangle.

18. Chuck DeVore, "New Yorkers and Californians Can't Stop Moving to Texas," *Washington Examiner*, May 30, 2018, www.washingtonexaminer.com/opinion/new-yorkers-and-californians-cant-stop-moving-to-texas.

19. Christopher Hooks, "Texas is a Purple State Now. The Proof is in Last Night's Results, *Texas Observer*, November 7, 2018, www.texasobserver.org/texas-is-a-purple-state-now-the-proof-is-in-last-nights-results/.

20. Elaina Plott, "The Race in Houston is the Future of Texas Politics," *The Atlantic*, September 2, 2018, www.theatlantic.com/politics/archive/2018/09/this-race-in-houston-is-the-future-of-texas-politics/569158/.

21. Daniel C. Vock, "The End of Local Laws? War on Cities Intensifies in Texas," *Governing*, April 5, 2017, www.governing.com/topics/politics/gov-texas-abbott-preemption.html.

22. Zelinsky, *The Cultural Geography of the United States*.

23. When Texas gained independence from Mexico, the area between the Nueces and Rio Grande River was a disputed territory claimed by both Texas and Mexico. When Texas entered the Union in 1845, the U.S. government exploited this dispute to provoke war with Mexico.

24. Dave Mann, "Party Hopping," *Texas Monthly*, May 2017, www.texasmonthly.com/politics/party-hopping/.

25. Ronald Brownstein, "The Prosperity Paradox Is Dividing the Country in Two," CNN, January 23, 2018, www.cnn.com/2018/01/23/politics/economy-prosperity-paradox-divide-country-voters/index.html.

26. United States Elections Project, "2016 November General Election Turnout Rates," www.electproject.org/2016g.

27. Ibid.

9

MOUNTAIN WEST: ARIZONA, COLORADO, AND NEVADA

David F. Damore
Robert E. Lang

In 2012, the Brookings Institution Press published *America's New Swing Region: Changing Politics and Demographics in the Mountain West*.[1] The volume, edited by Ruy Teixeira, examined how the increasing urbanization and diversification of the Mountain West is reshaping the politics in a region that had been a Republican stronghold for decades. Since the book's publication, majority-minority New Mexico has trended further Democratic, while Idaho, the least urbanized and diverse state in the region, has remained solidly Republican. Besides regaining the 4th Congressional District in 2018, the Democrats have made few inroads in Utah. However, in the region's other three states—Arizona, Colorado, and Nevada—the effects of demographic change and urbanization on these states' politics are being realized. The Democrats have made substantial gains in Colorado and Nevada (both states have voted Democratic in the last three presidential elections and both have Democratic governors), while the party is poised to do the same in Arizona in the coming years.

As we explore in this chapter, the political shifts occurring in Arizona, Colorado, and Nevada are largely a story of scale and disruption. Each state features a fast growing and diversifying population center that accounts for half (Denver), two-thirds (Phoenix), and three-quarters (Las Vegas) of these states' total populations. The relatively recent emergence of such large-scale metro regions in states that are otherwise sparsely populated challenges the rurally oriented politics and policies that have long defined the Mountain West.

Yet, as this analysis reveals, the contexts in which each of the region's million-plus metros operates differ demographically, politically, and structurally. The Democratic shift in Colorado has as much to do with increasing diversity in Denver as it does with Democratic strength along the Northern Front Range of the Rockies and the fact that Colorado has one of the highest shares of college-educated adults in the country. Like Arizona, Colorado's rural spaces are populated by Native Americans and Latinos, while in Nevada diversity outside of Las Vegas is limited and largely Latino. All three states contain a smaller metro region that constitutes 10 or more percent of the state's population. But, whereas in Arizona, Tucson, with a population exceeding a million residents, votes much more Democratically than Phoenix, Colorado Springs, the second-largest metro in Colorado, is a bastion of conservatism and Republican voting. In Nevada, Democratic voting in Las Vegas is bolstered by shifts in Reno that have moved the state's second most populated metro from red to purple. At the same time, Las Vegas's development is hindered by its remoteness from state government and strong Dillon's Rule limitations on local governments, while Phoenix and Denver benefit from being their states' seats-of-government and being afforded greater local autonomy.

STATE OF PLAY: ARIZONA

Arizona is an emerging swing state. Long a mainstay of a western Libertarian-based conservatism, as best expressed by former Arizona Senator Barry Goldwater,[2] the Grand Canyon state elected a Democratic Senator, Kyrsten Sinema, to a long-held Republican seat in 2018. The voting patterns revealed in that election inform the state's political regions, as represented in figure 9-1.

As one of the fastest-growing states (Arizona's population increased by over 12 percent between 2010 and 2017), Arizona and its politics are in flux. New arrivals from states such as California and the Midwest, and a high rate of population increase among Arizona's

FIGURE 9-1. Arizona

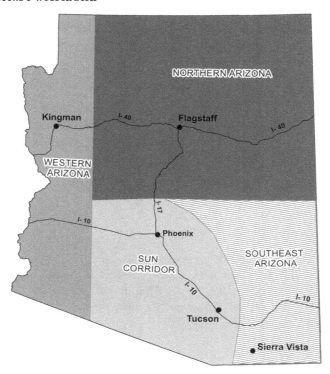

Latino community, account for most of the state's population gains in recent years. Thousands of young native-born Latinos are turning eighteen and becoming voter eligible every year, replacing a much older and more conservative population of retirees that is leaving the voter rolls due to death. The net effect of Arizona's changing demographics is a state shifting from red to purple, with the 2018 U.S. Senate election reflecting this shift.

With more than 7 million residents as of 2017 (see table 9-1), Arizona ranks fourteenth in the United States, overtaking both Massachusetts and Indiana this decade. Arizona currently holds eleven votes in the Electoral College, and is on track to gain a new U.S. House seat after congressional reapportionment following the 2020 census. During the prior decade, Arizona's population surpassed older, eastern states such as Maryland, Missouri, and Wisconsin.

TABLE 9-1. Demographic and Economic
Comparison between Arizona and Metros

	Arizona	Share in Phoenix (%)	Share in Tucson (%)
Population	7,016,270	67.5	14.6
White	54.7%	68.3	13.8
Black	4.1%	82.8	11.5
Asian	3.2%	80.8	12.5
Latino	31.4%	66.7	17.3
Foreign-Born	13.2%	72.8	13.4
College Educated	29.3%	71.0	16.6
Jobs	3,165,129	73.2	14.4
GDP	$279,435	75.5	12.4

Sources: 2017 American Community Survey 1-Year estimates as aggregated by censusreporter.org, Department of Commerce, Bureau of Economic Analysis, 2015 Real GDP (millions of chained 2012 dollars) County Level Data, U.S. Department of Labor, Bureau of Labor Statistics 2017 County Level Data.

Arizona's emergence as an urbanized and populous state is a bit of a shock considering it was the last continental U.S. territory to enter the Union, in 1912. Even in the mid-twentieth century, Arizona was still sparsely settled, with just over 750,000 residents as of the 1950 census (or about a tenth of its current population).[3] But interstate highways, jet travel, and air conditioning remade Arizona, along with the larger Sun Belt.

In their book *Boomburbs: The Rise of America's Accidental Cities*, Robert Lang and Jennifer LeFurgy observed that the city of Peoria, Arizona, had surpassed its namesake Peoria, Illinois, in population.[4] Peoria, Illinois, has long been used as a bellwether for insights into Midwestern and, more generally, middle-of-the-road American, tastes. Hence, the old vaudeville expression "but will it play in Peoria" served as a standard reference to see if a show developed in New York City had broader national appeal. Lang and LeFurgy speculated that Peoria, Arizona, may provide a better test market for middle-American tastes than the old Peoria, Illinois.[5] Likewise, Arizona may be a new bellwether state that reflects a larger political shift in the Sun Belt that extends eastward to Georgia and North Carolina.

Sun Corridor

The Arizona Sun Corridor "megapolitan area" is comprised of three core counties: Maricopa (Phoenix), Pima (Tucson), and Pinal (between Maricopa and Pima, but within the Phoenix metropolitan area based on commuting patterns).[6] The three counties are the first, second, and third most populous in Arizona and, as detailed in table 9-1, together they account for over 82 percent of Arizona's total residents and an even larger share (88 percent) of the state's GDP. The Sun Corridor is also more diverse than the rest of Arizona, although there are sizeable Latino and Native American rural populations throughout the state. For example, table 9-1 shows that the Sun Corridor accounts for over 90 percent of Arizona's foreign-born population.

The Sun Corridor exhibits diverse politics, especially in the urban centers and close-in suburbs of Phoenix and Tucson. For instance, a 2006 project at Arizona State University (ASU), applied geographer James Vance's concept of "urban realm theory" to the Sun Corridor, to delineate ten distinct urban realms.[7] Analysis of electoral data within the realms found that the East Valley of metro Phoenix, which includes cities such as Mesa, Chandler, and Gilbert, is the most conservative urban realm in the Sun Corridor (Tempe, home to ASU, is the only blue city in the East Valley). The most liberal realm is the Tucson Valley, which includes Tucson and the University of Arizona.[8] The data in table 9-2, detailing the strong Democratic margins in Tucson, are consistent with this analysis. Except for the 2018 U.S. Senate race, Republican candidates tend to perform much stronger in metro Phoenix, in large part because of the large Republican margins in Pinal County.

Like Dallas-Fort Worth (as noted in chapter 8), Phoenix and Tucson are not naturally paired into a common urban complex. Just as Dallas and Fort Worth had a long-standing rivalry, where each city looked upon the other with some disdain, Phoenix and Tucson represent very different visions of urban Arizona. Tucson sees Phoenix as departing from the Arizona spirit to build within the limits of the So-

TABLE 9-2. Comparison of Electoral Outcomes between Arizona and Metros

Election	Arizona Outcome	Phoenix Vote Share [%]	Phoenix Outcome	Tucson Vote Share [%]	Tucson Outcome
2018 Gubernatorial	+14.2 Rep	65.2	+15.1 Rep	16.3	+2.8 Dem
2018 U.S. Senate	+ 2.3 Dem	65.2	+3.0 Dem	16.4	+15.5 Dem
2016 Presidential	+3.5 Rep	65.2	+4.1 Rep	16.2	+13.7 Dem
2016 U.S. Senate	+13.0 Rep	65.3	+16.2 Rep	16.2	+3.5 Dem
2014 Gubernatorial	+11.8 Rep	61.7	+11.8 Rep	18.0	+4.9 Dem
2012 Presidential	+9.1 Rep	64.6	+11.1 Rep	16.6	+6.9 Dem
2012 U.S. Senate	+3.0 Rep	64.5	+5.7 Rep	16.7	+14.4 Dem

Source: Data from Arizona secretary of state's website.

noran Desert. Tucson limits urban growth and never built a beltway around the region. Meanwhile, relatively water-rich Phoenix (with supplies from the Salt River and Central Arizona Project) created a lush, sprawling desert environment—almost a Disney Desert.[9] Phoenix remains pro-growth and added three beltways (or loops) around the urban realms within its metropolitan area.[10]

Political tensions once ran so high with Phoenix that liberal Tucson considered secession from Arizona.[11] These tensions were exacerbated by the passage of the Support Our Law Enforcement and Safe Neighborhoods Act, more commonly referred to Senate Bill 1070, in 2010, requiring proof of citizenship if an individual is stopped by law enforcement. The bill raised such concerns in Tucson that "the Sheriff of Pima County, which includes Tucson, calls it [SB 1070] stupid and refuses to enforce it."[12] The bill also endangered Phoenix's competitive position as a place to relocate California businesses in that most Californians took offense to the harsh measure, not unlike the way Northern industries once viewed racially intolerant cities in the South such as Birmingham.[13]

Yet, Tucson and Phoenix are on track to merge into a megapolitan area (and an official U.S. census combined statistical area) by 2040.[14] Commuting patterns in booming Pinal County will link the two regions into an extended version of the Dallas-Fort Worth Metroplex.

While the Sun Corridor projection of a unified metropolitan region anchored by Interstate 10 (see figure 9-1) appeared over a decade ago, the anticipated merger between Phoenix and Tucson remains a current topic of discussion and planning within the region.[15] For example, in 2015, Tucson renamed its economic development agency "Sun Corridor, Inc."

Within the next decade, Phoenix and Tucson are likely to merge politically. Metro Phoenix is growing so diverse, urban, and populated with expatriate Californians that it is now liberal enough so that Tucson does not feel compelled to secede from Arizona. Still, there are parts of the Phoenix metropolitan area that are likely to remain conservative even as the region in general shifts blue. Phoenix's East Valley, which on its own has more than 1 million residents, will resist the Sun Corridor's overall leftward gains given its high proportion of Mormons and Midwestern baby boomer retirees. But the Sun Corridor so dominates Arizona politics, with four in five voters, that even if the region turns a light blue, it should prove enough of a shift to make Democrats competitive at the state level in the 2020s.

Some of the consequence of the state's shifting politics can be gleaned from table 9-3, which summarizes the partisan composition of state government and Arizona's congressional delegation. While the last Democratic governor of Arizona was Janet Napolitano, who served from 2003 to 2009 before resigning to become U.S. Secretary of Homeland Security, since 2010 the Democrats have increased their representation in the lower chamber of the Arizona legislature, and the party has more than held its own in the state's nine-member U.S. House delegation. These outcomes are due in part to the fact that Arizona uses an independent redistricting commission that is required to consider potential competitiveness when drawing district boundaries.

Structurally, Arizona's metro regions also are well positioned to shape their own destinies. In terms of local autonomy, Arizona ranks twenty-seventh, and like many western states, the state's two million-plus metro regions are not overly fragmented (see table 9-4). Moreover, Phoenix is the state's capital, and to help develop and promote the region's economic, transportation, and resource needs, local governments work together through the Maricopa Association of Governments.

TABLE 9-3. Partisan Composition of Arizona State Government and Federal Delegation

		State Government				Federal Delegation			
		Upper House		Lower House		U.S. Senate		U.S. House	
	Governor	Dems	Reps	Dems	Reps	Dems	Reps	Dems	Reps
2019–20	Rep	13	17	29	31	1	1	5	4
2017–18	Rep	13	17	25	35	0	2	4	5
2015–16	Rep	13	17	22	38	0	2	5	4
2013–14	Rep	13	17	24	36	0	2	5	4

Sources: Data from National Conference of State Legislatures, "State and Legislative Partisan Composition" for various years, and Arizona secretary of state's website.

TABLE 9-4. Metro Governance Fragmentation and Autonomy in Arizona

Governance Fragmentation

Metro	Number of Counties in Metro	Number of General Purposes Governments in Metro
Phoenix	2	35
Tucson	1	6

Governance Autonomy

Local Government Autonomy Score	−0.025
Local Government Autonomy Ranking	27

Sources: Data for Governance Fragmentation from 2017 Census of Governments. Data for Governance Autonomy from Harold Wolman, Robert McManmon, Michael Bell, and David Brunori, "Comparing Local Government Autonomy Across States," in *The Property Tax and Local Autonomy,* edited by Michael Bell, David Brunori, and Joan Youngman (Lincoln Institute of Land Policy Press, 2010), pp. 69–114.

Northern Arizona

Northern Arizona, which includes Coconino and Yavapai Counties and the Native American lands that cover the northeastern part of the state, is a sparsely settled, blue-tinted political section. The biggest city/metro area, Flagstaff, is home to Northern Arizona University and supported Democratic U.S. Senate candidate Kyrsten Sinema with 62 percent of its vote in 2018.[16]

The two Native American counties that contain the Navaho and Hopi Indian Reservations often split their vote with Apache County to the east, a more liberal area. Navaho County includes the nonreservation cities of Winslow and Holbrook, which are mostly white and more conservative.

Yavapai County, in particular the Prescott Valley, is the most conservative part of Northern Arizona. By contrast, Sedona (which is partly in Coconino County) is liberal and attracts the kind of migrants drawn to desert landscapes and artistic enclaves. Sedona and its surroundings are very much a part of the Cappuccino West (see the Colorado State of Play section in this chapter).[17]

Western Arizona

The three Arizona counties that border the Colorado River form Western Arizona; these are Mohave in the north; La Paz in the center; and Yuma in the south. Western Arizona is mostly conservative, although Yuma County shares a border with Mexico, maintains a large Latino population, and is more politically moderate.

Mohave County, including the city of Kingman, is the reddest part of Arizona. For example, in the 2018 U.S. Senate election, Republican candidate Martha McSally received 70 percent of Mohave's vote, her best performance among all Arizona counties.

Western Arizona, north of Yuma, is older, whiter, and less diverse than the rest of Arizona. Colorado River resort/retirement communities, such as Lake Havasu City and Bullhead City, attract less affluent migrants than those who retire to places such as Sun City Arizona in the Phoenix metropolitan area. The demographics of these places should continue to favor Republicans for the near future.

Southeast Arizona

Southeast Arizona includes counties that lie east of the Sun Corridor. The area is conservative and votes Republican in most elections. Cochise is the most populous county and contains southeast Arizona's largest city—Sierra Vista. Fort Huachuca, which borders Sierra Vista, is home to many military personnel and military retirees. This area is especially conservative.

More liberal parts of southeast Arizona include the city of Douglas, which borders Mexico and has a large Latino community. Bisbee, once essentially a mining ghost town, is now an arts colony with an active bohemian scene. Bisbee is by far the bluest part of southeast Arizona. It is another Arizona city that qualifies as the Cappuccino West (defined in the Colorado analysis presented below).[18]

Conclusion: Arizona State of Play

Arizona's changing demography and politics suggest that the state may soon join Nevada and Colorado in shifting to bluer politics. This may seem counterintuitive to those who remember Arizona as the land of Barry Goldwater and the only state outside the South that qualified for federal monitoring under the 1965 Voting Rights Act. Arizona is now a swing state. And as Arizona continues to grow, it is likely to become bluer as expatriate Californians and minorities living in the Sun Corridor exert their political preferences.

EXPERT ANALYSIS: ARIZONA

Arthur C. Nelson, associate dean for research and discovery and a professor of planning and real estate development at the University of Arizona, provided expert analysis for Arizona. Nelson's research interests focus on metropolitan development patterns, urban growth management, urban planning and infrastructure, and suburban redevelopment. He was interviewed on May 10, 2018. Note that some of the quotes provided by Nelson have been edited for clarity.

Intrastate Political Dynamics

Arizona's political dynamics are primarily shaped by its three metropolitan regions, Flagstaff, Tucson, and Phoenix, with Flagstaff and Tucson tending to be more left of center compared to Phoenix. Even with these differences, Nelson indicates that most elected officials tend to be moderate, but this may change due to Phoenix's growth patterns. Nelson predicted that in the coming decades, "90 percent the population growth in Phoenix will be nonwhite. And to the extent that nonwhite voters are center left, that will change the voting dynamics in Phoenix. It already has changed in Phoenix, and it's going to change every year going on out. So, whereas Tucson might now be center left, Phoenix, in ten, fifteen years, could be characterized about the same." At the same time, Phoenix will continue to have "far right" pockets attracted to the politics embodied by former Maricopa County Sheriff Joe Arpaio.[19]

Nelson suggested that the state's blueward shift is being delayed because of uneven voter participation:

Now, my sense is that roughly 75 percent of registered Republicans vote in the off-year. Now, they're only one-third of the electorate, but they are such a voting bloc in the off-year elections that they pretty much dominate the off-years. So, the only competitive advantage the Democrats and Independents have, which are roughly equal in size—Democrats are a little smaller in number than Independents—but they together comprise about two-thirds of the electorate. The only time they really tend to flex their muscle is during the presidential election.

Nelson adds, however:

Even though Democrats vote far less than Republicans, the numbers will be to their [the Democrats'] advantage so much that, by the end of the next decade, they will be dominating politics in this state unless Republicans find a way to reach out to minorities and bring them into their party. I don't see that happening, but that is a way for them to maintain control, if they want to.

In the short term, however, the partisan differences in political participation between presidential and midterms can create policy dissonance. For instance, in 2016, 58 percent of voters supported a ballot measure raising the state's minimum wage. But, as Nelson noted, the Republican dominated legislature "hated the idea" and the legislature "actually tried to sue the citizens in court, and they failed." In Nelson's view, the episode was a consequence of the fact that "the legislature, because of the people voting for legislators often in off years, is, in fact, out of tune with the sizable majority of Arizonans."

More generally, Nelson indicated that there is a statewide 55-45 split in favor of same-sex marriage, LGBTQ rights, and access to abortion, with two-thirds support in the metro regions. On other social and cultural issues, Nelson suggested that there are subtle differences. For example, like in many western states, "Arizonans would certainly want to have the right to bear arms. But they also want to restrict that ability in social settings." On immigration, Nelson suggested that attitudes are "really bifurcated between the perception of illegal immigration across the Mexican border versus general immigration from around the world" and that there are noticeable differences between the state's two largest metros: "Even though Tucson is only sixty miles from the border, it's a lot more relaxed about border patrol, border security than Phoenix is." He also noted that employers "are struggling to find qualified, highly skilled labor in computer sciences and engineering and such, and so many of them need to import people from overseas to fill their positions. And they're the ones who are complaining about the H1-B limitations."[20]

Structural Features of State Government

Nelson indicated that "Arizona, as well as most of the Mountain West states, have strong governors," and the position has been further enhanced by the fact that "the governor in this state has been historically a strong person," such that "a strong-willed, a strongly opinionated person who is not a whacko person, but a strong personality, a populist kind of personality, can win elections, whether Republican or Democrat." Yet, because of stronger Republican turnout in nonpresidential elections, "Republicans have always outdone Democrats in statewide elections, except when you have a popular, a strongly minded person like [former Democratic governor Bruce] Babbitt." At the same time, Republican influence in state politics is mitigated by the fact that district boundaries for the state legislature and the U.S. House are drawn by an independent commission that "tends to avoid gerrymandering. So even though Republicans dominate the state elected offices, it's nowhere near what it could be" because districts are "designed to represent political and social interests."

Nelson also suggests there is an ongoing tension between state and local governments. Nelson characterizes Arizona as a "home rule state with qualifications." That is, "local governments by constitution and state statute have much wider reign in how they make decisions, or at least you would think, because what really happens is the legislature, which is Republican dominated, and the Republican governor will sign their legislation, continually reins in the ability of locally elected officials to make decisions." As a consequence, "every legislative session, some power or, to some seemingly innocuous power, or two are simply taken away from locally elected officials."

Metro Power in State Government

Nelson was unequivocal in his assessment about Phoenix's dominance of Arizona politics:

Let's face it, Phoenix is the state of Arizona. They completely dominate the legislature. They basically elect the governor, and it is growing at a much faster pace than Tucson. And at the end of World War II, Tucson might have arguably been considered the more influential of the two metropolitan areas, maybe even through the seventies, but that changed; that Phoenix dynamic just makes it so much bigger. . . . Phoenix in 2050 will have 8 million people there to Tucson's 1.4 [million].

Yet, despite the differences in scale between Phoenix and Tucson, Nelson expects:

There will be interesting coalitions of legislators who represent voters connecting between metro Tucson and parts of metropolitan Phoenix. Probably the more educated, higher income parts; Tempe, Mesa, perhaps, would align more frequently with the interests of Tucson and vice versa, and that sort of Phoenix-Tucson coalition could influence legislative affairs. But it's also the case where sometime in the 2020s, the state will flip legislatively to Democrats. The resulting dynamic is likely not to be Tucson versus Phoenix so much as Tucson plus [liberal] pieces of Phoenix versus [the more conservative areas of] Phoenix.

The little influence that Arizona's nonmetro regions have in state politics stems from the fact that "rural legislators elected to office usually are able to get reelected more frequently and hold office longer than metropolitan politicians. And as they simply outsurvive other politicians and stay in office, they become the committee chair; maybe not speaker or senate president, but they become the powerful committee chairs."

Nelson also noted that, despite Phoenix's size, it is far from monolithic in its preferences, which can create divisions within the Phoenix delegation:

Maricopa County, where Phoenix is, is spatially larger than many states, and when you look at aerial or satellite imagery of the Phoenix metropolitan area, you clearly see there are large sections of exurban, even rural development. It is dominated by suburban interests, and its urban interests are limited to maybe Phoenix downtown and other immediate neighborhoods, maybe Tempe, and that would be about it. So, it really is a microcosm in many ways of the entire country because in that single county you've got the full spectrum.

Nelson clearly sees Phoenix as emblematic of the country's future. "We're becoming a nation increasingly of highly centralized economies and decisionmaking. And give it to mid-century and this nation will be basically dominated by a few large metropolitan interests. Phoenix will be one of them. . . . It's only a matter of time before the large urban areas will also dominate national politics. They already dominate national economies, but it takes a while for politics to catch up."

STATE OF PLAY: COLORADO

The tension between the blue and red sections of Colorado is so palpable that Republican-leaning counties in the northeastern Great Plains section of Colorado tried (and failed) to break away from the rest of the Centennial State to form the fifty-first state of the union. In a series of November 2013 county ballot referendums, voters in six of the counties (Elbert, Lincoln, Logan, Moffat, Sedgwick, and Weld) that were part of the secession movement rejected a proposal to exit Colorado, while voters in five counties (Cheyenne, Kit Carson, Phillips, Washington, and Yuma) voted to secede.[21]

That much of the Great Plains part of Colorado fails to politically and culturally identify with the Front Range—an extended megapolitan area that runs along the front of the Rocky Mountains from the south in Colorado Springs to the border with Wyoming in the north—is not unexpected given the physical geography of the state.[22] Frank Popper, the urban planner and geographer from Princeton University, observed that: "Colorado is the kind of state that can only be drawn up by bureaucrats working for the federal government back in Washington, D.C. The state is a rectangle that is a third in the Great Plains and two-thirds in the Rocky Mountains. It is not an organic space that formed via local identity with an industry or geography that bound people to a place."[23] As depicted in figure 9-2, these geographic features motivate much of the state's internal political dynamics.

Great Plains

Popper's observation accounts for the alienation of interests expressed by people living in the pancake-flat Great Plains section of a state known for its mountains and ski areas. Even the architectural reference of Denver International Airport, which is built in the Great Plains, is that of snow-capped mountains.

As detailed in figure 9-2, the plains and the mountain parts of

FIGURE 9-2. Colorado

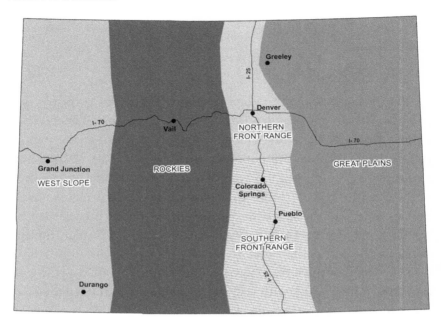

Colorado form a political divide. The plains are solidly a part of red America, while large sections of the Front Range urban corridor that includes Denver, Colorado's capital, and Boulder vote Democratic. The political split between metro Denver, which accounts for just over half of Colorado's population, and the more rural and sparsely settled Great Plains is stark, and explains why the eleven plains counties made the official effort to separate their jurisdictions from the rest of Colorado. In subsequent years, these tensions have remained, and after the Democrats' strong showing in 2018, local elected officials in Greeley revisited the succession idea.[24]

Northern Front Range

While the entire Great Plains section of Colorado votes strongly Republican, Colorado's Front Range region is more complicated. There is a definite split in Front Range politics north and south. The Northern

Front Range, anchored by the million-plus Denver metropolitan area, is the bluest and most progressive section of Colorado.

Denver is an affluent and highly educated region that contains a semi-diverse population. Note that the term *semi-diverse* is applied here in relative terms to other big metros in the Mountain West, such as Las Vegas and Phoenix, which feature much greater diversity than Metro Denver. The Front Range—north and south—remains majority white, but given the region's share of the state's population, it contains the vast majority of the state's Asian, Black, Latino, and foreign-born residents (see table 9-5).

Denver also differs from Las Vegas and Phoenix in that it is Denver's majority non-Hispanic white residents that account for many of the Democratic-leaning voters in the region. Denver is both affluent and educated. As the data in table 9-5 details, the Denver metro contains 56 percent of Coloradans with a college education, and the region generates over 60 percent of the state's GDP. Data from the Brookings Institution indicates that Denver continues to be a top destination for young, college-educated migrants.[25] In addition, Denver

TABLE 9-5. Demographic and Economic Comparison between Colorado and Denver

	Colorado	Share in Denver (%)
Population	5,607,154	51.5
White	68.2%	48.5
Black	3.9%	72.5
Asian	3.1%	70.7
Latino	21.5%	55.2
Foreign-Born	9.8%	64.4
College Educated	41.2%	55.8
Jobs	2,911,081	54.7
GDP	$307,912	60.9

Sources: 2017 American Community Survey 1-Year estimates as aggregated by censusreporter.org, Department of Commerce, Bureau of Economic Analysis, 2015 Real GDP (millions of chained 2012 dollars) County Level Data, U.S. Department of Labor, Bureau of Labor Statistics 2017 County Level Data.

has created a pattern of urban development, centered by an extensive and expanding rail system that serves to intensify the region's overall development density.

In short, Denver is an educated, densifying, cosmopolitan metropolis with an international airport that features direct flights to places like China, and its physical setting and built environment are almost European in look and feel. Given these characteristics, the region votes strongly Democratic. As tables 9-6 and 9-7 detail, except for the 2014 U.S. Senate election, the only statewide victory for a Republican presidential, senatorial, or gubernatorial candidate during the decade, Democratic candidates have carried the region by double digits. Also factoring into Colorado's blueward shift is the fact that other parts of the Northern Front Range, including once conservative places such as Fort Collins (home to Colorado State University), are now voting more Democratic.

Denver's ability to coordinate regional policy initiatives is attributable to greater local autonomy (see table 9-8) and the creation of institutions structured to overcome regional governmental fragmentation, such as the Denver Regional Council of Governments and the Metro Mayors Caucus. Because Denver also is the state's capital, much of the state's workforce is drawn from the region.

TABLE 9-6. Comparison of Electoral Outcomes between Colorado and Denver

	Colorado	Denver	
Election	Outcome	Vote Share [%]	Outcome
2018 Gubernatorial	+10.6 Dem	52.4	+19.8 Dem
2016 Presidential	+4.9 Dem	52.5	+15.4 Dem
2016 U.S. Senate	+5.7 Dem	53.2	+14.3 Dem
2014 U.S. Senate	+1.9 Rep	51.5	+6.3 Dem
2014 Gubernatorial	+3.3 Dem	51.5	+12.2 Dem
2012 Presidential	+5.4 Dem	51.3	+13.2 Dem

Source: Data from Colorado secretary of state's website.

TABLE 9-7. Partisan Composition of Colorado State
Government and Federal Delegation

		State Government				Federal Delegation			
		Upper House		Lower House		U.S. Senate		U.S. House	
	Governor	Dems	Reps	Dems	Reps	Dems	Reps	Dems	Reps
2019–20	Dem	19	16	41	24	1	1	4	3
2017–18	Dem	17	18	37	28	1	1	3	4
2015–16	Dem	17	18	33	32	1	1	3	4
2013–14	Dem	19	16	36	29	2	0	3	4

Sources: Data from National Conference of State Legislatures, "State and Legislative Partisan Composition" for various years, and from Colorado secretary of state's website.

Southern Front Range

The more modestly scaled Southern Front Range tells a different political story. Somewhere along the I-25 Corridor (which runs the length of the Front Range) near Castle Rock, blue Front Range politics shift to red. The region is anchored by Metropolitan Colorado Springs, the second-largest metro region in the state, with a population over 700,000. Colorado Springs is predominately white and, politically, is the anti-Denver. Home to the United States Airforce Academy (and many military retirees) and several conservative national associations such as Focus on the Family, Colorado Springs has nurtured and attracted a red-leaning voting base. This pattern holds true for the entire Southern Front Range, which extends south to the border with New Mexico and includes the Pueblo metropolitan area.

Rockies

West of the Front Range, the Colorado Rockies exhibit a complicated but generally blue-leaning voting pattern. The region is still sparsely settled compared to the rest of Colorado and is dotted with small towns and ski resorts. Interestingly, it is the high-amenity and affluent villages that have developed around ski resorts that are clearly

TABLE 9-8. Metro Governance Fragmentation
and Autonomy in Colorado

Governance Fragmentation

Metro	Number of Counties in Metro	Number of General Purposes Governments in Metro
Denver	10	53

Governance Autonomy

Local Government Autonomy Score	0.204
Local Government Autonomy Ranking	15

Sources: Data for Governance Fragmentation from 2017 Census of Governments. Data for Governance Autonomy from Harold Wolman, Robert McManmon, Michael Bell, and David Brunori, "Comparing Local Government Autonomy Across States," in *The Property Tax and Local Autonomy,* edited by Michael Bell, David Brunori, and Joan Youngman (Lincoln Institute of Land Policy Press, 2010), pp. 69–114.

part of blue Colorado. A 2001 analysis conducted by Kris Rengert and Robert Lang showed that these parts of the west, often proximate to national parks and monuments and ski areas, feature a cosmopolitan and often liberal-oriented local population.[26] They labeled such places the Cappuccino West—or a place where one could find a fashionable caffeinated beverage as a symbol of their relative culinary sophistication and, thus, connectivity to urban America.

By contrast, the Cowboy West, or the more traditional west, that developed from extractive industries such as farming, energy production, and mining, were far more conservative in orientation when compared to the trendy and tourist-driven Cappuccino West. Rural Colorado, especially in the Rockies, has plenty of places that qualify as being a part of the Cappuccino West and are, thus, blue-leaning places. In the northern and central Rockies, places such as Aspen represent the high-amenity or Cappuccino West. The southern Colorado Rockies also have scenic places, but a part of the Democratic vote in this area is due to a significant rural Latino population.

West Slope

Beyond the Colorado Rockies lies the West Slope, which overall represents a Republican section of the Centennial State. The northern West Slope, which in physical form comprises a red rock country that looks like eastern Utah and in many ways (including religion) is more connected to the Beehive State than the rest of Colorado, is especially conservative. The region's biggest city, Grand Junction (named for the confluence of the Colorado and Gunnison Rivers), is an agricultural-and-trade-based city that is solidly in the Cowboy West.

There is a small section of the West Slope that is part of the Cappuccino West. The area extends from hyper-wealthy Telluride (which has a ski area and a film festival) down through Silverton and south to Durango. These places are, in essence, the only blue parts of the West Slope. In any of the aforementioned cities, one could easily get a cappuccino and enjoy many other such urban-oriented amenities all in a small-town setting.

Conclusion: Colorado State of Play

For decades, Colorado was a solid red state anchoring an extended Republican-voting region in the Mountain West. This is no longer the case. Driven by increased growth that has attracted a highly educated and diverse population, metro Denver, along with the Cappuccino West, has rapidly shifted the state from red to blue. The state's changing voting behavior is but one indicator of Colorado's changing politics. The state is increasingly pushing for increased renewable energy; it was one of the first states to legalize recreational marijuana; and the Denver metro region is a paragon of urban development. The fact that eleven conservative Great Plains counties wanted to leave the state is evidence of the degree to which Colorado's traditional politics have been displaced.

EXPERT ANALYSIS: COLORADO

Professor of political science at Metropolitan State University of Denver Robert Preuhs provided expert analysis for Colorado. Preuhs's research examines minority representation and political behavior, the effects of demographic change on public policy, and Colorado politics. He was interviewed on May 18, 2018. For clarity, some of Preuhs's quotes have been edited.

Intrastate Political Dynamics

Preuhs sees the urban/rural divide as the defining feature of Colorado's politics, particularly in statewide elections. "It's much like a lot of states, that is we have a strong urban Denver metro support for Democratic candidates and that's held over the last three, four, elections . . . and in the rural areas, which encompass maybe about 30 or 40 percent of the state's population, that is primarily Republican and has supported Republican candidates, again, over the last several elections, particularly since 2000."

Preuhs added that much of Colorado's shift from a red to a purple state is attributable to "a growing metropolitan area, particularly the Denver area, with a huge influx of interstate migrants, so we've benefited from immigration in terms of population expansion. And they have been primarily young, relatively affluent for their age group, and well-educated. And so those kinds of differences emerge in terms of political orientation, and it has tended to solidify Denver's more liberal orientation versus rural Colorado's more conservative orientation."

Denver's increased liberalism contrasts to the conservatism in the state's western and eastern swaths:

The west side of the Rocky Mountains tends to be fairly conservative, fairly rural, although some growing metropolitan areas due to both tourism but also resource extraction, oil, gas in particular. Their demands tend to be based on transportation, high-profile issues like gun control, and environmental protection versus resource extraction. . . . On the other side is what we call the Western Slope and Eastern Plains, and the Eastern Plains tend to be as equally conservative as the Western Slope. Primarily rural farming, it butts against Kansas and Nebraska, and the usual kind of rural, farmer elements out there with more recent resource extraction finds as well.

Colorado's urban/rural divide often manifests itself in cultural and social issues such as LGBTQ rights and immigration. The state's urbanization has resulted in "a growing LGBTQ population as well as larger support." At the same time, until it was invalidated by the U.S. Supreme Court, Colorado had in place "a state ban on gay marriage while allowing for civil unions, so it's kind of that purply area as well, but there's a clear rural/urban divide." In 2018, Democrat Jared Polis was elected governor, the first openly gay man to win a governorship in the country's history.

Preuhs suggested there is an urban/rural and Republican/Democratic divide over immigration, as well. "In Colorado, we've had long-standing differences between Republicans and Democrats. . . . Historically, the Republican Party has been strongly supportive of restrictive policies regarding immigration, and perhaps the most prominent person in that discussion was Tom Tancredo, a [former] member of Congress." Preuhs does see some Colorado Republicans shifting on the issue. For instance, Tancredo's replacement in the U.S. House, Mike Coffman, who lost his reelection bid in 2018, "moderated his position on immigration," an indication, in Preuhs's view, of a split between the party's "establishment" wing and the "fairly conservative elements of the Republican Party" that support hardline immigration policies.

On other social and cultural issues, Preuhs suggested that the state's "libertarian streak" tends to cut across the state's urban/rural and partisan divisions. This is most evident in "policies like marijuana legalization [the state legalized recreational use of marijuana in 2012], as well as gun rights tend to be a little bit less clear in terms of the defining differences between rural and urban Colorado but also across the parties, as well."

Moving forward, Preuhs anticipates that continued population growth will push Colorado further leftward. Specifically, he noted that "the growth of the metropolitan area, Denver metro area, has outpaced rural Colorado and that will continue, and I think those general trends of self-selection and policy preferences being more liberal and metropolitan residents are going to continue." Increased growth and political participation in the state's Latino community also will expedite this shift:

> You also have native birth rates fairly high, particularly among Latino populations, and the voting rates, relatively rough voting rates, in Colorado Latinos place them about, well, they're about 20 percent of the population and they're about 13, 14 percent of the voter base in Colorado, but that should increase as both younger voters, mostly as younger, under eighteen, folks who make up a plurality of school-age kids, become eligible to vote. So, between migration and the diversity of the voting bloc, in particular Denver and the growth, we will probably see a bit more weight toward the liberal spectrum, favoring Democrats.

At the same time, Preuhs indicated that not all of the expected growth will translate into increased Democratic support. "The counter to that, the slight counterbalance to that, is that we do see, given the growth, particularly the growth in our economy based on some of the elements of energy extraction, we have seen growth in exurbs and far suburbs that tend to be fairly conservative still, but I don't think that growth tends to outweigh the more core urban Democratic voters' growth."

In the near term, however, Colorado will continue to be a purple state, as evidenced by the closely divided state legislature and congressional delegation (see table 9-7). Preuhs suggests that the state's politics are moderated by the fact that Independents are a plurality of registered voters, while the Republicans and Democrats are more-or-less evenly split. As a consequence, "a good deal of Colorado politics is trying to make sure that you can appeal to independent, unaffiliated voters . . . [statewide candidates] need to be able to kind of bridge that gap between core Denver type voters and a bit more conservative suburban voters, and some of those most conservative rural voters."

Structural Features of State Government

Preuhs indicated that, institutionally, the governorship has "middling" power. In terms of budget power, the "governor can propose a budget, but the budget does originate from the state legislature," and while the governor does have the line-item veto, the governor "has not used it extensively." Preuhs also suggested that the fact that the attorney general, treasurer, and secretary of state are elected independently fragments executive authority. In addition, Colorado's legislature meets annually, and as noted, the legislature tends to be closely divided (see table 9-7), in part because the boundaries for state legislative districts are drawn by an appointed commission (the legislature draws the districts for Colorado's U.S. House seats). In 2016, Colorado voters supported another proposal designed to increase moderation in the state's politics by allowing unaffiliated voters to participate in the state's primary elections

Preuhs suggested that the cities "are generally left to their own" and classified the state as having a fair amount of home rule. At the same time, he indicated that "there has been some contention recently, particularly in terms of natural resource extraction and fracking issues." The decisions of some localities to ban fracking set in motion a debate about "how much power the city has in the proper place of the policy decisionmaking at the state level or within the community local government level." After the state Supreme Court overturned local fracking bans, in 2019 the Democratic controlled legislature passed legislation granting local governments greater authority to decide where drilling can happen in their localities. The bill was signed into law by Governor Polis.

Preuhs also cited the 1996 *Romer v. Evans* (517 U.S. 620) Supreme Court case as another example of a salient conflict between the state and more liberally oriented local governments. In 1992, Colorado passed an amendment to the state's constitution preventing local governments from recognizing homosexuals as a protected class. The measure, which was struck down by the U.S. Supreme Court, repealed ordinances in the liberal enclaves of Denver, Aspen, and Boulder that prohibited discrimination against homosexuals.

Metro Power in State Government

Although Denver is Colorado's economic and demographic engine, Preuhs indicated that Denver's ability to exert authority is constrained. "Denver tries to exert power within the state legislature, but it's often a dynamic with push back from rural areas as well as our second-largest metro area, Colorado Springs, and it's fairly conservative, historically a conservative bastion. So in terms of raw power, Denver is somewhat limited in terms of its attempts to exert power."

Preuhs offered the example of transportation policy as a policy area where Denver's priorities conflict with the rest of the state. "Denver itself tends to push for more multi-modal transportation and mass transit whereas it gets push back," and state government "then responded with some extension of lanes on highways, as well as rural transportation networks, but primarily roads. So, that is as much influence that Denver has in terms of getting its voice heard. They also tend to get push back" from legislators from outside the region.

STATE OF PLAY: NEVADA

Despite its massive footprint and hyper-urbanization, Nevada has very little privately held land.[27] As a consequence of the large federal land holdings in the state, the vast majority of Nevada's population is proximate to the California border, and hundreds of miles of largely uninhabited basin and range separate Las Vegas from the rest of the state (see figure 9-3). These features of the state's topography underpin the Three Nevadas—colloquial shorthand for the demographic, geographic, economic, cultural, and partisan differences between Southern Nevada, home to Las Vegas, and its suburbs, Reno and Carson City in northern Nevada, and the Rurals (the state's sparsely populated, sprawling eastern and northern rural counties).[28] In fact, these regional differences are so deep-seated that they underlie Nevada's economic development efforts.[29]

In developing their guide to Nevada in the 1930s, Works Progress observers described the state as "the great unknown."[30] These writers offered an understandable yet now erroneous comment that, "Nevada is large, its people content with their way of life, so it is unlikely that

FIGURE 9-3. Nevada

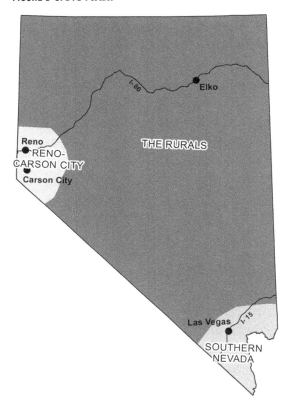

even large numbers of visitors will change its essential quality."[31] Fast forward to present-day Nevada and you have a state that, in fact, is transformed by large numbers of migrants from around the country and across the globe who relocated to the Silver State for economic opportunity and social mobility.[32] This transformation is all the more remarkable considering it occurred in just one of Nevada's nearly 200 valleys—the Las Vegas Valley—way down in the far southern corner of the state.

When Las Vegas emerged as a tourist and convention destination after World War II, it did so in a state dominated by rural and northern interests. Mining, banking, and ranching called the shots, and the provision of government services to Las Vegas was anything but a priority. Geographically advantaged by the establishment of state government in Carson City, a short drive from Reno, in the ensuing decades, northern and rural powerbrokers used their control over the levers of power to minimize Las Vegas's influence.

Even as Las Vegas's population boomed, and the metro grew to become the twenty-eighth largest urban center in the nation, with a roster of global gaming companies with international brands, gubernatorial candidates from Southern Nevada were pummeled outside the region and taxes collected in the south continue to be siphoned away to pay for schools and infrastructure elsewhere in the state.[33] That these resources are stripped out of one of the most diverse metros in the country and are redistributed to benefit a largely white population further exacerbates regional animosities.

Indeed, as the data in tables 9-9 and 9-10 make clear, Nevada is now a majority-minority state that leans Democratic. However, the state's diversity and Democratic electoral strength primarily reside in its million-plus metro, Las Vegas. In contrast, the state's other two regions are overwhelmingly white, and the rural counties in particular vote strongly Republican. During the last decade, Washoe County, where Reno is located, has shifted from a Republican stronghold to a swing county that regularly delivers split partisan outcomes, as it did in 2016 when Hillary Clinton and Republican U.S. Senate candidate Joe Heck carried the county.[34] In 2018, however, Washoe County swung toward the Democrats and, in so doing, altered the state's political dynamics.

The 2018 governor's race featured two regional candidates, Republican Adam Laxalt, who has strong familial ties in northern Nevada, and Democrat Steve Sisolak, the former chair of the Clark County Commission, where Las Vegas is located.[35] During the campaign, Laxalt warned that Sisolak would favor Southern Nevada.[36] Sisolak, in an effort to demonstrate that he would be the governor for all of Nevada, campaigned heavily in Reno,[37] and his campaign received a significant boost when he was endorsed by the nonpartisan but progressive mayor of Reno, Hillary Schieve.[38] Mayor Schieve's endorsement sent an important signal to the region that the state would be better served by the southerner Sisolak than the northerner Laxalt. Sisolak won the election and carried Reno and Washoe County. Sisolak's victory was not just a first for a Nevada Democratic gubernatorial candidate since 1994; he became the only member of the Clark County Commission ever elected to lead the state.

Southern Nevada

During the 1990s and the 2000s, Nevada was the fastest-growing state in the country. Driven by migration from neighboring Arizona and California and retirees from the Midwest and the Northeast, as well as substantial migration from abroad, the vast majority of this growth occurred in Southern Nevada. As a consequence, the region's population grew from less than 750,000 in 1990 to nearly 2 million by 2010, and the share of Nevada's population residing in the region increased from 62 percent in 1990 to 72 percent in 2010. Today, with a population exceeding 2.2 million residents, the Las Vegas region is home to nearly three of four Nevadans, and when its voters are mobilized, the region is able to drive statewide electoral outcomes (see table 9-9). For instance, in 2016, Catherine Cortez Masto won election to the U.S. Senate despite winning just one of Nevada's seventeen counties— Clark. Similarly, a 2016 ballot initiative requiring background checks for private gun purchases and transfers passed despite losing in every county but Clark (see chapter 1).

However, absent robust registration and get out the vote efforts by Nevada Democrats and allied interests, particularly organized labor, turnout in Clark County can drop precipitously, allowing rural voters, who register and turn out at much higher rates, to exert outsized influence in statewide elections. This was most evident in 2014. With no U.S. Senate election to draw national resources to the state and the Democrats' failure to seriously challenge popular Republican incumbent governor Brian Sandoval, the GOP won three of Nevada's four U.S. House seats, all six of the state's constitutional offices, and majority control of both chambers of the statehouse (see tables 9-10 and 9-11).

Given these dynamics, the most important number in Nevada politics is Las Vegas's share of the electorate (see table 9-10). When Southern Nevada constitutes two-thirds or more of the electorate in competitive elections, it is difficult for Republicans to offset the Democratic advantage in the region. To this end, in 2018 voter turnout in

TABLE 9-9. Demographic and Economic Comparison between Nevada and Las Vegas

	Nevada	Share in Las Vegas (%)
Population	2,998,039	73.5
White	48.80%	63.8
Black	8.90%	94.2
Asian	8.30%	88.3
Latino	28.80%	79.7
Foreign-Born	19.90%	85.5
College Educated	24.90%	71.6
Jobs	1,384,608	73.2
GDP	$135,100	72.3

Sources: 2017 American Community Survey 1-Year estimates as aggregated by censusreporter.org, Department of Commerce, Bureau of Economic Analysis, 2015 Real GDP (millions of chained 2012 dollars) County Level Data, U.S. Department of Labor, Bureau of Labor Statistics 2017 County Level Data.

TABLE 9-10. Comparison of Electoral Outcomes between Nevada and Las Vegas

	Nevada	Las Vegas	
Election	Outcome	Vote Share (%)	Outcome
2018 U.S. Senate	+5.0 Dem	67.1	+14.2 Dem
2018 Gubernatorial	+4.1 Dem	67.1	+13.3 Dem
2016 Presidential	+2.4 Dem	68.2	+10.7 Dem
2016 U.S. Senate	+2.4 Dem	68.0	+10.9 Dem
2014 Gubernatorial	+46.7 Rep	61.7	+37.4 Rep
2012 Presidential	+6.7 Dem	68.1	+14.6 Dem
2012 U.S. Senate	+1.2 Rep	67.9	+9.0 Dem

Source: Data from Nevada secretary of state's website.

TABLE 9-11. Partisan Composition of Nevada State Government and Federal Delegation

| | | State Government | | | | Federal Delegation | | | |
| | | Upper House | | Lower House | | U.S. Senate | | U.S. House | |
	Governor	Dems	Reps	Dems	Reps	Dems	Reps	Dems	Reps
2019–20	Dem	13	8	29	13	2	0	3	1
2017–18	Rep	11	10	27	15	1	1	3	1
2015–16	Rep	10	11	15	27	1	1	1	3
2013–14	Rep	11	10	27	15	1	1	2	2

Sources: Data from National Conference of State Legislatures, "State and Legislative Partisan Composition" for various years, and Nevada secretary of state's website.

Clark County was robust, with the share of the votes cast in Las Vegas matching that of the 2016 presidential election. The Democrats picked up a U.S. Senate seat with Jacky Rosen's victory over incumbent Republican senator Dean Heller, maintained control of the region's three U.S. House seats, won five constitutional offices, and expanded the party's majority in the Nevada legislature by picking up seats in the rapidly diversifying suburbs, the GOP's last foothold in the Las Vegas Valley.

Perhaps more significant, in term of the state's interregional dynamics, after the 2018 election, both U.S. Senators and four of the six constitutional officers are from Southern Nevada. Also noteworthy is the fact that the Democratic-led Nevada legislature became the first female majority legislature in the country's history. During the 106th Congress, the only white male in the state's congressional delegation represents the safe Republican 2nd District that encompasses the rest of the state.

Also, note that, unlike other million-plus blue voting metros, such as Austin, Denver, and Tucson, that feature high shares of college-educated, Nevada has one of the lowest shares of college-educated adults in the country, and the share of college-educated in Las Vegas is below its population share (see table 9-9). In this regard, Las Vegas is largely a working-class city that lacks clusters of "creative class" jobs.[39]

Moreover, despite its demographic, economic, and political clout, the region's advancement is hindered by the limited capacity of state government—the Nevada legislature meets every other year for 120 calendar days—coupled with strong limitations on the powers afforded to local governments. As table 9-12 indicates, Nevada ranks thirty-third among states in local government autonomy, and although Southern Nevada has just six general purpose governments, suggesting limited structural fractionalization, disputes between the city of Las Vegas and Clark County over issues ranging from the trivial (the exclusion of city officials from events on the Las Vegas Strip, which is located in the county) to efforts by Las Vegas to annex parts of the county are not uncommon.[40] As a consequence, only recently has Southern Nevada begun to overcome internal divisions to develop a regional policy agenda focused on building Interstate 11, which connects Las Vegas to Phoenix, establishing the UNLV School of Medicine, and constructing Allegiant Stadium, where the Las Vegas Raiders and UNLV play football.

TABLE 9-12. Metro Governance Fragmentation and Autonomy in Nevada

Governance Fragmentation		
Metro	Number of Counties in Metro	Number of General Purposes Governments in Metro
Las Vegas	1	6

Governance Autonomy	
Local Government Autonomy Score	−0.098
Local Government Autonomy Ranking	33

Sources: Data for Governance Fragmentation from 2017 Census of Governments. Data for Governance Autonomy from Harold Wolman, Robert McManmon, Michael Bell, and David Brunori, "Comparing Local Government Autonomy Across States," in *The Property Tax and Local Autonomy,* edited by Michael Bell, David Brunori, and Joan Youngman (Lincoln Institute of Land Policy Press, 2010), pp. 69–114.

Reno and Carson City

While Reno is not technically Nevada's state capital, Carson City,[41] which is the capital, is within Reno's political and economic sphere of influence. In fact, Carson City lies within Reno's U.S. census-designated CSA and, thus, maintains a commuter relationship with the Reno metropolitan area. Reno and Carson City are not "Twin Cities," but like Dallas and Fort Worth (on a much smaller scale), they do form a mini metroplex. Moreover, there are even state government functions that one would expect to be housed in the capital that are located in Reno—such as the offices for the state agency for higher education that are located on the campus of the University of Nevada, Reno.

Despite representing a minority of the state's population, for decades the region and the Rurals maintained a powerful northern Nevada Republican alliance that mitigated Las Vegas's influence in state politics. For a number of reasons, however, this alliance is fraying. Nevada's dominant industry—gaming—was so stigmatized for decades it was hesitant to exercise its influence beyond defending a narrow set of interests in Carson City. With broader acceptance of gaming, the industry is more engaged in promoting Southern Nevada's interests in areas such as K-12 funding and transportation policy. To satisfy growing demands for equitable resources in the south, K-12, higher education, and infrastructure appropriations have been reduced in the rural counties, while appropriations directed to Reno have either been maintained or increased.

Term limits imposed on Nevada legislators during the prior decade eliminated an important source of northern Nevada institutional influence, and every ten years redistricting of the sixty-three-member Nevada legislature reapportion more seats to the south.[42] Southern Nevada's increased diversification and urbanization also has reduced the share of Republicans elected to the statehouse from the region. Coupled with the articulation of a more unified policy agenda, Las Vegas's delegation to Carson City is less susceptible to being cross-pressured to vote party over geography. Until recently, the acquiescence of Clark County Republicans to northern priorities was a key factor undermining Southern Nevada's influence in state government.[43]

Under former governor and Reno resident Brian Sandoval, the state provided substantial tax abatements to lure business from outside Nevada, as well as from Las Vegas,[44] to invest in Reno and the surrounding area. These efforts, particularly the Tesla battery plant and other tech-based businesses, attracted Californians to the region seeking jobs, lower housing costs, and access to the region's outdoor activities. While migration into the region has challenged Reno's penchant for limiting growth,[45] these new residents, coupled with a growing Latino population, have shifted Washoe County from a Republican stronghold to a swing county that is increasingly voting for Democratic candidates.

In contrast to many state capitals that tend to vote for Democrats, Carson City remains reliably Republican. Its limited diversity also creates a mismatch between the race and ethnicity of the pool of potential state employees and the people served by state government. Thus, not only is Nevada's capital geographically remote from the state's population center, the demographic profile of much of the state workforce is much less diverse than Nevada's population.

The Rurals

Nevada's rapid growth, urbanization, and increased liberalism, first in Las Vegas and, more recently, in Reno, have significantly reduced the influence of the Rurals in state politics. As a point of comparison, the Southern Nevada city of Henderson, the second largest in the state, has more residents than the fourteen rural counties combined. In contrast, the largest city in the rural counties is Elko, in the heart of Nevada's mining region, with a population of just over 20,000, or roughly the equivalent of the number of residents in one of the dozens of master planned communities dotting the Las Vegas Valley. Although the rural counties have little ethnic and racial diversity, mining in eastern Nevada and ranching in central and western Nevada have attracted some Latinos and the region has pockets of Native Americans, but not in large enough concentrations to alter those counties' partisan voting habits.

Instead of fortifying the Rurals, Reno now provides a cushion for Las Vegas's liberal politics. Even when Republican candidates carry

Washoe County in competitive statewide elections, the margins are not sufficient to offset the Democratic strength in the south. To be sure, despite strong voter turnout that typically provides the GOP with a 2-1 advantage in the rural counties, the Rurals are now politically dominated from what are two rather modest-size urban physical spaces. The Las Vegas Valley and Truckee Meadows in northern Nevada represent just 2,000 square miles of urban space in a state that covers 109,000 square miles. There is no other state where 2 percent of the physical space contains 90 percent of a state's population and is able to exert political dominion over the other 98 percent of the land area.

The alienation felt by residents of the rural counties is often expressed in terms of the threats to the "real Nevada" from California colonizers and their Southern Nevada enablers. A staple of rural conservative rhetoric for decades, in 2018 this messaging was embraced by Republican candidates up and down the ballot. The parties' candidates warned that electing Democrats would lead to higher taxes, unfettered immigration, and the imposition of liberal, Hollywood values on the Silver State.[46]

The outcomes of the 2018 elections suggest just how disconnected this view is from the reality of Nevada's demographic and economic landscape. Not only is Nevada one of the most urbanized and diverse states in the country, it is dependent upon California for population growth and visitors to fuel its economy. In fact, an analysis of the 2010 U.S. census found more eligible voters in the state who were born in California than in Nevada.[47] Moreover, Nevada has provided tens of millions of dollars in tax abatements to induce California companies such as Apple and Tesla to invest in the Reno area. The states even share what is one of the West's most picturesque settings, Lake Tahoe, and more recently, the NFL Raiders relocated from northern California to Las Vegas.

Conclusion: Nevada State of Play

The juxtaposition of one of the most diverse million-plus metros—Las Vegas—in the middle of a state with deep rural roots and the historic legacy of the wide-open West, peopled mostly by whites results in some of the starkest demographic, geographic, and political fissures in the United States. By some estimates, in 2060, the country's demography will look like Las Vegas does today,[48] while the state's rural counties demographically look like America of 1960 and, in some instances, express political values that seem straight out of 1860—such as comments by a Republican state legislator suggesting that if his constituents wanted him to, he would, reluctantly, vote to reinstate slavery.[49]

At the same event, Assemblyman Jim Wheeler—himself a native of Southern California—suggested that he and other rural Republicans were working on a plan to either make Las Vegas a district—a status that would deprive the million-plus metro of representation in state government—or to trade the region to either Arizona or California. After Wheeler was pushed out as Republican Assembly caucus leader following the 2019 legislative session that saw the advancement of significant Democratic priorities, his replacement, Assemblywomen Robin Titus, another rural legislator, suggested that one of her priorities is to get her colleagues to accept that "Clark County is not that evil monster that we think it is." She confided that there is a "need to embrace Clark County." Titus then offered, "I think for me it's recognizing that the folks in Clark County need things that I don't necessarily see, and I need things that they don't."[50] Denial, anger, bargaining, depression, and at last, acceptance, the final phase of the grief cycle.

EXPERT ANALYSIS: NEVADA

Expert analysis for Nevada was provided by Michael Green, an associate professor of history at UNLV. Green, a native Nevadan, has written extensively on the politics and history of the Silver State. He was interviewed on April 17, 2018. Some of the quotes from Green that follow were edited for clarity.

Intrastate Political Dynamics

Green indicated that regionalism is much more salient north of Las Vegas. He suggested that this is the case because so many Las Vegans are new to Nevada and are less concerned about state politics. He recalled a conversation with a lifelong northern Nevadan who explained that "a northern Nevadan will only vote for a southern Nevadan if there's not an alternative." As a consequence, "people of Clark County tend to vote by party," while people in Reno are "more likely to vote by region."

Green also suggested that Democratic support in Las Vegas was a consequence of the region's diversity and the extensive voter mobilization efforts led by organized labor, particularly the Culinary Union.[51] In contrast to the Democratic strength in Las Vegas and the emerging Democratic shift in Reno, Green characterized the Rurals as being "redder than a bleeding ball."

Structural Features of State Government

Green suggested that Nevada's penchant for limited state government stems from the preferences of the framers of the Nevada constitution. These limitations, however, are largely reflected in the limited capacity of the Nevada legislature, which meets every other year for 120 days. In contrast, the Nevada governor is a strong office with "a degree of power that most other governors would envy," and this power asymmetry allows governors to "massage the legislature to get more things done."

Discussions about moving the capital from Carson City occur on occasion, but due to "inertia" and a belief among some that it is better for the legislature to be remote, these proposals get limited traction. Likewise, efforts to amend the Nevada constitution to implement annual sessions go back to the late 1950s, but these efforts have failed due to procedural hurdles (a proposed constitutional amendment must pass the Nevada legislature in two successive sessions before it is put before the voters). In the absence of annual sessions, the legislature "has more special sessions because they can't get their work done," and relies heavily on the Interim Finance Committee (IFC), a committee composed of legislators from both chambers, to address budget issues when the legislature is not in session. Green suggested that because the IFC is allowed to alter budgets after the fact this could potentially prompt legal challenges to its decisions.

Green noted that while Nevada is a modified Dillon's Rule state, the sheer size and scope of Las Vegas relative to the rest of Nevada has resulted in Clark County becoming more powerful. As a consequence, it is not uncommon for people to "leave the legislature to serve on the Clark County Commission."

Metro Power in State Government

Green indicated that Las Vegas's influence was "less than it should be" largely because of the tendency of Southern Nevadans to vote party, while Reno and Carson City and the Rurals tend to vote to protect their regional interests. Green noted, though, that the implementation of legislative term limits is changing this dynamic by weakening the seniority of northern legislators. "Before term limits, northern Nevadans stayed there longer. Legislators from Reno and other surrounding areas could go home" at the end of the day, while Southern Nevada legislators have to relocate to Carson City during the legislative session. Still, Green suggested that the mismatch between Southern Nevada's economic and political power persists. "Southern Nevada has the overwhelming majority of the state's population, and tourism funds the bulk of what goes on in Nevada," but the region "has more economic than political power."

CONCLUSION: THE MOUNTAIN WEST

Combined, the three Mountain West swing states have the same number of Electoral College votes as Michigan and Wisconsin. However, after the 2021 U.S. census, Arizona and Colorado are likely to gain their tenth and eighth U.S. House seats, respectively, while Michigan, as well as Ohio, another Midwestern state that is trending against the Democrats (see chapter 6), are likely to lose House seats. Thus, as the country's changing demography continues to reshape the geography of political competition, the Mountain West and its million-plus metros should provide the Democrats with opportunities to expand the western "Blue Wall" from the coastal states into the country's interior in the coming decades.[52]

Despite these states' general blueward trajectory, as the analysis presented in this chapter demonstrates, the influence of the Mountain West metros is contingent. Las Vegas, by virtue of its size and demographic distinctiveness relative to the rest of Nevada, is best positioned to drive electoral and policy outcomes. However, for decades, an alliance between the state's other regions undermined Las Vegas's influence, and institutionally, Las Vegas's ability to assert its interests is hindered by limited home rule and the limited capacity of state government. Moreover, it is only in the last few years that the Las Vegas region has created an organization, the Southern Nevada Forum, tasked with developing and articulating the region's policy priorities. In contrast, Denver and Phoenix have developed much stronger institutions for coordinating regional policy initiatives, and both metros have the additional advantages of having more home rule and state government established in their regions.

Yet, whereas Democratic voting in Las Vegas is being bolstered by the changing political landscape in Reno, Colorado Springs, Colorado's second-largest metro region, provides a conservative counterweight to Denver's liberalism. As a consequence, the Democrats' ability to win in Colorado requires not just strong margins in Denver but also increasing support along the northern Front Range and in liberal pockets of the West Slope. Moreover, the large number of registered nonpartisans, coupled with the use of a redistricting commission to draw the lines for state legislative districts, and the recent enactment of open primaries, have a moderating effect on Colorado's politics.

In Arizona, the increasing geographic and political consolidation between Phoenix and Tucson, coupled with liberal pockets in the north and along the border, will improve the Democrats' prospects in the state in the coming years. Also aiding the Democrats is the fact that Arizona uses an independent commission to draw the boundaries for its U.S. House and state legislative districts, which has allowed the Democrats to maintain representation in government despite Republican control over the governorship and Republican majorities in both chambers of the statehouse. At the same time, uneven patterns of voter turnout among Democratic leaning constituencies and strong Republican support in parts of Phoenix and in some of the state's hinterlands will keep the GOP competitive in Arizona in the near term. Eventually, though, the state's growing density and diversity will win out.

These interstate differences also have important implications for the states' issue environments. The saliency of environmentalism versus natural resources extraction, particularly fracking, and differing attitudes about diversity acceptance and immigration are the clear fault lines dividing rural and urban Colorado. Although a major industry in Nevada, mining's concentration in the rural counties tends to shield the industry from sustained scrutiny. And while the Rurals have loudly announced their opposition to the state's increasing liberalism, rural voters and legislators have little ability to alter the Silver State's increasingly stronger ties with California, given that just 10 percent of Nevadans live outside of the state's urban centers and each of these regions shares a border with California. Arizona, which earlier in the decade made national headlines after the passage of SB 1070 (2010), is selectively embracing more liberal policies. In 2016, a ballot measure increasing the minimum wage passed, but unlike in Colorado in 2012 and Nevada in 2016, Arizona voters opposed an initiative that would have legalized recreational use of marijuana. In 2018, Arizonans voted down a measure that would require the state to generate 50 percent of its energy from renewable sources. In the same election cycle, a similar measure passed in Nevada with nearly 60 percent support.

Moving forward, we anticipate that much of the expected Democratic shift in Arizona, Colorado, and Nevada will occur in the region's fourteen fast-growing, large-scale urbanizing suburbs, or boomburbs.[53] Arizona's Sun Corridor is home to Mesa, the nation's most populous boomburb. With over a half million residents, Mesa has more people than Atlanta. Henderson, Nevada, a boomburb that was incorporated in 1953 and is now the state's second-largest city, is larger than Cincinnati, St. Louis, and Pittsburgh.

Many boomburbs in the Mountain West are density built, often around light rail. Consider Tempe, Arizona, which is home to ASU's main campus. Tempe not only has several station stops in its downtown and at ASU, it is now building a secondary street-car system that links Valley Metro (Phoenix's light-rail system) to its neighborhoods via the Mill Avenue Corridor. Lakewood, Colorado (a Denver boomburb), used its half dozen light rail stops to build a series of higher-density nodes based on a land-use plan borrowed from Arlington, Virginia.[54]

Mountain West boomburbs are also diverse. For instance, North Las Vegas, Nevada (population 244,949 in 2018), is home to a large foreign-born population (much of it Latino). Lang and LeFurgy suggest that this type of boomburb, what they call a New Brooklyn, operates as an international gateway that adds additional diversity to places that already have large shares of minority and foreign-born residents.[55] Because of their density and diversity, the Mountain West boomburbs are poised to vote more Democratic compared to the whiter and sprawling suburbs located farther from the region's metro cores.

NOTES

1. Ruy Teixeira, ed., *America's New Swing Region: Changing Politics and Demographics in the Mountain West* (Washington: Brookings Institution Press, 2012).

2. Barry Goldwater, *The Conscience of a Conservative* (Eastford, CT: Martino Fine Books, 1960, Reprint 2011).

3. Yet unlike Mountain West neighbors such as Nevada and New Mexico, Arizona had already seen major population gains since the early twentieth century. The boom was noted in the Works Progress Administration Guide to Arizona in 1940, *Arizona: A State Guide*, compiled by Workers of the Writers' Program of the Works Project Administration of the State of Arizona (1940), p. 54.

4. A "boomburb" is defined as a suburb that had a population exceeding 100,000 by the 2000 census and experienced double-digit population growth every decade since 1950. See Robert Lang and Jennifer LeFurgy, *Boomburbs: The Rise of America's Accidental Cities* (Washington: Brookings Institution Press, 2007).

5. Ibid.

6. Robert Lang (then at Virginia Tech) and John Stewart Hall (from Arizona State University) named the "Arizona Sun Corridor" megapolitan area in 2006. Robert Lang was, at the time, a distinguished visiting professor in the ASU Department of Public Administration. Lang led a graduate-level public administration studio class at ASU that developed the Sun Corridor geography and gathered its data. The initial studio analysis and report was turned into the ASU College of Public Programs (now the Watts College of Public Service & Community Solutions) in June 2006. See Grady Gammage Jr., John Stuart Hall, Robert E. Lang, Rob Melnick, Nancy Welch, and Michael W. Crow, "Megapolitan: The Arizona Sun Corridor" (Phoenix: Morrison Institute for Public Policy, May 2008).

7. Vance's urban realm theory was developed to explain large, extended urban systems that are linked via economy but may be seen as semi-autonomous subregions within a larger metropolis. Vance, a geographer at the University of California, Berkeley, first applied the concept in the 1960s to the San Francisco Bay Area. James

E. Vance, *This Scene of Man: The Role and Structure of the City in The Geography of Western Civilization* (New York: Harper & Row, 1977).

8. Robert E. Lang and John Stewart Hall, "The Megapolitan Future," *Arizona Republic*, May 4, 2008, M1.

9. Jon Talton, "Phoenix 101: Tucson," *The Rogue Columnist*, January 3, 2011, www .roguecolumnist.com/rogue_columnist/2011/01/phoenix-101-tucson.html.

10. The Phoenix freeway loops are: Loop 101 (around Central Phoenix), Loop 202 (around East Valley); and Loop 303 (around West Valley).

11. Lourdes Medrano, "Fed Up with Phoenix, Tucson Talks Secession from Arizona," *Christian Science Monitor*, May 3, 2011, www.csmonitor.com/USA/Poli tics/2011/0503/Fed-up-with-Phoenix-Tucson-talks-secession-from-Arizona.

12. Ibid.

13. Robert E. Lang and William E. Brown Jr., "Phoenix—the New Birmingham," *Las Vegas Sun*, May 16, 2010, E1.

14. See Lang and Hall, "The Megapolitan Future"; Gammage Jr. and others, "Megapolitan: The Arizona Sun Corridor"; and Nelson and Lang, *Megapolitan America*.

15. Catherine Reagor, "Could Population Growth Propel Phoenix and Tucson to Merge?" *Arizona Republic*, April 21, 2019, www.azcentral.com/story/money/real-estate/catherine-reagor/2019/04/21/could-phoenix-and-tucson-merge-2040-popu lation-growth/3509155002/.

16. Coconino also has the youngest county population in Arizona, with a median age of thirty.

17. Kris Rengert and Robert E. Lang, "Cowboys and Cappuccino: The Emerging Diversity of the Rural West," *Census Note Series*, Fannie Mae Foundation, March 2001.

18. Ibid.

19. Arpaio served as Maricopa County Sherriff from 1993 to 2016, winning election five times and surviving two recalls. After Arpaio was held in contempt of court for failing to comply with judicial orders requiring that his office stop racially profiling Latinos and other minorities, Arpaio was pardoned by President Trump in 2017.

20. H-1B visas allow U.S. employers to hire, temporarily, high-skilled immigrants in specialized fields such as technology, engineering, and medicine. The number of H1-B visas is capped annually. See Neil G. Ruiz and Jill H. Wilson, "The H-1B Visa Race Continues: Which Regions Received the Most?" Brookings Institution, *The Avenue*, April 2, 2015, www.brookings.edu/blog/the-avenue/2015/04/02/the-h-1b -visa-race-continues-which-regions-received-the-most/.

21. Matt Ferner, "Colorado Secession Vote Fizzles: Rural Counties Split on 51st State Initiative," *HuffPost*, November 13, 2013, www.huffpost.com/entry/51st-state -initiative-rejected_n_4220891.

22. See Nelson and Lang, *Megapolitan America*.

23. Frank Popper, interview with Robert E. Lang, UNLV, August 24, 2018.

24. Sara Kuuth, "Five Years After Weld and 10 Other Counties Tried to Secede From Colorado, Feeling of Divisions Still Linger," *Greeley Tribune*, November 18,

2018, www.greeleytribune.com/news/five-years-after-weld-and-10-other-counties
-tried-to-secede-from-colorado-feelings-of-division-still-linger/.

25. William H. Frey, "How Migration of Millennials and Seniors has Shifted since
the Great Recession," Brookings Institution, January 31, 2019, www.brookings.edu/
research/how-migration-of-millennials-and-seniors-has-shifted-since-the-great
-recession/.

26. Rengert and Lang, "Cowboys and Cappuccino: The Emerging Diversity of the
Rural West."

27. To facilitate its growth, Las Vegas needed an act of Congress, the "Southern
Nevada Public Land Management Act" (1998), to develop federal lands in the Las
Vegas Valley.

28. For a detailed analysis of the Three Nevadas, see David F. Damore, "'Senator
Spineless' and the Campaign against Demography," in *Cases in Congressional Campaigns: Split Decision*, edited by David Dulio and Randall Adkins (New York: Routledge, 2020), pp. 49–68. Nevada has six cities with a population of 50,000 or more.
Although three of these cities, Las Vegas, Henderson, and North Las Vegas, are located in Clark County, the combined population of these cities is less than half of
the county's population and, as a consequence, with more than a million residents,
unincorporated Clark County contains the largest share of Nevada's population. The
three largest cities in the north are Reno, Sparks, and Carson City, with a combined
population of roughly 400,000. Elko, with a 2017 population of just over 20,000, is the
largest city in the Rurals.

29. "Unify, Regionalize, Diversify: An Economic Development Agenda for
Nevada," Brookings Institution, Brookings Mountain West, and SRI International,
2011, p. 8.

30. *The WPA Guide to 1930s Nevada,* Nevada Writers Project of the Works Progress Administration (University of Nevada Press, 1991), p. 3.

31. Ibid., p. 5.

32. Non-native-born Nevadans constitute just a quarter of the state's population,
the lowest share of native-born residents in any state in the country.

33. Michael W. Bowers, *The Sagebrush State*, 5th ed. (University of Nevada Press
2018), pp. 168–69. Also note in table 9-9 that Las Vegas's share of Nevada's GDP and
jobs is commensurate with the region's population share. However, because of the
state's low property taxes and the fact that Nevada does not levy a state personal,
business, or corporate income tax, taxes and fees assessed on economic activity
associated with gaming and tourism are the major sources of state revenue. For
example, the Live Entertainment Tax assessed primarily in Las Vegas generates
more than twice as much general fund revenue than the mining tax, even though
Nevada is one of the leading gold-producing states in the country. See Fiscal Analysis
Division, Legislative Counsel Bureau, "Fiscal Report, Eightieth Nevada Legislature,"
February 2019, p. 17, www.leg.state.nv.us/Division/Fiscal/Fiscal%20Report/.

34. For example, in 2010, Democratic U.S. Senator Harry Reid and Republican
gubernatorial candidate Brian Sandoval carried Washoe County. In 2012 and 2016,

the Democratic presidential candidates and the Republican U.S. Senate candidates won Washoe County.

35. Adam Laxalt, who is the grandson of former Nevada Republican governor and Senator Paul Laxalt, and former New Mexico Senator Pete Domenici, a fact that was not revealed until prior to his 2014 attorney general run, moved to Nevada in 2011. When the elder Laxalt was governor in the 1960s, his budgets disproportionately favored the northern branch of the state university in Reno (now the University of Nevada, Reno) at the expense of the southern branch in Las Vegas (what is now UNLV). In protest, students on the southern campus built a shantytown on campus and hung an effigy of Governor Laxalt from a campus building. See Laurie Furth, "Oh, The Things We Did," *UNLV Magazine*, Fall 1997, pp. 11–13.

36. Hugh Jackson, "Laxalt to Southern Nevada: Buzz Off," *Nevada Current*, October 29, 2018, www.nevadacurrent.com/2018/10/29/laxalt-to-southern-nevada -buzz-off/.

37. Michelle Rindels, "Sisolak Launches Ad in Reno Touting Investments in UNR During His Time as a Regent," *Nevada Independent*, October 23, 2018, https:// thenevadaindependent.com/article/sisolak-launches-ad-in-reno-touting-invest ments-in-unr-during-his-time-as-a-regent.

38. Riley Snyder, "Reno Mayor Makes Pitch for Sisolak in New Campaign Ad," *Nevada Independent*, October 19, 2018, https://thenevadaindependent.com/article/ reno-mayor-makes-pitch-for-sisolak-in-new-campaign-ad.

39. Richard Florida, "Where to Find a Creative Class Job in 2020," *CityLab*, March 2, 2012, www.citylab.com/life/2012/03/where-creative-class-jobs-will-be/1258/.

40. See, for example, April Corbin, "Las Vegas' Plan to Annex Small Portions of Clark County Fuels a Flare-up," *Las Vegas Sun*, January 4, 2018, https://lasvegassun. com/news/2018/jan/04/las-vegas-move-annex-parts-clark-county-fuel-anger/; Richard N. Velotta, "Stratosphere Owner Says Casino Is on Las Vegas Strip," *Las Vegas Review Journal*, December 17, 2017, www.reviewjournal.com/business/ business-columns/inside-gaming/stratosphere-owner-says-casino-is-on-las-vegas-strip/; John Katsilometes, "Carolyn Goodman: Let's Just Move the Welcome to Fabulous Las Vegas Sign," *Las Vegas Review Journal*, March 30, 2017, www.review journal.com/entertainment/entertainment-columns/kats/carolyn-goodman-lets-just-move-the-welcome-to-fabulous-las-vegas-sign/; John Katsilometes, "Dividing Line: Why Las Vegas City Leaders Aren't Invited to Ceremonies on the Strip," *Las Vegas Sun*, July 3, 2016, https://lasvegassun.com/news/2016/jul/03/dividing-line-why-las-vegas-city-leaders-arent-inv/; and James Dehaven and Ben Botkin, "Las Vegas' Big 'Party' Banner Irritates County Leaders," *Las Vegas Review Journal*, May 12, 2015, www.reviewjournal.com/local/local-las-vegas/las-vegas-big-party-banner -irritates-county-leaders/.

41. In 1969, Carson City and Ormsby County were consolidated and the county was dissolved.

42. The Nevada legislature, with twenty-one members in the state senate and forty-two members in the state assembly, is the fourth-smallest state legislature in

the country. After the 2011 redistricting, forty-four of the state's legislative districts are in Clark County.

43. Bowers, *The Sagebrush State*, p. 91.

44. Switch Communications, a Las Vegas data center company, received millions of dollars in tax abatements from the Governor's Office of Economic Development to build a data center outside of Reno, a rare instance of a state subsidizing a business already operating in a state to invest elsewhere in the state.

45. Kris McLean, "Opinion: Gigafactory Hiring Hurt by Housing Shortage, Says Panasonic Official," *Reno Gazette Journal*, September 16, 2019, www.rgj.com/story/opinion/voices/2019/09/16/reno-sparks-housing-shortage-impacts-hiring-says-panasonic-official/2316160001/.

46. Damore, "'Senator Spineless' and the Campaign against Demography."

47. William H. Frey and Ruy Teixeira, "America's New Swing Region: The Political Demography and Geography of the Mountain West," in *America's New Swing Region*, edited by Ruy Teixeira (Washington: Brookings Institution Press, 2017), p. 45.

48. Jed Kolko, "40 Years From Now, the U.S. Could Look Like Las Vegas," *FiveThirtyEight*, June 2, 2017, https://fivethirtyeight.com/features/40-years-from-now-the-u-s-could-look-like-las-vegas/.

49. Editorial, "Jim Wheeler's World," *Las Vegas Sun*, November 3, 2013, https://lasvegassun.com/news/2013/nov/03/jim-wheelers-world/.

50. Megan Messerly, "Wheeler Steps Down as Assembly Republican Leader; Titus to Take His Place," *Nevada Independent*, June 4, 2019, https://thenevadaindependent.com/article/wheeler-steps-down-as-assembly-republican-leader-titus-to-take-his-place.

51. David F. Damore, "Demography Realized? The 2016 Latino Vote in Nevada," in *Latinos and the 2016 Election: Latino Resistance to the Election of Donald Trump*, edited by Gabriel R. Sanchez, Luis Fraga, and Ricardo Ramirez (Michigan State University, 2020), pp. 257–59.

52. Damore and Lang, "The End of the Democratic Blue Wall?" p. 10.

53. Lang and LeFurgy, *Boomburbs: The Rise of America's Accidental Cities*.

54. Ibid., p. 156.

55. Ibid., p. 61.

10

FROM BLUE METROS TO BLUE STATES

David F. Damore
Robert E. Lang
Karen A. Danielsen

A new kind of suburbanization is sweeping through
politics, from Richmond to Atlanta, Houston, Denver
and elsewhere, and Democrats are starting to breach
Republicans firewalls in elections.[1]

—*Sabrina Tavernise and Robert Gebeloff*

Reporting in the *New York Times* in the wake of big Democratic wins in the 2018 midterm elections, Sabrina Tavernise and Robert Gebeloff take stock of the results by suggesting that a blue wave swept the nation's suburbs. Every metropolitan area they cite is covered in this book. They also note the same blue wave happened "elsewhere." This chapter summarizes and extends our findings, including the idea that the suburbs for decades formed a Republican firewall that Democrats are now breaching. We begin by reviewing our analysis and highlighting the primary implications of our findings. Then we assess the consequences that our case studies suggest for national-level political competition and state-specific policymaking. This is followed by a discussion of urbanizing suburbs and their role in tipping the balance of power within the thirteen swing states. The chapter concludes by considering how interstate migration from mostly blue states contributes to demographic and political change in the Sun Belt swing states.

SUMMARY AND IMPLICATIONS

Despite the ubiquity of the red state, blue state, swing state trichotomy, such a framework obscures how intrastate political competition motivates many of the salient fissures defining contemporary American politics. This book unpacks these dynamics by examining how demographic, economic, and partisan differences between million-plus metros and the balance of their states affect electoral and policy outcomes. While this analysis considers thirteen swing states that have at least one million-plus metropolitan area and where the 2016 presidential election was decided by ten points or less, this approach can be generalized to other contexts, particularly at lower levels of analysis, to understand how geography conditions the policies and preferences of elected officials and their constituents.

As we lay out in the first two chapters, geography shapes both the composition and dispersion of a state's diversity and, by extension, the sociocultural milieu in which a state's political and policy competition transpires. Often the differences originate in the degree to which states and their localities were settled by Northern or Southern interests. This is particularly true for the eastern and middle parts of the country. Despite differing dispersions, diversity in these spaces and the resulting cultural divisions are defined typically by a Black/white dialectic. In the recently urbanized Mountain West, the Texas Triangle, Northern Virginia, and most of the Florida Peninsula, there exists greater diversity within diversity and differing patterns of its dispersion. These differences promote distinctive sociocultural attitudes and values.

Yet, as the state case analyses suggest, increasing urbanization, diversification, and migration and the confluence of these factors with economic productivity are powerful forces reshaping traditional patterns of political behavior. The transformations are threefold.

First, increasingly, electoral outcomes and policy preferences are less a function of North/South sectionalism and are more attributable to population density and proximity to major population centers. Regardless of region, the denser and more diverse the locality and the closer said locality is to a million-plus metro, the greater the Democratic support.

Second, the blue state, red state model undergirded by an urban/ rural divide is shifting to a within-state split between major metros versus smaller cities and rural areas. This analysis of these twenty-seven metropolitan regions suggests that fast-growing, large-scale urbanizing suburbs, or boomburbs, often constitute the tipping point between blue and red America.

Third, despite continued urbanization, demographic diversification, and an accelerating clustering of economic productivity in million-plus metros, the endurance of rural-oriented electoral and policymaking institutions often underrepresent and underserve the needs and interests of the large-scale urban complexes driving the country's population and economic growth.

RUST BELT VERSUS SUN BELT: THE CURRENT AND FUTURE DEMOCRATIC PATH TO POWER

In 2016, Hillary Clinton tried to expand the Electoral College map by contesting several Sun Belt states, such as Arizona, North Carolina, and Georgia, while also hoping to hold traditional Democratic northern strongholds such as Michigan, Pennsylvania, and Wisconsin. The strategy failed. Building from an insight offered by journalist Ron Brownstein,[2] Robert Lang and David Damore suggest that Clinton and the Democrats were caught between a fading Rust Belt Blue Wall and an emerging Sun Belt Blue Wall.[3] The analysis presented in this book reflects this thesis and suggests that the Democrats' weakening position in Pennsylvania and the Midwest, and the party's improving prospects across the Sun Belt, are driven by divergent urbanization and diversification patterns.

Democrats are less competitive in much of the Midwest because the region grows so slowly, lacks large shares of minority voters, and its major metros are not large enough to counter the Republican dominance in the smaller cities and rural spaces. Michigan and Pennsylvania exemplify this point. Grand Rapids and Pittsburgh, which are million-plus metros with little diversity, support Republicans more than denser and more diverse Detroit and Philadelphia. And unlike states such as Colorado and Minnesota or metros such as Austin, Denver, and Raleigh, Michigan and Pennsylvania lack sufficient shares of college-educated whites to offset the strong Republican support among noncollege-educated whites.

After the 2021 reapportionment, Rust Belt state representation in the U.S. House and, by extension, the region's clout in the Electoral College, will drop. Although still considered a swing state, the trajectory is akin to Ohio. Barack Obama narrowly carried Ohio in 2008 and 2012, and had John Kerry won the state in 2004 (he lost it by less than 120,000 votes), he would have won the presidency. As the analysis of Ohio presented in chapter 6 indicates, the state is trending away from the Democrats due to a lack of diversity, its small share of college-educated whites, and population decline, most notably in metro Cleveland, the most Democratic part of the state.[4]

The opposite dynamics hold for Sun Belt swing states—Arizona, Colorado, Florida, Georgia, Nevada, North Carolina, and Texas.[5] Within the Sun Belt, Colorado and Nevada (see chapter 9) shifted most strongly to the Democrats in the past decade. Although Colorado and Nevada have smaller populations than other Sun Belt swing states, they provide a template for what is likely to unfold in coming years.

In Nevada, the shift from a Republican-leaning to a Democratic-leaning state offers a textbook example of the political consequences of increasing density and diversity. Mobilization of the Latino electorate in Las Vegas, aided in large part by organized labor and other liberal-oriented grassroots groups, significantly contributes to Democratic success in the Silver State.[6] Moving into the 2020 election cycle, similar efforts are being made in Arizona and Texas to increase registration and participation among voter-eligible Latinos. The Democrats' path in Florida is similar. Although the Sunshine State is politically more complicated (see chapter 5) than the Mountain West states and the GOP has long held power in state government, growth in the Latino electorate along the I-4 Corridor and in Jacksonville should nudge that state toward the Democrats.

Democrats are also reaping the political benefits of increasing density and diversity in Colorado. However, unlike in Nevada, which features low educational attainment, support among Colorado's large share of college-educated whites has been an equally important driver in Democratic success. Although not considered part of the Sun Belt, Virginia, principally Northern Virginia, which is home to large concentrations of foreign-born and college-educated minorities, has all these characteristics. Not surprising, in little more than a decade, Virginia shifted from Republican to Democratic control (see chapter 3).

In sum, the Democrats' improving prospects in the Sun Belt and the party's weakening position in the Rust Belt result from two sides of the same coin. In the Sun Belt, Democratic ascension stems from population growth and demographic diversification within economically dominant million-plus metros. By contrast, the absence of these drivers in the Midwest and in the western half of Pennsylvania benefits the GOP.

Yet, as the state case study analyses make clear, while these general patterns determine the relative size of the blue metros and the red states voting blocs, besides Nevada, where the million-plus metro so dominates, each state has its own patchwork of partisan support. For example, Minnesota's Iron Range region remains relatively liberal, while counties bordering the Dakotas tend to be conservative. In Colorado, the rural Republican vote is blunted by liberal pockets of the Cappuccino West (see chapter 9), a necessity for Democrats given Colorado Springs's conservatism. Democrats' emerging rebirth in the Lone Star State hinges not just on winning its thirteen boomburbs but also on improving turnout along the Mexican border and in the urban cores. In Wisconsin and Arizona, liberal Madison and Tempe augment Democratic support in Milwaukee and Phoenix, respectively. But given these states' differing latitudes, as Phoenix booms, it is becoming more Democratic while the opposite happens in Milwaukee. Because North Carolina lacks a single dominant million-plus metro region, growing Democratic strength is less concentrated and is dependent on improving the party's margins throughout the nearly 200-mile long "Carolina Piedmont" running along I-85 (see chapter 4).

Collectively, the states featured in this book hold the balance of power in the Electoral College and the U.S. Senate, and winning major metros within these states by larger margins goes a long way to gaining majority control in the U.S. House of Representatives. Perhaps more important, though, are the implications that our analysis has for state policymaking. Dysfunction and gridlock in Washington, D.C., means that states and localities are taking on more policy demands that traditionally were under the purview of the federal government.[7]

The COVID-19 epidemic exemplifies this point. The lack of preparation and slow response by the Trump administration and Congress to the pandemic forced cities and states to not only develop and implement policy on the fly but also to compete for limited medical supplies and absorb the brunt of the crises' economic and healthcare fallout.

Within many states, however, a clear blue metros, red states split exists between the initial scope of actions taken by Republican-led state governments and the policies being implemented by local leaders.[8] In notable contrast to efforts by these same state governments to rein in local autonomy, Republican governors in states such as Florida, Georgia, and Texas deferred to local government officials to develop their own policies limiting economic and social activity. Mayors of big cities and urbanizing suburbs, including some Republicans, in turn, banded together to vocally criticize the lack of uniform state standards as insufficient and likely to undercut local efforts to contain the pandemic.

In Texas, for instance, the Republican mayors of Fort Worth and the boomburb Arlington and the Democratic mayor of Dallas sent a joint letter to Texas governor Greg Abbott stating their belief that "a statewide approach to limiting nonessential business or commerce—rather than allowing a patchwork of regulations in neighboring cities and counties—is imperative to slowing the spread of COVID-19, which does not stop at county lines or city limits."[9] The mayors' message is clear: urbanized suburbs see their interests inextricably linked to their regions' principal cities—fortifying the urban-boomburb versus exurban-rural political identities that animate the blue metros, red states divide.

Indeed, one clear theme running through the analyses of these cases is the degree to which state policymaking institutions often hinder the interests of million-plus metros. These discussions indicate that redistricting machinations, weak and divided legislative bodies, limited home rule, and increased state preemption of localities are often used by Republican-controlled state governments to control their states' major metros. This is most apparent in Michigan, North Carolina, Ohio, Texas, and Wisconsin. In other instances, Republican-controlled state governments impose the policy preferences of the hinterlands even though such directives may harm the reputations and economies of their state's million-plus metros. The state cases also suggest a propensity of Republican-controlled states to perpetuate tax and spending policies that deprive major metros of infrastructure resources or operational funding, particularly for education, commensurate with their contribution to state coffers. Intra-metro fragmentation also encumbers the ability of million-plus metro regions to develop and implement regional policy priorities, a dynamic exemplified by Dallas and Houston, and until recently, Las Vegas.

These effects, however, are not universal. In states like Florida, that grant localities greater autonomy, conflicts between major metros and the state government are less salient. In Arizona and Colorado, because million-plus metros are the site of state government, Phoenix and Denver are better positioned to effectuate their policy goals. Perhaps with the exception of Portland, Oregon, Minneapolis's Metropolitan Council provides the most cohesive framework for metro governance in the country. The recent shifts in partisan control of state government in Nevada and Virginia demonstrate just how quickly states' governing priorities can change in response to election results. Thus, while blue metros, red states politics have implications for representation in Washington, within-state political competition between major metros and the rest of their states affects everything from tree removal to bathroom access, from funding for English learners and light rail to renewable energy mandates and economic development priorities, to gun control, reproductive rights, and voter eligibility.

URBANIZING SUBURBS: THE NEW POLITICAL BLUE LINE

Suburbs within million-plus metros form the main battle line between red and blue politics. In fact, how far the "blue line" (or the point at which Democrats win a majority of the vote) reaches into the suburbs determines the overall metropolitan vote share gained by Democrats. If Democrats win distant suburbs and the major metros contain a significant share of the state's total vote, then Democratic candidates for governor, senator, or president often prevail.

Our thesis, as developed in the first two chapters, is that higher population density plus significant demographic diversity equals more Democratic voters (or D + D = D). Not all suburbs represent equal targets for Democratic candidates. We find that fast-growing, urban-izing, large-scale suburbs constitute the most blue-shifting parts of million-plus metros. By contrast, remote, less dense, and whiter sub-urbs remain GOP strongholds.

Light rail is a key metric gauging the extent to which suburbs urbanize. In their 2007 book on large, urbanizing suburbs labeled boomburbs, Robert Lang and Jennifer LeFurgy document the influ-ence light rail has on neighborhoods. At the time the book appeared, rail projects were spreading throughout the United States. Lang and LeFurgy focused on rail's impact in several boomburbs to highlight the change they saw in land-use patterns and housing types around train stations—known in urban planning circles as transit-oriented development (TOD). They found that places such as Plano, Texas, and Lakewood, Colorado, were redirecting planning efforts around rail to accommodate mixed-use (multifamily and commercial space) and denser development. They note:

> Just about every boomburb mayor interviewed would like to have light-rail transportation in his or her city, reflecting a shift in pro-jection of growth from out to up: light-rail projects would promote real estate development in downtown. Light-rail projects are un-derway in Tempe and Mesa, Arizona, Lakewood, Colorado, and Mesquite, Texas.[10]

The boomburbs book appeared over a decade ago and reflected conditions in the mid-2000s. Since then, light rail, TOD, and the den-sity and diversity that accompanies such development has flourished to a remarkable degree in urbanizing suburbs. Almost half the boom-burbs with over 100,000 residents that Lang and LeFurgy identified in 2007 now contain some form of rail—light rail, heavy rail, or street-cars. Most boomburbs are transitioning to more densely built places in the process.

Boomburbs are becoming "built out," or running out of "green-field" space to accommodate lower-density, single-family subdivi-sions.[11] Many are reaching the limits of annexable space and are now forced to "infill" commercial districts with mid-rise, mixed-use development. In the process, many boomburbs are becoming significantly more urban in look, function, and politics.

Boomburbs are a common type of urbanizing suburb. They are mainly found in Sun Belt states around fast-growing major metros. These are incorporated suburban cities exceeded 50,000 residents by the 2000 census and gained population at a double-digit rate in every decade between 1970 and 2000. There are 137 boomburbs in the United States.[12] Boomburbs have become so ubiquitous in the Sun Belt that they now account for sixteen of the most populous twenty-five municipalities in the "Southwest Megapolitan Cluster" (Southern California, Southern Nevada, and Arizona's Phoenix/Tucson Sun Corridor).[13]

Table 10-1 shows select boomburbs from ten of our thirteen swing states. The table also includes three urbanizing suburbs that are not boomburbs (they grew too slowly to qualify as booming) from Michigan, Ohio, and Pennsylvania. The three were added so that examples of urbanizing suburbs can be shown for all thirteen swing states. Still, the fact that no such cities exist in these states despite their size is indicative of the slow growth of those states. Table 10-1 also profiles a similar-sized traditional big-city against each boomburb. These cities provide a context for how large many boomburbs have grown in that they now surpass better-known older cities. For instance, a suburb such as Henderson, Nevada, is now more populous (with 310,390 residents) than not only St. Louis, Missouri, but also Pittsburgh, Pennsylvania, and Cincinnati, Ohio. Also note that the populations of the first four boomburbs listed in table 10-1 surpass multiple big cities that anchor NFL franchises. In 2020, Henderson, Nevada, became the home of the team headquarters and practice facilities for the Las Vegas Raiders.

The politics in urbanizing suburbs trend blue. Consider one recent example from the Democratic Michigan primary held on March 10, 2020. Michigan was a critical state for Democrats in the 2016 presidential election. Democrat Hillary Clinton lost Michigan to Republican Donald Trump by less than 11,000 votes (or 0.2 percent)—making it the closest margin among the three Rust Belt states that gave the GOP the Electoral College votes needed to win. Michigan's 2020 Democratic primary helped former Vice President Joe Biden solidify his hold on the party's presidential nomination following a strong performance

TABLE 10-1. Selected Boomburbs and Urbanized
Suburbs in the Thirteen Swing States

	2018 Population	Metro Area	Comparable Traditional City	2018 Population
Boomburbs				
Mesa, AZ	508,958	Phoenix	Atlanta, GA	498,044
Arlington, TX	398,112	Dallas	New Orleans, LA	391,006
Henderson, NV	310,390	Las Vegas	St. Louis, MO	302,838
Chesapeake, VA	242,634	Virginia Beach	Buffalo, NY	256,304
Pembroke Pines, FL	172,374	Miami	Providence, RI	179,335
Cary, NC	168,160	Raleigh	Jackson, MS	164,422
Lakewood, CO	156,798	Denver	Springfield, MA	155,032
Sugar Land, TX	118,600	Houston	Lansing, MI	118,427
Round Rock, TX	128,739	Austin	Topeka, KS	125,904
Clearwater, FL	116,478	Tampa	Rochester, MN	116,961
Sandy Springs, GA	108,797	Atlanta	Green Bay, WI	104,879
Brooklyn Park, MN	80,610	Minneapolis	Scranton, PA	77,182
Waukesha, WI	72,549	Milwaukee	Canton, OH	70,458
Urbanized Suburbs in MI, OH, and PA				
Sterling Heights, MI	132,964	Detroit	Columbia, SC	133,451
Parma, OH	78,751	Cleveland	Racine, WI	77,432
Upper Darby, PA	82,716	Philadelphia	Lawrence, MA	80,376

Note: Only the largest boomburb in each metro is included.

Sources: Boomburbs (2007) and 2018 U.S. census estimate.

in Super Tuesday contests on March 3. Vermont's Independent senator Bernie Sanders won the 2016 Michigan Democratic primary, which
proved a bad omen for Hillary Clinton's loss in the state that fall.

Just ahead of the 2020 Democratic Michigan primary, the Republican mayor of Sterling Heights, Michael Taylor, endorsed Joe Biden in
the primary and for the presidency over Donald Trump, the incumbent president within his own party.[14] Taylor's endorsement made

national headlines. A Republican mayor of an urbanizing suburb in a key swing state gave an endorsement to a candidate from the opposite party. Biden went on to win the primary held on March 10, 2020, with 52.9 percent of the vote, over second-place finisher Bernie Sanders, with 36.4 percent. Expect urbanizing suburbs, especially Sun Belt boomburbs, to play an outsized role in future statewide and presidential elections. Winning the boomburbs by big margins often means winning states and perhaps the nation.

Not all large-scale urbanizing suburbs are incorporated cities. In fact, many of the most densely built and diverse suburbs lie within unincorporated areas of what Robert Lang calls "mega counties."[15] These places are the county-level equivalents of boomburbs and are most commonly found in the south, from Virginia's suburbs outside of Washington, D.C., to suburban Atlanta, Georgia. Lang documented the growth of mega counties from 1950 to 2000. He found that places such as Loudoun County (population 406,850) and Fairfax County (population 1,150,795), Virginia; metro Washington, D.C.; Gwinnett County (population 927,781) and DeKalb County (population 756,588), Georgia; and metro Atlanta grew from small towns and rural hamlets in the mid-twentieth century to large quasi-urban complexes by the first decade of the twenty-first century. And as mega counties boomed, their population diversified and their built densities intensified. For instance, Fairfax County, Virginia, is home to the third-largest, non-downtown office and retail complex in the United States,[16] and now links to the Washington Metro rail system via the new Silver Line.

Note that Tysons Corner, Virginia, is the largest office cluster in the United States that lies outside an incorporated city. Tysons Corner is located in McLean, Virginia, a "census-designated place."[17] CDPs are areas with significant population concentration and business activity that do not fall within incorporated cities.[18] Robert Lang and Dawn Dhavale determined that most CDPs with populations over 50,000 are found in the biggest, fastest-growing suburban counties, especially those in the south and, thus, they constitute rough proxies for boomburbs in million-plus metros such as Northern Virginia, Charlotte, North Carolina, and Atlanta, Georgia.

As suburban mega counties densify and diversify, their politics tend to shift in favor of the Democrats. Consider Loudoun County,

Virginia, and DeKalb County, Georgia. Loudoun was once a reliably Republican suburban county of the type the GOP counted on to dominate Virginia politics for decades. Yet as waves of suburban (and now quasi-urban) growth swept over this once sleepy exurb, its politics shifted blue. It was a key county in 2006 when the Democrats retook the U. S. Senate, as Jim Webb defeated Republican incumbent George Allen.[19] In the 2008 presidential election, Loudoun helped elect Barack Obama president, the first Democrat since Lyndon Johnson in 1964 to win the county.[20] By 2016, Hillary Clinton won Loudoun by an even bigger margin than President Obama did in 2012. And in the most recent 2019 statewide Virginia legislative election, Democrats so dominated the county that the *New York Times* did a long article on Loudoun's politics. The story was reported out of South Riding, Virginia, a CDP and planned community in unincorporated Loudoun.[21] As the *New York Times* noted, one in four residents in Loudoun County is an immigrant and President Trump's politics played poorly in that community.[22]

DeKalb County, Georgia, is another mega county with a now solid Democratic base. Located just east of the city of Atlanta, DeKalb was, until the 1960s, a smaller suburban/semi-agricultural county. But by the next decade, two big transportation improvements better linked DeKalb to Atlanta. First was the completion of the I-285 Beltway (locally known as the "Perimeter").[23] In the 1970s, DeKalb became one of only two counties (the other being Fulton) to approve rail service from the Metropolitan Atlanta Rapid Transit Authority (MARTA). MARTA is a heavy-rail commuter line, and access to it helped transform DeKalb into a far more urban place. DeKalb is now Georgia's most diverse county, with an African American majority. From a swing county in the 1980s, DeKalb shifted solid blue by the 1990s. In 2016, Hillary Clinton won four in five votes in DeKalb as the county helped make Georgia a more competitive state than it has been in recent presidential cycles.[24]

Finally, we are not the only observers who see the urbanized suburbs as the new political battle line. *Washington Post* columnist George Will, commenting on Arizona politics, called the state, "a loose brick in the Republicans' red wall."[25] The reason the once solidly GOP-voting Arizona is now in play? Urbanized suburbs:

Under its current master, who holds it on a short leash, the Republican Party has difficulties in the suburbs, where education levels are inconveniently (for Republicans) high and women have a peculiar abhorrence of ignorance coarsely expressed. Phoenix, the nation's fifth-largest city has suburbs that are cities: Tempe is larger than Providence, R.I., Scottsdale is larger than Salt Lake City, Mesa is larger than St. Louis [actually it's even bigger than Atlanta], Glendale is larger than Des Moines.[26]

Will notes that Hillary Clinton nearly beat Donald Trump in the 2016 presidential election in Maricopa County (home to Phoenix), and that it contains many new migrants who bring along their politics to Arizona. That Maricopa County will have well over 300,000 more residents in 2020 than it did just four years ago should give Republicans cause for concern. The largest share of Maricopa's migrants come from blue states such as California and Illinois.

BLUE "INVADING" RED: MIGRATION PATTERNS IN THE SWING STATE VOTE

Many of the case analyses in this book note the degree to which undervoting by Democratic-leaning constituencies creates a gap between public opinion and what Stephen Klineberg calls "politically effective opinion" in chapter 8. Certainly, higher rates of engagement among less-habitual voters would reduce this gap and elect more Democrats. Equally important for the party's prospects are the political shifts caused by interstate migration. Although the internet and rising housing costs[27] have helped slow the pace at which Americans relocate,[28] migration does continue, particularly from expensive and congested regions such as California and the Northeast to places with less-expensive housing and lower taxes.

Historically, the United States was peopled by an east-to-west movement. Throughout the late-nineteenth century, the U.S. Census Bureau even mapped an actual western "frontier line" to show the extent that the nation was settled. The frontier line map was part of a census document titled "Progress of the Nation."[29] Some east/west movement remains. Yet, domestic migration patterns divide east and west. People living in the Northeast and Midwest mostly move to southern states such as Florida, North Carolina, and Georgia, while the main migration shift in the west is from California to Mountain West states such as Arizona, Colorado, Idaho, Nevada, and Utah. The Tax Cut and Jobs Act of 2017 (see chapter 2) may further accelerate movement from California and the Northeast to lower-tax states because of a $10,000 cap on state and local tax deductions.[30]

Throughout this book, especially in the case study chapters, we document recent interstate movement as it pertains to politics. We note, for example, where Californians have shifted a state's politics by moving to places such as Arizona or Nevada. We also document transformative international migration patterns and how they shape state politics in places such as Texas and Florida. In the book *Diversity Explosion: How New Racial Demographics are Remaking America*, Brookings Institution demographer William Frey projects that geographically expanding diversity will continue to the mid-twenty-first century.[31] Frey predicts that by 2060, the majority of states will be either mostly minority or majority minority in composition based on current census definitions.[32]

We find evidence in our case analysis suggesting that change in politics due to the diversity explosion is already occurring across much of America. As noted earlier, because Loudoun County, Virginia—once solidly part of the cultural South—now has a quarter of its residents born outside the United States, Loudoun's diversity is certainly remaking politics in Old Dominion, as evidenced by Virginia's 2019 blue-wave state legislative election.

Starting with Bill Bishop's 2009 book, *The Big Sort: Why the Clustering of Like-Minded Americans is Tearing Us Apart*, [33] a literature emerged that cautioned against America becoming a divided public sphere where people shut out opinions they prefer not to hear. Bishop's divided discourse idea now applies to "social media bubbles" where news is micro-targeted to reflect and reinforce existing opinions.[34] Thus, people do not need physical propinquity, as suggested by Bishop, to filter out information that cuts against their political views. Yet, place still matters. People vote in a place or precinct, and face-to-face contact with other community members still shapes opinion and provides a collective context for political action. This is especially important in local grassroots political networks focused on voter registration and get-out-the-vote campaigns.[35] Thus, the manner in which migration patterns interact with local context has the potential to affect policy agendas and elections.

Finally, a new book on American political migration is raising alarm that blue state residents are leading a "liberal invasion of red state America."[36] Conservative columnist Kristin Tate shows that progressive-leaning tax refugees from California to Massachusetts are moving to low-cost states such as Florida, Nevada, and Texas.[37] She is angered by the fact that blue-state migrants seek lower taxes and housing costs and fewer regulations in red states but then go on to shift their adopted states' politics toward higher taxes as they demand more services and amenities. Tate cites many of the same sources and data we do concerning migration of, for instance, tech workers from California to Texas, but paints a dire picture where America is on the road to universal high taxation and regulations as state after state shifts from red-to-purple-to-blue.[38]

The reality is that many blue state migrants are affluent enough to move to red states, while most red state residents cannot afford to relocate to a blue state. That is because most wealthy states are blue. Data compiled by *USA Today* in advance of the 2018 midterm election that ranked all fifty states based on their wealth showed that all the top dozen states but Alaska voted for Democratic candidate Hillary Clinton.[39] Conversely, Republican Donald Trump won all but two— New Mexico and Maine—of the twenty least affluent states in 2016.[40]

Blue state residents can and are moving to red states. Many of these migrants are either retirees or work in emerging tech industries found in what were once red million-plus metros, from Phoenix, Arizona, to Jacksonville, Florida. If the trend persists, much of the Sun Belt may shift blue in state and presidential politics, further solidifying the blue metros, red states divide.

FROM THE URBAN/RURAL DIVIDE TO THE MAJOR METRO/REST OF STATE DIVIDE

The idea of an urban/rural divide extends back at least to the 1928 presidential election. Republican Herbert Hoover defeated Democrat Al Smith in a landslide even as Smith won the dozen largest U.S. cities. A form of the city/country electoral split persists into the 2020s, a century later. However, the new political battle line runs not between the city and country but, instead, through the suburbs, especially urbanizing suburbs within million-plus metropolitan regions. It splits major metros from exurbs, small towns, and rural areas.

American suburbs are now so large-scale and varied that it is impossible to declare that either party maintains a lock on the suburban vote. Republicans continue to hold the line in conventional suburbs that are auto-dominated, mostly white, consist mainly of single-family detached homes on large lots, and lie toward the metropolitan edge. But Democrats are rapidly gaining ground in urbanizing suburbs, especially in the Sun Belt, where multifamily housing mixes with commercial uses that are increasingly served by new transit systems.

The more cosmopolitan suburbs are home to a growing educated and diverse population, whose residents often identify with the interests of the urban core. There are many such suburbs, dozens of which exceed 100,000 people and match traditional big cities in urban characteristics such as foreign-born populations and major commerce. According to Peter Taylor and Robert Lang, these places represent a still-emerging urban form.[41]

Urbanizing suburbs can consume entire counties that may lack incorporated cities but nonetheless have city-like development recognized by the census as CDPs. Clark County, Nevada, home to big incorporated cities and suburbs such as Las Vegas, Henderson, and North Las Vegas, also maintains several CDPs that exceed 100,000 people, and in one case—the Paradise CDP—surpasses 200,000 residents.[42]

A review of the most current census data for county population estimates as of July 1, 2019 (released in March 2020), shows that the biggest urbanized suburbs we cover in the book remain the fastest-growing places in the United States based on numeric change.[43] In fact, the five counties adding the most people over the past year all lie in our twenty-seven million-plus metropolitan areas.[44] The counties are found in the Phoenix, Las Vegas, Houston, Dallas, and Austin metropolitan areas. Sun Belt urbanized suburbs—both incorporated and unincorporated—lead the nation's growth and are projected to continue that trend in the 2020s.

Urbanized suburbs are not simply overgrown countrified enclaves that politically align with smaller metros and rural areas.

They are America's new big cities—born mostly over the past half-century in the booming Sun Belt. A key urban quality they now share with older big cities is politics. Urbanized suburbs are quickly turning blue, and as goes these new cities so goes their metros, states, and the nation.

NOTES

1. Sabrina Tavernise and Robert Gebeloff, "How Voters Turned Virginia from Deep Red to Solid Blue," *New York Times*, November 9, 2019, www.nytimes.com /2019/11/09/us/virginia-elections-democrats-republicans.html.

2. Ronald Brownstein, "Has the Balance of Power Shifted from the Rustbelt to the Sunbelt?" *The Atlantic*, November 8, 2016, www.theatlantic.com/politics/archive /2016/11/campaign-efforts-rustbelt-and-sunbelt/506873/.

3. Robert E. Lang and David F. Damore, "The End of the Democratic Blue Wall?" Brookings Mountain West Policy Report, December 2016, p. 9, https://digital scholarship.unlv.edu/brookings_pubs/45/.

4. Like Ohio, Missouri was for decades considered a "political bellwether." See David Brian Robertson, "Bellwether Politics in Missouri," *The Forum* 2, no. 3, article 2 (September 2004). From 1904 to 2004, the state voted for the winning presidential candidate in every election except 1956. Yet Missouri's Southernness, slow-growth, and low education and minority population levels, now make it a solid red state. Ohio appears to be following a similar political track.

5. The term *Sun Belt* was coined by Kevin P. Phillips in *The Emerging Republican Majority* (New York: Arlington House, 1969) to label the growing political and economic power of western and southern states, a theme that is later amplified in Kirkpatrick Sale's *Power Shift: The Rise of the Southern Rim and Its Challenge to the Eastern Establishment* (New York: Random House, 1976).

6. See David F. Damore, "Demography Realized? The 2016 Latino Vote in Nevada," in *Latinos and the 2016 Election: Latino Resistance to the Election of Donald Trump*, edited by Gabriel R. Sanchez, Luis Fraga, and Ricardo Ramirez (Michigan State University Press, 2020), pp. 211–30; David F. Damore, "'Senator Spineless' and the Campaign against Demography," in *Cases in Congressional Campaigns: Split Decision*, edited by Randall E. Adkins and David A. Dulio (New York: Routledge, 2020), pp. 49–68; and David F. Damore, "It's the Economy Stupid? Not so Fast: The Impact of the Latino Vote on the 2012 Presidential Election in Nevada," in *Latinos and the 2012 Election*, edited by Gabriel R. Sanchez (Michigan State University Press, 2015), pp. 181–98.

7. Bruce Katz and Jennifer Bradley, *The Metropolitan Revolution: How Cities and Metros Are Fixing Our Broken Politics and Fragile Economy* (Washington: Brookings Institution Press, 2013).

8. Ronald Brownstein, "The Pandemic Is Dividing Blue Cities from Their Red States," *CNN*, March 31, 2020, www.cnn.com/2020/03/31/politics/red-states-blue-cities-coronavirus/.

9. Ibid.

10. Robert E. Lang and Jennifer B. LeFurgy, *Boomburbs: The Rise of America's Accidental Cities* (Washington: Brookings Institution Press, 2007), p. 18.

11. Robert E. Lang and Jennifer B. LeFurgy, "Boomburb 'Build Out': The Future of Development in Large, Fast-Growing Suburbs," *Urban Affairs Review* 42, no. 2 (March 1, 2007), pp. 533–52.

12. Lang and LeFurgy, *Boomburbs*, p. 8.

13. Karen A. Danielsen and Robert E. Lang, "Polycentric Metropolitan Regions: The Emerging Integration of Southern California, Central Arizona and Southern Nevada into an Urban Polycentric Southwest Triangle," in *Polyzentrale Metropolregionen*, edited by Ranier Danielzyk, Angelika Munter, and Thorsten Wiechmann (Berlin: Verlag Dorothea Rohn, 2016), pp. 362–85.

14. Justin Wise, "Michigan GOP Mayor Ditches 'Deranged' Trump. Endorses Biden for President," *The Hill*, March 10, 2020, https://thehill.com/homenews/campaign/486833-michigan-gop-mayor-ditches-deranged-trump-endorses-biden-for-president.

15. Robert E. Lang, *Edgeless Cities: Exploring the Elusive Metropolis* (Washington: Brookings Institution Press, 2003).

16. Robert E. Lang, Edward J. Blakely, and Megan Zimmerman-Gough, "Keys to the New Metropolis: America's Big, Fast-Growing Suburban Counties," *Journal of the American Planning Association* 71, no. 4 (Autumn 2005), pp. 381–91.

17. Robert E. Lang and Dawn Dhavale, "Reluctant Cities: Exploring Big Unincorporated Census-Designated Places," *Census Note 03:01* (Alexandria: Metropolitan Institute at Virginia Tech, July 2003).

18. Ibid.

19. Robert E. Lang and Thomas W. Sanchez, "The New Metropolitics: Interpreting Recent Elections using a County-Based Regional Typology," Metropolitan Institute 2006 Election Brief, December 2006, www.researchgate.net/publication/230820734_The_new_metro_politics_Interpreting_recent_presidential_elections_using_a_county-based_regional_typology.

20. David Leip, "Dave Leip's Atlas of U.S. Elections," https://uselectionatlas.org/.

21. Tavernise and Gebeloff, "How Voters Turned Virginia from Deep Red to Solid Blue."

22. Ibid.

23. Lang, *Edgeless Cities*.

24. In 2012, Democratic President Barack Obama lost Georgia by a 7.8 percent margin. Hillary Clinton closed that gap to 5.2 percent in 2016.

25. George F. Will, "A Loose Brick in the Republicans' Red Wall" *Washington Post*, March 25, 2020.

26. Ibid.

27. See chapter 8.

28. Thomas Cooke, "Americans are Moving Less and Less—and It Could Dramatically Reshape Society," *Fast Company*, December 7, 2019, www.fastcompany.com/90439810/why-are-americans-moving-less-and-less.

29. Robert E. Lang, Deborah Epstein Popper, and Frank J. Popper, "'Progress of the Nation': The Settlement History of the Enduring Frontier," *Western Historical Quarterly* 26, no. 3 (Autumn 1995), pp. 289–307.

30. Chris Edwards, "Tax Reform and Interstate Migration," *Cato Institute Tax and Budget Bulletin* 84 (September 6, 2018), www.cato.org/sites/cato.org/files/2019-09/tbb-84-KY-fixed.pdf). Edwards sees the 2017 Tax Law as mostly impacting retirement movements.

31. William H. Frey, *Diversity Explosion: How New Racial Demographics are Remaking America* (Washington: Brookings Institution Press, 2018).

32. Ibid.

33. Bill Bishop, *The Big Sort: Why Clustering of Like-Minded America Is Tearing Us Apart* (Boston: Mariner Books, 2009).

34. Dominic Spohr, "Fake News and Ideological Polarization: Filter Bubbles and Selective Exposure on Social Media," *Business Information Review* 34, no. 3 (September 2017), pp. 150–60.

35. Lisa Kashinsky, "Retail Politics Still Key to Wooing New Hampshire Voters," *Boston Herald*, July 6, 2019, www.bostonherald.com/2019/07/06/retail-politics-still-key-for-candidates-wooing-new-hampshire-voters/.

36. Kristin B. Tate, *The Liberal Invasion of Red State America* (New York: Regnery Publishing, 2020).

37. Ibid.

38. Ibid.

39. Grant Suneson, "Wealth in America: Where are the Richest and Poorest States Based on Household Income?" *USA Today*, October 8, 2018, www.usatoday.com/story/money/economy/2018/10/08/wealth-america-household-income-richest-poorest-states/38051359/.

40. In the case of Maine, Trump won a single electoral vote out of the rural 1st Congressional District.

41. Peter J. Taylor and Robert E. Lang, "The Shock of the New: 100 Concepts Describing Recent Urban Change," *Environment and Planning* 36, no. 9 (September, 2004), pp. 951–58.

42. The Las Vegas Strip, the region's largest commercial center, is found in Paradise, as is the University of Nevada, Las Vegas, and McCarran International Airport. Paradise contributes so much to the regional economy that it is the only CDP in the United States that is included in an official census name for a metropolitan area—the Las Vegas-Henderson-Paradise MSA. Other Clark County CDPs exceeding 100,000 include Spring Valley, Sunrise Manor, and Enterprise.

43. U.S. Census Bureau, Population Division, "Annual Estimates of the Resident Population for Counties in the United States: April 1, 2010 to July 1, 2019." The current U.S. estimated population just ahead of the 2020 census is 328,299,522. The U.S. population passed the 300 million mark in April 2006.

44. The counties are Maricopa County, Arizona (83,011 people added), Clark County, Nevada (40,600 people added), Harris County, Texas (33,280 people added), Collin County, Texas (30,425 people added), and Travis County, Texas (27,382 people added).

Epilogue
THE VIEW FROM WASHINGTON
Molly E. Reynolds

In the preceding chapters, the authors explored how the rural/urban divide within states has consequences for the representation and advancement of the policy priorities of metropolitan areas within states, focusing on thirteen states and, within them, twenty-seven metro areas with populations over 1 million. But policies affecting these states and metro areas, and the people who live in them, are not made only at the state level. What happens in the halls of the U.S. Capitol affects the lives of individuals living in the states under study here. By the same token, the political choices made by voters in red states with blue metros can have consequences for how things work in Washington—but that influence of the legislators selected by voters is filtered through long-standing and powerful congressional institutions.

This epilogue begins by providing an overview of the kinds of congressional districts observed in the thirteen states under study here and discussing their partisan makeup, as well as the partisan breakdown of the Senate seats in these states. Next, it traces changes in the ideology of House members from red states with blue metros over time and analyzes how this ideological change fits in with polarization in the House as a whole. The chapter continues with an analysis of the role congressional institutions can play in shaping the influence of legislators from red states with blue metros as well as an evaluation—

relying on the example of the cap placed on the state and local tax deduction in the 2017 tax law—of how certain policy issues can divide House members from the swing states analyzed here from their same-party colleagues. The epilogue concludes with a discussion of how redistricting—both the process to come after the 2020 census and several mid-decade, court-ordered rounds that have occurred since 2010—have and will shape the representation of red states with blue metros in Congress.

THE BASICS: REPRESENTATION OF RED STATES AND BLUE METROS IN THE U.S. CONGRESS

In the 116th Congress, legislators from the thirteen states under study here comprise roughly 43 percent of the membership of the House of Representatives, or 185 members. Of those, approximately 44 percent are Democrats and roughly 55 percent are Republicans.[1] In some recent years, the share of votes won by Democrats nationally has not translated into an equivalent share of seats.[2] The 2018 election did not see an especially large discrepancy for Democrats on this metric nationally; however, Democratic House candidates received approximately 54.5 percent of the two-party vote, as compared to 54 percent of House seats. While we do, on average, observe divergence between votes and seats when we examine state-by-state results, there was no discernable difference between red states with blue metros and other states on this metric. In both cases, Democratic congressional candidates received an average of 52 percent of the vote and an average of 48 percent of the two-party vote.[3]

As the preceding analysis suggests, however, these seats are not evenly distributed across types of districts within states. Using David Montgomery's measure of congressional district density, we see in table E-1 that Democratic districts in these states tend to be urban or suburban, whereas Republican districts are more likely to at least partially contain rural areas.

In red states with blue metros, roughly 85 percent of the Democratic districts are sparsely suburban, densely suburban, or an urban-suburban mix. This is a slightly larger share than the 71 percent of all seats held by Democrats that fall into these three categories (dis-

TABLE E-1. Distribution of Types of Congressional
Districts by Party, 116th Congress (%)

	Share of Democratic Districts in Red States with Blue Metros	Overall Share of Democratic Districts	Share of Republican Districts in Red States with Blue Metros	Overall Share of Republican Districts
Pure Rural	4	4	23	29
Rural-Suburban Mix	9	11	4	45
Sparse Suburban	27	22	25	18
Dense Suburban	35	29	9	8
Urban-Suburban Mix	2	20	1	1
Pure Urban	3	15	0	0

Sources: David Montgomery, "CityLab's Congressional District Index," November 20, 2018, www.citylab.com/equity/2018/11/citylab-congressional-density-index/575749/; Clerk of the U.S. House of Representatives.

played in the second column)—a difference driven largely by the fact that red states with blue metros contain relatively few purely urban districts. Of the thirty-four purely urban seats (all of which are held by Democrats), only two, Pennsylvania's 2nd and 3rd Districts, are in states under study here.

For Republicans, meanwhile, approximately 65 percent of the seats held by the party in red states with blue metros are purely or partially rural, as compared to 74 percent of all GOP-held seats nationwide. Conversely, Republican strength in the suburbs is somewhat stronger in red states with blue metros than it is nationwide; 35 percent of the party's seats in those states are in sparsely suburban, densely suburban, or urban-suburban mix districts, as compared to only 27 percent overall.

When Democrats gained control of the House of Representatives after the 2018 elections, moreover, the states under study here were well represented in the set of seats that changed hands. Party control of forty-four seats changed hands in 2018, with Democrats winning forty-two races previously held by Republicans and Republicans picking up two seats held by Democrats. Of these, nineteen, roughly 43 percent, were in the thirteen red states with blue metros analyzed here. As expected, the seats gained by Democrats tended to be in suburban areas; nearly all were in sparsely suburban, densely suburban, or urban-suburban mixed areas, with just one (Virginia's 7th District, in which Abigail Spanberger defeated David Brat) characterized as a rural-suburban mix. The results in the two seats previously held by Democrats but picked up by Republicans also conform to our expectations. Minnesota's 1st District, now represented by Republican Jim Hagedorn, is a mixed rural-suburban seat, while Minnesota's 8th District, now represented by Pete Stauber, was one of the relatively small number of purely rural seats held by Democrats.

In the Senate, meanwhile, the twenty-six senators are divided neatly along party lines, with thirteen Republicans and thirteen Democrats. The relationship between density and partisanship, however, is not as strong for Senate seats as it is for House districts. Table E-2 displays two population figures: the share of each swing state's population that lived in a metro area in 2018 and the share that resided in one of the specific twenty-seven metros with populations over one million that are the focus of the preceding chapters. Shown alongside those population figures are the number of Democratic senators from each state.

First, we see that in each of the states under study, a significant majority of the population lives in a metro area; Wisconsin, which ranks last on this metric, still saw roughly three-fourths of its population residing in an MSA in 2018. When we examine the share of these states' residents who live in the large metros on which the analyses in the previous chapters focuses, however, we see substantially more variation. In some states, like Arizona, Nevada, and Virginia, a sizable majority of the population lives in a metro area with a population of over 1 million. But in other states—like Colorado, Michigan, Ohio, and Pennsylvania—the figure is closer to half, and in North Carolina and Wisconsin, it is a notable minority.

Comparing the share of a state's population in each of these categories to the number of Democratic senators who represent it in Washington yields weak trends that depend on which population metric is used. States in which a higher share of the overall population lives in

TABLE E-2. Number of Democratic Senators by
Metro Share of State's Population, 2018

State	Number of Democratic Senators	Share of Population Living in an MSA [%]	Share of Population Living in MSA Over 1 Million [%]
Arizona	1	95	82
Colorado	1	87	51
Florida	0	97	63
Georgia	0	83	63
Michigan	2	82	54
Minnesota	2	78	62
Nevada	2	91	74
North Carolina	0	81	37
Ohio	1	80	50
Pennsylvania	1	89	50
Texas	0	89	67
Virginia	2	88	73
Wisconsin	1	75	29

Note: Differences between the "Share of Population Living in MSA Over 1 Million" presented in the table and the population data presented in chapters 1 through 9 result from the use of different years (2017 opposed to 2018) and different data sources (American Community Survey 1-Year estimates versus U.S. Census Annual Estimates of the Resident Population).

Source: Annual Estimates of the Resident Population, Estimated Components of the Resident Population Change, and Rates of the Components of the Resident Population Change for States and Counties: April 1, 2010 to July 1, 2018.

a metro area tend to have fewer Democratic senators, but the correlation is relatively weak ($\rho = -0.18$). At the same time, states in which a larger percentage of the population lives in a large metro area tend to have more Democratic representation in the Senate; though, again, the correlation is slight ($\rho = 0.23$). While not as strong as the trends for the House just discussed, the Senate data does suggest more densely populated areas are more likely to send Democrats to Washington.

POLARIZATION AND RED STATES WITH BLUE METROS

Political science research provides strong evidence that, over roughly the past forty years, the political parties have polarized substantially, especially at the elite level. In Congress, this trend has been accompanied by the tendency for nearly all policy issues to divide liberals and conservatives along ideological lines; in previous decades, a given topic could produce a coalition that involved members of both parties in a way that is rarely seen in today's politics.[4] While the legislating that does happen in Congress continues to be bipartisan, polarization has also made it more difficult for Congress to attack big, national problems, leaving more issues gridlocked.[5]

How has this polarization played out in the states under study here? Using political scientists' workhorse measure of congressional ideology for the current Congress (where negative values indicate a more liberal member and positive values correspond to conservative voting records), we can examine how the delegations from red states with blue metros have changed over the period in which polarization has increased (measured here beginning with the 97th Congress, in 1981).[6] In figure E-1, we see the 1st-dimension NOMINATE score for Republicans from red states with blue metros in solid gray as compared to their same-party colleagues in dotted gray. For Democrats, the same data is displayed in black with the solid line indicating the mean ideology for members from states with blue metros and the dotted line denoting their co-partisans representing other states.

These trends across the two parties yield interesting, though different, conclusions. For Republicans, we see that members from both the swing states under study here, and from other states, have generally become more conservative over time; this is consistent with the broader trend among Republican legislators.[7] Republican members from red states with blue metros, however, have been, on average, more conservative than their colleagues for almost the entire period of rising polarization in Congress.[8] This trend is driven in part by the fact that Texas is included in the set of states of interest; Texas has had a consistently more conservative group of Republican House members

FIGURE E-1. Average Ideology of House Members from Red States with Blue Metros versus Other States, by Party, 97th–116th Congress (1981–2019)

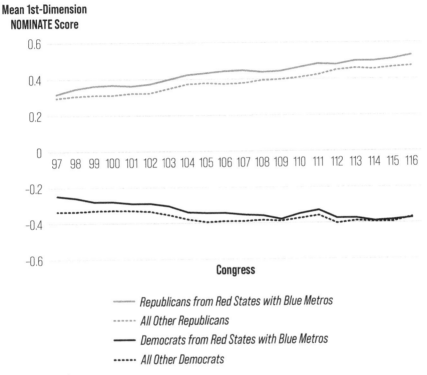

Mean 1st-Dimension NOMINATE Score

Congress

——— *Republicans from Red States with Blue Metros*

······ *All Other Republicans*

——— *Democrats from Red States with Blue Metros*

······ *All Other Democrats*

Source: Voteview.com.

than other states since the early 1980s and, since 2005, had either been or been tied for the largest Republican delegation in the country.

For Democrats, on the other hand, we see—as expected based on the overall movement of the party over time—a smaller movement to the left by both groups. Notably, however, the Democratic legislators from red states with blue metros are, through the 107th Congress (2001–02), more moderate than their same-party colleagues from other states.[9] Since approximately 2003, however, Democratic House members from the states under study here look roughly the same ideologically as their co-partisans from other states. The extent that Democratic members from red states with blue metros were once a moderating force in their cause has disappeared, then, at the same time as their Republican colleagues in these thirteen states have become more conservative.

What might explain this change among Democratic legislators? Other research demonstrates that while polarization in Congress over the past forty years has largely been driven by Republican representatives moving to the right, the slight shift among Democrats to the left has been associated with demographic change in the makeup of their caucus. Specifically, the number of African American, Asian, Latino, and female members of the House Democratic caucus has increased over time, and because legislators from these demographic groups tend to be more liberal, the average position of a Democratic representative has shifted similarly.[10]

In figure E-2, we see that over the past roughly forty years, legislators from red states with blue metros have come to represent a larger share of the Democratic party's nonwhite and non-male legislators. In 1981, for example, only 18 percent of Democratic women came from the states under study here; in 2019, it was 43 percent. Similarly, the share of the party's nonwhite members hailing from red states with blue metros grew from 25 percent in 1981 to 38 percent in 2019—and has been as high as 42 percent between 2007 and 2010. Similarly, the share of the states' delegations that fall into these demographic groups has also grown. In 1981, just 1 percent of the Democratic members from the states of interest were women and 4 percent were nonwhite. By 2019, those figures had grown to 20 percent in both cases. As the delegations from our swing states of focus have become more diverse and to represent a greater share of the party's diversity, we would expect them to also become more liberal.

FILTERING THE URBAN/RURAL DIVIDE: THE ROLE OF CONGRESSIONAL INSTITUTIONS

Once House members and senators from red states with blue metros reach Washington, their ability to represent the interests of their constituencies is filtered through a range of different congressional institutions. In the House, that includes the power of the majority party leadership to determine what bills get considered on the floor. These decisions are generally made with an eye toward main-

FIGURE E-2. Diversity of House Democratic Caucus
from Red States with Blue Metros

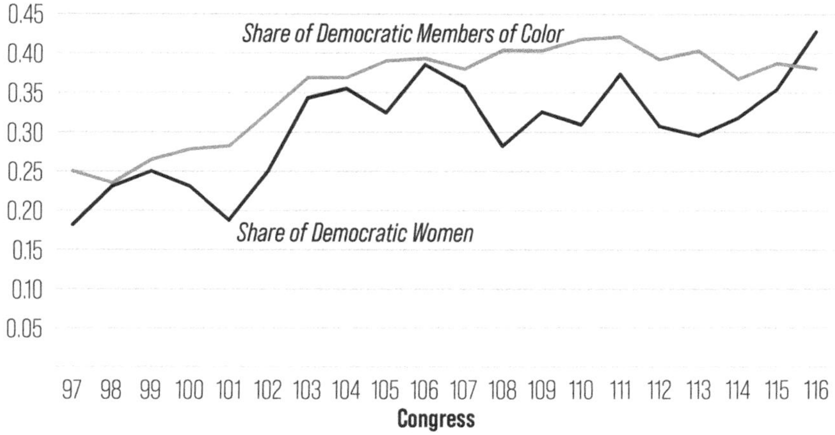

Source: Office of the Historian, U.S. House of Representatives.

taining the party's majority, and doing so involves creating a strong party brand that is distinct from the minority party's reputation.[11] For vulnerable members, however, this effort to generate a strong party image can be at odds with their desire to build personal brands that may appeal to swing voters. Party leaders, then, must balance these competing concerns as they construct a floor agenda. News reports discuss these tensions on a range of legislative issues that Democratic leaders considered bringing or have brought to the floor in 2019, including a minimum wage increase, prescription drug prices, and a trade agreement with Canada and Mexico.[12]

If Democratic leaders are making decisions about their legislative agenda with the concerns of vulnerable Democratic members in mind, what might that mean for the policy concerns of Democratic legislators from red states with blue metros? Only roughly 40 percent (fourteen of thirty-four) of the seats currently held by Democrats that stand to be competitive in the 2020 elections are in the states under study here.[13] In addition, the competitive districts held by Democrats do not perfectly mirror the party's seats in red states with blue metros. As we have seen, roughly 85 percent of the red state-blue metro districts held by Democrats are in sparsely suburban, densely suburban, or urban-suburban mix areas. Among the set of competitive seats, only 62 percent fall into these three categories. This difference is driven, in part, by the fact that roughly 35 percent of Democrats' marginal districts are in pure rural or rural-suburban mix areas, as compared to just 12 percent of the party's seats in red states with blue metros overall. To the extent that shoring up support for these members from more rural areas is a focus of Democratic party leaders in Congress, then, suburban legislators may find themselves looking for common policy ground with their rural colleagues to advance their priorities. For Republicans, the picture is slightly different. Nearly all (fourteen of nineteen) competitive seats for 2020 are in the states under study here. To the extent that leaders would use their relatively limited procedural rights on the House floor to protect their vulnerable members, their efforts are likely to benefit legislators from red states with blue metros. At the same time, if the majority party Democrats are utilizing their power to limit credit-claiming opportunities for Republicans from marginal districts—such as by denying them opportunities to amend bills on the House floor—legislators from the states under study here are likely to be affected.

A second way the influence of legislators from red states with blue metros is filtered through congressional institutions involves committee assignments. While the tangible benefits for rank-and-file members of committee service appear to be small, service as a committee chair is associated with greater legislative effectiveness and greater financial resources for one's future campaigns; being an Appropriations subcommittee chair also leads to more benefits for one's district.[14] Both Republicans and Democrats consider five committees to be especially powerful, designating them as "exclusive": Appropriations, Energy and Commerce, Financial Services, Rules, and Ways and Means.[15] There are 129 Democrats and ninety-four Republicans in total across these five panels; Democrats from red states with blue metros hold 36 percent of their party's seats, while Republicans from the same states occupy 49 percent of theirs. These figures are roughly in line with the share of seats in both parties that legislators from the states under study here occupy in the House as a whole. On the Democratic side, 35 percent of the party comes from red states with blue metros. On the Republican side, approximately 52 percent of the conference hails from these states (including twenty-three members from Texas). The influence of House members from the states focused on in this analysis, then, have influence on powerful committees in roughly the proportion we would expect by examining the distribution of seats in their parties as a whole.

In the Senate, meanwhile, the potential influence of legislators from red states with blue metros is filtered through a different set of institutions. While party leaders—especially the Majority Leader—have substantial influence over how the Senate operates on a day-to-day basis, perhaps the most significant institutional feature shaping the chamber is the filibuster, or the need to garner sixty votes to end debate on most measures.[16] Among other consequences, the existence of the filibuster empowers the more moderate members of the minority party, whose support is often sought by the majority party when the latter is attempting to build a sufficiently sized coalition to ensure passage of a bill. In the current Senate, where Republicans hold fifty-three seats, we might expect this bloc to consist of the seven Democratic senators who have the most moderate scores on the same measure of ideology discussed in the previous section (1st-dimension NOMINATE scores). Of these seven Democrats, three—Michael Bennet of Colorado, Mark Warner of Virginia, and Kyrsten Sinema of Arizona—hail from states under study here. The bloc of the most moderate Republican senators, meanwhile, also includes two—Martha McSally of Arizona and Rob Portman of Ohio—who represent red states with blue metros. The interests of these senators and, by extension, of red states with blue metros, might receive some additional attention as the result of the Senate's institutional structure, but they are likely to find themselves in competition with some colleagues from other states.

A CASE STUDY IN POLICYMAKING ACROSS THE URBAN/RURAL DIVIDE: THE SALT CAP

In addition to seeing their influence shaped by aspects of the internal organization of Congress, legislators from red states with blue metros may also find themselves in tension with their colleagues on certain policy issues—especially ones where the incidence varies across geographic space. Consider, for example, the state and local tax deduction. The Tax Cuts and Jobs Act, passed in 2017 as the signature legislative achievement of the Republican congressional majority during the first year of President Trump's term, limited the amount of one's state and local taxes that could be deducted from one's federal tax liability to $10,000. As news coverage during the debate indicated, this change would not be felt equally across all taxpayers; high-income individuals residing in states with higher state and local taxes (SALT) and in which voters tended to support Democrats were expected to be hit the hardest.[17] Since the law was enacted, Democrats have sought ways to relieve these voters in high-tax states from the cap, including an unsuccessful vote in the Senate that would have allowed states to pursue workarounds to the limit and the introduction of legislation in the House that would temporarily increase the cap.[18]

When we examine the geographic distribution of those who benefit from the deduction, we see how the issue might divide members from red states with blue metros from their same party colleagues from other states. In 2016, in the average congressional district in a red state with blue metros, 28 percent of tax returns claimed $8,800 in state and local tax deductions; in all other states, an average of 32 percent of returns took an average of $12,400 in SALT deductions.[19] For House members from the swing states under study here, then, the SALT issue may not be as salient as it is for their colleagues from other states.

An analysis of the incidence of the deduction in districts held by each party across the two types of states, moreover, suggests that this divide may be particularly problematic for Democrats. For seats held by Republicans in the current Congress, there was no discernable difference in either the average share of tax returns in a district claiming the SALT deduction or the average amount of the deduction in 2016. But in districts represented by Democrats, both the average percentage of returns taking the deduction (28 percent) and the average size of the deduction ($9,200) are lower in districts in the swing states under study here than in Democratically-held districts in other states (35 percent and $14,800).[20] As legislators look ahead to a potential change in party control in the Senate and the presidency after the 2020 elections, House Democrats from red states with blue metros may find themselves under pressure from their same-party colleagues to act on an issue that is less salient for them and their constituents. Indeed, three states, Florida, Nevada, and Texas, have no state income tax, and among the other ten states, only Minnesota (9.6 percent) and Wisconsin (7.65 percent) have state income tax rates greater than 6 percent.[21]

LOOKING AHEAD: REDISTRICTING AND REAPPORTIONMENT

The legislative agenda is not the only thing that may change following the 2020 elections. The redrawing of congressional districts following the 2020 census will affect the red states with blue metros under study here—and, specifically, their representation in Washington—in several ways. Some of the states—like Michigan, Minnesota, Ohio, and Pennsylvania—are projected to lose a congressional seat, while others—such as Arizona, Colorado, Florida, North Carolina, and Texas—are expected to gain one or more representatives.[22]

In nine of the thirteen states, responsibility for drawing congressional district lines rests with the state legislature and governor. (In three of the remaining states—Arizona, Colorado, and Michigan—independent redistricting commissions are used, while in North Carolina, the state legislature draws the lines but the governor cannot veto them.) In the states listed in table E-3, then, the intrastate distribution of power, including between Democratic-leaning metro areas and Republican-leaning rural areas, will be of particular importance in shaping the state's congressional delegation.

Of the three states under study here that are projected to lose seats and in which political actors will be responsible for redistricting, Democrats are already guaranteed to have a say in the process in two (Minnesota and Pennsylvania) in the form of a Democratic governor. In Ohio, Republicans would have full control over the process absent a change in state legislative control after the 2020 election. In the states expected to gain seats, meanwhile, Republicans will have more influence unless there is a change in state legislative partisanship.

Importantly, in several of the states under study here, the coming post-2020 reapportionment is not the only way in which redistricting has affected the relative partisan representation of red states with

TABLE E-3. Current Partisanship of State Legislatures and Future Partisanship of Governors in Selected Red States with Blue Metros

State	Current Partisanship of Legislature in 2019	Partisanship of Governor in 2021
Florida	Republican	Republican
Georgia	Republican	Republican
Minnesota	Divided	Democrat
Nevada	Democrat	Democrat
North Carolina	Republican	N/A
Ohio	Republican	Republican
Pennsylvania	Republican	Democrat
Texas	Republican	Republican
Virginia	Democrat	Democrat
Wisconsin	Republican	Democrat

Source: National Conference of State Legislatures; National Governors Association.

blue metros in Washington. Since 2012—the first congressional election conducted under new lines drawn after the 2010 census—four of the thirteen states explored here have been required by courts to make additional adjustments to their congressional districts. Those mid-decade efforts have been at least neutral, and in some cases beneficial, for Democrats. In several of the cases, the successful court challenges were made under *state* constitutional provisions. Given a ruling by the U.S. Supreme Court that partisan gerrymandering is a nonjusticiable question outside the reach of federal courts,[23] state constitutional challenges are likely to be increasingly important in setting the direction of redistricting plans in 2020.

In Florida, a new map was used for the 2016 congressional elections after the existing lines were held by the Florida Supreme Court to be unconstitutional under the state's constitution. The revised boundaries created three new districts that favored Democrats and put one Democratic incumbent in a GOP-leaning seat.[24] Democrats netted a one-seat gain with the new map in 2016 before picking up two additional seats in districts that became more favorable to the party in 2018. Virginia also underwent a redrawing of its congressional district lines before the 2016 election after federal courts ruled that the prior arrangement had concentrated too many Black voters in a single district.[25] Under the new map, the state's delegation shifted from 8-3 in favor of Republicans to 7-4 thanks to a Democratic victory in a new, Richmond-centered district.

In addition to the two states that saw new lines for 2016, a new map was drawn in Pennsylvania ahead of the 2018 midterms. There, thanks to a challenge under the state constitution filed by the League of Women Voters, the Pennsylvania Supreme Court produced a new map that reduced the number of districts carried by President Trump in 2016 from twelve to ten. Shifts in favor of Democrats were concentrated in the blue metros in the Philadelphia suburbs and the Lehigh Valley.[26] Democrats ultimately gained a net of three seats in the 2018 election, producing an evenly split 9-9 delegation; this included pickups in suburban Philadelphia (the new 5th and 6th Districts) and the Lehigh Valley (the new 7th District).[27]

North Carolina, meanwhile, has seen not one but two sets of adjustments to the congressional map approved by its state legislature post-2010. In 2016, the General Assembly was forced by federal courts to redraw the district lines on the grounds that the previous map was an unconstitutional racial gerrymander. While the 2016 map produced the same 10-3 Republican-Democrat breakdown that the 2012 lines had, it did result in two Republican incumbents, George Holding and Renee Ellmers, running against each other in a primary contest (ultimately won by Holding).[28] A second round of litigation seeking to declare the 2016 map—which maintained a 10-3 delegation in favor of Republicans in 2018—as illegally gerrymandered under the *state* constitution was successful in 2019. A new map approved by the state legislature in November 2019 would place two incumbent Republican members of Congress in Democratic-leaning, metro-based seats. The new lines consolidate metro-dwelling Democratic voters in Raleigh (the 2nd District, currently held by Holding) and Greensboro (the 6th District, currently represented by Mark Walker), rather than splitting them across multiple districts, making the possibility of additional Democratic representation in North Carolina's congressional delegation after the 2020 elections significant.[29] (As of this writing, Holding has already announced that he plans to retire.)

The 2020 elections and the redistricting process that will follow them have the potential to shape the representation of the red states—and the blue metros within them—that are analyzed in the preceding chapters. Potential changes in the makeup of the U.S. Senate, where four of the six most competitive seats are in the swing states under study here, as well as in the occupant of the White House, could reshape the range of achievable legislative outcomes. Existing structural features of congressional institutions and the overall trends in polarization within the House and Senate, meanwhile, will affect the influence that legislators from these areas find themselves with in Washington.

NOTES

Thanks to Clara Hendrickson for helpful comments.

1. Of the remaining two seats, one is held by Justin Amash, Independent, of Michigan, who left the Republican Party in 2019. The second, Wisconsin's 7th District, is vacant as of this writing but was previously held by a Republican and is rated as "likely Republican" for the 2020 election by the Cook Political Report.

2. Jonathan Rodden, *Why Cities Lose: The Deep Roots of the Urban-Rural Divide* (New York: Basic Books, 2019).

3. Total votes for Democratic House candidates are from the Federal Election Commission.

4. Nolan McCarty, *Polarization: What Everyone Needs to Know* (Oxford University Press, 2019).

5. James M. Curry and Frances E. Lee, "Congress at Work: Legislative Capacity and Entrepreneurship in the Contemporary Congress," in *Can America Govern Itself?* edited by Nolan McCarty and Frances Lee (Cambridge University Press, 2019), pp. 181–219; and Sarah Binder, "Legislating in Polarized Times," in *Congress Reconsidered,* 11th edition, edited by Lawrence C. Dodd and Bruce I. Oppenheimer (Washington: CQ Press, 2017), pp. 189–206.

6. This analysis represents the portion of the 116th Congress prior to December 2019, when Representative Jeff Van Drew of New Jersey switched parties from Democrat to Republican.

7. McCarty, *Polarization.*

8. A t-test of whether the mean values for Republicans are statistically different across the two groups reaches conventional levels of statistical significance (p < 0.10) for all Congresses since 1985.

9. A t-test of whether the mean values for Democrats are statistically different across the two groups reaches conventional levels of statistical significance (p < 0.10) for all Congresses between 1981 and 2002.

10. McCarty, *Polarization*.

11. Gary Cox and Mathew T. McCubbins, *Setting the Agenda: Responsible Party Government in the U.S. House of Representatives* (Cambridge University Press, 2005); and Frances E. Lee, *Insecure Majorities: Congress and the Perpetual Campaign* (University of Chicago Press, 2016).

12. Erica Werner and Mike DeBonis, "House Passes Long-Sought $15 Minimum Wage Legislation," *Washington Post*, July 18, 2019; Sarah Ferris, Heather Caygle, and Adam Cancryn, "Pelosi Drug Plan Hits Resistance from Left," *Politico*, October 22, 2019; Sabrina Rodriguez, Megan Cassella, and Sarah Ferris, "Battleground Democrats Make USMCA Push Amid Impeachment Furor," *Politico*, November 14, 2019.

13. *Competitive* is defined here as seats rated as "Lean Democratic," "Democratic Toss Up," "Republican Toss Up," and "Lean Republican" by the Cook Political Report as of March 27, 2020.

14. Christopher R. Berry and Anthony Fowler, "Congressional Committees, Legislative Influence, and the Hegemony of Chairs," *Journal of Public Economics* 158 (2018), pp. 1–11; and Christopher R. Berry and Anthony Fowler, "Cardinals or Clerics? Congressional Committees and the Distribution of Pork," *American Journal of Political Science* 60, no. 3 (July 2016), pp. 692–708.

15. Judy Schneider, "House Committees: Categories and Rules for Committee Assignments," *Congressional Research Service*, October 17, 2014.

16. For an explanation of the history and mechanics of the filibuster, see Molly E. Reynolds, "What Is the Senate Filibuster, and What Would It Take to Eliminate It?," *The Brookings Institution*, October 15, 2019, www.brookings.edu/policy2020/voter vital/what-is-the-senate-filibuster-and-what-would-it-take-to-eliminate-it/.

17. Alicia Parlapiano and K. K. Rebecca Lai, "Among the Tax Bill's Biggest Losers: High-Income, Blue State Taxpayers," *New York Times*, December 5, 2017.

18. Doug Sword, "Senate Rejects Repeal of State and Local Tax Deduction Cap Rule," *Roll Call*, October 23, 2019; and Doug Sword, "House Democrats to Move on Temporary 'SALT' Cap Increase," *Roll Call*, December 4, 2019.

19. Data on SALT deductions by congressional district is from Tax Policy Center, "Congressional Districts Ranked by Percentage of Returns With State and Local Tax Deduction, 2014 and 2016," October 7, 2019, www.taxpolicycenter.org/statistics/con gressional-districts-ranked-percentage-returns-state-and-local-tax-deduction -2014.

20. T-tests of whether these averages are statistically different from one another yield p-values of $p = 0.000$ in both cases.

21. Katherine Loughead, "State Individual Income Tax Rates and Brackets for 2020," *The Tax Foundation*, February 4, 2020, https://taxfoundation.org/state-individ ual-income-tax-rates-and-brackets-for-2020/.

22. Ted Mellnik and Reuben Fischer-Baum, "What's New for the 2020 Census?" *Washington Post*, April 2, 2019, www.washingtonpost.com/graphics/2019/national/ census-2020-technology/.

23. *Rucho, et al. v. Common Cause, et al.* 588 U.S., __ (2019).

24. Mary Ellen Klas, "Florida Supreme Court Approves Congressional Map Drawn by Challengers," *Miami Herald*, December 2, 2015.

25. Bill Bartel, "Virginia Gets New Redistricting Maps for 2016 Elections," *Tribune News Service*, January 8, 2016.

26. Nate Cohn, Matthew Bloch, and Kevin Quealy, "The New Pennsylvania Congressional Map, District by District," *New York Times*, February 19, 2018, www.nytimes.com/interactive/2018/02/19/upshot/pennsylvania-new-house-districts-gerrymandering.html.

27. Two districts in suburban Pittsburgh, now numbered PA-14 and PA-17, essentially swapped Republican and Democratic control.

28. Jorge Valencia, "Q&A: Takeaways from NC's 2016 Congressional Redistricting," *WUNC*, February 19, 2016, www.wunc.org/post/qa-takeaways-ncs-2016-congressional-redistricting.

29. Amy Gardner and Ted Mellnik, "Democrats Would Likely Gain Two Seats Under New Congressional Map Approved by North Carolina Legislature," *Washington Post*, November 15, 2019.

Appendix

Each of the state analyses presented in chapters 3 through 9 incorporates extensive quotes provided by state political experts. These data are used to provide contextual understanding for each state's political and policy environment. The state experts were interviewed by a research assistant utilizing the same set of questions (see chapter 1). The interviews were recorded and then transcribed. The following table lists the state political experts, their titles, and the dates they were interviewed.

STATE EXPERTS

State	Name	Title	Interview Date
Arizona	Arthur C. "Chris" Nelson	Associate Dean for Research and Discovery and Professor of Planning and Real Estate Development at the University of Arizona	May 10, 2018
Colorado	Robert R. Preuhs	Professor of Political Science at Metropolitan State University of Denver	May 18, 2018
Florida	Brian Fonseca	Director of the Jack D. Gordon Institute for Public Policy at Florida International University	May 15, 2018
	Sean D. Foreman	Chair of the Department of History and Political Science and Professor of Political Science at Barry University	May 8, 2018
	Darryl Paulson	Emeritus Professor of Government at the University of South Florida	May 3, 2018
	Richard D. Phillips	Associate Professor of Sociology and Religious Studies at the University of North Florida	May 16, 2018

State	Name	Title	Interview Date
Georgia	Charles S. Bullock III	Richard B. Russell Professor of Political Science at the University of Georgia	May 7, 2019
Michigan	Thomas Ivacko	Associate Director of the Center for Local, State, and Urban Policy at the Gerald R. Ford School of Public Policy at the University of Michigan	April 24, 2018, March 24, 2020
Minnesota	William Stancil	Research Fellow, Institute of Metropolitan Opportunity, University of Minnesota Law School	October 2, 2019
Nevada	Michael Green	Associate Professor of History at UNLV	April 17, 2018
North Carolina	Mary Newsom	Director of Urban Policy Initiatives at the University of North Carolina, Charlotte	May 23, 2018
Ohio	Kyle D. Kondik	Managing Editor, *Sabato's Crystal Ball* at the University of Virginia	May 18, 2018
Pennsylvania	William H. Frey	Senior Fellow at the Metropolitan Policy Program at the Brookings Institution	May 6, 2019
Texas	William Fulton	Director of the Kinder Institute for Urban Research at Rice University	May 1, 2018
	Calvin "Cal" Jillson	Professor of Political Science at Southern Methodist University	May 2, 2018
	Stephen L. Klineberg	Founding Director, Kinder Institute for Urban Research and Professor Emeritus of Sociology at Rice University	May 24, 2018
Virginia	Thomas W. Sanchez	Professor of Urban Affairs and Planning at Virginia Tech	April 17, 2018
	Geoffrey Skelley	Associate Editor, *Sabato's Crystal Ball* at the University of Virginia	May 31, 2018
	William S. Antholis	Director and CEO of the Miller Center for Public Affairs at the University of Virginia	May 31, 2018
Wisconsin	Katherine J. Cramer	Professor of Political Science and the Natalie C. Holton Chair of Letters & Science at the University of Wisconsin-Madison	April 23, 2018

Index

Figures and tables are indicated by *f* and *t* following the page number.

Zelinsky   Cultural Geography of th United States

Exploring the Beloved Country

Not Yet a Placeless Land

CPSIA information can be obtained
at www.ICGtesting.com
Printed in the USA
LVHW031559151122
733218LV00001B/60

9 780815 738473